About The Author

Ian Wishart is an award-winning investigative journalist, with extensive experience in newspaper, magazine, radio and television journalism since 1982. He is also the author of the No. 1 bestseller, *The Paradise Conspiracy*, and *Ian Wishart's Vintage Winebox Guide*. *Lawyers, Guns & Money* is his third book.

For Matthew & Melissa

LAWYERS, GUNS & MONEY

A TRUE STORY OF HORSES & FAIRIES, THE BANKERS & THE DECEIVED

IAN WISHART

Howling At The Moon
Productions Ltd

This book is dedicated to the broken hearts, broken promises, broken homes and broken dreams of all of those affected by both the Winebox Inquiry and the film and bloodstock investigations.

First edition published 1997 (August) by
Reprinted 1997 (September)
Howling At The Moon Productions Ltd,
PO Box 16–233, Sandringham
Auckland. New Zealand

ISBN 0-9583568-4-X
Typeset in Berkeley

Cover concept by Ian Wishart, Heidi Robertson & Mark Smith
Cover photo by Mark Smith
Edited by Steve Bloxham
Book design and layout by Graeme Leather
Printed in Australia by Australian Print Group

Contents

Warning!

PLEASE NOTE: This book is about civil lawsuits filed in the High Court at Auckland and Jersey, in the Channel Islands. In those proceedings an allegation of fraud was made. This does not and did not mean fraud in the criminal sense.

Allegations of fraud in that sense are not made in this book, unless otherwise specified.

This book traces an investigation into <u>allegations</u> of "deception" or "concealment" practised on a group of investors. They are allegations of fraud in the civil sense.

It should be pointed out also that the defendants in this case have steadfastly denied these allegations. Readers should not make any assumptions, and should maintain an open mind.

Prologue

"The Right Honourable gentleman is indebted to his memory
for his jests, and to his imagination for his facts."

– RICHARD SHERIDAN, BRITISH MP, 1751–1816

April 1992, Auckland:

The cars swept up the driveway to the rural retreat one at a time but linked by a common purpose. The faces of the occupants remained largely hidden by the trees lining the carriageway, although to any hidden watchers it would have been almost irrelevant – most of the men meeting here secretly on this day, while each powerful, were not well known publicly.

The dappled April sunlight played shadow-games in the craggy lines of one particular face though. It was a face worn down and aged beyond its years. And yet for him, and most of the others who'd gathered, the ordeal hadn't really even begun.

Half an hour away, the city of Auckland – home to a third of New Zealand's three and a half million citizens – buzzed on the horizon as a new work day dawned. Out here though, the noise and the pace of the city could not intrude. The only sounds: the crunch of car tyres and footsteps on gravel, and the occasional chirp of a bird or an insect.

It was an inspired choice of locations. The long drive meandered to a halt in front of a rambling farmhouse mansion, and a converted stable now provided extra parking. Behind, visitors could glimpse the vines of St. Nesbit's winery stretching down into a valley and up the other side, clusters of Cabernet Sauvignon and Merlot grapes hanging like purple icicles from the branches, sparkling as the last of the morning dew captured the sunlight. It would be harvest time soon.

St. Nesbit's was the passion of prominent Auckland lawyer, Tony Molloy and his Dutch-born wife, Petra. Molloy, with a doctorate in law under his belt and a Queens Counsel by trade, was a specialist tax lawyer by day and a vintner of premium wines by night and weekends. Although small in terms of turnover, the vineyard's reds are highly prized, earning St Nesbit's five-star accolades in New Zealand and Australia.

But it wasn't wine, or even wineboxes, that they'd gathered to discuss. From the elegant porch, guests who chanced a look through the large leadlight windows could see the living room had been converted into a conference room. Against the far wall, a whiteboard stood ready to play its part.

There would be repercussions from today's rendezvous. They were inserting dynamite into the cracks of a political tectonic plate, and the earthquakes that began here, at an exclusive vineyard south of Auckland on April 22 1992, would reverberate through the country for the next five years.

One of the guests would bear a personal cost as well: the price of being seen at this clandestine gathering – particularly in the presence of the man with the craggy face – would be his career. Alan May was a top fraud investigator with the Inland Revenue Department's Auckland office, but he would discover that even a reputation as an IRD "golden boy" couldn't save him from the witch hunt that would follow.

Introductions were brief. May, whose attendance was unofficial and in his own time, was joined by two investigators from the Serious Fraud Office, Geoff Downey and Neil Morris. The invitation had been extended to the man in charge of the SFO, Charles Sturt, but Sturt had declined the offer, sending two of his staff instead.

The man with the well-worn face grinned briefly as the group made small talk. Winston Peters was instantly recognisable to everyone in the room, but if his appearance was a surprise none of the three public servants were prepared to show it. The two SFO investigators, in particular, remembered one of the guests later, "sat on the couch looking like two rejects from the KGB – expressionless, emotionless and impassive."

Peters' barrister, Brian Henry, was one of the prime movers behind the meeting, and he too watched quietly from the sidelines, searching the faces of those around him for signs of reaction. This discussion, he thought, would spell out in words of one syllable for the benefit of the IRD and the SFO, the fraud he believed was present in a series of major financial deals involving bloodstock and movies.

Molloy, as host, was to be assisted in this operation by two more lawyers. Chris Dickie and Peter Edwards were partners in a mid-size city lawfirm, McVeagh Fleming & Co, who'd been investigating the deals for a long time.

Too long, thought Dickie to himself as his mind drifted back to the events of the previous few weeks that had led to this meeting. "Weeks!," he muttered to himself. Hell, if you measured this investigation by the old nuclear Doomsday Clock, the past month was merely minutes to midnight in comparison with an inquiry that had begun four years earlier into events going as far back as 1982.

And yet, as "midnight" ticked ever closer in this operation, no-one was sure whether – at the crucial moment – the clock would chime, or explode.

August 1992, Parliament:

"The Inland Revenue Department determined those transactions to be a sham. . .Why has it not acted on what is clearly massive, criminal, fraudulent activity? What immunity from prosecution do those perpetrators of fraud have in this country?

"What pressure was brought to bear on the Commissioner of Inland Revenue? Was he threatened by those two gentlemen from Russell McVeagh McKenzie Bartleet & Co?

"Because of inaction, inexplicable inaction, I have referred this matter to the Serious Fraud Office." – Winston Peters, MP

March 1994, Parliament:

"If the Inland Revenue Commissioner David Henry can find no evidence of tax fraud in the Magnum Corporation transaction alone, he should resign or be sacked.

"Decisions by the Serious Fraud Office and Inland Revenue Department not to prosecute have been made behind closed doors and I ask what right have they to be judge and jury away from the scrutiny of justifiably suspicious New Zealand people?

"Who knows what favours are being called in, or bribes are being paid, even as we speak, to save the reputations of some of New Zealand's so-called leading business figures and top political campaign donors." – Winston Peters, MP

July 1995, the Fay Richwhite tower:

The manuscript landed with a thud on Sir Michael Fay's desk, sliding a couple of centimetres before coming to rest in front of the multi-millionaire. Across the table from him, three sets of eyes waited for a reaction.

John Hughes, a silver-haired former Detective Inspector in the New Zealand Police Force, probably felt a sense of triumph in the moment. A boutique private security consultant now, he'd been searching for a copy of a book that a TV journalist was rumoured to be writing on the winebox and related issues.

Hughes had been part of the police team that put Arthur Allan Thomas behind bars for the Crewe murders in the early 1970's. He'd led the manhunt to find the killer of Swedish tourists Urban Hoglin and Heidi Paakonen in 1989. Latterly he'd come to public notice as the security consultant to millionaire businessman Alex van Heeren who'd nabbed a British security team in controversial circumstances that had been tracking van Heeren through Auckland.

Hughes drank in the view from Fay's 27th floor office, but not for long. His eyes flicked back to the cover page of the manuscript.

"Uncorking The Genie – by Ian Wishart," was printed in large type across the page.

The second set of eyes belonged to one of Hughes' boys – the man who'd found and delivered the package to the Fay office, a fact of which the private eye was quietly proud. He could still rattle cages in this city, still shake the gorillas out of the trees. Fay had wanted Wishart's book. Now he had it.

The third set of eyes watched more cautiously. Rhys Harrison QC was well known to journalists in town as a defamation law specialist, acting on behalf of magazines like North & South or Metro. But he wasn't here today to guard media freedom. Harrison was here as Fay Richwhite's hired legal gun, lead counsel for the merchant bank at the Winebox Inquiry.

And still they all watched in silence, as Fay flicked through the manuscript, particularly portions that had been tagged with yellow Post-It notes.

Finally, the merchant banker lifted his gaze from the page and looked at each of the men sharing this moment in time.

"How do we stop it from coming out?"

July 1995, later the same day:

The cellphone on the seat beside the driver was flashing furiously, but he couldn't hear it ringing. He didn't need to really: the dashboard lights were going bananas and the Dire Straits cassette in the car stereo suddenly sounded like a flock of strangled seagulls. It was, after all, a digital cellphone with a signature tune of electronic interference far more effective than any annoying ring tone.

As he reached for the phone, he wondered if it would be the managing editor of the publishing company he'd been dealing with. The guy was supposed to have rung by midday with contract details for the new book, but had missed the deadline. Better late than never, thought the journalist.

"Yeah, Wishart speaking."

"Gidday," replied the voice of Spook, a shadowy informant who'd been across the journalist's investigations since 1992. "I've got some news for you," he said furtively. "I hear you're working on a book."

A string of earthy Anglo-Saxon profanities pranced through his mind, but Wishart didn't give them voice as he listened to Spook. The journalist had, after all, deliberately kept him in the dark about the book's existence because of the absolute need for secrecy about the project. How the hell had he found out about it?

"I also hear that you gave it to someone," Spook continued, "someone you trust, who has secretly slipped a copy to Michael Fay."

Wishart's nerves were a wreck. It was definitely time to pull the car over and stop. Spook explained there'd been a top level meeting in Fay Richwhite earlier in the day to discuss the crisis caused by the existence of the book draft that was to become The Paradise Conspiracy. *Spook, Wishart had known for some time, had a highly-placed mole within the merchant bank.*

"Someone at Fay Richwhite has told your publisher they'll be sued for millions if they handle it, and the publishing company's not going to touch it."

It was a long, guttural scream of rage that rent the cool night air.

August 1995, Auckland:

The merchant banker grimaced as he clambered from the vehicle. It was a beautiful weekend morning with the sun glinting on the water off St Heliers beach, but it was largely lost on Michael Fay. He had good reason to scowl.

Across the road he could see a familiar face, someone he wouldn't mind having a word to.

"Charles Sturt?" he inquired, thrusting out his hand. "Michael Fay. I have some information I'm sure you'll find interesting."

October 13 1995, Auckland:

Wishart's cellphone was ringing. It had been ringing repeatedly for hours, the publication of The Paradise Conspiracy *that morning creating massive interest and demand. For the 48th time that day, he answered it.*

"Howling At The Moon Productions, hello?"

"Yeah, Ian," said the lawyer on the other end of the line, "I thought I should let you know that I was speaking to a lawyer who works inside the Serious Fraud Office today.

"I'm told that Fay Richwhite got a draft of your book a couple of months ago. Not the whole book, just selected portions, but it was enough to set them on fire. Fay came to see Sturt, told him it was explosive but not to worry, they'd fixed it so that it would never get published in New Zealand.

"I guess Fay was wrong," the lawyer laughed.

June 1996, the Winebox Inquiry:

The politician slumped back in the chair, trapped in hesitation's vice-like grip. The question hung in the air. No one breathed.

"Mr Peters!," the Fay Richwhite lawyer had snarled between tightly-clenched teeth. "I will ask you for about the eighth or ninth time. I want an answer. Are you alleging, before this Commission of Inquiry, on oath, that Sir Michael Fay, David Richwhite, any of the Fay Richwhite directors or employees in any way influenced Mr Sturt or Mr Henry in the performance of their statutory duties investigating the winebox transactions. Yes or no?"

The man who would be king looked anything but. Beaten, cowed, punch-drunk. Lurching from answer to answer with rage appearing to cloud his judgment. Fay Richwhite's QC, Rhys Harrison, knew he had Winston Peters on the ropes, and was playing it for everything he was worth.

In the public gallery sat the skeletal figure of David Richwhite, joint chief executive of the now-privatised merchant bank. The strain of four years fighting Peters and the winebox investigation appeared to be taking its toll on one of the richest men in New Zealand. He looked almost cadaverous. Beside him sat the company's public relations adviser Michelle Boag. Both could sense blood on the floor. They had waited a long time for this.

On the media benches it was standing room only, and even those standing weren't guaranteed a view over the phalanx of television and newspaper photographers who'd formed a human barricade in the front row.

Rhys Harrison's pursuit of Peters had been relentless this June Friday afternoon. In the northern hemisphere they were commemorating the 1944 D-day invasion; in the Auckland hearing room of the Winebox Inquiry Fay Richwhite's legal attack on the outspoken politician would become equally decisive. The question had been asked over and over again. "Where's the evidence that my clients corrupted Serious Fraud Office director Charles Sturt or Inland Revenue Commissioner David Henry?"

Repeatedly, Peters had pointed out that he had no evidence that fell within the Winebox Inquiry's strict terms of reference. The answer wasn't good enough for Harrison, who wanted nothing less than a complete exoneration for Fay and Richwhite. Naturally this wasn't acceptable to Peters, who looked around for any straw he could clutch at to keep the issue alive.

"He's dead meat," grinned one journalist on the media bench, North & South's David McLoughlin.

And then Peters stirred. "Yes, Mr Harrison. I believe it is a possibility, though it is not the central part of my allegation. It isn't my allegation, Mr Harrison. You have sought to make it one."

"Don't play with words, Mr Peters," chided the QC. "I am asking you a question. You know full well that you are on oath and you are bound to give an answer!"

"No!," snapped the MP. "With respect, I am here to give evidence on the allegation I made and I will not be intimidated by verbal gymnastics to say otherwise."

It was all too much for the inquiry's ringmaster, Sir Ronald Davison. "All right Mr Peters, let's have an end to this. Before this inquiry you are entitled to be asked questions and you will answer those to the best of your ability!"

Rhys Harrison paused only momentarily before laying another lash across the politician's back.

"I will repeat the question for the ninth time. Mr Peters, do you say on oath today that Mr Sturt or Mr Henry were influenced in the performance of their statutory duties relating to the winebox transactions by Sir Michael Fay, Mr David Richwhite, or any other Fay Richwhite director or employee – yes or no?"

"Yes," replied Peters. "I have always believed that."

Incompetence, he said, had already been proven at the inquiry, and the question was whether the incompetence had a more sinister root cause.

"I have always admitted the possibility of corruption. I don't have any explanation for that massive level of incompetence."

"So, you have no evidence to support an allegation of corruption involving those two senior civil servants and my clients, isn't that it?"

"No, Mr Harrison. When two civil servants prepare notes for their Minister claiming to have conducted investigations which have been proven demonstrably not to be true – in one case the investigation didn't start until a month later – I begin to believe that there is something corrupt going on."

The atmosphere crackled with the tension.

"I have asked you," demanded the QC angrily, "and don't try to duck it because you can't answer it, what evidence you had to implicate my clients in the corruption of two senior civil servants. If you haven't got it, can you say so?"

"You want more?" snapped Peters. "I have just given you one example of both civil servants doing that. The second piece I want to give you, for you have asked for it, is the head of the Serious Fraud Office who gets a series of disks, scores of them, and approaches Citibank, the very people who could not be relied upon to give a true attestation of what is –"

Peters was cut short by the jack-in-the-box response of SFO lawyer, Willie Young QC. The Paul White affair had been ruled out of bounds several times earlier, but somehow the ball always ended up in play again.

"Sir," objected Dr Young to Commissioner Davison, "that should never have been put on the brief of evidence. I touched on it, Mr Peters started off, we stopped yesterday. In my submission it is quite disgraceful for this approach to be taken by Mr Peters to have a free hit on material that he is well aware is not material to this inquiry."

But push was about to come to shove as the seething tensions sought some form of release. You couldn't have so much fear and loathing in one inquiry room without the cork blowing off. Back in 1994, Serious Fraud Office director Charles Sturt had told the inquiry he'd never met Sir Michael Fay or David Richwhite.

"No, and I do not know Sir Michael Fay or Mr Richwhite personally. I am pleased you have brought this matter up, because I have heard also information that I was a close friend of both gentlemen. I have spoken to neither gentleman at all and would not even know them to speak to."

In the face of the Fay Richwhite legal barrage, Winston Peters remembered the Sturt denial, and proceeded to tell the mysterious story of a woman he called Mrs X, who had phoned him after Sturt gave evidence. She was, said Peters, effectively accusing the head of the Serious Fraud Office of perjury.

"This person has told me that they were present when Mr Sturt came to Michael Fay's home, whereupon he met the Fay babysitter, and that is when they established an acquaintanceship."

To say that shockwaves rumbled through the hearing room would be an understatement. Winston Peters was claiming to have evidence that Charles Sturt had lied on oath when he said he didn't know Sir Michael.

"Mr Peters," asked Rhys Harrison in a tone of utter disbelief, "are you making an allegation of criminality on the basis of something you were told about somebody going to somebody's home to do with babysitting?"

In short, Peters appeared to be doing just that, clutching at a half-remembered conversation with a previously unnamed witness.

"This witness is a Marcia Read."

Marcia Read, the former head of the Phobic Trust, had just written a book on anxiety disorders and panic attacks. Right now, a number of people in that inquiry room could have used her advice.

Rhys Harrison, however, had other things on his mind right now.

"Do you have any evidence, with a capital E, which would tell this Commission that Mr Sturt lied on oath when he said: 'I do not know Sir Michael Fay or Mr Richwhite personally?' Do you have any evidence that that was a lie?"

When Marcia Read took the stand, she confirmed she'd called Winston, but said there'd been a misunderstanding and she had not personally seen Sturt or Fay together. Moreover, the actual story was that Charles Sturt's wife was running an exclusive daycare centre whose clients included the Richwhite family.

The Sturt family per se was obtaining fee income from the Richwhite family, but any potential conflict of interest implications were overlooked in the general acknowledgment that Winston Peters had got it wrong about Fay knowing Sturt.

July 1996, Auckland:

If one thing was sticking in the journalist's craw big-time, it was the suggestion that no relationship existed between the head of the Serious Fraud Office and the controversial merchant banker. It had been true when Sturt said it in 1994, but by the time Peters was being beaten around the ears over it in mid-1996, there was evidence that Fay had personally revealed to Sturt that he'd tried to shut down publication of an explosive book.

Wishart now wanted proof.

The weapon of choice was a state of the art Sony tape recorder. The medium was a phone line, and the target was that legal beagle from the Serious Fraud Office. The lawyer agreed to speak, provided he was not quoted directly, which is why the person is not named here.

"I've been doing research for a new book," I told the lawyer, "and one source said someone in Fay Richwhite had actually contacted the Serious Fraud Office and spoken to the director or yourself [I added the lawyer's own name to increase the pressure] about the book prior to its launch."

"Well," said the lawyer carefully. "You can take this as I say it. It wasn't me. All right? You can read into that what you like about who was approached.

"Certainly there had been informal discussions between the director and Fay somewhere, on a walk somewhere along St Heliers, or something like that."

"Why would Fay approach him?" I asked.

"It was put to me that they had not met before, and they just ran into each other while they were out walking one Sunday morning."

"So what was the thrust of that first discussion then?"

"What I understood from that was that the book had been seen by Michael Fay, and something about 'steps had been taken to stop it from being published'."

I was staggered that Fay would admit – to the head of a law enforcement agency that he'd never met before – that he'd taken steps to prevent the book from being published.

"It seems like an incredibly sensitive sort of thing for Fay to be revealing to Chas Sturt," I queried.

"I know that!" the lawyer exclaimed down the phone. "Let me put it this way. Sturt has always denied that he knew Fay and I've just taken that at face value. I don't know the man well enough to know who he knows and who his friends are. And it was raised that there'd been a meeting somewhere, and it was a casual meeting, and it was raised and it was discussed."

"Was there any sort of request or suggestion made to Sturt as to what he should do about this book?"

"No, I just think it was information that was relayed to him as far as it was passed on to me."

"In other words, 'Wishart's doing something, watch out, we've seen it'?" I asked.

"Yeah, it was put in more colourful terms than that," chuckled the lawyer. "I certainly know that it excited Sturt . Let me put it that way. The fact that it was something that he'd been mentioned in that was too hot to print – he got carried away with that."

I hung up the phone, dazed, but with a growing sense of outrage. Within minutes I was dialling another number.

"Dickie speaking."

"Chris, it's Wishart, I hope I didn't disturb your evening. I need to play this down the phone to you."

I hit the play button on the cassette recorder. When it finished, the voice on the other end of the phone was grave. "I need to see you in my office. Twenty minutes. Bring the tape."

Dickie and I had been working together on these investigations for four years, each protecting the other's back, to some extent. Late-night excursions had long ago become par for the course.

It was a little after 10.00pm by the time I arrived downtown and rendezvoused with the lawyer. As we elevated up to his 15th floor eyrie, he said little and his face was grim.

It wasn't until we reached the lawfirm's partners' lounge that he decided to open up. "Ian. What you have just played me down the phone is something I found devastating. Absolutely incredible. Have you made a copy?"

"Not yet."

He ducked out of the room momentarily and returned with another micro-cassette recorder.

"It is imperative that we make a copy now, and that that copy goes into safe keeping. What you have there is, in my opinion, dynamite."

After we'd made the dub, the lawyer finally relaxed a little. "What are you going to do with it?"

"I'm not sure," I answered, still reeling at the enormity of all that I'd heard. "But when the time is right, New Zealand will find out about this tape."

The evidence left me with more questions than answers. Certainly there is now proof that Charles Sturt has met Sir Michael Fay. There is evidence that Sir Michael wanted to stop, and I believe did try to stop, publication of *The Paradise Conspiracy* after obtaining an unauthorised version.

Welcome to *Lawyers, Guns & Money*. I hope you find the rest of this book, our second major investigation after *The Paradise Conspiracy*, equally explosive.

CHAPTER 1

The Rendezvous

"A little rebellion now and then is a good thing."
– THOMAS JEFFERSON, 1743–1826

The short, feisty lawyer looked at the faces congregating in the vineyard's old farmhouse, and let his memory wander. He had witnessed the passage of more than a few special moments in time since his world debut some 44 years earlier. Most of them had long since faded to grey on the image screen of his mind, but a few stood out like beacons. Personal moments that had helped shape his identity and define his life.

The son of two doctors, the slopes of a dormant volcano in Auckland's exclusive Remuera had been home for his formative years. "The silver spoon was certainly visible in my upbringing," Dickie once confided to a colleague. "I went to a private primary school, Kings Prep, where the school motto was 'Manliness Prevails'. Went to Kings College, had the compulsory overseas trip in my last year. Fell straight into University, and from there straight into a partnership. But probably throughout that time I was very conscious of a lack of genuineness, artificiality."

As the young Dickie propelled himself through University, he discovered the silver spoon was beginning to leave a bitter taste in his mouth. In joining the Auckland University Underwater Club, he came into regular contact with students from the other side of the tracks.

"I went along, very embarrassed and shy, and I remember being staggered within the first half-hour – first of all by the fact that I was mixing with girls as well as guys, and secondly that they were all from quite a different background to me but they were all absolutely neat people. Absolutely genuine."

It was there, too, that Dickie first fell in love. "Her name was Trish, but my twin sister, à la Remuera, used to call her 'Trash', which just made me all the more angry because she was absolutely not. She was a very genuine person, she just didn't speak 'proper', according to my dear twin sister," he said with a grin.

Revenge is a dish best served cold, however, and the chance arose at the twins' 21st birthday party, by necessity a shared occasion. "Of course, I invited some of my diving friends and one of them, a particularly good fellow from engineering, arrived in a pair of shorts and bare feet. My sister hit the roof!

Those were great times, and they certainly influenced my attitude towards people."

It was at University, too, that Chris Dickie first made contact with a young Tony Molloy. Over the old wooden desks in the law school library, the late afternoon sun would invariably give way to darkness as the pair studied silently together. Dickie, who never really considered himself a scholar, used to call it quits by seven or eight o'clock, but Molloy would linger on, hungry for the knowledge buried in fusty old law texts.

Now, two and a half decades later, the two amigos were back working together. If Molloy was the brains behind the team, Dickie was the brawn, like the cartoon dog Muttley, who would delight in sinking his teeth into a villain's leg whilst giggling maniacally. Not that Dickie didn't have the intellectual firepower. It was simply much easier to leave the joining of the dots to the specialist tax QC, while Dickie indulged his taste for the brutal cut and thrust of law. He had developed a reputation as a pit-bull – someone who wouldn't let go.

Perhaps that was why the midnight phone call that had led to this morning's vineyard meeting had come a few weeks earlier from Brian Henry. Dickie had known of Henry but, in a city where lawyers use their reputations to mark their territory in the same way that lions use trees, this was hardly surprising.

Aware that Henry had close ties to the National Party and, in particular, Winston Peters, Dickie also knew that Henry had been sniffing around the edges of his own investigation, along with a couple of competitive and combative business journalists, Frances O'Sullivan and Jenni McManus. Nevertheless, despite this cursory knowledge, the two lawyers were not what one would call "well acquainted" in March 1992.

Thus, when the late night call shattered his first hour of sleep, Chris Dickie was quite startled to find Brian Henry introducing himself down the line.

"I have some crucial information to give you. Can you come into my office straight away?"

Dickie blinked, and the baleful glow of the LEDs on the bedside clock-radio flickered in his eyes as he did so. For all he knew the midnight caller could have been "The Jackal" and he wouldn't have been any the wiser. His wife, Sue, was pondering this point as well.

The lawyer had become embroiled in a game of international intrigue, where his quarry were mixing with the kind of people who had security teams armed with Uzi machine-guns. It was a web that spun from New Zealand and Australia out to Hong Kong, through Japan, America, Ireland and Britain to the Channel Islands tax haven of Jersey, but Dickie and Molloy had yet to positively identify the spider in the middle of it all and that was part of the problem. The spider remained hidden inside a tightly woven core of tax haven companies.

"Don't go!" Sue warned. "It could be a set-up."

Like a sailor to a siren, however, Chris Dickie couldn't resist it. "Yeah, I'll be there," he groaned, dragging himself from the bed.

Half an hour later in downtown Auckland, a lone light in an office window beckoned Dickie to his second-floor rendezvous with the voice behind the phone call.

"I might be able to help you in respect of the offshore companies," said Brian Henry cutting right to the chase. The offshore companies Dickie and Molloy were investigating generated little or no paperwork, and yet somebody had to be controlling them. They suspected a code of some kind, but had never been able to prove it. Now Brian Henry had stepped into the fray.

"I am prepared to act as an intermediary for you to get an understanding of how the codes work and how the system operates."

Henry claimed to have a source, a senior lawyer, who had personal knowledge of the secret control of offshore companies. Such control would be in direct violation of tax laws.

That was the bait, but it would take more than that to hook Dickie in the wee small hours. The two men fenced a while longer, dancing around the edges of what they knew, each testing the other, not knowing whether to trust. Or not.

Two days later Brian Henry had phoned again.

"The person has agreed to meet you, but only through me. Tell me everything you know, and I'll get it confirmed or denied for you."

"Not good enough," retorted Dickie, who had no intention of playing Chinese Whispers when the stakes were so high. The danger of information getting muddled or confused in the retelling was high, and the result didn't bear thinking about.

"Look," pleaded Dickie. "I'm prepared to stand naked on a desert island, so that he can see I have no hidden tape recorders, but I have to meet him face to face or I'm not going to understand the detail. It's direct or nothing!"

Ironically, the threat worked. Brian Henry got back in touch a short time later.

"The idea of you standing naked is too frightening for words," he grinned. "He'll meet you face to face. My chambers, ten past five tomorrow evening. And wear some clothes!"

CHAPTER 2

Deep Throat

"Laws are like spider's webs, which stand firm when any light,
yielding object falls upon them, while a larger thing breaks
through them and escapes."
– SOLON, 638–559 BC

Chris Dickie was nervous. Was this a mountain being overcome or just another foothill? He barely had time to ponder as the elevator whisked him up two floors and deposited him outside the chambers of Brian P. Henry, Barrister.

He knocked and was ushered into the office he'd only seen previously in the dark. A huge wooden desk could be glimpsed through a doorway, and antique timber and glass cabinets with legal memorabilia and learned works and treatises. But by far the oddest decoration was a man with a craggy face. Winston Peters, still a National Government politician at this point, was sitting beside Henry's desk. Dickie knew that Peters and Henry worked as a team, but he hadn't expected to see Winston Peters at such a hush-hush meeting.

The turn of a handle and the creak of the door ended any chance for the lawyer to speculate further. The mysterious source had arrived.

Paul Darvell. Well-known would be an understatement. Notoriety, or perhaps even infamy, would be a better description. As a senior partner in the lawfirm Rudd Watts & Stone, Darvell had been close to the movers and shakers for a long time. So close, in fact, that when the Serious Fraud Office swooped to arrest Equiticorp boss Allan Hawkins and his colleagues on fraud charges, Paul Darvell – Equiticorp's lawyer – was one of the bigger fish netted that day. In 1992, their High Court trial had become the biggest show in town, although Darvell would be acquitted at the end of that year.

Brian Henry had been representing another of the accused, and that's how he'd come into contact with Darvell.

He became the equivalent of Watergate's "Deep Throat" – the shadowy character with a penchant for even shadier carparks who kept *Washington Post* reporters Bob Woodward and Carl Bernstein briefed on how to crack the Nixon conspiracy.

Darvell had once been close to the centre of the web himself, but in the brutal backroom power struggles that determine corporate and political direction in this country he had come off second-best.

When Equiticorp disintegrated amid the detritus and aftermath of the '87 stockmarket crash, the subsequent criminal trial left Darvell feeling like a scapegoat being fed to the ravenous public wolves. He felt he was being made to take the rap for the sins of the entire legal profession, and his anger was fuelled by others in legal circles who were gloating about Darvell's predicament.

But whoever decided to make an example out of such a formerly powerful individual as Paul Darvell was playing a very dangerous game. Not only did he know the legal tricks being used to con the tax department and other law enforcement agencies, but he also had first hand involvement in some of the schemes.

Rudd Watts & Stone are the solicitors who act for Cook Islands tax haven company European Pacific. Paul Darvell was one of the partners who helped European Pacific devise their schemes.

European Pacific's lawyers, and the IRD and Serious Fraud Office lawyers, had made much of the fact at the Winebox Inquiry in 1995 and 1996 that European Pacific had consulted the best legal brains in the business, including Paul Darvell, and been given a clean bill of health on the allegedly fraudulent Cook Islands tax credit deals.

Imagine the surprise then when, on the 6th of June 1996, IRD counsel Bruce Squire QC took this question-line with Winston Peters.

"Is it fair to suggest to you," said Squire, "that the net result of your evidence in this regard is that the statements that you personally have made about the winebox transactions – the fact that they are 'demonstrable fraud' to use your term in some respects – are in fact entirely based on the advice you got from [Brian] Henry and Dr Molloy?"

"Well, no," replied the politician. "I had others who were saying that."

"Right," said Squire, looking annoyed. "Who else?"

"Well, there was a man who could be regarded as the doyen of professional circles in the '80s."

"Yes?"

"One Paul Darvell," said Peters, revealing for the first time the identity of his Deep Throat. In a series of discussions, Darvell briefed Peters on the Magnum and JIF tax credit deals, which involved a total of US$1.2 billion and were alleged to involve a fraud on the revenues of New Zealand and Japan. Darvell, a man who'd helped design the schemes, told Peters "this is all shonky!"*

There was a delicious irony here, in the sense that one of European Pacific's own lawyers was the man ultimately responsible for delivering the winebox to Winston Peters. The irony was made even more delicious by the fact that Darvell and Brian Henry had done a secret deal to keep the Rudd Watts partner's involvement in providing the actual documents secret, even from Peters, who suspected but never knew for sure.

---

* Documents subsequently released at the Winebox Inquiry suggest Darvell wasn't as strong on the issue when he briefed the Commission of Inquiry privately. However, Dickie and Henry, who were both present, back up Peters' recollections.

"I believe he was the man that made the winebox documents available to me," the MP told the inquiry hesitantly. "For I could not – have not – been able to identify any other person specifically.

"Mr Darvell, to me, seemed to know a fair bit about the winebox documents and what they meant." Peters later told Brierley Investments Ltd's QC, Jim Farmer, that he regarded Darvell's views as "pretty serious". He also told the inquiry of a comment that Equiticorp founder Alan Hawkins made to him:

"If I am guilty, then all of these guys are too."

Jim Farmer wanted to know what Peters thought Darvell meant by "shonky".

"Illegal. A jack-up, a fix, a device, but not within the law."

TVNZ's *60 Minutes* programme had discovered Paul Darvell's true role in 1995, but the man was by this time dying of cancer. For humanitarian reasons, *60 Minutes* opted not to unmask Darvell as the source of the winebox.

At the March 1992 meeting with Peters and Dickie, the Rudd Watts partner looked weary and strained, but showed no sign yet of the illness that would eventually steal his life. Some would say the tumour had been caused by the stress of his arrest and subsequent acquittal on criminal charges arising from Equiticorp.

The small talk didn't last long. At this point in time the winebox wasn't on the agenda. It was bloodstock and movies – the favoured tax dodges of the '80s – that Chris Dickie wanted to know about. He was desperate to find out how the offshore companies were secretly controlled from New Zealand. As it turned out, Darvell was desperate to tell him.

Rather than create a paper trail for the New Zealand Inland Revenue Department, Police or the Serious Fraud Office to follow, tax haven companies were essentially controlled via gentlemen's' agreements.

"If you think the days of doing business with a handshake and a promise to honour your word are gone, you're seriously mistaken," he explained. "Suppose, for argument's sake, a secret Hong Kong company was having its chain yanked from Auckland. How do you ensure that any old Tom, Dick or Harry doesn't just ring up and clean out your tax haven bank account on the strength of a phone call? The secret is in the mechanism for authorisation, and the mechanism is simple.

"ACME Dodgy Trusts Ltd in the Netherlands Antilles, which administers the secret Hong Kong company on behalf of the New Zealand owners, is essentially taking part in a game of 'Simon Says'.

"It has authorisation to take phone calls from only two New Zealanders. One of those calls might come from a company executive in Auckland. The other might come from a lawyer or accountant. The phone calls must be made within the same timeframe, and the instruction must match exactly. If Simon doesn't say it right, the people at ACME Dodgy Trusts Ltd won't carry out the instructions. There's usually a password involved as well."

The wheels were spinning at high speed inside Dickie's head. He had seen faxes to a Hong Kong accountancy firm from men he was pursuing in relation to alleged bloodstock fraud. They had used a codename – "Project Topaz". Now it all made bloody sense.

"Project Topaz". The very name reeked of a Robert Ludlum novel. Where the hell had Paul Carran dragged up that sobriquet?

He fought the urge to swear out loud, and opted instead simply to clench and unclench his fists to relieve the tension.

Paul Carran, the solicitor from Russell McVeagh McKenzie Bartleet & Co, was one of the keys to solving the mysteries of the spider in the web, as far as Chris Dickie was concerned.

A law graduate from Wellington's Victoria University with Honours, Carran had gained his Masters from the University of London before returning to practice in New Zealand in the mid-1970's.

Promoted to a full partner at Russell McVeagh in June 1982, a lawfirm biography noted Paul Carran's expertise in "the fields of company law, commercial law and entertainment law."

New Zealand in the 1980's, and Auckland in particular, was the closest thing in the western world to commercial anarchy. Success was defined by how big and how tough you were.

At the cutting edge were the lawfirms. Financial deregulation had brought with it new opportunities, and new loopholes to explore. Ironical as it may seem, the abolition of rules resulted in an exponential explosion in the number of lawyers. One of the biggest and toughest firms around was Russell McVeagh McKenzie Bartleet & Co. More than a century old, its alumni ran New Zealand.

If success can be measured by the number of Russell McVeagh graduates on a board of directors, then perhaps it's no surprise to discover that a number of very successful companies were almost top heavy with current or former lawyers from the firm. Even Winston Peters had once worked there.

Paul Carran was himself on the boards of more than 20 companies, although most of those were special purpose private investment vehicles. But two other men in particular with connections to the firm were fast developing reputations as company directors – Robin Lance Congreve and Geoffrey Thomas Ricketts.

Born in Blenheim in 1944, young Robin Congreve completed his Masters degree in Law at Wellington's Victoria University, before topping it off with a Ph.D from the University of London. A tall dark-haired, sophisticated man, his intellect on tax law was so hot you could fry eggs on it.

Becoming a Russell McVeagh partner in 1976, Congreve spent ten years with the firm as a specialist tax adviser to the business community, before going solo as a consultant to the firm and his existing clients in 1986. He told Sir Ronald Davison 's Winebox Inquiry in 1995 that he had been feeling burnt out after a decade of intense tax practice and wanted to go into business on a more general basis.

Congreve was, in effect, a kind of Rumpelstiltskin in reverse: when it came to keeping profits out of the tax department's clutches, he could turn gold into straw, and among the finance houses to benefit from Dr Congreve's fisco-legal medicine was merchant bank Fay Richwhite & Co. Ltd.

Asked by Commission of Inquiry lawyers whether it was true that he was "instrumental" in many of the tax deals set up by Fay Richwhite, Robin

Congreve replied "I think it flatters me," but conceded that "I was an early and probably enthusiastic user and recognisor of the opportunities that followed deregulation. . .and it may have been possible for people to think that I was the 'eminence grise', or whatever the expression was, of that area."

Geoff Ricketts, balding and bespectacled, looked older than Congreve but was in fact nearly two years his junior. A partner in Russell McVeagh since 1973, the young lawyer had also strayed into the orbit of Fay Richwhite.

Chris Dickie knew Ricketts well. His wife, Fran Ricketts, had been bridesmaid at Dickie's wedding, and Geoff and Chris had become good friends. Ricketts had returned from overseas just after he qualified, and called on Dickie to get a briefing on the legal scene in Auckland.

As Dickie would later remark to colleagues, the close personal ties between them all would become the first casualty of the bloodstock and film investigations.

While Ricketts and Congreve were associated with merchant bankers Fay Richwhite & Co and served on the board of subsidiary Capital Markets Ltd, the pair also did a Batman and Robin twosome for other leading corporate lights.

When Lion Nathan was formed in 1988, for example, three of its directors had Russell McVeagh connections, and two of the three were Congreve and Ricketts. On the Mace Trust Management Ltd board, half the directors had worked at Russell McVeagh, including Robin Congreve and Geoff Ricketts. Congreve also served on the board of Freightways Holdings Ltd. Both men, of course, would later be found on the board of the Bank Of New Zealand.

Along with deregulation, the election of a Labour Government in 1984 ushered in the era of the corporate consultant. It had begun with Roger Douglas' much heralded "Economic Summit", which brought together business, union and political leaders for a pow-wow on where the country should be going.

One of the rising stars at the summit was a man named Michael Fay. With a desire to deal only with the best and biggest, the summit gave Fay Richwhite a chance to plug in at even higher levels of influence.

In the book *Michael Fay – On A Reach For The Ultimate*, marketing consultant Iain Morrison wrote of a discussion with the Fay Richwhite team just after Prime Minister Sir Robert Muldoon had called the snap election.

Fay Richwhite's Wellington manager, he wrote, Bill Birnie, described Muldoon "as a pain in the neck. Fay Richwhite had come up with a number of different packages and Muldoon could see right through them. They admired Muldoon for his intellect. However, they felt that with a change of Government these schemes would be able to proceed.

"They were looking forward to this. They believed a new Labour Government would be so preoccupied with getting established that they would be able to swing the deals that Muldoon had emphatically rejected. They saw it as a new era of opportunity, as long as the National Government fell and Lange took the Treasury benches."

Muldoon himself was scornful of the brash Aucklanders and their entourage, and critical of the way they gained influence after the economic summit.

"You can go back to the time of the first Labour Government," he told the authors of *On A Reach For The Ultimate*, "and find a number of people who became the darlings of Cabinet. I guess the original Sir James Fletcher would be the most obvious. He got alongside the ministers and the Prime Minister in a personal way and profited from it accordingly.

"It works more easily with Labour Cabinets because the ministers feel flattered by the attention. Fay did this at least as well as others with past governments."

Giving his interview for the book on the eve of the 1990's, Sir Robert looked with hindsight at what had followed in a general sense.

"Now, if you look at the state-owned enterprises, you see directors and chairmen, people of this description, who got there by deliberately putting themselves alongside ministers in a social capacity.

"Mind you, the Fay Richwhite people did it with both sides of the House. They did it with some of the younger members of the National Party caucus. We were talking about some new ideas for a health scheme, and my young friend Ruth Richardson said we should get a businessman to run it.

"I asked who she would pick as chairman. She suggested David Richwhite. So they got their arms around both sides. A few years earlier she wouldn't have known David Richwhite from somebody out in the street."

Sometimes the relationship between business leader and politician appears a little murkier than simply wide-eyed adoration. In his 1994 book, *Where's The Gold?*, former Goldcorp boss Ray Smith wrote of the circumstances surrounding Goldcorp's 1987 public share float.

Demand was so great for the 50 cent shares, he said, that long-standing clients only ended up with an average allocation of 1500 shares each in the new company. Smith claims he was approached by Customs Minister de Cleene.

"He quietly suggested that he and Roger Douglas, then Minister of Finance, would be most grateful to receive a share allocation and subsequently a substantial allocation of 50,000 shares each was made via another sharebroker to some obscure company.

"I have no way of knowing," Smith wrote, "who the actual shareholders of those companies were; it may not even have been the two ministers. There was no suggestion that we would get a payoff of any kind. It was just nice to know that the Ministers of Customs and Finance possibly owed me one. They at least were sensible enough to stag their shares at close to $0.85."

If Ray Smith's allegations are true, Roger Douglas and Trevor de Cleene stood to make up to $17,000 clear profit each on the deal, without having had to have put in a cent in the first place.

On February 27, 1987, Goldcorp's official launch party was held at Ray Smith's Takapuna home. "There was unlimited Moet, spit-roasted pork and lamb, oysters and crayfish. The guest list included our friends, bankers and large investors; two special guests were Roger Douglas and Trevor de Cleene."

In May 1994, during research for TVNZ's *Eyewitness* programme and what subsequently became *The Paradise Conspiracy*, I rang Douglas and de Cleene for comment.

"I can't remember if I bought any or not, to be honest. Could've. I honestly can't remember, to be honest," burbled Sir Roger, before adding that he certainly wouldn't have personally sought an allocation. "I don't remember, you're probably better to ring Trevor. I can't remember it at all, to be honest, but I'm not going to say it didn't happen."

As for his alleged attendance at the Goldcorp launch party, Sir Roger searched for the right words to describe the situation, and failed.

"Ah, I ah, actually ah, I, I didn't have any, I was there for about half an hour to be honest, ah I had a, I launched a book, I was invited, I didn't go to the opening at all, to be honest, ah, but ah, I think Trevor might have been more involved in that than I was. I was invited, and I went to his home, which was after the sort of launch, and I was there for half an hour."

As to the claim that he'd had a parcel of 50,000 shares, he was more definite.

"I'll tell you what, there is no way I have ever invested that much in shares in my life, so I certainly didn't do that!"

The phone call to Trevor de Cleene resulted in a more hostile reception. A lawyer by trade, he stated that he'd had some correspondence with Ray Smith about another passage in an early draft of the book, and warned him it could be libellous.

"I'm not saying anything. He wrote to me about another matter, not connected with this. I'm not saying what it was about. You people have to make your own mind up. All I'm saying is I warned him then about libel and, frankly, I'm warning you about libel.

"I have been many years in Parliament and haven't had the good fortune to be libelled. As I can conduct my own affairs, I'm actually looking forward to it.

"I'm not saying anything – why should I? The answer is no comment. Anything you do, you people, is at your own risk."

For their part, Fay Richwhite denied having a strategy to get close to politicians in a bid to score business deals. Instead, they responded, theirs was a natural progressive relationship over time.

When State-Owned Enterprises Minister Richard Prebble came looking for aggressive young business leaders to shake up the Post Office, it was Fay Richwhite's door he knocked on. Michael wasn't home, he was away playing with yachts. David agreed to take some time out to conduct a hard-hitting review of the Post Office Savings Bank, and he was helped in his toils by 31-year-old Bill Birnie from Fay Richwhite's Wellington office.

Also tapped on the shoulder, Robin Congreve, the Russell McVeagh consultant and Capital Markets director who would go on to be described by *Metro* magazine in 1987 as "pivotal in reshaping a wide range of New Zealand companies and finance houses to enable them to thrive in the new age of deregulation. . .regarded as one of the top tax brains in the country, a man with a special ability to find the most profitable solutions for companies and rich individuals with the most complex tax problems."

Following the Richwhite/Birnie recommendations, Richard Prebble then appointed Robin Congreve as chairman of the new Post Office Bank. Despite their close relationship to Postbank through Congreve, Birnie and Richwhite's involvement, Fay Richwhite & Co took a thumping when the state asset was sold, losing to a bid almost double their own from ANZ Bank.

Both Congreve and Ricketts would receive a hefty tarring and feathering at the hands of rebel National MP Winston Peters in 1992 over their dual roles as Fay Richwhite and Bank of New Zealand directors, and what Peters alleged was their involvement in fraudulent schemes as he campaigned for an inquiry into the BNZ.

This, then, was the Russell McVeagh McKenzie Bartleet & Co that Chris Dickie had come to know, along with its high profile whiz-bang tax and commercial lawyers. Even other Russell McVeagh staff held the firm's tax section – to which Carran and Congrev belonged – in a mixture of absolute awe and absolute fear. One senior partner told how the office doors of the tax lawyers would be deadlocked, so that no other partner in the firm could gain access to their files. They were the only section in the lawfirm to adopt such stringent security. Which was all very well, except when the tax lawyer concerned was on holiday or away, and one of their clients phoned wanting an update on his case.

"Try explaining to the irate client why you can't access his file and tell him what's happening!" the lawyer exclaimed with a shrug.

But Russell McVeagh would be involved in another venture in the early 1980's that would come to have an effect on Chris Dickie's investigations, and it resulted from the visit of a Saudi Arabian prince, His Royal Highness, Prince Nawaf bin Abdul Aziz Al Saud.

At the time in question, Saudi Arabian and, in fact, Middle Eastern money of any origin was at the centre of all sorts of mysterious schemes, some of them apparently tied to the notorious Bank of Credit and Commerce International, BCCI, which finally collapsed in 1991 because of massive fraud.

Prince Nawaf himself, a member of the Saudi royal family, had surfaced on the fringes of the BCCI controversy when he purchased shares in one of Washington DC's biggest banks, Financial General – later renamed First American. At the same time, an Arabian consortium fronting for BCCI was taking Financial General over illegally.

One of the kingpins in the BCCI team was Kamal Adham, the former chief of Saudi intelligence and an adviser to the royal family. Both Adham and the Prince had begun their buy-in's on the recommendation of the same person, Saudi diplomat Hassan Yassin. There is no evidence to suggest the Prince had any involvement with BCCI, the story merely serves to underline the strange places that Arab cash was turning up in. *

---

* BCCI, by all accounts, had only one New Zealand investment, a car haulaway venture run by businessman Matt Thompson, the founder of lame duck airline Skybus in the 1970's. BCCI's money was to be used to bankroll the airline. Thompson eventually ended up gun-running for Libya's Colonel Gaddafi, but died in a drunken stunt when he was pretending to hang himself whilst standing on the kitchen table of his London apartment. Unfortunately, a table leg gave way, and the entrepreneur was killed.

Two years later the Prince was in New Zealand on a spending spree. He snapped up a Coromandel farm for $1 million, but substantially more cash was injected into a bright new investment venture.

"New Zealand and Saudi Arabia," intoned the New Zealand Herald's front page lead, "have joined hands in an investment plan which will see millions of dollars pour into this country in the next 10 years.

"In the most significant moves yet by any country to invest in New Zealand, Saudi Arabian interests will take half shares in an equity investment company which will help to bankroll this nation's future."

So what was the magic investment carpet from which many riches would be sprinkled by this wealthy Arabian knight? A company to be known as the Saudi New Zealand Capital Corporation, or Saudicorp, as it would later be shortened to. The deal was signed in Los Angeles, and the $20 million company would be 50 percent owned by Prince Nawaf, 25 percent by New Zealand's government-owned Development Finance Corporation, and the remaining 25 percent would go to private business interests in New Zealand.

Saudicorp's brief was to help bankroll the DFC into funding "projects which are beneficial to the economy." DFC General Manager John Hunn called it a stimulating beginning to the 1980's.

"Development of New Zealand's economic resources and potential during the next decade could well be limited by a shortage of private venture capital. This joint venture is an ideal way to introduce overseas investment capital while furthering New Zealand's interests."

At a time, in 1997, when tens of billions of foreign dollars pour into New Zealand each year, the setting up of a twenty million dollar company in 1981 seems almost quaint – even more so given that it was front page news. Looking back in time, however, you could almost say it was the moment that the little boy pulled his finger out of the dyke. What started as a trickle sixteen years ago has become a flood.

Russell McVeagh would become solicitors to Saudicorp, and Robin Congreve would later end up serving as chairman of it as well. Eventually, Saudicorp's path would cross Chris Dickie's.

This then, is a rough thumbnail sketch of the historical canvas that Dickie's investigations had been set against. For the McVeagh Fleming lawyer and his close friend Tony Molloy QC, seeking answers to the collapse of a bloodstock investment partnership and the tax implications of some movie deals, it would be a long and painful process of joining the dots before they would begin to appreciate the bigger picture. Part of that painful process would hinge around the April 1992 vineyard meeting.

CHAPTER 3

The Grapes Of Wrath

"History, is indeed little more than the register of the crimes,
folies and misfortunes of mankind."
– EDWARD GIBBON, 1737–1794,
THE DECLINE AND FALL OF THE ROMAN EMPIRE

The aroma of freshly brewed coffee drifted into the makeshift conference room from the old farmhouse kitchen, tendrils of fragrance from the Arabica beans invisibly swirling around the vineyard's guests until they could take it no more.

On a vast rustic timber table lay a veritable feast of salads, meats, cheeses, bread and, of course, bottles of St. Nesbit's finest red.

It had been a morning of legal scene-setting on the bloodstock transactions, but lunch and a glass of Cabernet found Chris Dickie recounting, on a more informal level to some of those gathered, his own entrapment in the proceedings four years earlier.

There are moments in time, outwardly indistinguishable from any other moment, which can have profound and lasting effects on an individual's – or even a country's – future. Dickie could clearly remember that quarter-past four on a November afternoon in 1988 was one of those moments.

Chris Dickie didn't know it at the time, of course.

It was the urgent trill of the phone, on the corner table at the top of the stairs on the other side of a locked front door, that occupied Dickie's attention. He fumbled with the keys, twisted and pushed, and clambered up the staircase.

"Dickie speaking," he puffed into the mouthpiece.

"Yeah, Chris, it's John Taylor. We've got a problem."

It wasn't so much the words as the tone of voice that had told Dickie the worst. John Taylor was a top executive at Anzon Investments Ltd, a blue-chip corporate investment company. The pair had known each other for a year or two after meeting as negotiators on opposite sides of some friendly corporate raiding. "John was a delightful person to deal with," Dickie would later remark. "I held him in high esteem."

Back in 1986, one of Anzon's subsidiaries, Anzon Capital Ltd, had been pushing an investment scheme based on bloodstock, supposedly the finest horseflesh in the world. A company called Buckingham Enterprises Ltd had been established in February of that year, with the aim of buying top brood mares. In a glossy twenty-eight page prospectus, the promoters revealed their masterplan. "Anzon Capital Ltd and [consultant] Mitchell McLeish will establish over the next three years a sizeable and high quality bloodstock breeding operation in New Zealand, Australia, USA and Ireland in conjunction with the top studs and management in those countries."

Anzon saw numerous advantages for investors. There would be benefits from spreading the breeding risk across both northern and southern hemisphere bloodstock industries, and European bloodlines would find their way downunder more easily.

"By breeding in Ireland, England and USA where the bloodlines are strong and well developed, the Partnership should be able to generate above average profits. The Partnership will also be able to transfer selected bloodstock to its Australasian operations to strengthen its bloodlines and increase the profitability of those operations faster than would otherwise be the case."

Despite the success of champion sire *Sir Tristram* – described by bloodstock consultant Mitchell McLeish as "a fluke", NZ bloodstock was, by and large, not on a par with the top European and American studs.

"The very very best of our horses could go up [to the northern hemisphere] and compete. The odd freak that we get could go up and compete and probably be quite competitive just below top level," he said. Examples of such freaks include names like *Horlicks* and *Balmerino*. The rest of them weren't in the race. So to speak.

Buckingham Enterprises Ltd and Company wasn't an ordinary company. It comprised two entities: "Buckingham Enterprises Ltd", an ordinary shelf company, was one and the "Company" referred to was the other. The "Company" was not a company, it was a group of investors who'd joined together and pooled their money in the project.

It had been established as a "special partnership", which meant the investors were silent partners, not allowed by law to have any say in the management of the partnership. That task would be handled by Buckingham Enterprises Ltd.

If you like, Buckingham Enterprises Ltd and its staff and advisers were the engine, the driving force of the project, while the "and Company" were the fuel. Altogether, Buckingham Enterprises Ltd and Company was a vehicle on a one-way track to disaster.

As part and parcel of the deal, the investors also had to make a written promise to Westpac – Buckingham's banker.

If, for some unforeseen reason, the partnership went under, the investors each had to guarantee that they would pay the bank an additional sum equivalent to double the original investment. In other words, if the partnership disappeared down the gurgler taking your $10,000 stake with it, you would not only lose that $10,000, but you'd have to write a further cheque to Westpac for another $20,000 on top of that, plus interest.

But of course, with investments in horses with Kentucky Derby-winning bloodlines, nobody believed for a moment that this venture could fail. Nobody, that is, until that phone call to Chris Dickie from Anzon's John Taylor.

Taylor didn't waste words. "Chris, you're an investor in the Buckingham partnership. I don't know how to say this – I've just discovered Buckingham is an absolute disaster. The bank, Westpac, haven't been paid."

Christopher Dickie's world caved in.

"They must have been paid, dammit! They must have been!"

"No," Taylor replied quietly. "Chris, I believe that only two payments were ever made on time. The bankers are owed millions and millions, and they're going to look to everybody – you included – under their guarantees."

Dickie had lowered the phone back onto its cradle in a state of shock. A naturally cautious person, he was not the kind of investor to throw money around flamboyantly. Hell, he laughed bitterly to himself, he'd only ever made two investments before this. The first was back in the 1960's, when he bought a parcel of Yates shares for £300. He'd sold those many years later for a modest sum, and later invested in a kiwifruit orchard, but throughout the boom years he hadn't put a cent in the stockmarket.

All around him lawyers, accountants and other professionals had been dabbling in film finance, to attract significant tax breaks offered by the Government of the day as an incentive to make movies, but Chris Dickie had stood aloof.

The pressure to have a financial fling continued to build in those pre-crash days, however. July 31st 1986 was budget night, and the Labour Government's financial fairy godmother, Sir Roger Douglas, was poised to turn the Cinderella bloodstock investment industry back into a pumpkin at midnight, by removing the tax advantages for any schemes not already fully subscribed by that time.

All around the country, the final days of July saw a mad scramble by the promoters of various similar schemes to sew up as many investors as possible before the Government's budget-imposed witching-hour.

"I can remember July 31st as clear as anything," Dickie would later remark wistfully. "It was a beautiful sunny Thursday, and I'm sure the Good Lord looked down at me and said 'you're a miserable little sinner, and I'm going to pay you back!' "

In the preceding few days Dickie had seen a number of his colleagues in various Auckland lawfirms rush to secure their own places in Buckingham before it closed, and he'd had the chance to look over people's shoulders at the prospectus. But it was during lunch in a restaurant on the 31st that fate finally intervened. "As luck would have it, sitting at a table opposite me was David Rouse of Anzon."

"Chris, haven't you got involved in Buckingham yet? We've written to you. Come on, this is the best thing since sliced bread. You can't afford to miss it, we're closing at five tonight – you're crazy if you're not in!"

The lawyer and history were on a collision course. Hindsight would suggest that envy played no small role in the decision to get involved. Being a commercial lawyer, he'd had many an opportunity to press his nose up against the window panes of some wealthy friends who'd also become clients.

"I had been with these people in circumstances and lifestyles that I certainly don't enjoy the privileges of – all the bells and whistles, the helicopter rides, the expensive overseas trip that I was shouted by these clients as a 'thank you' for a job I'd done, their magnificent homes and cars.

"They worked incredibly hard but they played even harder! I went to parties like I'd never seen before and suspect I never will again, parties complete with a crane lifting a girl up, hidden inside a cake, to a first floor window.

"The interesting thing about these friends in particular was that they were very down to earth. They certainly called a spade a spade. They weren't the toffee-nosed, double-barrelled names talking with lisps in their voices – they were good, solid businessmen."

Pulling his nose back from the window-glass, Chris Dickie had paused to reflect on his own circumstances, which he referred to – somewhat self-deprecatingly – as "a solicitor on an average income, doing an average job, living in an average house." His friends had done well in some special partnerships already, including some run by Fay Richwhite.

Always the bridesmaid, never the bride, thought Dickie, remembering his own tenuous connections to the jet-set. When Michael Fay and David Richwhite had first started out in business together in the mid 1970's, after quitting the doomed Securitibank, they'd set up shop in what Dickie called "a pokey little office" leased to them by his father-in-law.

He'd seen the two lads around, and he knew his wife's father, at that time secretary of the United Permanent Building Society, was sending a little bit of work Fay Richwhite's way. But Chris Dickie hadn't moved in their circles.

Dragging himself back to his current dilemma, he weighed up the dynamics of investing in bloodstock. The fact that he knew nothing about horses except which way they pointed was neither here nor there.

"I've only ever had two experiences with a horse prior to that day. One of the animals once stepped on my foot on a gravel road – hell that hurt! And the other time was that I had sat on the bonnet of a Morris Minor at the top of the Ellerslie racecourse on Ladies Mile road, with my very close friend, now deceased, Jim Fletcher.*

"I remember being staggered by the power of these horses as they galloped up in the steeplechase. I can remember that as clearly as anything – the impression of the incredible power of these magnificent animals.

"And those were the only connections I'd ever had with a horse. I didn't know anything about them," he chuckled.

Dickie made his investment decision on the hoof, so to speak. David Rouse's personal hard-sell succeeded where two years of sharemarket boom and hype had failed. Dickie signed on the dotted line with just hours to spare, sinking $10,000 into the venture. He'd largely forgotten about it in the interim and, like many of the other investors, had just assumed that his horses were out there somewhere, eating grass, mating and racing.

---

* Fletcher was tragically murdered when he disturbed a teenage intruder at his Papamoa Beach holiday home in the Bay of Plenty.

To say that John Taylor's phone call two and a half years later had come as a shock would be a gross understatement. Dickie and his wife, Sue, had just returned from Auckland's Jean Batten International Airport, after seeing off daughter Joanna on an overseas excursion to Sweden. A generally melancholy air had already overtaken the couple, without the news that they might just have lost $30,000.

That evening marked the end-of-year partners' dinner for the McVeagh Fleming lawfirm, but the atmosphere of bonhomie and festive season good cheer was lost on Dickie. All he could think of was horses, and every mouthful of sirloin tasted like jellimeat.

"I kept thinking 'this cannot be true. It can't be true!' We had bought millions of dollars of top quality horses. I mean, we had bought the best bloodstock in the world, and there were competent people behind it.

"I was frightened, because clearly John's comments were to be taken very seriously, and that night I just simply didn't eat at the restaurant. I was praying like hell that I was right and John was wrong. As it turned out, I couldn't have been more wrong."

Events had moved swiftly over the following days. Westpac Bank, now owed millions by the three hundred or so investors in Buckingham Enterprises Ltd & Co, was moving to call in those debts. Sensing impending financial doom, the investors gathered for a special meeting at the International Hotel in downtown Auckland city.

Grabbing his coat from the back of the office door, Chris Dickie was running late. He wanted one of his legal partners in the McVeagh Fleming lawfirm to come with him, but there were no takers.

"I don't think anything hit me until I walked in that door. I can tell you this: it was a late afternoon, it was sunny, and I can remember walking up the stairs to where the meeting was to be held and hearing this incredible noise.

"The room was chocker, absolutely packed to the gunwales with people standing all around the sides, from front to back it was absolutely jam-packed with sweating, grunting, angry humanity."

The lawyer's eyes scanned the room, settling briefly on John Taylor who was standing near the front. A brief flicker of acknowledgment passed between the two men, before Dickie resumed his hunt for a vacant seat. Surprised to find one he bounded across before anyone else could grab it. If there was going to be bad news, he wanted to be sitting down when he heard it. A blonde woman next to him nodded a greeting.

"Have you got many units in this?" queried Dickie.

"Oh yes, just a few," she murmured in an Irish lilt, in what would prove to be a massive understatement. She was the biggest single investor.

The minutes of the meeting don't capture the flavour of the missiles being directed at the partnership bosses, but they do record the main points.

"Westpac were owed $1.1 million in terms of principal and interest with another $241,000 due on 31 January 1989. Westpac have advised that they would like partners to lend money to the partnership [to cover the arrears]. If this does not happen then Westpac will move to call up the amount owed in terms of individual guarantees of partners.

"After considerable discussion," noted the minutes dryly, "it was moved that the General Partner [the executive team] be instructed to advise Westpac that the special partners [the investors] are not prepared to make an advance to the partnership."

It was during one of these rapid-fire sorties against the executive team, that Chris Dickie's attention was momentarily diverted by the late arrival of a new face.

"It was about three quarters of an hour into the stoush, and I can remember the doors opening and in walked the solicitor representing the Buckingham partnership, Paul Carran. He just waltzed up the front and sat there. I didn't know who he was then, and I remember thinking 'how rude!' for the partnership's solicitor to turn up late, because clearly it was a critically important meeting."

Dickie didn't realise he would spend the next seven to nine years of his life tracking Carran's movements and activities.

From his vantage point towards the back of the room, Dickie spent most of his time just quietly observing the hellish scenario unfolding before them. He couldn't put his finger on it, but he felt that not every card was being laid on the table.

"It just didn't add up, no way did it add up. Here I was listening to them trying to explain these enormous debts, and for some reason it was setting off alarm bells inside me. I think that's the moment that I realised there was something much bigger going on."

Others shared his concerns on a more general level. Time and again, the same questions kept cropping up – where had the money gone, why had the investors only been told now when Westpac had virtually never been paid?

"The feeling of that meeting was one of absolute disbelief. They were shattered, they were in a state of shell-shock, and you've got to remember that none of us had received a bean out of the investment in the intervening two years, not a bloody cent! It wasn't like they'd paid us and forgotten to pay the bank. Something was seriously wrong."

Flaring tempers needed cooling off. John Taylor poured oil on troubled waters by setting up a special committee to identify what had gone wrong with the partnership, and to examine the Westpac issue in more detail. Chris Dickie found himself invited to join the investigation group.

Over a cool beer on that warm summer evening, the lawyer mingled with a small group of investors who'd hung around. They wanted to know if he would take them on as clients.

It very quickly became apparent, once the investors refused to throw good money after bad, that Westpac was going to take the investors to the cleaners if it had to. Not only had they defaulted on the first million and a quarter, now the bank could see there was no chance of the remaining loan repayments being made either.

"The investors were about to be sued by the bank," Dickie explained to an inquisitive neighbour. "The bank had made a demand and was clearly determined to proceed with those demands. There was a large amount of money involved, and it was inevitable that if the bank was successful a considerable number of the investors would have been bankrupted.

"Taking Buckingham as an example, the liability of each investor was twice the amount they'd subscribed for plus interest. Unbeknown to the investors though, until after that meeting, only two payments had ever been made to the bank on time by Buckingham's management, so clearly the partnership was totally insolvent."

Formed on March 3, 1986, it was set up not as a normal company or an ordinary partnership, but as a special partnership, under the Partnership Act 1908.

In an ordinary partnership, such as a legal or accounting firm, each partner is jointly and severally liable for the debts of the partnership and, as all lawyers know, that liability is unlimited. If a lawyer rips off a client, the other partners in that firm have to dig into their own pockets and make good the loss.

In a special partnership there's a major difference. Provided that you, as a special partner, play no role in the management of the firm, your liability is limited to the amount of your original investment, and not a cent more. If you invested $10,000 and the special partnership went bust, your liability would be limited to that $10,000.

With Buckingham, however, there was a catch. Even though, under law, the special partners had this protection, as explained earlier they had to sign those rights away before Westpac Bank would agree to give Buckingham an overdraft.

While their liability wasn't unlimited, special partners had been required to sign a guarantee to pay Westpac a further 200% of their original investment if things went sour. In return, according to the prospectus, the banks would provide up to $10 million in loan finance.

Not being allowed to have a say in the management of Buckingham, the special partners also had to sign powers of attorney allowing a "general partner" – Buckingham Enterprises Ltd (as opposed to Buckingham Enterprises Limited and Company) – to run the special partnership as it saw fit.

"The General Partner," stated the prospectus, "will not contribute to the capital of the Partnership and will neither share in the profits nor bear any losses."

The company behind the bloodstock promotion, Anzon Capital Ltd, had appointed two of its own directors, John Taylor and Chris Kirkham, to the board of Buckingham Enterprises Ltd, while the other two directorships went to accountants Keith Goodall and Robert Nurse. These men would have the responsibility of guiding the Buckingham partnership's fortunes, including the purchase, breeding and sale of world class horses.

It is important at this point to understand the structure of the these partnerships. A "general partner", usually a limited liability company, was responsible for the day to day management of the investment, but shared none of the profits or losses.

The "special partners", the investors, could play no role in the management but incurred all the liabilities and enjoyed all the profits. The special partners were totally and utterly dependent on the management abilities of the general partner. As such, when things became messy, the investors directed their legal battle against the general partner because those executives were the people solely responsible for the management.

One of Chris Dickie's first major discoveries on the special committee set up to unravel the mess was that Buckingham appeared to be missing $2.96 million of its capital funds. The initial capital of the partnership was to have been $7 million, according to the glossy prospectus. Seven thousand units of $1000 each. The problem was, Dickie and his committee of disgruntled investors could only find just over $4 million paid up. They retraced the dots to the very beginning of Buckingham Enterprises Limited and Company. This, they thought, would be Ground Zero of the investigation.

There had been one extra protection built into the Buckingham Partnership, and it came in the form of a statutory supervisor. This was a form of watchdog to ensure, as the prospectus put it, that no units in the scheme were allotted to any investor until "the Statutory Supervisor is satisfied that subscription monies in respect of such applicants have or will be paid in terms of this Prospectus."

The supervisor for Buckingham was accounting firm subsidiary KMG Kendons Trustee Company Ltd; the parent accounting firm has since become Coopers and Lybrand.

In the court proceedings that would later follow, it was alleged that Kendons had made an "unfortunate error":

"The statutory supervisor, contrary to the terms of the prospectus, contrary to what all the clients were told would be the rules, allowed nearly $3 million worth of subscriptions to be acquired but not paid for," Chris Dickie would later allege. It would become one of the central themes of his investigation.

"Within a short period of time it was clear to me that the liability of this room full of people to Westpac had to be looked at in terms of the legal documentation, because that's how they acquired the liability.

"The documents say they were liable for twice the amount of *subscribed capital* [author's emphasis] – and that's the original and subscribed capital of the partnership. It was a formula.

"Therefore the central question must be, 'what was the capital of Buckingham?' "

It was no idle question. If the investors were being held liable for double the $7 million total capital plus interest accruing daily, and yet they'd only invested $4 million of that themselves, then the person or persons who held the remaining $3 million worth of capital needed to be found so they could be hit with their fair share of the burden.

Who had the cash? The answer could best be described as a set of Russian dolls, and it would lead to the heart of what would later be alleged in court and in parliament to be a massive fraud against the investors and the Inland Revenue Department.

Little did Chris Dickie know, but the journey he was about to embark on would, over the course of nine years, nearly destroy his life, his career, his friendships and almost his marriage. If you had suggested to him the steps he would one day have to take to protect his family and the evidence, the nights he would spend wondering if he would survive until dawn, the self-confessed "average" Auckland lawyer would never have believed it.

CHAPTER 4

The Missing Millions

"All progress is based upon a universal innate desire on the part of
every organism to live beyond its income."
— SAMUEL BUTLER, 1835–1902

The young model blushed, she couldn't help it. "You want me to what?" she
asked quietly, as the director eyed her expectantly.

"I need you to rub this on your breasts. It's aniseed, and horses love it. Trust
me, it'll be OK, he won't bite."

The young Irish woman gave a toss of her dark Celtic hair and smiled
ruefully. Dressed in skin-tight jeans and a risqué loose fitting T-shirt, she could
have been forgiven for her earlier assumption that she'd been hired to provide
some extra visual appeal for the viewers of this promotional video.

Instead, she deduced, she'd obviously been mistaken. She was here to
seduce the horse. "Yeah, OK, I'll be out in a minute."

The director shot a glance back over his shoulder as he left the caravan. She
was beautiful, no doubt about it, and this – he congratulated himself – would
be a winning shot. Hot enough to drive a man to invest in horses, he chuckled
quietly as he made his way towards the director's chair.

"Buckingham video, take 7," came the call a few moments later, "and
action!"

Kelly, leading the colt, came to a stop just a few metres in front of the
camera. As if on cue, the magnificent-looking animal dropped its nose down the
front of her shirt, nuzzling her breasts in a bid to get at the aniseed. Kelly
couldn't help laughing, it tickled and the whole thing was ridiculous anyway.
Somewhere on set the still cameras were clicking as well, their motor-drives
whirring continuously.

"Cut! That's a wrap, perfect everybody!" barked the director with a big grin
and a noticeably faster heartbeat. Sure as hell beats a bimbo on a Ferrari bonnet.

Half a world away, in mirror-glass corporate totem poles in glittering
Auckland city, dark-suited men couldn't get hold of the videos fast enough. No
sooner had the promoters from Anzon found some more, than they were
snapped up by eager prospective punters.

One investor was more than a little peeved when his copy with the girl and
the horse on the front cover vanished from his desk one afternoon.

"It was really raunchy-looking," he complained later, "and I'm quite certain the person stole it because they thought it was a pornographic movie about the horsey-set. They would have been bitterly disappointed, because inside were the rolling emerald hills and dales of Ireland, no tits and bums anywhere."

For a while there in 1986, they'd been having video evenings up at the Anzon offices every Friday, part of a massive sales push to attract investors to bloodstock. The plan was for New Zealanders to buy shares in the best horses in the world, from top stud farms in the USA, Australia and Ireland.

"They were very good sales pitches," agreed the investor. "We were seeing unspeakably beautiful countryside, gentle hills and those ancient rock walls and then these magnificent horses being led out to the strains of stirring, dramatic music. It was all very upmarket, lots of sweeping vistas and galloping herds, must have cost them a fortune in helicopter time.

"By the end of it I wanted those horses, boy did I want those horses. Worst decision I ever made."

Christopher John Kirkham was one man who remembered the Buckingham video more clearly than most. He looked around the packed meeting room in the Park Royal hotel, full of angry investors, and sighed inwardly. A lynch mob in suits and ties, all baying for blood.

A former New Zealand hockey rep, he'd managed to retain his boyish good looks and his athletic appearance despite long ago trading the rough and tumble of the sports field for the rough and tumble of the boardroom.

All that, mind you, had been a lifetime in the past. After a university degree and a string of marketing and management positions, he'd found himself working as the Development Finance Corporation's Auckland manager.

The DFC, with its reputation for financing cutting edge – some would argue get-rich-quick – projects, placed Kirkham in close contact with the movers and shakers in Auckland's entrepreneurial set, and it led him into industrial giant Fletcher Challenge's investment bank, Challenge Corporate Services Ltd, later to become Broadbank.

The former hockey-rep's first introduction to mega-lawfirm Russell McVeagh had come during this time, during a film investment project. Travelling to London, Kirkham met up with Robin Congreve, who introduced him to another Russell McVeagh lawyer, Paul Carran. Kirkham and Carran would begin to work very closely together.

When Anzon Investments was set up in mid-1985, the brainchild of Chase Corporation and businessmen David Rouse and John Taylor, Chris Kirkham had eventually jumped across to become managing director of Anzon Capital Ltd, the group's investment bank.

In 1985 the grass had certainly been a lot greener. Now the green grass was gone, eaten by expensive bloodstock no doubt, and in its place was the dusty taste of failure.

Back then, of course, it had been the thrill of the chase and the spoils of victory that Chris Kirkham and other yuppies had feasted on. The doing of the deal was all important, and the adrenalin would always kick in with the certain knowledge that another deal lay just over the horizon, waiting to be hunted down, trapped, and skinned of the fat fees and commissions that accompanied such things. Others had smiled when they heard Chris Kirkham's nickname, "Mr Dial-a-Deal".

"The idea was," businessman Stephen Lunn – a colleague of Kirkham's – had once joked, "that you found a phone box and you put Mr Kirkham in it with a bag of 20 cent coins, and he would dial-a-deal."

" 'Dial-a-deal' was Mr Kirky," chuckled Lunn. Apparently, he could sell icecream to the Eskimos. Except now the tables had been turned. Icecream-eating Eskimos had become harder to find, and Chris Kirkham's bloodstock dealings were in danger of being hunted down, trapped and skinned of the facts by this stroppy middle-aged lawyer with the Napoleon complex.

"Chris," the lawyer had asked, "I just want to get this straight in my head. Exactly how much was Buckingham's capital?" Kirkham had given the same answer each time. Four million dollars, he'd said. Why wouldn't bloody Chris Dickie leave it at that? Not that Kirkham would ever use that language, no matter how pushy the legal Bonaparte became.

"He was," Dickie had once remarked, "never once rude to me. Not once in the entire investigation, despite the fact that I clearly was the hunter and he clearly was included amongst the prey.

"He was always polite, you could always go and see him, but he could give our politicians a real lesson. He'd say everything about nothing, and he would only ever tell you things that he thought you already knew. The guy was, and remains, an enigma."

Cat and mouse they may have been, but in the early days of the investigation they were ostensibly working together, on the subcommittee set up after the initial crisis meeting. It became a routine though; the cat would ask what Buckingham's capital was, and the mouse would reply $4 million, not $7 million.

"It was not as if we were just simply talking about $2,966,000 – we were talking about the fact that this had interest running with it. We had a bank demand for around $8 million, with penalty interest clocking up every day! We needed to find out who'd subscribed for that capital because they were the ones who should have been paying, not the rest of us. We had our own debts to worry about."

Dickie tried to play on one of Chris Kirkham's weak points. The Anzon Capital managing director was also, in his personal capacity, a special partner in Buckingham, and therefore just as exposed as everyone else to Westpac's magic repayment formula.

"Taking advantage of my 'working with Kirkham', quote unquote, in the flavour that I was generating, I would go up to see him. I would wear mufti and be relaxed and laid back. But I smelt a rat.

"I knew all was not well in Gotham City, and I said to him it was going to be essential for me to sit in his office, in peace and quiet, away from my law office, so that I could actually sit and look at his copies of the investors application forms so that our investors' committee could deal with the bank.

"I was taking advantage of the fact, as I say, that the bank was attacking him, as well as everybody else."

Anzon's offices were in a high rise next to the Auckland High Court. Dickie had phoned through to let Kirkham know he was on the way. As the glass elevator crept up the side of the Anzon building, the lawyer savoured the view out over Auckland city.

When the elevator doors opened Dickie caught a glimpse of the foyer to Kirkham's office, where the documents he'd asked to inspect had been laid out on a table for his perusal.

A striking looking woman, with jet-black hair and immaculately groomed, was just laying out the last of the papers as Dickie walked in. Glenda Griffin, Kirkham's executive assistant, glanced at the lawyer briefly as he entered.

"As I walked in she was closing a drawer in a cabinet, and then she returned to the table and finished setting out the forms. By this time I already had a list of all the investors in Buckingham, so I just sat down and spent the next two hours going through and ticking off two things: firstly the name of the person, and secondly the number of units that they were taking."

Chris Kirkham was on the phone, a long and involved conversation from the snippets that Chris Dickie caught through the doorway to the investment banker's personal office. Glenda Griffin was back at her desk, and Chris Dickie couldn't help but be distracted by her. He'd first noticed her during one of the investors' meetings, always wearing either black or red. She really was, thought Dickie, quite stunning.

She was also, he noted, as sharp as tacks. Whereas Chris Kirkham had often seemed muddled at the meetings, Griffin always had the answers to questions, or could lay her hands on the relevant paperwork.

More than anything else in the world right now, Chris Dickie desperately wanted to find out what the super-efficient Glenda had put back in the filing cabinet as he was coming in. He soon had his chance.

Griffin had had to go out, and after a while Chris Kirkham as well had made his excuses.

"You'll be all right here for a few minutes?," he asked Dickie on the way out, "I've got to pop out briefly."

"Yeah, I'm fine here, this is going to take ages," the lawyer replied, grinning on the inside. He could feel the adrenalin starting to surge through him as he mentally worked through the ramifications of what he was about to do.

As the lift doors sealed Chris Kirkham in the glass elevator for his journey to the ground far below, Chris Dickie was already moving toward the filing cabinet in Glenda Griffin's now unguarded office.

Was this breaking and entering, theft or commercial espionage?, the lawyer pondered momentarily. No, dammit, if whatever was in that drawer was related to the case it belonged to him and the rest of the investors.

"When I yanked open the filing drawer I found a folder with a brown envelope. If this envelope pertained to Buckingham it was my property. Kirkham was only the manager – my employee.

"There was a feeling that had developed by this time that we hadn't been told the full picture. This was our business, and I was bloody-well going to find out! We knew we'd had millions of dollars worth of horses that suddenly weren't worth anything, and we had a massive sum of money, nearly $3 million, gone! Vanished!"

Wild horses, as it turned out, couldn't have dragged Dickie away from that envelope, and he later described his decision to rifle through Glenda's drawer as one of the best of his legal career.

"I opened the envelope, and it blew me away. If you go and buy a magazine from a shop and you open it, the first thing that will often hit you is the smell of clean pages and clean printer's ink.

"My parents, as doctors, used to say that the sense of smell is a stronger sense of recall than eyesight – you can be walking down a road and a scent will suddenly hit you, taking you back to an event that you haven't thought of for years. This envelope did that for me.

"Before I even took out the papers in the envelope, the smell of fresh print hit me, and I knew they had to be investor subscription certificates like the one I'd been delivered years earlier."

Nervously looking around, Dickie made sure he was alone before furiously flicking through the certificates. There were six of them in all, originals not copies, and they totalled $2,966,000.

The blood drained from Dickie's face, and his stomach was churning. Here was the missing cash. Shit, what a bonus! His eyes darted across the pages, looking for the name of the subscriber – the mystery investor who would now be liable for almost half of the debt owed to Westpac. According to the documents it was some outfit called Wicklow, whoever they were.

If what had just happened could have come straight from the script of a thriller movie, what followed next could have come from a silent movie.

Chris Dickie wasted no time, he scooped up the certificates and fled the office, or at least that was the plan.

"In my rush to get out of the building I ran straight into the glass doors at the bottom and knocked myself out. It was like something out of Mr Bean!"

Dickie's not sure how long he lay there in the foyer, surrounded by the certificates, but it was a dishevelled and stunned Dickie who lurched into the foyer of his own McVeagh Fleming lawfirm a little later.

The receptionist stopped talking mid-sentence, and one of Chris Dickie's legal partners looked equally shocked. "What the hell's happened to you?" he asked, peering at the massive bump on Dickie's forehead.

"Can't stop to talk, missing certificates, I've got them, need to copy them. Wicklow."

If McVeagh Fleming staff weren't sure what Dickie was raving about, the lawyer remains adamant that his gibberish wasn't the result of the knock to the head, but because of euphoria about his discovery and panic about the need to copy the papers and return them to the Anzon office before Kirkham or Griffin returned.

"I was holding literally millions of dollars in my hands. I was holding the Wicklow certificates. I photocopied those mothers in a matter of seconds and took off back."

Whether God happened to be smiling down on the "miserable little sinner" or whether it was just good luck, Dickie was mightily relieved to discover Kirkham's office was still empty when he returned. He had been ready for anything.

"There was certainly an adrenalin rush, but if Kirkham had bounced me I probably would have punched him in the face – I had absolutely no qualms about it! Indeed, subsequently, I told his lawyer that I'd 'pinched' these certificates, and I used the word 'pinched', and he said 'yes, I know, we've been considering what action to take'.

"I remember saying to him 'Be my guest, be my guest boy!' I wasn't thinking any particularly high thoughts: this was my bloody partnership and somebody wasn't telling me the whole story!"

It was February 1989, and Chris Dickie assumed he'd cracked the case, found the missing investor, and that everyone would now pay their fair share of the debt and that would be it. Nothing could have been further from the truth. His discovery that a partnership called Wicklow had subscribed for the missing $2.96 million was merely the unmasking of the first "Russian Doll".

When the bloodstock tax minimisation loophole had been closed off on July 31, 1986, most of the attention was focused on Buckingham. It was the partnership being furiously promoted in the weeks leading up to Budget night.

It is now clear, however, that Anzon Capital Ltd and Buckingham Enterprises Ltd had been working quietly on other plans. Also born on July 31, 1986 were six smaller investment schemes, collectively called the Wicklow Bloodstock Partnerships. Each of the six had a capital of only $625,000, and each had taken a stake in Buckingham, with one big proviso.

Whereas the special partners had been required under the partnership rules, by Buckingham's Statutory Supervisor, to sign guarantees to pay Westpac a further 200% of their original investment, the Statutory Supervisor apparently let the Wicklow partnerships take stakes in Buckingham without signing any guarantees, without – in fact – Wicklow even paying out the $2.966 million they'd subscribed for. Effectively, Wicklow had been given that stake for nothing!

It was no wonder that the Buckingham partnership had collapsed under a mountain of debt. It was, essentially, under-capitalised.

"When you buy a horse," noted Dickie, "it's not like buying a box of tissues. It costs me nothing to keep that box sitting on my desk, but if you buy a horse you've got to feed it. If it's a mare, it's got to be bonked!, and the service fee costs you a bloody fortune."

Dickie leaned over and thumped his forefinger into his desk as if to make the point, a scowl creasing his face.

"The service fees on these things, some of the fees were over a hundred thousand dollars a screw!"

Not to mention the routine veterinary bills for top of the line horses, and the agistment – or babysitting – fees payable to the overseas studs where the horses were being stabled on behalf of their New Zealand owners.

Buckingham's management had, quite simply, bought more horses than they could afford to feed and service. In the Buckingham prospectus, investors had been told that only $10 million would be spent on bloodstock purchases, while a further $6 million would be retained as working capital to cover the day-to-day expenses.

The investors had dutifully signed up by July 31, 1986, to qualify for the wondrous scheme they'd been presented with. Twenty-four hours later, far from having a six million dollar surplus in its bank accounts, on August 1, the Buckingham partnership had gone two million dollars into overdraft.

"They had no money," muttered one disgruntled investor, "they were in trouble the day they started."

One who shares that view is Mitchell McLeish, a bloodstock expert who was intimately involved with the partnership.

"It was always supposed to have a capital of $17 million, and not $10 million, but all they ever raised was $10 million, so that was bloody disastrous. We'd overspent for the amount of money that was raised. It was like a pack of bloody cards falling over."

Financial analysts going through Buckingham's accounts have subsequently confirmed the partnership was "totally insolvent" on day one, the definition of insolvency being an inability to pay the bills as they fall due. There wasn't a lot of point in selling off the horses either, because they were the only income-producing asset that the partnership had left.

When he got hold of the Wicklow prospectus, Chris Dickie desperately searched its pages for clues. Finally he found one.

"It is proposed that in August 1987 the approval of partners in the Buckingham Partnership and the Ermine Partnership will be sought for those partnerships to effectively pool their interests in their bloodstock with the Wicklow Partnerships.

"This will be effected by the Ermine Partnership and the Buckingham Partnership selling interests in bloodstock they own to the Wicklow Partnerships and, conversely, the Wicklow Partnerships selling interests in bloodstock they own to the Buckingham Partnership and the Ermine Partnership.

"The advantage to all Partnerships of this concept of pooling their bloodstock interests is that the risks of bloodstock breeding are spread over a much greater number of mares, stallions and markets, thus reducing the impact of industry risks on them."

From starting as an innocent investor in the Buckingham deal, Chris Dickie had now flushed out Wicklow and Ermine, the remaining two players in what would become a triple-pack of trouble. Ermine, Buckingham and Wicklow. Like dominoes, as one fell over the next began to wobble.

Working backwards from the big bang, Chris Dickie knew he needed to find the location of bloodstock's "Ground Zero" – the moment the nightmare began.

CHAPTER 5

The Amazing Mr McLeish

"A government was overthrown not in the clear light of democratic
day – where its abuses might have compelled its recall anyway –
but in the shadows of myth and factional intrigue. Public
ignorance, democracy's lethal draft, was served and drunk."
– ROGER MORRIS, LEN COLODNY & ROBERT GETTLIN, *SILENT COUP*, 1991

The year was 1984. Deregulation was nigh, and at Challenge Corporate Services Ltd, an investment bank, they'd just sold their half share in the tax haven company that later became European Pacific, of winebox fame. Challenge was looking for new deals, and its bright new star, Christopher John Kirkham, had some fresh ideas.

They centred on bloodstock investment partnerships, something the boys over at Fay Richwhite had been pushing on their own behalf for some years.

As the authors of *On A Reach For The Ultimate* noted, "there was money to be made in the bloodstock and horse racing industry, another sector where Michael Fay could mix it with a 'glamour set'."

The trick would be in tax write-offs of the kind enjoyed by cattle farmers, deductions originally introduced by the Government as an incentive to increase livestock and land productivity. But Queen Street farmers could use the deductions too.

"Fay probably was the first person to see that potential," they wrote, "He worked out the concepts and, with his Fay Richwhite team, filled in the fine detail. His logic was that if cattle farmers could get tax deductions on cheap cattle, why couldn't horse owners get the deductions on a horse?

"Horses were worth a lot more money, so if you had one animal worth many thousands of dollars you should be able to get a bigger write-off against other sources of income."

Challenge Corporate Services wanted to see whether it could get on the bloodstock gravy train, by investing its own money in horses, and it put Kirkham in charge of assessing the possibilities.

"It was definitely not done with the intention of having New Zealand investors, members of the public, getting involved," confirmed one source. "That's not how all this started."

In 1984 they hired Christchurch-based breeder and bloodstock consultant

Mitchell McLeish, a man who would later receive glowing descriptions in the various prospectii.

"He has had a lifetime of experience in the international bloodstock industry and is very well versed in the English and Irish bloodstock industries. He has strong connections with Barronstown Stud and Coolmore Stud in Ireland and with several other Irish, English and USA breeders."

Chris Dickie, after years of investigations, still hoots with laughter at the mention of McLeish, his mental images of the man no doubt enhanced by the many meetings they ended up having.

"You've gotta meet Mitchell McLeish, oh yes," he would cackle uncontrollably, pausing only to remove his glasses and wipe a tear from his left eye. "Oh shit yes, you've gotta meet Mitchell McLeish – talk about the gift of the Blarney Stone! He's quite unique."

It is easy to get the impression that the feeling may be mutual: McLeish describes Dickie's investigations as "a joke". They are two of the main protagonists in this story, yet each appears to have enjoyed the other's company.

As Dickie puts it, all of McLeish's Christmases had come at once. Here was a man familiar with the horsing world, and who was suddenly being asked by a subsidiary of Fletcher Challenge, New Zealand's largest company, to travel the world profiling bloodstock.

He poked his nose in and made himself known at the premiere Irish studs, Coolmore and Barronstown, and he was said to be "matey" with top Australian breeder Colin Hayes, at the Lindsay Park stud near Adelaide, but it was his expense accounts that really boosted his reputation.

"Boy, did he use that expense account!" exclaimed one investigator later hired to follow the money trail. "We worked out that his expenses in the first year would have been the equivalent of sending a person around the world eight times!

"He stayed at the best hotels, and there was no question of travelling economy class. This was, in Mitchell McLeish's mind, essential, because he was moving with the movers and shakers and trying to keep up appearances."

At the same time, back in Auckland, Chris Kirkham and Russell McVeagh lawyer Paul Carran were working through the construction of what would become the Ermine bloodstock partnership.

Their target pool of preferred investors were partners in Russell McVeagh itself and the accounting firm Lawrence Anderson Buddle. These were people with high incomes and, at 66 cents in the dollar, high marginal tax rates that could use some downward leverage.

Documents from the time provide snapshot images of how the planning for Ermine was unfolding at this time. A memorandum from Paul Carran to his Russell McVeagh partners spelt out where things were at by May 1, 1985.

"Chris Kirkham at Challenge Corporate Services Limited and I have spent a year developing the proposals and we have now been successful in bringing most of the important elements together.

"Part of the analysis shows that for Partners having already sheltered down to $38,000 or so, this investment still shows very high returns at lower taxable incomes."

Unfortunately for Paul Carran and Chris Kirkham, they'd done what others in the bloodstock business try to avoid at all costs: they'd left their run too late. The year it had taken them to stitch together the Ermine proposal was too long for their partners to wait. By the time they'd done the deal and come to the partners for cash, the partners had already gone elsewhere to minimise their taxes, and Ermine hadn't figured in their plans.

The end result was that at the 12th hour they suddenly realised that they'd bought these horses, but they hadn't got the capital, because a lot of the partners had made other arrangements. So all of a sudden they had to issue a prospectus and get members of the public involved. It was a move that ultimately plunged them into litigation. In a 1993 Statement of Claim filed in the High Court at Auckland, investors painted a background to the scheme.

The main points included that capital would be raised from investments by partners in the legal and accounting firms, and that further capital would be raised by borrowing. This money would be used to purchase bloodstock, although some of the horses might be leased.

"Because of depreciation allowances permitted by the Inland Revenue Department on bloodstock," noted the Statement of Claim, "an investor would be entitled to claim tax deductions in respect of depreciation on the purchased stock, as well as claiming in respect of rental payments on any leased stock."

As well as the tax benefits outlined, "significant taxable profits would be generated from the breeding of bloodstock." In other words, this was to be a genuine, money-making commercial proposition. Further down the page, the claim document noted that additional investment was envisaged over the following 2–3 years, so that more horses could be purchased.

There were also "'possibilities' for 'purchasing our own stud property and even floating part of the operation on the stockmarket'."

Although by early June 1985 a number of partners in Russell McVeagh and Lawrence Anderson Buddle had taken the plunge and invested, the Statement of Claim noted their numbers were "insufficient to enable the plan to proceed. By a process at present unknown to the Plaintiffs, the plan was modified."

The modification, now allowing *clients* of the two firms to take part, was a June 14 unsigned memorandum from accountant Keith Goodall, and addressed to various branches of the accounting firm throughout New Zealand, inviting subscriptions from staff or their clients.

By mid-July 1985, Ermine Holdings Ltd & Company Special Partnership was seeking a $4 million loan from Equiticorp, and two days later, on July 18, the partnership was legally born. Things were moving rapidly.

McLeish, who'd managed to chalk up a $71,000 expense account, was back and giving accountant Keith Goodall from Lawrence Anderson Buddle something to scream about.

"Look, McLeish is something else!" Goodall protested, "his expense accounts are beyond belief."

"Keith had come in during the very early days of my investigation, when I was on the committee," Chris Dickie would later recall, "and we were talking about McLeish and Goodall was just sitting there pulling his hair out. Clearly McLeish's expenses, from Goodall's point of view, were out of control and it caused him immense worry."

This, then, was the chaotic picture emerging by the time Ermine's public prospectus was issued a few days later on July 23, 1985.

"The object of the Partnership," would-be investors were told, "is to purchase thoroughbred bloodstock for breeding purposes.

"The local bloodstock industry is following international trends with large annual increases in average sales prices. In the United Kingdom, the Tattersall's Highflyer sale at Newmarket saw a 43% increase on last year's figures. Similarly, Trentham sales this year were up approximately 40%.

"The overall quality of bloodstock offered for sale in New Zealand last year was by far the best ever seen and is predicted to improve as more discerning buyers visit New Zealand."

The promoter's statement in the prospectus attributed the stronger NZ market to the arrival of top-class stallions like *Sir Tristram*, *Imposing* and *Bletchingly* and, in Australia, "stallions such as the extremely well bred and performed Danzatore and Godswalk".

"International breeders are taking an active interest in our bloodstock industry and, as a result, it is expected that more proven stallions and mares will be sent to Australasia.

"The aim is to improve the overall Australasian standard of bloodstock which can be traded with the established northern markets. English and Irish mares over the past few seasons have been responsible for a high proportion of group races won in both New Zealand and Australia.

"The Partnership intends to purchase impeccably bred Irish, English and Australian broodmares together with local mares. Shares in top stallions in Australia and New Zealand will be purchased. Yearlings are to be sold at select sales at Trentham, Sydney and Newmarket (United Kingdom)."

So much for the fluff, now the Ermine prospectus was getting down to business, with a four paragraph section entitled "Operations Plan" detailing what investors could expect for their money.

Ermine was shopping for 10 mares, and also stated "three shares in *Godswalk* will be sought."

Back in earlier centuries, horse breeders came up with a plan to divide stallions into "shares". Each stallion would comprise forty shares, which at the time was thought to represent the maximum number of mares a stallion could cover in a season. The breeder would walk his horse from farm to farm, and farmers who'd purchased a share would have one of their mares join the stallion for a romantic interlude in the clover.

Today, stallions are still sold as a forty-share parcel, but they can now mate with as many as ninety mares in a season. Not only do shareholders get their own mares covered, but as a syndicate they can sell their stallion's services to outsiders for considerable pots of dosh – £100,000 a time – a far cry from the days of yore.

"It's to do with veterinary work, really," notes Mitchell McLeish. "In the old days it was a hit or miss event. You didn't know whether the mare had a proper follicle or not, you just knew she was in heat so you'd cover her maybe four or five times, where today a stallion only covers maybe one and a quarter times per pregnancy.

"In 1984, horses were standing for as much as US$1 million per service."

Godswalk was the pride and joy of Colin Hayes' Lindsay Park stud in Australia. A champion sprinter from England, he'd sired stakes winners in six countries, and was in a similar league to New Zealand's Sir Tristram, although perhaps not quite as sought after.

Earnings figures for 1984/85 showed *Godswalk's* average yearling price was $156,000, with a high of $330,000. In contrast, *Sir Tristram's* average was $192,500, with a high of $750,000.

Colin Hayes, meanwhile, was to be involved with Ermine, according to the promoter's statement, which described him as one of Australia's leading trainers and a world record-holder for the number of winners in one season.

"He is also well known for his association with Robert Sangster, and the Partnership is expected to benefit from this association in the future."

Hayes and two others, Mitchell McLeish and New Zealand's Okawa stud owner Tom Lowry, made up Ermine's advisory panel.

Tom Lowry's stud would host "approximately two" of the mares, four would be agisted [farmed] at Lindsay Park, and four at one of the Irish studs selected by McLeish.

This then was the picture painted in the Ermine prospectus, designed to lure clients of Russell McVeagh and Lawrence Anderson Buddle. When Keith Goodall's June 14, 1985 memo hit the desks of his accounting colleagues, they in turn consulted their clients. Among them, Auckland couple Graeme and Pat Hadlee.

"Our accountant," explained Graeme Hadlee over a coffee one autumn afternoon, "was a chap by the name of Rod Partington, and we were, like a lot of other companies at that stage, making quite a lot of money and needed something to reduce our taxation."

The opportunity had come in a rushed phone call from Partington to Hadlee.

"I've got this thing, it's just been put on the market, I don't know much about it myself but it looks bloody good!," the accountant had explained. No, he hadn't had the chance to go through the prospectus in detail, but Keith Goodall had told him it was definitely worth getting into. "It closes tonight. The Budget's tonight and all the applications have to be in tonight."

A year earlier, in 1984, Partington had offered them the chance to invest in the London stage musical *Starlight Express*, but the Hadlees had missed the deadline by the time they finally made up their minds.

"I can still remember sitting out there in the chair," sighed Pat Hadlee, gesturing toward the sun deck with its panoramic vista framed by the Rangitoto Island volcano, "and thinking gee what a neat play, on roller skates and all that, and I thought it would be quite fun to invest in Starlight, because I'm a lot more cultural than agricultural.

"I don't know which end of horse is which, so I would've been much happier investing in a stage show. So when this bloodstock thing came along I thought fine, OK, it's a similar thing to *Starlight*, but with horses."

In retrospect, she noted, "I'd have far rather invested in Mickey Mouse than bloody bloodstock, that's for sure!"

Pat had been rung by her husband and told to get over to Partington's office straight away. "Graeme said 'just sign the papers', and I thought 'that's a real dumb blonde wife thing to do, just get over there and sign the papers and don't ask any questions!'"

Nevertheless, the self-confessed blonde mother-of-three did just that, asking just one question of Rod Partington when she reached his office.

"Fine, what are we doing?"

"Oh, it's just a tax thing," mumbled the Lawrence Anderson Buddle partner, "and the Budget's tonight."

Graeme had already been and gone, so Pat Hadlee simply added her own moniker to the papers and walked out. A five minute visit that would cost seven years of her life.

Each had put in $10,000, matching the sum that Partington himself had personally invested. Over the next 12 months, all any of them would see was a mailout to investors.

"We only got the one big mailing," Graeme Hadlee recalled some years afterward, "we got beautiful pictures of horses – gorgeous horses – I thought I owned all these bloody horses, I couldn't believe it!

"I remember showing them to the kids and saying 'look, we own a share of this horse!', and the kids were going 'yahoo, Dad's rich, buy us another pair of Reeboks!'. And that's about as much as it meant."

Under the terms of the Ermine prospectus, the special partners were to share some special tax breaks. They included 33% depreciation on each broodmare or, in the case of stallions, depreciation at 50% a year.

"For the two years ended July 1985 and 1986 the deduction for taxation purposes (inclusive of depreciation) should be equal to approximately 150% of the special partners' capital contributions," noted page 11 of the prospectus.

"Any deductions in future years will be set off against income received by the Partnership from the sale of bloodstock."

How, you may well ask, could an investor get a tax break of 150% if the horses were only being depreciated at 33% or 50%? Good question – it works like this: The depreciation allowance applies to all the bloodstock that Ermine buys. If, for example, it buys $6 million worth of horses, then it is that $6 million that is being depreciated at – let's say – 33%. At the end of year one, the partnership as a whole will enjoy $2 million worth of tax writedowns.

Now, if the investors have only provided $1.4 million of the partnership's funding but are entitled to all the profits and all the losses, you can see they'll get back almost 150% of what they put in. The balance of Ermine's funding, $5 million, was in the form of a loan, and the bankers weren't investing for the sake of tax breaks, they wanted interest on that loan. Therefore they allowed the tax breaks applying to their $5 million to be spread among the special partners.

These calculations are rough, done simply to illustrate the tax rebate mechanism. Obviously actual tax rebates would differ from year to year depending on numerous variable factors. There was nothing illegal in these tax breaks, nor would people have rushed to invest if they thought there was.

"I saw it not as tax evasion, or a tax loop or tax anything!" said Pat Hadlee. "I just saw it as 'you've made a lot of money, invest in this', and I knew that we weren't going to make money for a while, but eventually the horses would do well and we would have to deal with that problem when that came around."

This, then, was the picture emerging on July 31, 1985 – or the picture available to investors at least. However, it's alleged in a Statement of Claim filed with the High Court that something very different was going on behind the scenes, out of sight of the special partners in Ermine or prospective investors.

It is this, they say, that began the bloodstock fraud.

CHAPTER 6

Hello, I'm Mr Ed

"Never look a gift horse in the mouth."
— ST. JEROME, C.342–420

Imagine, for a moment, that you are part of a syndicate buying the best racehorse breeding stock in the world. Along with hundreds of others, you have pooled your funds and created a large purse with which to go shopping, alongside the likes of the Aga Khan.

The executives managing your combined millions travel the world on your behalf, stopping in at the best stud farms in Ireland, the United States and Australia. They buy horses.

That's how it is supposed to work. But what if something else was happening? What if somebody is running a secret company, unbeknownst to the investors, which will be slipped into the purchasing process as an intermediary. The secret company buys – for argument's sake – five brood mares from the studs at a cost of half a million dollars.

The secret company, on the same day, then sells those five mares to you investors for a million dollars. Except, you don't realise that you've bought the horses from this secret company – you were told you'd bought a million dollars worth of horseflesh direct from the stud.

The mystery company secretly pockets the half million dollar commission it made on the deal, and you've ended up with overpriced horses.

Get the picture? It really is that simple.

But who was behind it, and why did it take a seven year legal battle for the facts to emerge? Why did New Zealand's so called premier crime fighting agency, the Serious Fraud Office, not do a thorough investigation?, and why have there been allegations in Parliament and/or at the Winebox Inquiry of a cover-up of the issues behind the bloodstock and film deals?

On July 31st, 1985, the very same day that Ermine breathed life, banking records obtained by investigators show payments of US$2.3 million were made by the Ermine partnership to a company called Zorasong Ltd. The payment was for "bloodstock acquisition". But Zorasong was not a stud farm.

Zorasong was a secret company, registered in Britain but controlled via Hong Kong. Who owned or controlled it? That would be the $64 million question that Chris Dickie would pursue for nearly a decade.

So what had been going on behind the scenes, and why was Ermine buying horses from a company with paid up capital of a mere six dollars?

During the conceptual development of Ermine in early 1985, Carran and Kirkham had sent McLeish off to the overseas studs to look at prospective bloodstock purchases, while back in Auckland they concentrated on getting the deal structured properly.

McLeish traded on the fact that he was representing Challenge Corporate Services, a sub-unit of the massive Fletcher Challenge, New Zealand's largest company. Mixing with magnates like Robert Sangster and John Magnier, McLeish found the Challenge link was an impressive calling card at the studs in Ireland, North America and Australia. But he got a shock when Chris Kirkham told him there'd been a change of plan. McLeish was told to drop Challenge out of the introductions and tell the studs he was purchasing the bloodstock on behalf of a Hong Kong company called Two Song Fong Ltd. Naturally, Mitchell McLeish was not impressed and made his feelings clearly known down the phone line.

More than a decade later, McLeish still laughs grimly at mention of the name Two Song Fong Ltd. "The only reason I was unhappy about Two Song Fong was just the way it sounded. You've got to remember that in those days I had no idea about shelter companies and tax havens. Sure, I knew they existed and I knew the people that we were dealing with were in tax havens from Liberia to all over the place, because that's the way these types of people operate.

"But Two Song Fong Ltd came as a shock to me, because I actually felt at that stage that I was dealing for the Fletcher Group. I'd been gone about three months I think, trying to do some deals, and all of a sudden we weren't Fletchers – we were some outfit I'd never heard of and I thought would have absolutely no credence with [horse] sellers.

"They could feel happy that they were going to get paid from New Zealand's largest company, but some outfit in Hong Kong?" He leaves the point hanging, to emphasise it.

When he arrived back in New Zealand, however, McLeish found Paul Carran ready with an explanation. Carran told him the purchasing sleight of hand was a necessary ingredient of structuring the tax breaks and the financial package. He smoothed ruffled feathers slightly by explaining that rather than Two Song Fong Ltd, they would use a company in Hong Kong called Zorasong. At least it sounded less like a Chinese laundromat and more like a real company.

McLeish was also informed of the existence of Bonshow Ltd, a Hong Kong shelf company that would ostensibly provide a half million US dollars to Ermine. This loan would later be alleged to be fictitious, and designed only to mislead the New Zealand Inland Revenue Department by inflating Ermine's costs, on paper, and therefore inflating its tax breaks.

In the High Court Statement of Claim filed by investors in the Ermine partnership, it was alleged: "The acquisition of Zorasong on Russell McVeagh's instructions had not been effected on behalf of, or on the instructions of, Challenge Corporate Services Ltd."

The Statement of Claim named accountants Keith Goodall and Robert Nurse from Lawrence Anderson Buddle as joint first defendants with three directors from Challenge Corporate Services: Colin Graham Perrin, Albert Barrie Downey and Dennis Albert Ferrier. The second defendants to the action were Russell McVeagh McKenzie Bartleet & Co.

In the document, angry investors spelt out their other allegations.

"Carran and/or members of the Russell McVeagh tax team formulated or knowingly agreed to and helped provide for. . .the price to be paid for the bloodstock [to] be inflated by means of purchase through certain concealed companies, including Zorasong Limited, with the aid of Bonshow Limited, a HK$2 company incorporated in Hong Kong on 23 April 1985."

The plaintiffs alleged that ultimate control of the companies lay in New Zealand, but that "the price inflation, and the profitability, and the location of the ultimate control and direction of those companies, as well as the identity of those in whom the ultimate beneficial interest therein was vested would be kept concealed from any person who might have a duty, or a legitimate need, to inquire."

What this carefully-worded paragraph of legalese meant was this: the prices of the horses were being artificially jacked-up through the aegis of tax haven companies. The use of a tax haven meant that investigators could not penetrate the corporate veil to see who really owned, controlled or benefited from these secret companies, but it was alleged that control was being carried out from New Zealand.

Just to hammer the point home, the Statement of Claim crystallised the allegation further, saying "that the operations, assets, control, and ultimate beneficial ownership of those entities deliberately were concealed from the New Zealand Commissioner of Inland Revenue, and from any other persons whose duties or legitimate interests might require them to inquire."

Important ingredients in the concealment, the plaintiffs pleaded, included the fact that both Zorasong and Bonshow were located offshore, and controlled via offshore nominees "associated with Deloittes, chartered accountants, in Hong Kong and England."

Why was all this important? Because investors in Ermine were not told in the investment prospectus that they were buying horses from a Hong Kong entity being run by the people they had entrusted their money with.

When Ermine purchased US$2.3 million worth of horses from Zorasong on July 31 1985, included in that figure were five horses from the Lindsay Park Stud near Adelaide, in South Australia. Ermine was charged NZ$1.7 million for those five horses alone.

The most expensive was top stallion *Godswalk*, priced at $750,000 for just three of its 40 shares. A similar small slice of the stallion *Gielgud* knocked Ermine back $300,000. Bringing up the rear were the mares *Moonlight* and *Adaptable*, priced at $245,000 each, and lastly *Crystal Bright* at $160,000.

That's what Ermine investors paid for those horses. But the documents tell a different story.

In a 1991 letter to Chris Dickie, Australian accountant Robert Williams confirmed he had acted as Secretary to the syndicate that had owned *Gielgud* back in 1985. He says three shares in the stallion were sold to Zorasong on July 30 1985 for just over A$90,000. At the exchange rate on the day, that would have been just NZ$116,000. A far cry from the $300,000 paid by Ermine to Zorasong 24 hours later.

But the Statement of Claim goes further. It alleges that all of the five horses had been grossly overpriced in the 24 hours they were owned by Zorasong, which had purchased them from Lindsay Park Stud for a total of only NZ$791,000, not the $1.7 million that Ermine investors were told about.

"The markup of approximately NZ$908,000" it was alleged, was taken by Zorasong and "had been determined by Carran, Goodall, Kirkham and Perrin." It stayed hidden from Ermine investors, said the plaintiffs, by virtue of the concealment mechanisms already spelt out.

From the Irish studs on that same day, Zorasong bought six horses for NZ$2.5 million, including top class mares *Hard to Tell* and *Rustic Lace*. By the time the six mares were in Ermine's hands, a short time later, their prices had increased to just ten thousand dollars shy of three million.

So what went wrong?

During 1986 international bloodstock prices crashed.

It happened in what the industry labelled "Sunday, Bloody Sunday".

Before dealing with the events of that day, it is probably important to spell out again the way the bloodstock industry works. Investors might own a mare for breeding purposes. Each year they would pay very big money to have their mare serviced by a top stallion.

In many cases, the service – or nomination – fees ran over $100,000. If the mare's owners didn't have that money they would have to borrow it from the bank. They hoped to repay the mortgage by making a profit on the sale of the resultant colt or yearling.

Depending on the quality of the parents, the yearlings could be very valuable.

"In 1982 for example the top-priced yearling* sold in the world made $13.1 million. The bloodstock market was terribly overheated," according to Mitchell McLeish. "Both the Arab and American economies had been very strong. It was really fuelled by the Arabs, because they wanted desperately to win a Derby. They'd been at the game, and they'd probably spent about a billion US dollars, and they still hadn't won one."

With all the pressure, however, something had to give.

"There was an indication, in the July sales earlier in 1986, when sales fell back sharply – around 23 percent – but you sometimes get that in a sale. But on Bloody Sunday, the very top end of the foal market fell 90 percent that day, which has never happened since or before."

---

* In 1996, the top-priced yearling fetched less than $2 million.

McLeish was there. He watched it unfold and saw the horror in human terms that was left in its wake.

"It was just an utter sense of desperation. I mean, fellows shot themselves afterwards. They actually committed suicide. The whole farm, everything, was gone, in the space of one night. They probably owed a fortune, most of the guys, in nominations and the horses were making about 10 percent of their cost. It was just staggering."

In plain terms, investors who'd borrowed huge money to get their mares pregnant in the expectation of making several times as much money from the sale of the yearlings suddenly found no buyers for the young horses, and banks looking for repayment.

Amid the carnage, a close friend of McLeish's gave it all away. Irish bloodstock agent Paul Doyle, a son of the legendary agent Jack Doyle, decided he had nothing left to live for.

"He swallowed a shotgun. He went off in the car on his own and didn't come back," said McLeish, his voice melancholy as he remembered the day. "Left young children and a young wife. It's not a part of my life that I like to remember that much."

The desperation was palpable.

"It really was. That sale comes along in November and you've just got your mares back in foal as of the first of October. The stallion fees were still enormously expensive, because they hadn't had any adjustment at all. The stallion fees do adjust to the market, but you're always two years behind with the yearling market and at least a year behind for the foal market, so not only have you just lost the service fee of the foal you had at the sales, but there was no possibility of you – unless you were a very wealthy man – meeting your high nomination that the same mare was carrying for the following season.

"You had to be there, really. There were stunned silences."

An Ermine foal that McLeish had had high hopes for was passed in at £20,000.

"She was a filly, and we were struggling to get a bid at all, and by this stage I'd realised that the bloody market was crazy and we'd have to do something. We decided to buy them back – our own stock – and she was one of them."

Fortunately for the partnership, the filly went on to sell the following year as a yearling for £160,000. One of the lucky ones. There were not many happy endings.

There was a combination of factors that had combined to superheat the thoroughbred breeding industry. Perhaps the biggest, already alluded to, was the strength of the world economies and a fierce desire by the Arabs to breed a Derby-winner.

But a second factor would have to be the quality of the bloodlines as well. The world's top stallions of the day were *Northern Dancer* and his progeny, and they're regarded as "the grandfathers of our modern racehorses". But *Northern Dancer* and the next generation are dead. While his bloodline is still strong, in 1997 it no longer has what McLeish calls "the aura". The top stallions in the

United States are now standing for less than US$200,000 a service, compared with triple that or more in the past.

Australasia's top stallion, *Dane Hill*, despite being a champion sire, is considered second rate in Europe and commands only £15,000 per service in the northern hemisphere, and $100,000 when he's down under.

But perhaps one of the main reasons that the bubble burst in November 1986 came back again to the Arabs on one hand, and short-sighted and greedy breeders on the other.

"It wasn't just the fact that they hadn't won a Derby. While they were buying up all this bloodstock they were building up a huge capital bank of horses – really high quality horses. And if they liked the way something was running they'd go off and buy the mare. The Arabs had bought so many of the well-bred mares that that level of stock wasn't available any more."

By selling off the mares capable of producing top foals and yearlings, the breeders had cut themselves off at the knees. At the end of Sunday, Bloody Sunday, the Ermine partnership, whose investors had unwittingly bought high, found itself with overpriced bloodstock and no one buying.

"For the New Zealand partnerships," confirmed McLeish, "that was the end of them! I mean, the Buckingham partnership – because of the way it was structured – was a tax deal really, first and foremost.

"They had to buy foals, which I wasn't terribly keen on, in July because that was our balance date. We'd purchased in July with the idea of selling in November, just to get our money back and get the tax break, and then to buy more mares and things at that time. But with the foal market falling through the ground like that, that was one of the major reasons Buckingham failed."

Not that Buckingham's promoters weren't trying to put a brave face on it. In a November 1986 report to punters, director Chris Kirkham described it like this: "The bloodstock market has been on a tremendous upswing but, like any commodity, this inevitably had to level off. The general trend this year has been a downturn in average prices.

"One of the beneficial effects of these lower yearling prices will be that for 1987 service fees in the northern hemisphere will reduce by 30-50 percent. Big stakes in racing make people want to buy horses and this is continuing. New buyers are constantly appearing and the demand is generally buoyant for sound horses with good pedigrees."

Kirkham also had theories on what had caused the market "correction".

"All markets in 1986 were dominated by the Arab buyers, which comprised five major families, the Maktoum family* being the most notable. These Arabs are responsible for 38 percent of the entire revenue of the Select Yearling Sale in Keeneland and fifteen percent of the recent US Broodmare/Foal Sale. They also purchased two out of the top ten lots in Europe this year.

"One factor which affected several of the sales in 1986 was the low profile

---

* The ruling family of Dubai.

adopted by the Sangster team. This low profile was caused by over-spending in the previous year, especially on the high-priced yearlings at Keeneland where [Robert] Sangster was the buyer of the US$13 million yearling [by *Northern Dancer*'s son *Nijinsky*], as well as the withdrawal from the Sangster syndicate of three important members.

"The Sangster team's cashflow was even further impaired when their stable produced no top racetrack performances ending in a successful stallion syndication. Consequently, the buying pressure was absent at Keeneland Sales resulting in fewer high prices.

"Overall," concluded Kirkham, "notwithstanding the very bad foal sale, the [Buckingham] partnership emerged in a solid position."

Yeah. Right. Significantly, by December 1987 – a year later – Kirkham's tone had become a lot more sober. He described the events of 1986 as "nothing short of disastrous."

It is also perhaps significant, in an international context, to note that the two leading studs in the United States, Spendthrift and Gainsway, both folded in the aftermath of the crash. They were the oldest and largest farms in Kentucky. One of them stood eighty stallions. Their collapse devastated the world bloodstock industry.

"They just fell on their asses," said McLeish [no pun intended]. "The stallions had cost too much and the syndication had gone mad. There were horses being syndicated for ridiculous sums. *El Gran Senor*, he got syndicated for $40 million. He got beaten by a nose in the Derby, and would have been syndicated for US$80 million if he'd won.

"Twas a great game," he remarked wistfully in his Irish lilt. "But you'd want to have a head for heights, you know."

So that's the picture the NZ bloodstock collapse is set against, and that's without taking into account the price inflation of the horses under the table. It is important to remember, throughout this story, that none of the investors were ever told about the mysterious company Zorasong, or its secret role clipping the ticket as the horses went through on their way from the studs to the partnerships. The prospectii and promotional material for the Ermine, Buckingham and Wicklow syndicates indicated to investors that they were purchasing their bloodstock direct from top international studs.

It's also important to remember that Chris Dickie, who at the start of 1989 was just beginning his investigation on behalf of disgruntled investors, knew nothing of this either for the entire first year of his investigation. He actually missed the first hint of Zorasong's existence even though he was holding the evidence in his hands.

It had come during his search of Chris Kirkham's office for the Wicklow subscription certificates. While rifling through the drawers of Kirkham's secretary, Dickie found a document, a horse sale contract, headed "Zorasong to Buckingham". The name of the horse involved was *Mourwara*. While he recognised the horse, the name Zorasong meant nothing to him and certainly wasn't one of the studs, so Dickie put the contract back in the drawer and forgot about it. He would spend the next five years mentally kicking himself around Kirkham's office in his nightmares, because he would soon discover just how crucial Zorasong was to his entire investigation.

"To this day I am still shattered by that," he sighed over a beer one afternoon. "If ever, *ever* I am asked to do an investigation for anyone else ever again, I will photocopy every bloody thing, because you never know when it is going to be relevant."

CHAPTER 7

Buckingham Palace

"Four legs good, two legs bad."
– GEORGE ORWELL, 1903–1950, *ANIMAL FARM*

December 1988 passed. With Christmas, and a long, hot summer, it was easy for Dickie to forget the gathering storm awaiting his return to work. But the problem, of course, wasn't going anywhere, especially with an impatient Westpac Bank beginning to rattle the cages.

The lawyer had been appointed to a special committee to negotiate with Westpac, but when Dickie, John Taylor and the rest of the committee stepped from the lift into the opulent, marble-endowed 27th floor foyer of the Westpac Tower in Auckland, they discovered it was all downhill in more ways than one. There to greet them was Glyn Boyt, a senior loan manager at the bank's Auckland office. Not originally involved in approving the loans, Boyt had been brought in as troubleshooter by the bank as it struggled to deal with the crisis.

Dickie was eager to share news with Westpac of his Wicklow discovery – the missing $2.966 million in share subscriptions that would spread the debt burden more fairly for investors in the Buckingham partnership. Up to this point, the members of the public who had put their names to $4 million of Buckingham's capital were being held liable for up to triple their investment.

Buckingham's balance sheet, as at February 28, 1989, showed share capital of $4 million. Against that Kirkham had applied a trading loss of $5.3 million, and also the drop in the value of the bloodstock, which had tumbled up to $4.6 million in worth. It meant that with capital of $4 million, Buckingham's investors were facing a loss of $5.9 million on which the bank would be imposing penalties.

But if the share capital figure was really $7 million, then the deficit becomes only $2.9 million – a much easier debt to repay. The lawyer felt sure the bank would welcome the discovery that Wicklow owed the bank some of that money. No such luck.

Across the table from Boyt, Dickie began his pitch.

"Mr Boyt, the amount which the partners guaranteed was twice the amount of their capital, that it bears to the original and subscribed capital of the partnership. The capital of the partnership is $7 million. It is not four as you say, because look –"

He didn't get the chance to finish his explanation or even lay down the documents that proved his case. Glyn Boyt was on his feet and, with a face like thunder, leaning across the table menacingly.

"Don't you be a smartass young lawyer with me," he snarled, thrusting his finger just centimetres from Dickie's chest. "You borrowed the money, and you're going to pay it!" At that moment the noise of a pin dropping in that room would have sounded like a herd of stampeding elephants. Nobody said a word.

The banker also indicated he wasn't interested in Dickie's documents. Westpac was going to play hardball.

In a fury, Dickie opened his mouth and uttered one of those immortal lines that he would later come to regret. Very much.

"Well if you are going to take action against the investors, I want to be the first to know!"

And this was the committee's first meeting with Westpac. Not that investors were being given any clue to the behind-the-scenes fracas in the committee's official reports. Indeed, the picture in January and February 1989 appeared to be one of rapprochement and civility.

"The bank is as anxious as partners to straighten out the matter," noted Dickie in a report to investors in February 1989, "and recognises that they should sometimes run with clients rather than close in. Also, in a fire sale situation, it was made clear that the Partnership's bloodstock could realise as low as one fifth of the real value."

Buckingham's bloodstock consultant, Mitchell McLeish, was dead against a fire sale, and warned that any move to sell the herd before October 1, 1989, "would be a disaster".

Chris Kirkham agreed, spelling out to partners that while they owned valuable horses, they were only valuable as long as you didn't try to sell them.

"The partnership was established on the 3rd March 1986 and the partnership acquired most of its bloodstock in July 1986," Kirkham wrote in a special report.

"At that time bloodstock prices were buoyant and, as subsequently became evident, were at their peak prior to the disastrous foal sale in Ireland in November 1986. Since that sale the partnership has experienced difficulties in selling its interests in progeny due to the falling prices experienced worldwide in the bloodstock industry."

Horse breeding, he noted sagely, is a cyclical industry with peaks and troughs. "Prices may not increase significantly for another two or three years.* These factors must be taken into account in attempting to value the partnership's bloodstock for sale in the next 12 to 18 months."

---

* One of the mares purchased privately by McLeish and his colleagues was producing foals worth £1,000,000 and US$1,000,000 respectively in the mid-1990s. "That's still in a bad market," he told the author. "If we were back in the early 80s these horses could have been making five or six million apiece."

Buckingham, he pointed out, had significant bloodstock holdings in Australia, and a major sale was approaching in Sydney at Easter. The only problem? Fallen business angel Laurie Connell, whose shonky Rothwells Bank had collapsed, forcing him to dump his own collection of horses on the market, thereby driving prices down further.

"Even if [Buckingham's] bloodstock is sold off individually in an attempt to avoid the sales being seen as a dispersal sale," continued Kirkham, "there is a substantial risk that any sale of the partnership's broodmares will be immediately perceived by the bloodstock agents in Australia as a dispersal sale. Rumours of this may already be in the market."

Putting the Australian problem to one side for a moment, Kirkham attempted to address the Irish problem.

"The partnership also holds percentage interests of bloodstock in Ireland. When [Buckingham] was established the concept was that the partnership would obtain the benefit of high leverage from borrowings from Westpac Securities Ltd and would then invest its equity and debt capital [partners' funds and bank loans] in as many mares in Ireland as possible.

"In order to achieve this the partnership bought percentage interests in mares rather than purchasing 100% of any mare. This has the advantage of spreading the risks of farming bloodstock over a wide band of mares and reducing the impact on the partnership if a mare fails to get into foal or aborts or has an injured or defective foal.

"The converse effect of the foregoing is that if the partnership chooses to attempt to sell its percentage interest in the mares it has an extremely limited market upon which to do so. The most likely buyers are the owners of the other interests in the mares.

"Clearly, they are in an extremely strong position to make a low offer for the percentage interest and may, in fact, discourage the sale of those interests to their competitors. It is impossible to sell the percentage interest in open auction."

But the sting, for already disillusioned Buckingham investors, came in the tail as Kirkham raised and then dashed their hopes.

"The only realistic market for the sale of these percentage shares is to retain a bloodstock agency in Ireland to attempt to locate a buyer or buyers who may be prepared to buy such a limited interest in the mares. The most likely buyers for such mares would be other investment partnerships being established on the same principles as Buckingham.

"The difficulty with this is that at the moment most of those partnerships are established in Australia, and before Australian investors will undertake such an investment the bloodstock must be agisted [farmed] in Australia. Consequently, this market is excluded from this possibility."

Kirkham also raised the option of swapping the percentage shares in various mares for one whole mare, and on-selling that horse at an auction, but he didn't think the other co-owners would cooperate.

All told, the partnership owned nine mares in the Southern Hemisphere –

seven of those outright – and 23 mares in the Northern Hemisphere in varying percentages from as low as 8.7% to as high as 50%. According to Kirkham their combined values were somewhere between an estimated low of $2.8 million and a high of $4.3 million.

Westpac Securities was owed almost eight million dollars, and sundry creditors a further three-quarters of a million.

This left the partnership nursing a loss of up to $5.9 million, even after a fire sale, and meant that partners who'd already lost ten thousand dollars each, would have to contribute a further $14,700.

Among the other options being considered was an adjustment of the repayment schedule, and another $3 million loan. Alternatively, the partners could attempt a partial payment of the outstanding base debt, and seek a "discharge of liability" to the extent of that payment. There were legal difficulties with that solution.

As 1989 grew older, the pressure began to take its toll. In a report to partners dated 14 April, Kirkham signalled that time was running out.

"At the last special meeting of partners, the majority was of the view that the Partnership's Committee take its time to explore ways of disposing of the bloodstock over a period of time, with a view to maximising the return from the disposal of the bloodstock. However, there was also a significant minority view at that meeting which wished the bloodstock to be disposed of forthwith on the basis that interest was still running on the $8 million loan, which would far outweigh any possible increase in price of bloodstock gained by waiting.

"Since the last meeting, the pressure from the latter group has increased immensely, as has the pressure from Westpac. The situation has now been reached where Westpac is preparing to call up the guarantees of each individual partner, and this is expected shortly."

For Chris Kirkham, who'd been instrumental in the horse partnerships from the very beginning, the next paragraph must have been a hard one to write.

"The situation has now been reached where it is obvious that the partnership can no longer continue, even for a short time, as it has no funds and its northern hemisphere broodmares are currently foaling and incurring new stud fees as they go back into foal.

"It is therefore impossible to allow business to continue while in an insolvent state. Therefore there is no option but to sell the bloodstock forthwith and pay the proceeds from the sale of the bloodstock to Westpac, and negotiate with Westpac on the best possible terms for the payment of the deficit remaining, payable under each partner's guarantee."

Turning the page of Kirkham's report, there was more bad news for investors. Two months earlier they'd been told their bloodstock was worth between $2.8 million and $4.3 million. Now, Kirkham revealed an offer was on the table to buy out Buckingham's bloodstock for just $2 million.

The group making the offer comprised a handful of Buckingham's largest investors, including Bob Wilson and Murray Carter. The other two shareholders were to be consultant Mitchell McLeish and Chris Kirkham himself.

"Messrs Wilson and Carter have suffered heavy losses from their Buckingham investment," wrote Kirkham, "being the largest and second largest partners in the partnership with a combined capital investment of $500,000."

The new group, calling themselves Scorten Investments, figured they could take over the bloodstock, pay off the trading debts, and turn the business around to make a profit over a five year period. If they could salvage something from the debacle they'd be happy.

Of the $2 million they were offering for the horses, however, the two hundred partners in Buckingham would only receive $800,000 from the deal – a drop in the bucket against the $8 million debt to Westpac Securities. This was because the studs in Australia and Ireland were owed substantial sums of money for babysitting, feeding and servicing the herds.

Eight hundred grand in the hand for horses that the partners had paid more than $6 million for! What the hell had gone wrong? Part of the answer could be found in the Kirkham report.

"In the manager's report to the last meeting, the low valuation of the bloodstock of the partnership totalled NZ$2.79 million. Recent discussions with [the Coolmore Stud's vet] have indicated that the NZ$600,000 low valuation attributed to the Irish yearlings is [still] excessive, as many of the foals are now not well conformed and not even their pedigree can make up for the conformation faults."

It is fair to say that the various Irish breeding ventures involving the partnerships and their promoters had a string of unfortunate mishaps.

In a letter to a disgruntled Ermine investor in February 1988, Chris Kirkham explained that a yearling by the top mare *Hard to Tell* "was knocked over outside the sales ring immediately prior to its sale, hit its head on the railing and received considerable injury to its back, completely incapacitating the horse.

"The *Rustic Lace* colt was actually sold but was returned to us by the purchaser as, in the purchaser's opinion, it had failed a medical check as it had a wind defect. The horse is now back in Ireland and we have had the full expertise of the Coolmore vets brought to bear on the problem, and they have indicated that it is a minor problem and that the horse will probably grow out of it but if it does not, then minor surgery will correct it.

"As Mr McLeish has pointed out in his report, Tommy Stack, who is caring for both these colts, considers the *Rustic Lace* colt to be a very fine racehorse. This horse is also eligible for the Magic Million race to be run later in 1988."

Years later, McLeish would reminisce about the vagaries of fortune when it came to the Ermine thoroughbreds. "Ermine had a bit of bad luck. It had an awful lot of money tied up in one mare, *Hard To Tell*, and one of its star foals got hurt on the day of the sales. The last foal had made eight hundred and sixty thousand guineas, by the same sire, and this one couldn't be sold, so that really knocked us to bits.

"Our second best horse went to the sales at Goffs and made a lot of money, and then he got spun on his wind, which is a veterinary thing. Most of the capital was tied up in two horses, so it was a bad stroke of luck."

The $400,000 Buckingham mare *Spirit in the Sky* gave birth to a foal that sold for more than 400,000 Irish guineas in the 1985 yearling sales, but its 1986 yearling lived up to the mare's name, dying before it could be sold. In 1987 the *Spirit in the Sky* yearling sold for just 36,000 guineas, and in 1988 the mare gave birth to a foal worth only nine thousand.

All up, the sales of Buckingham's yearlings in Ireland raised a total of only 1.1 million guineas in the 1987, 88 and 89 years.

The same mares, in 1985 alone, produced yearlings worth 3.4 million and in 1986 yearlings worth 2.7 million. Unfortunately, Buckingham didn't own the progeny in 1985 and 1986, so shared nothing. Buckingham's first year in the income stream, 1987, saw sales of only half a million guineas.

The figures illustrate the horrendous impact of "Sunday, Bloody Sunday" in November 1986. When Kirkham, Carran and McLeish had been doing the budgets for their proposed bloodstock partnerships back in 1985 and 1986, it must have seemed like a licence to print money. But by April 14, 1989, it was anything but. Kirkham was recommending to the partners that they accept the buyout offer by the new company.

"On the basis of the partnership receiving $800,000 from the sale of this bloodstock and assuming the worst case, which is that partners would have to contribute the remainder of the $8 million loan, then partners would collectively have to pay to Westpac $7.2 million which is equivalent to $17,850 per $10,000 of capital." Oh joy, groaned two hundred partners.

The relationship with Westpac, meanwhile, was beginning to get tense. In April, 1989, Chris Dickie had sent out a letter to investors urging them to put money into a legal trust fund operated by his lawfirm, McVeagh Fleming, pending a possible partial repayment to the bank of the outstanding debt. Dickie enclosed a copy of a letter he'd received from Westpac's Loans Administration manager, Glyn Boyt.

A few days later, Westpac sent its own letter to the investors.

"We have not been privy to the letter circulated by the Committee but advise that the copy of Westpac's letter was used without our knowledge or consent," Boyt wrote, somewhat testily. It was the second tremor between Westpac and Dickie in what would become an earthquake of litigation.

The lawyer was finding he'd become a touchstone for the cause. The list of investors wanting to investigate possible legal action quickly grew. As complaints and documentation poured in, Dickie set aside a room inside McVeagh Fleming to handle it all. It quickly became known as "Buckingham Palace", and would soon become the nerve centre for the massive operation that was to follow.

In another letter to investors, Dickie warned that "the current offer to purchase stock raises immediate questions as to the reasons for the substantial depreciation in the value of the bloodstock. . .and the most important issue, namely the inevitable shortfall with the bank loan and each special partner's purported guarantee for twice the original capital contribution together with interest.

"A number of partners have requested the writer to act for them and, to that end, we propose to instruct a QC to prepare an opinion as to the effect of the guarantee. It is the writer's view that we cannot undertake any meaningful negotiation with the bank until we know the strength of the legal argument relating to a defence or partial defence under the guarantee."

Events were now moving at speed, and gaining a momentum that would become impossible to stop. A Special Partners' Meeting had been called for May 1, 1989 in Auckland – at this point only a matter of days away. Buckingham investors were to receive yet another missive in the mailbox, this time from another group of investors urging them to rally to the cause.

"It is likely that the next meeting. . .will be the most important in the history of the partnership and its business," they wrote. "It is also likely that the result of the meeting will be actions which will seriously and permanently and adversely affect the financial affairs of each and every member of the partnership.

"The previous meetings have been poorly attended. It is doubtful that a majority of the members have attended at any of the previous meetings, or that the members attending plus the proxies received for the meeting have, together, constituted a majority."

They urged everyone to make an effort to attend the May Day meeting, particularly as "you may by now have been served with a notice of Westpac Banking Corporation which demands payment of that part of the debt to that bank which the partnership owes and which the bank claims that you have guaranteed. The time for making payment in terms of that notice may have expired by the date of the meeting on 1st May 1989."

The begging letter did the trick. At ten past three on Monday, May 1, a hundred and three partners filed into the Fitzroy Room at Auckland's Park Royal Hotel, armed with a further 74 proxies.

As an opening shot, Chris Dickie revealed he was resigning from the special committee set up to negotiate with Westpac. It had outlived its usefulness, he told the assemblage.

He also revealed 61 partners were now paying two hundred dollars each into the legal kitty for an opinion from Dr Tony Molloy QC on "all aspects surrounding the Westpac guarantee."

John Taylor reported on the bloodstock situation. The Australian horses that had cost the partners $1.8 million to buy were now worth only $1.2 million. The Irish horses, which were only owned in portions, carried debts imposed by the studs hosting them. "A total of $950,000 is required to be paid by the investor group in order to achieve a clear title to these animals," said Taylor. "Therefore, for practical purposes, the Irish bloodstock has no value." He noted that the Irish horses had cost investors $5 million to buy.

The offer on the table from Bob Wilson's group, Scorten Investments, to assume the stud liabilities and pay $800,000 cash for the horses, was accepted by a 75% majority, conditional on Wilson, Carter, McLeish and Kirkham finding the finance to pull it off.

In a tug-of-war for the hearts, minds and wallets of the investors, however, Westpac got back in the act the following week. In another blunderbuss letter to all partners, Glyn Boyt noted the expiry of the bank's May 1 deadline, and sounded doubtful about the bloodstock rescue deal.

"Based on a settlement date for the sale of bloodstock of June 15, 1989, the total liability of the partnership on that date will have increased with accrued interest to $8,628,850.21.

"The liability per unit [of one thousand dollars invested] will increase from $2,085.56 to $2,140.09 on June 15, 1989.

"The receipt by Westpac of the $800,000 from bloodstock sales on that day would reduce your liability per unit invested to $1941.68 on which interest will continue to accrue and compound until it is paid at approximately ninety cents per day per unit invested."

The minimum investment in Buckingham had been ten units, or ten thousand dollars, so partners with ten units were being told that their indebtedness was growing by nine dollars a day. "The effect of compounding interest will see your liability escalate alarmingly in the event that delays occur in payment," wrote Boyt darkly. The bank's taxi meter was veritably spinning, and it was the investors who felt they were being taken for a ride.

Inside Buckingham Palace, Chris Dickie was plotting. OK, so the bankers were being bastards, but that's par for the course. Not unreasonably, Westpac wanted its cash. The sticking point seemed to be over who owed what.

Surely, thought Dickie, this could all be sorted out with some civilised discussion and compromise on all sides.

Even looking at the Wicklow purchase of a $2.9 million stake in the Buckingham syndicate, the McVeagh Fleming legal team did not suspect anything sinister. They thought it was a simple mistake by the statutory supervisor and the bank that had allowed $2.9 million worth of shares to be sold but not paid for.

Dickie's investigations, at this stage, were centred on Wicklow. One of his largest clients had been an investor in both Buckingham and Wicklow, and had passed on the Wicklow prospectus to Dickie at a very early point in the investigation.

The document stated that Wicklow had no contingent liabilities, but Dickie's discovery of Wicklow's unpaid stake in Buckingham gave the lie to that claim. Wicklow had a contingent liability of almost three million dollars long before it started seeking funds from investors in 1987. That liability dated back to a sequence of events that had taken place on Budget Night, July 31, 1986.

Realising that Buckingham's subscription was going to close undercapitalised, that night Russell McVeagh lawyer Paul Carran had engineered the creation of six small Wicklow partnerships, despite the fact that he was halfway across the world.

Dickie had become aware of this following an anonymous phone call from a man who told him to go and stand beside his fax machine. Within seconds it began spewing out a copy of a Paul Carran's instructions.

"Through the machine came this extraordinary document, which Carran had sent from Barronstown stud in Ireland on the night of July 31. A telegram which instructed Anzon to form the Wicklow partnerships and subscribe for the balance of the [unfilled] capital in Buckingham."

The first inklings of under-subscription for Carran had actually come a few days earlier. A legal file note dated July 29, 1986, records a phone conversation with Paul Carran, who was in Dublin with Chris Kirkham and phoning from the Cashel Palace Hotel. The file note lists tasks for "Erich and Brendan" who are told:

"Paul wants you both to spend the next three days working on Buckingham only – top priority. He wants you both to help Robin at Anzon – go up and see her this afternoon to go through it with her.

1. Paul wants to know the following urgently:
2. What amount of money in respect of the application has been applied for?
3. How many applications and the guarantees have been approved by Westpac?
4. Get ready to do allotment by 31 July 1986. Deed of Accession is to be ready to be signed under Power of Attorney by Anzon by 31 July 1986.

Paul needs the above information so that he can remit the moneys out of the account and draw down Westpac money on July 31 1986 (NZ time). He needs to know how much money they have."

The document goes on to remark on a *Sunday News* article.

"Re: the clobbering of Special Partnerships. In Paul's view it is rubbish. He is not too worried about it so far as Buckingham is concerned – it is crying wolf. In Paul's view it does not affect Buckingham. It does affect other partnerships but not Buckingham, as it has been done well."

There had, in fact, been considerable publicity for the Buckingham Partnership in the two weeks leading up to the 31st.

"Buckingham Buys Best" trumpeted an *Auckland Star* headline on July 18.

"The New Zealand thoroughbred industry has taken another major step into the international arena with the purchase of some of Europe's most sought-after bloodlines.

"Newly formed partnership Buckingham Investments (sic) has bought 30 top mares and 21 foals from the Barronstown Stud in Ireland."

Barronstown's co-owner, David Nagle, was naturally delighted at such a spend-up.

"By world standards the collection of mares in this deal is unique. Their progeny will qualify for the major select sales in the USA and Europe, such as the Keeneland sales, where the average yearling price in 1985 was more than $1 million."

In the *New Zealand Herald* of the same day, the focus was on Anzon Capital director and bloodstock promoter Chris Kirkham.

"Mr Kirkham said when offers for Buckingham's 7,000 units of $1,000 each close on July 31, the partnership would be the largest in New Zealand, with funds in excess of $13 million available.

"He would be disappointed if Buckingham produced a maiden pre-tax profit of less than $3 million.

"Mr Kirkham said Anzon Capital intended to have $50 million worth of high quality bloodstock under its control by the end of 1988."

Dickie grabbed a beer from the lawfirm's fridge, and sat down to read through the Wicklow documentation. The six Wicklow partnerships were much smaller than Buckingham and set up as ordinary partnerships, rather than special partnerships, now that the Government had closed the tax loopholes relating to the latter.

Where Ermine had borrowed from Equiticorp, and Buckingham had borrowed from Westpac Securities, the Wicklow syndicates were borrowing from Chris Kirkham's old haunt, the DFC Bank, a taxpayer funded venture-capital provider.

In the offering memorandum to keen investors, the start-up date of July 31, 1986 was noted, along with the fact that "each partnership had subscribed for units in the Buckingham Partnership. The partnerships do not have any outstanding debts, contingent liabilities, claims or actions against them,"

From the subscription certificates he'd swiped from Kirkham's office, Dickie could see how many units Wicklow had taken in Buckingham. Five of the Wicklow partnerships had taken 500 units each. The sixth had subscribed for 466.

"It struck me as a very precise figure," said Chris Dickie. "You don't just go '500' five times and then suddenly pluck 466 out of thin air."

The total of 2,966 units in Buckingham, at a thousand dollars each, matched exactly the unpaid capital in Buckingham of $2.966 million. But then Dickie began to smell a bigger rat.

He believed then, and still does today, that some of the Wicklow documents may have been backdated. That's because the final figure of Buckingham's shortfall couldn't have been known on the night of July 31, 1986. Some of the private investors subscriptions didn't arrive in the office until August 1, and yet here Wicklow had magically subscribed on July 31 for exactly the amount that Buckingham found it needed a few days later. Dickie and his legal team made the issue of backdated documents one of the bullets in the their legal guns very early in the piece.

Westpac Bank, meanwhile, was doing its own plotting. Dickie didn't realise it, but the angry comment he'd made to Westpac's Glyn Boyt – "I want to be the first to know" – was about to boomerang back. The bank decided to sue Chris Dickie in his capacity as an investor, in a test case which would determine the liability of all the bloodstock partners to make payments to Westpac Securities forthwith.

By July 1989, 182 Buckingham partners were now on Chris Dickie's client list to fight Westpac through the courts. On July 18, Boyt sent out another "taxi meter" letter, reminding partners that their personal liabilities were increasing at the rate of at least $9.80 a day, and in some cases up to 30 times that figure.

At the same time, Chris Dickie was served with the lawsuit. Westpac was seeking a summary judgment against Dickie for the full amount the bank claimed he owed, plus interest. A clearly irked Dickie spelt out his response in a letter to his Buckingham clients.

"For reasons which would be clearly understood by those clients who are solicitors, it is clear that in issuing proceedings against the writer the Bank is endeavouring to 'gag' the steps being taken by our firm to protect your position.

"The Bank had already been formally advised of the list of clients for whom we were acting and, quite frankly, now that proceedings have been issued, we consider it utterly inappropriate that they should have written to partners, let alone sued the solicitor who is acting for those parties.

"You may rest assured that the threatening and, indeed, unprofessional conduct now shown will be dealt with in the appropriate manner."

The "manner" of choice was legal action of their own. Backed by a legal opinion from Tony Molloy QC on the enforceability of the Westpac guarantees, and the documentation indicating Wicklow's original partners – Anzon Capital Ltd and Anzon Investments Ltd – should be sharing the liability, Dickie and the McVeagh Fleming team began preparing a massive lawsuit of their own: At that stage, two hundred and six partners in Buckingham would sue Westpac.* The gloves were off.

---

* This number became a movable feast. At any given point in time, the number of people listed as being represented depended on a number of variables. Investors drifted in and out of the litigation process at various times, some deciding to settle rather than fight, while others who'd been sitting on the fence opted to join in.

CHAPTER 8

The Domino Theory

"I'd much rather have that fellow inside the tent pissing out,
than outside pissing in."
– PRESIDENT LYNDON JOHNSON, 1908–1973,
REFERRING TO FBI CHIEF J. EDGAR HOOVER

The gargoyles guarding Auckland's old High Court building peered down at the lawyer making his way towards the court's entrance. Constructed in the mid-nineteenth century, the imposing court had fallen into disuse in the early 1980's pending a major refit.

During the renovation a large chunk of the old court had broken off, forcing a major re-think of the plans if there was to be a chance of saving any piece of the historic building at all. The front facade, with its gargoyles depicting the grey visages of long dead jurists and politicians, was saved.

Not that Chris Dickie was in a mood to admire the way the early sunlight was playing on the sculptures and figurines. It was August 17, 1989, and the lawyer was in court to defend himself from a rapacious attack by Westpac Bank.

The Bank, still sticking to its claim that Buckingham's capital was only $4.032 million dollars, argued that Dickie was personally liable on a ratio of 10/4032 – ten units out of 4032 units paid up.

The McVeagh Fleming defence argued that the capital was $7 million, and Dickie's share of the debt should be worked out on the ratio of 10/7000th's. They also argued that Westpac shared some of the blame – or in their words "caused or connived" – for Buckingham's collapse and therefore some of the liability, because the bank advanced money to the partnership earlier than the date set down in the documentation for loan drawdown. This meant, they claimed, that funds advanced earlier should not be included in the total guaranteed by the partners.

It was a novel argument, but it seemed to be on fertile ground, with the Court indicating it might strike out Westpac's summary judgment claim on the spot.

Clearly panicked at the prospect, the Bank gained an hour's adjournment to give it time to bring in more senior lawyers to handle their case.

Warning Westpac that it could ultimately face an imposition of hefty court costs if it failed to prove that Dickie had no defence to the Bank's claim, the Court decided to allow a full hearing on the issue.

"The Court was concerned," wrote Dickie to his clients the following day, "that if the plaintiff was not given the opportunity to present full argument, that the matter would be appealed."

The proceedings against Dickie were adjourned until mid-October 1989.

"It has had the unfortunate result," noted the lawyer's letter, "that we are unable to file the representative action which we were ready to do, as to do so now would be to provide the Bank with [ammunition] which we do not wish to give them at this stage."

Dickie and Molloy did not want to tip their hand to Westpac in regard to the bigger picture.

Molloy, in particular, felt very confident of the partners' chances, spelling out the main points in a lengthy legal opinion that was so confidential that clients were initially only allowed to read it in Dickie's office, and couldn't take copies or notes.

"In view of the Bank's own recognition that the advances of $7.8 million were made before Buckingham had become entitled to them under the Agreement," wrote Molloy, "there appears to be no way in which liability can be established by the Bank against the special partners as guarantors.

It appeared, said the QC, that the Bank's original financing offer was on the basis that only 18 mares would be purchased, and the loan required would be $7 million.

"However, the Bank was advised by the promoter on or about July 21, 1986, that Buckingham had already purchased many more mares than this, namely 27 with 21 foals at foot."

Not only that, but Buckingham's promoters were negotiating with Westpac to borrow almost $1.5 million more to fund more bloodstock purchases. In addition, the number of investment dollars trickling in from partners was a lot less than expected – only $2.1 million compared with the required target of $4 million. The Bank had asked for, but not been given, "a satisfactory cash flow and repayment projection."

It all added up, argued Molloy, to negligence on Westpac's part for continuing to prop up a shaky partnership.

"The Bank knew, or should have known, that the Buckingham promoter was still stitching the project together. Clearly the integrity and viability of the project had not been established."

The Court, and the participants, held their breath. Finally, in December 1989, a written judgment was handed down. Case dismissed. Dickie was ecstatic. He wasn't off the hook in terms of liability, but he was off the hook in the sense that the Courts had no intention of dancing to Westpac's tune on the timetable and sum involved. The Court felt the dispute should be resolved in a more appropriate legal manner than a summary judgment application, which is the judicial equivalent of a softball-bat beating.

Westpac Securities, however, had no intention of giving up. It was off to the Court of Appeal.

Something Dickie and his clients would learn at a very high cost over the next seven years was that when you take on corporates with deep pockets, you can expect them to string proceedings out for as long as possible. It's part of a strategy aimed at wearing members of the public down through the high cost of keeping a lawyer ticking over filing papers every few weeks.

The only thing in Dickie's favour was that he was a lawyer too, and could play that game as well as any of his colleagues. He was also mindful of the fact that this was a·"must win" case. While Westpac has singled him out for special treatment, the punishment would be meted out to two hundred others if he lost.

"You will remember," he wrote to his clients just before Christmas, "that at the outset of the Buckingham problems there was a major concern that a summary judgment application could be successfully brought by the Bank against any one partner.

"If that action had been successful then, like a pack of falling cards, each of the partners would ultimately have had to have made full settlement to the Bank."

United, they stood. Divided, they would be hunted like rats and made to suffer. It was perhaps little wonder that the partners quickly contributed to a $200,000 "fighting fund" to pay for a class action lawsuit against Westpac.

In the meantime, investors in the six Wicklow partnerships were having similar nightmares, except in their case the banker was the DFC, not Westpac. DFC's Christmas present to Wicklow investors was to issue a demand for full payment or face summary judgment proceedings in the High Court.

The McVeagh Fleming legal team headed the financier off at the pass, filing a class action lawsuit against the DFC as well, on behalf of 83 Wicklow investors. The filing of the lawsuit meant DFC could no longer proceed with summary judgment until the main case had been thrashed out in Court.

There was a further twist to the Wicklow case.

In April 1990, the High Court granted leave for the existing defendants, who now included the DFC, the promoter – Buckingham Enterprises Ltd – and the directors of Anzon Corporation, to have the lawfirm Russell McVeagh joined to the proceedings as a third party.

Under court rules, defendants may ask the court to join a "third party" to the proceedings, provided there is some factual relationship between the legal action the defendant faces from the plaintiff, and the defendant's cause of action against the third party.

A person being sued for negligence by somebody might join his insurance firm as a third party, so that if the judgment goes against him his own claim against the insurer can be heard simultaneously, without a further expensive court hearing.

Russell McVeagh had been heavily involved as lawyers for Ermine, Buckingham and Wicklow, as well as being lawyers for Anzon Corporation. Paul Carran had been the Russell McVeagh partner acting for the horse syndicates.

Under partnership law, which governs New Zealand legal and accounting firms, the sins of one partner are deemed to be the sins of all, which meant that if Carran was liable for his involvement in any way then the whole of the Russell

McVeagh partnership would have to carry the can for any wrongful act or omission by Carran in the ordinary course of the business of the firm.

But being named as a third party marked the entry of the mega-lawfirm into the main ring for the first time. When it finally managed to escape the ring, years later, Russell McVeagh would be severely bruised by the experience. The blue-chip lawfirm came up against a streetfighter in Chris Dickie.

Not that it started off brutally. Dickie still had enough silver spoon left deep inside to try and find a civilised way through. He spent the weekend chewing it over and, on a lazy Sunday afternoon in that languid time that always follows lunch, he decided to see if the process could be short-circuited. Picking up the phone in the seclusion of his daughter's bedroom, Chris Dickie dialled his old friend Geoff Ricketts, the Russell McVeagh partner he'd once been close to.

"Geoff, I've got to get around a table with you. I've been going through the mathematics of this bloodstock business. It's not looking good and we've got to talk it through."

Ricketts didn't want to know. The issue was being dealt with by a committee inside Russell McVeagh McKenzie Bartleet & Co, he said. "I won't interfere."

Dickie was disappointed, but not surprised. It was a large lawfirm, they had a lot of issues on the boil. He'd secretly hoped that Ricketts would take advantage of their long friendship to perhaps stand back and take a look at the way things were developing. It wasn't to be.

Undeterred, Dickie and Tony Molloy opted for Plan B – a direct approach to Russell McVeagh through official channels. The mega-lawfirm sent down one of its partners, Frank Quin, to meet Dickie in McVeagh Fleming's offices. Dickie and Molloy had drafted a series of questions, each beginning with the words "Show us where we are horribly wrong. . ."

"Show us where we are horribly wrong in that the documents were not backdated, show us where we are horribly wrong when we say the capital of this company is seven million dollars, not four million, and show us where we are horribly wrong when we say that investors in Wicklow have incurred automatic and full liability for the unpaid capital in Buckingham."

They were all important questions, particularly the last because it meant that Wicklow should be fronting up with a cheque for the $2.9 million dollars worth of Buckingham shares subscribed for but not paid for.

And Dickie and Molloy really were hoping that they were horribly wrong, that somehow there would be an innocent explanation.

Frank Quin didn't say much, and didn't stay long. Despite an invitation to return with answers to the three questions, he never did.

Soon afterward, Tony Molloy was approached by a former senior partner at Russell McVeagh, who told him that he was indeed "horribly wrong" when it came to the allegation that some of the documents appeared to have been backdated. Molloy indicated he'd be delighted to remove the allegation if the lawyer could demonstrate where, specifically, it was wrong.

"I'll get back to you in four days," said the lawyer, who later was to become a judge, but he never did.

The backdating allegation was extremely serious, however. By this time Dickie had spoken to a woman named Dorothy Coates. She had once run a lawnmowing business in Hamilton, then moved into the commercial world in Auckland. She'd been headhunted across to Anzon Capital Ltd in Auckland in mid-July 1986.

She joined Anzon and found herself thrown from the sublime to the ridiculous. From dealing with the kind of money a lawnmower generates, she was suddenly dealing with millions of dollars. She remembered being blown away by it, but remembered also finding herself in the midst of some very sorry-looking bloodstock partnerships.

"Ermine, which was the first of the partnerships that Anzon Capital had done, that wasn't really fully subscribed, it had no money. We used to continually shift money around and draw down so called 'advances' from Anzon Investments all the time. Getting people to buy into these things was a 'major'.

"Really, from day one, I guess, you would say the whole thing revolved around getting money in, because the minute that the money got in and got into the bank, they were able to borrow against it – two for one borrowings from Westpac Bank – especially with Buckingham."

When Budget Night rolled around, there was controlled chaos at the offices of Anzon Capital. Some of the biggest investors, said Coates, people like Murray Carter from Shanton Apparel and businessman Bob Wilson, had given verbal assurances that they would subscribe.

"All these people had made verbal commitments to Paul Carran and Chris Kirkham, and the emphasis was getting Buckingham closed off and fully subscribed to, and the money into Westpac Bank before it closed.

"Once the bank closed, supposedly we weren't meant to accept any more money because it was all over then. I think the closing date for that special partnership had already been extended once because it hadn't been fully subscribed at the original date. But it wasn't fully subscribed for."

The bank had closed at 4.30pm that day, with a gaping hole in Buckingham's subscription level.

"We waited around for the Budget, and for Kirkham to call from Ireland to find out what the final result had been. There weren't a lot of us there that night. It was a nervous time."

Coates told Dickie that she was the woman who'd filled out Wicklow's applications to purchase shares in the Buckingham Partnership.

"That's great," said the lawyer. "Were you working on the night of July 31 then?"

"Nothing actually happened on the night," said Coates, dropping a bombshell, "except that on the schedule the shortfall in sales got written up – I think in the name of either Anzon Capital or Anzon Investments – so that on paper it was fully sold. "Kirkham was away, and it wasn't until Kirkham came back that I got instructed to write some cheques."

It was like a line from a TV whodunit – where were you on the night of the 31st? Kirkham, and Paul Carran, were comfortably ensconced in the Barronstown Stud in Eire that night, eighteen thousand kilometres away from Dorothy Coates and her desk.

And yet legally, the Wicklow subscription for a chunk of Buckingham should have been filled out on the night. Kirkham also gave Coates six cheques at the same time as he asked her to fill out the forms. The cheques were to pay Buckingham for the $2.9 million worth of shares, and they should have been banked. But Coates was told not to bank them.

"This was all getting rather intriguing," Dickie later recalled. "She then said to me, 'but Chris, they gave me the cheques, and I had to put them in my top drawer and not tell anybody. Kirkham gave them to me, that morning.'

"Those cheques are worth, with the interest, over eight million bucks," the lawyer continued. "I've got them sitting in my office. Eight million, man. The bastards just stuck them in a drawer. I believe Anzon just filled them out to fool the Statutory Supervisor. He had to see an application form, he had to see a power of attorney, and he had to see a cheque."

However, as the case increased in its momentum, people became more aware of what was happening and newspapers started to feature the sensational allegations.

Over a coffee with Dickie one afternoon, I began to wonder what was going through the minds of the people at Russell McVeagh.

"I don't know about you," I muttered to the lawyer, "but if I was a lawyer in a partnership situation whose firm was on the receiving end of these kinds of allegations, I would not be just simply requiring to know what was happening, I would be personally involved in looking at all the bloody documentation and finding out whether there was any basis for the allegations.

"Because Chris, and correct me if I'm wrong, my understanding is that if a liability is proven then all the partners in a lawfirm have to carry it."

Dickie didn't say anything for a moment, he was seemingly content to stare into the distance.

"I just don't know what, if anything, Ian, the partners were told. They may be as much in the dark as I am."

CHAPTER 9

A Deadly Game Begins

"In nature there are neither rewards nor punishments
– there are consequences."

– Robert Ingersoll, 1833–1899, *Lectures and Essays*

If what had happened up to this point contained largely the ingredients for a good courtroom drama, what followed over the next few months would turn the drama into a deadly thriller. For the first time in his investigation, Chris Dickie was about to know the meaning of fear. Real fear. The kind of fear that eventually saw him armed with a pistol.

His nerves hadn't been helped when he discovered, from one of the investors, that the people running the horse studs in Ireland had heavily-armed private soldiers guarding them.

The investor had wanted to pop over to Ireland during a trip to the UK and see some of the horses he'd invested in. Chris Kirkham had telexed across a letter of introduction to the Coolmore Stud. The telex, described by those who've seen it as "delightful", tells Coolmore who the investor is and says it would be nice if the stud could look after him for the morning, but adding that this particular investor "wasn't worth the whole day". Never judge a man by the size of the horse he owns!

When he got there, the investor was staggered to find guards armed with Israeli-manufactured Uzi submachine guns, a throwback, apparently, to the kidnapping of top racehorse *Shergar* a few years previously.

"It would have been 81 when *Shergar* was racing, and he was kidnapped, I think, in 82," recalled Mitchell McLeish. "They eventually found that he had been shot. They'd been tipped off where he was and they dug him up. They were DNA testing to make sure it was him.

"It was the IRA who took him, and the motive was the age old one – greed. You know, money. His value at the time was about £12 million sterling. He was an extraordinarily good racehorse."

The Irish Republican Army had heard that the Aga Khan owned *Shergar*. Rich Arab, top horse, lots of loot to bankroll more weaponry and ordnance in the struggle against British rule in Northern Ireland.

"I guess they figured that the Aga Khan didn't need the money and he would pay, but of course that wasn't what happened. The horse didn't actually belong to the Aga Khan. Although *Shergar* stood at that stud, he was already syndicated and there were a lot of owners and very few got paid out.

"It caused ructions in the insurance world because while the horse was presumed dead, nobody could prove it was dead. Lloyd's has spent 300 years figuring out how to get out of paying claims and they said 'hang on a sec, this horse is just missing and you're not insured for that. How do we know he's dead?'

"There's wonderful stories about it. People ringing up for ransoms, ransoms seemingly paid on the moors. People that got the money disappeared, it was as if everybody in Ireland had a theory on where he was and who had taken him."

Back in New Zealand, the heightened sense of unreality and danger slowly began to impinge on Dickie's investigation. It began with Dorothy Coates, the former Anzon employee who was proving to be a useful source on an apparently secret Cook Islands company, Investment Management Services Ltd.

Investment Management Services had haunted Dickie ever since Coates first mentioned it to him in 1989, because he wanted desperately to know what the hell the Cook Islands had to do with his bloodstock investment.

When he drew the existence of the company to my attention in 1992 it drew me like a magnet: this was a company that had been created by the Cook Islands Trust Corporation – European Pacific – my target in the winebox investigation.

Although, of course, I would later learn that IMS was not involved in the winebox deals as tabled in Parliament by Peters, at that time it occupied a not insignificant space on my whiteboard as I looked for the links between what at first appeared to be utterly separate events.

For Coates, the discovery of IMS had proved to be an unpleasant experience. "I stumbled across it [in 1986] because Anzon Capital – everytime they needed money, which was regularly – somebody like Chris [Kirkham] or myself would go upstairs and say to John Taylor or David Rouse 'we've got to pay this and we have to draw down some funds from Anzon Investments.'

"Now, that went on for a few months because there was no cashflow and not a lot of money coming in, and then Chris asked me to prepare monthly reports on the status of each of the partnerships, in terms of their capital value, their cash in the bank, it was just really a financial overview of how much money they had.

"At the time I did the first one, he asked me to put down as an asset that company, Investment Management Services. At the time I sort of looked at him, because I had never even heard of this company before.

"He said 'Don't worry, it's a Rarotongan company, it's offshore, but we have those funds sitting there.'

"And so each month I put this down on the little summary that I used to send upstairs, by way of financial reporting. It never became an issue until audit time, and the auditors asked me for the bank statements and documents to prove that that money was there."

As part of her efforts to locate the records she needed, Coates rang Deloittes Hong Kong and attempted to speak to staff member Mildred Li about this company that Deloittes was apparently administering. She got nowhere, and tried to phone her boss.

"Chris was overseas at the time, and when he rang I told him about this, and he asked me to ring Paul. I rang Paul Carran and pretty much got my hand slapped. I got told that I should ask no questions and that I was to refer anybody that ever questioned me about that company direct to him, which is exactly what I did."

"Was he surprised that you knew about it?" I asked her.

"I don't know whether surprised would be the right word. I think probably more angered that I'd had the audacity to ring him up and ask him about it. He was always so abrupt."

Her motives for helping Dickie were simple. "I've been to Dickie's office, off and on, over the last seven years. I've tried to be helpful simply because a lot of people that invested in a number of partnerships – myself included – which were onshore, standardbred, partnerships – we had partners who declared themselves bankrupt, I nearly lost my home and everything I had was literally at risk."

Coates felt that helping Dickie would in some way ease the lot of some of her friends. But word got out that she was talking to the lawyer, and she received a chilling wake-up call.

"Something particularly vicious happened during the course of our investigation," remembered Dickie. "One of Dorothy's two boys was disabled. She was attending a social function one day when a friend came up to her. She was informed by him that an undisclosed party had told him that if Mrs Coates spoke to Mr Dickie about the secret Cook Islands company, Investment Management Services Ltd, her younger son would be made an amputee also." *

"When you're a woman alone," explained Coates, "and you've got two young kids, it's not only bizarre: it's scary shit! Frankly, I just didn't want to venture any further.

"There has not been a year, that I've lived in Auckland, that I haven't been burgled. I run my office from here. Whilst a couple of times I could accept it, there have been three of those burglaries in particular where I haven't lost anything but I had a big mess! You get this uneasy feeling: why would people do that?"

Every year for a decade, Coates has been burgled. Some were just crooks, others remain unexplained. Then there was a phone call naming the school that her children attended.

Understandably, she backed away from talking to the McVeagh Fleming team any further. Understandably, Dickie and his lawyers decided to leave her alone.

---

* The identity of the person who originated the threat has not been revealed to the author, and readers should note that speculation on specifically who was ultimately behind the threat is pointless. The friend was reporting the existence of the threat to Coates out of concern for her welfare.

The lawyer then found himself on the receiving end of a threat. It came from a prominent lawyer.

"He telephoned me at work and advised me that if I continued with the Wicklow matter he would ensure that I would be financially ruined."

The stakes in the game were being raised, but this was only the beginning.

Perhaps sensing that Dickie was on the trail, Chris Kirkham and Paul Carran arranged in January 1990 for Zorasong to sell its bloodstock and company assets to a Channel Islands company called Kanasawa Ltd.

Dickie, of course, was still oblivious to Zorasong or its role, but it transpired that Zorasong had not only allegedly been involved in clipping the ticket on the partnerships' bloodstock purchases, but was a horse trading company in its own right.

Kirkham, Carran and McLeish had been buying their own bloodstock through Zorasong, which raises very serious issues in regard to conflicts of interest between their roles as promoters and advisers to the partnership, and their private venture.* But they too had been caught by the industry collapse. They owed big money, and were trying to restructure.

The bloodstock owned by Zorasong, as opposed to the partnerships, was to be sold to Kanasawa for a price equivalent to what's known in accounting terms as their "book value".

Book value reflects the worth of an asset after depreciation and other tax matters are taken into account. The horses, for example, might depreciate for accounting purposes at 33 percent a year, so that after three years they're listed in the book as worthless. Yet obviously a three year old race horse is still worth something!

Kanasawa immediately sold the assets on to Securelaunch Limited for their market value, about IR£2 million. The assets, according to Chris Kirkham in a later report, included about £200,000 worth of unpaid bonuses and service fees from the stallion shares owned by Zorasong – enough, argued Kirkham, for Zorasong to have repaid an overdue loan from the Allied Irish Bank before the sale to Securelaunch. Indeed, it might even have removed the need for the asset sale. But there was a fly in the ointment.

Paul Carran and Chris Kirkham may have been brilliant deal-makers, always juggling a new transaction, but this time they had too many balls in the air, and something had to give.

Coolmore Stud refused to recognise the sale, saying the shares in the stallions had not been transferred between Zorasong, Kanasawa and Securelaunch correctly. Coolmore refused to transfer the horses, and from that

---

* As an example of such a potential conflict arising, Kirkham and McLeish brought one of their European stallions down to New Zealand to service mares owned by one of the partnerships that were being agisted here. There is a golden rule in thoroughbred breeding that you don't mate different styles of horse: for example you don't put a steeplechaser with a trotter, or a trotter with a galloper. However, on this occasion the stallion crossed those lines, and the partnership was charged a service fee even though the progeny were arguably useless.

date refused to pay any income derived by the stallions. It was as if the horses had ceased to exist. This left Paul Carran, Chris Kirkham and Mitchell McLeish in the saddle without a horse.

"One of the reasons Coolmore have given for not transferring the shares," McLeish later wrote, "is that they do not know who is buying them. 'It could be drug dealers' or 'a massive international fraud'.

"This," said McLeish disgustedly, "is sheer bullshit!!! In fact, most of the shares in all of their stallions would be owned by nominee companies."

To add to their woes, the run of bad luck with the horses themselves continued when they received a fax signed by an Irish veterinary surgeon regarding their breeding mare, *Rustic Lace*.

"The above mare was found dead in her box at Barronstown Stud on the morning of November 9, 1990. A post-mortem examination was carried out which showed that the right lung was congested with blood.

"There had been a haemorrhage in the substance of this lung. There was also enlargement of the right side of the heart which would be consistent with the lung haemorrhage."

At least the horse was insured, the trio consoled each other.

Dickie was unaware of all this. There was enough other work on his plate to keep him occupied without Dorothy Coates' input, and enough new documentation pouring in to sink a battleship. In May 1990, investors in Buckingham voted overwhelmingly to begin a class legal action against Westpac Securities and the Statutory Supervisor who'd allowed Wicklow to subscribe without paying.

The idea was to step up the pressure on Westpac, in the hope that the bank would make an acceptable settlement offer. Still, there were signs that the investors were getting weary. It was now a year and a half since they'd first been told of Buckingham's collapse, and still Westpac's Sword of Damocles hung over them, with interest accruing at a minimum of ten dollars a day.

Then there were the legal fees, with McVeagh Fleming seeking contributions of hundreds of dollars from each investor every few months to put into the growing "fighting fund".

Mindful of the mutterings from the cheap seats, Dickie wrote to his clients again.

"On a personal note, the writer would like to express his appreciation to the kind and generous comments which have been made by many clients to the writer and Dr Molloy. It is clearly a team effort and the representative approach will provide the best means of endeavouring to obtain a satisfactory conclusion.

"The loss of the clients' investment and the necessity to issue proceedings is the reality which faces each client. We can only repeat Dr Molloy's delightful reminder to the meeting of the comment the entertainer, Maurice Chevalier, made when asked by a reporter what it felt like to be 90 years old. The reply was 'it's not so bad when you consider the alternative'."

When the class action was filed, it was "delightfully" done so in the name of Auckland's Mad Butcher, Peter Leitch.

"The Butch" had invested in horses not because he knew anything about it but, like the Hadlees before him, his accountant had recommended it.

"My accountant told me 'this is a bloody good way to beat the tax system', so I bought some shares in the thing and it was a bloody nightmare from then on."

And Leitch was certainly mad.

"The [Buckingham] partnership has performed dismally," said his Statement of Issues to the High Court. "It purchased interests in bloodstock for almost $10 million, and recently has sold those interests for about $700,000."

The issues paper stated Westpac was seeking to recover $8.4 million plus interest, divided equally amongst what the Bank argued were the 4,032 units that went to make up the $4 million capital, a debt burden of $2,083 per unit.

Leitch, a well known Auckland retail personality, had sunk twenty-seven thousand dollars into Buckingham's horsemeat for 27 units, which meant Westpac was stinging him for more than $56,000. That's an awful lot of Mad Butcher's special sausages.

Leitch and the McVeagh Fleming team argued that the true capital of Buckingham was $7 million, made up of 7,000 units. Dividing the $8.4 million by seven thousand, they arrived at a debt per unit of only $1,200, which meant the Mad Butcher's liability was only a further $32,000.

"We are pleased to advise," wrote Dickie, that the High Court proceedings against Westpac and Buckingham Enterprises Ltd (ie. the management company not the partnership [Buckingham Enterprises Ltd and Company]) has been filed and served. It is the culmination of 19 months' work in researching the circumstances relating to the investment and the various activities of many individuals and/or their companies."

Although the initial legal scrap was to have included the Statutory Supervisor, Dickie and Molloy decided not to at the 11th hour. It would, they decided, only prolong the legal action and incur more cost. "We have all recognised that the principal target is to resist the bank demand and accordingly the writ has been limited to that issue."

There was also some new information to hand that considerably strengthened their case against Westpac Securities. More correspondence had surfaced to reinforce the belief that Buckingham had been insolvent even before it began, and that Westpac knew this when it lent the Partnership cash.

The exact figures, said Dickie, showed Buckingham under-capitalised by 46 percent and over budget by 176 percent.

"Buckingham was clearly insolvent and was only kept afloat by the advancing of funds by Westpac at the request of the promoter. If this is so, then the advancing of funds in these circumstances was not simply careless but reckless, and placed the funds paid by you in extreme jeopardy.

"We are therefore claiming against the bank for the return of all subscription moneys, together with interest."

This was the equivalent of lighting a fuse under the giant bank, and the McVeagh Fleming team knew it.

"To put it bluntly, the Bank is now in a situation of real risk in not only losing its claim for payment under the guarantee, which is approximately $8.5 million together with interest, but in addition may be required to pay out all the subscription moneys paid by our clients, together with interest thereon.

"The total loss to the Bank could therefore be in excess of $15 million."

The class action was lodged in what's known as the "Commercial List" of the High Court, which is a fast-track, behind-closed-doors process for civil litigants designed to speed up the wheels of justice where time and money are an issue by making proceedings swift and less confrontational.

So that was the state of play with the class action lawsuit against Westpac. The other major legal action for Buckingham investors still ongoing was, of course, Westpac's writ against Chris Dickie for summary judgment. This was to have been heard in July 1990 in the Court of Appeal, but was delayed because of a prominent criminal case, the appeal against conviction of a teenage Auckland sex and bondage mistress and her associate for the murder of Peter Plumley-Walker. Instead, the Court of Appeal would consider the summary judgment issue in August.

But if Dickie and Molloy thought Westpac was going to roll over and waggle its toes in the air, they were seriously mistaken. The bank immediately filed papers in a bid to get the class action struck out on the grounds that it was "vexatious" and just a bid to "embarrass" Westpac. Then it went one step further.

Notwithstanding that Westpac was already on a hiding to nothing over the Summary Judgment issue against Chris Dickie, the bank lodged a Summary Judgment application against Peter Leitch as well. The Mad Butcher was on the receiving end of a grilling from the bank.

Dickie accused the bank of trying to subvert the course of justice, saying that using Leitch as a scapegoat to represent all the other investors was unfair, a view echoed somewhat by the High Court judge who'd been roped in to hear the latest stoush.

"Surely the others have a right to be heard. They may have other arguments," said the judge to Westpac's lawyers.

Justice Wylie decided that he couldn't decide whether to strike out the class action lawsuit until the Court of Appeal had ruled on whether Westpac's summary judgment bid against Dickie was dodgy or not.

Everything, he ruled, would go on hold until the Appeal judgment was handed down.

So by the end of August 1990, it had become a legal juggling act with four cases in train on Buckingham alone.

Westpac Securities Ltd v Dickie – a Summary Judgment action filed July 1989. Court of Appeal ruling imminent.

Leitch v Buckingham Enterprises Ltd and Westpac Securities Ltd – Representative action filed July 1990. The main action.

<u>Westpac Securities Ltd</u> v <u>Leitch</u> – Summary Judgment action filed July 1990 by Westpac against the representative plaintiff.

Motion by Westpac Securities Ltd to strike out the representative action on the grounds that the action is vexatious, and requiring that judgment be entered against each represented person for the full amount of the bank's demand.

On September 6, the Court of Appeal delivered its verdict in the Westpac/Dickie clash. It didn't look good. As they read through the judgment Dickie could see he'd lost on his first two points.

The Appellate judges did not agree that the early advance of cash by the bank to Buckingham was made outside of the special partners' guarantee obligations. Nor did they agree that the bank had "caused or connived" Buckingham's collapse.

Dickie's insides began to churn. OK, so he'd failed to get the partners' liability reduced to nil, but he knew they'd been tilting at windmills on that as far as the Summary Judgment issue went. But what about the 4/7th's issue – the capital of Buckingham and whether Wicklow was liable for the remaining 3/7th's – that was the fundamental bottom line, surely?

"I thought I'd lost everything," he remembered later. "I thought it was a total failure."

Two down, one to go. Would it be "Strike three, batter out!" or would he hit a home run? He kept reading, scanning rapidly for news of his fate.

"It is far from clear," began the judges, "whether the applications of the Wicklow Bloodstock Partnerships were accepted and units allotted to them. Most importantly, it is not known whether deeds of accession were executed on their behalf."

"Christ!" thought Dickie, "please don't tell me I've lost this one as well." It all came down to this. Two hundred partners who could be picked off like ducks in a shooting gallery if he failed to prevent Westpac from winning Summary Judgment against him. He turned the page.

CHAPTER 10

On The Trail Of Zorasong

"If a little knowledge is dangerous, where is the man
who has so much as to be out of danger?"
– THOMAS HUXLEY, 1825–1895

In the split seconds that it takes to find a new paragraph in a legal document, the lawyer's mind had already canvassed the options. Dickie knew that he was closing a chapter on his life as he turned that page. Whatever happened, it marked a new phase in both his work and private lives.

Losing, at this point, would cost him personally the best part of $30,000. It would take a long while to recover from a financial thumping like that.

Winning would not really be a win, it would merely be a form of prolonging the agony. But then again, as Chevalier had said, it was better than the alternative.

It was Judgment Day, and time to face the truth buried there on page 17 of the ruling.

"If [Wicklow] had become liable to contribute to [Buckingham's] partnership capital," opined the Court of Appeal judges, "then the failure of the general partner [Buckingham Enterprises Ltd] to complete the necessary documents, particularly the guarantees, is not to be visited upon the other special partners by way of increasing their liability to Westpac Securities.

"That company may have remedies elsewhere but it cannot look to those who have signed guarantees to pay the share of those who have not. In this state of uncertainty as to the amount for which Mr Dickie is liable, we would uphold the. . .refusal to enter summary judgment so far as it related to quantum."

Dickie breathed a sigh of relief. He realised he was shaking. Cradling his head in his hands he just sat motionless, waiting for the emotion to pass. The words of the judgment kept scrolling through his consciousness.

Westpac "may have remedies elsewhere, but it cannot look to those who have signed guarantees to pay the share of those who have not." In other words, Buckingham's private investors were liable only for 4/7th's of the debt.

This was not of course, a win on the merits of the case. Those merits would be debated, on all three main points, in the class action lawsuit against Westpac. But obviously the Court of Appeal believed there was enough merit to the Buckingham capital issue to stop the bank from taking further action against Dickie in a summary way.

The victories started flowing thick and fast over the remaining weeks of September 1990. Justice Sir Ian Barker ruled that the class action lawsuit could proceed.

"Last Friday, September 21, 1990," wrote Dickie to the clients, "we succeeded in obtaining an order of the High Court directing that the representative action proceed to trial, and that the two abovementioned summary judgment actions be adjourned indefinitely."

This meant the Mad Butcher was off the hook in terms of summary judgment action as well.

"We are confident," continued Dickie, "that our right to a full trial with full presentation of evidence and legal argument has now been achieved after an 18 month battle."

He made the point that his team still hadn't disclosed in court much of their hand in terms of legal argument or evidence. He also spelt out the dangers of straying too far from the protection of the group. The participants in class action lawsuits can be compared to a herd of antelope on the African savanna. The lions in the long grass always manage to find one antelope foolish enough to go it alone. So did Westpac.

"Shortly before the Court of Appeal hearing," wrote Dickie, "one of our clients – and fortunately it was only one – personally resolved to settle with the Bank for the full amount of the Bank's demand.

"This person held only ten units but had become concerned at the complexity of the issues, the various hearings and, with the overall uncertainty, decided to pay in full.

"A few days after that payment we obtained the Court of Appeal ruling which demonstrates that on the very worst scenario, he has paid at least twice as much as necessary and, on the most favourable scenario, need not have paid at all."

Patience is a definite virtue during litigation, explained Dickie. Otherwise, a fool and his money are soon parted.

It wasn't long before the news media got wind of the Court of Appeal judgment but, not appreciating the subtleties of the complex case, misreported it as a win to Westpac.

"Bloodstock management companies are welcoming a Court of Appeal decision which found a special partner liable for funds borrowed in their name," wrote one journalist.

"Westpac Bank sued Auckland lawyer Christopher Dickie, one of the special partners in bloodstock syndicate Buckingham Enterprises Ltd, promoted by Anzon Investments Ltd, in an attempt to recover $7.8 million.

"The syndicate includes 'The Mad Butcher', Peter Leitch, who has filed his own suit against Westpac alleging reckless and irresponsible trading by the bank."

The article concentrated on the Court turning down Dickie's bid to have the liability set aside because of Westpac's alleged "connivance", and did not record that Dickie had won the 4/7th's argument. It then quoted from the managers of other bloodstock partnerships.

"Strathmore Group Ltd chairman Dr Ray Thomson said although the decision did not directly affect his company's partnerships, it had important implications for financiers and promoters of bloodstock syndicates.

" 'Partners cannot get away with trying to blame financiers and promoters for the collapse of the bloodstock industry,' he said.

Towards the end, the Mad Butcher got another run.

"But Buckingham syndicate member Peter Leitch is hopping mad at the decision which could cost him $27,000 plus interest.

" 'I'll just have to work twice as hard now. I'm now working 12 hours a day and now I'll have to work 24 hours and seven days a week. Thank God the league season's finished,' he said."

Leitch got a fright to see his name up in lights, so to speak.

"I get the Sunday paper, and I'll never forget it, I get the Sunday paper and I'm on the bloody front page! I bank with the Westpac Bank, for heaven's sake!"

Elsewhere on the planet, the world was gearing up for war in the Middle East as Saddam Hussein invaded Kuwait and dug his troops in. But in Auckland, a phoney war of a different kind was coming to an end. What had begun as an ordinary, if very large, civil lawsuit over contractual issues was turning into something more sinister. Dickie and his team had located new evidence that would catapult their case into the stratosphere. It took them down a line of inquiry that would ultimately lead to the *National Business Review*'s infamous "Wogistan" article in February 1992*, to a meeting with the IRD and SFO in an Auckland vineyard and, even more importantly, to a series of parliamentary speeches by rebel MP Winston Peters.

Dickie called a meeting for 176 of the Buckingham clients for Thursday, December 6, 1990. "This is a critical meeting for you and you must attend. For reasons of confidentiality we do not propose to set out in this letter any details of the matters which will be raised at the meeting.

"Since our last meeting," he continued, "factual matters of extreme significance have been uncovered. This information is of a highly confidential nature and under no circumstances will be discussed over the telephone with clients. Again, this information presents a totally new perspective to the remedies available."

The previous day, December 5, Dickie had officially contacted investigators at the Inland Revenue Department's Auckland office for the first time. Although IRD staff had sent out feelers earlier in the year after media publicity about the civil suit, there had been little direct discussion. This was the opening of a line of communication that would ultimately have major repercussions on the IRD staff involved.

So what was the hot new discovery? Chris Dickie and Tony Molloy had stumbled across a company called Zorasong, and it had come courtesy of some investors in the Ermine bloodstock partnership.

---

* See *The Paradise Conspiracy*, Chapter 1.

Up to this point Dickie had resisted the entreaties from Ermine investors to do for them what he was doing for the Wicklow and Buckingham partners. The lawyer was just too busy to handle it. That hadn't stopped him sniffing around the Ermine partnership's documentation though, and talking to those involved.

As part of the procedure, Dickie and Molloy arranged to go up to the offices of Russell McVeagh McKenzie Bartleet & Co to inspect some documents.

"They were very courteous about it. It was an informal arrangement, there were no court orders or anything like that. In fact, at this point in time, Russell McVeagh wasn't a defendant in the proceedings. Tony and I went along and we were given very nice morning and afternoon teas, and we beavered away for a couple of weeks going through a mass of material. An absolute mass of material."

In doing so, however, Dickie was mindful of the earlier troubles he'd had getting hold of the missing Wicklow subscription certificates and the accompanying, unbanked, cheques for $2.966 million. He was mindful too of the fact that documents relating to that subscription appeared to have been backdated.

"I was feeling very uneasy about things and felt that we were not getting the full picture so, as a result, I took along a miniature photocopying machine, which fitted inside a small bag."

For Dickie, the excursion with the James Bond-style document copier was another covert operation in the same vein as his raid on Chris Kirkham's filing cabinet nearly two years earlier. The device came into its own when Dickie found a letter, which he later mailed to his clients for their edification.

It was dated September 23, 1985, and written by an Anita Cheng, the Secretarial Department Manager at giant accounting firm Deloitte Haskins & Sells in Hong Kong. She was writing to one Christopher Kirkham, at Challenge Corporate Services in Auckland.

"Dear Sir," the letter began. "ZORASONG LIMITED. We return to you herewith the following agreements duly executed by the subject company for your appropriate action:"

What followed was a list of sales agreements apparently involving Zorasong, some horse studs, and the Ermine bloodstock partnership. Chris Dickie was fascinated.

"There were several points that grabbed my attention. Firstly, the original of this letter was on the Russell McVeagh file. The original, not a copy. The original. The second thing was that the heading was 'Zorasong Ltd'. It wasn't Ermine.

"Now, you don't have to be a master of scrabble to understand the significance of the words 'we return to you herewith the following agreements duly executed'. The word 'return' means you are giving it back.

"It's not 'we are forwarding on to you', or any other word. It was 'return', and the word 'return' stuck out like dogs balls to me.

"The next thing that stuck out was the bloody contracts themselves – the actual fucking contracts!"

The letter specifically referred to the existence of contracts. Not only did

Deloitte
Haskins+Sells

Certified Public Accountants

26th Floor, Wing On Centre
111 Connaught Road Central
Hong Kong
Mailing Address G.P.O. Box 3348
Telephone 5-450303
Telex 73175 DHSHK HX
Facsimile 5-411911

Mr. Chris Kirkham
Challenge Corporate Services Limited
P.O. Box 7149
Wellesley
Auckland 1
New Zealand

September 23, 1985

Dear Sir:

ZORASONG LIMITED

We return to you herewith the following agreements duly
executed by the subject company for your appropriate action:-

 1. Agreement with Lindsay Park Stud Pty. Ltd. ("Lindsay") re
    'Crystal Bright';
 2. Agreement with Lindsay re 'Adaptable';
 3. Agreement with Lindsay re 'Moonlight';
 4. Agreement with Lindsay re 'Godswalk';
 5. Commission Agreement with Lindsay;
 6. Agreement with Russell J. Trim re 'Gielgud';
 7. Agreement with Robert Malcolm Robertson re 'Gielgud';
 8. Agreement with B.B.A. (Ireland) Ltd. ("B.B.A.") re 'Bold
    Maiden' and foal;
 9. Agreement with B.B.A. re 'East River';
10. Agreement with B.B.A. re 'Hard To Tell';
11. Agreement with B.B.A. re 'Transit' and foal;
12. Agreement with B.B.A. re 'Rally' and foal;
13. Agreement with B.B.A. re 'Rustic Lace';
14. Agreement with Ermine Holdings Limited and Company
    ("Ermine") re 'Moonlight';
15. Agreement with Ermine re 'Hard To Tell';
16. Agreement with Ermine re 'Rustic Lace';
17. Agreement with Ermine re 'East River';
18. Agreement with Ermine re 'Rally' and foal;
19. Agreement with Ermine re 'Bold Maiden' and foal;
20. Agreement with Ermine re 'Transit' and foal;
21. Agreement with Ermine re 'Crystal Bright';
22. Agreement with Ermine re 'Adaptable';
23. Agreement with Ermine re 'Gielgud';
24. Agreement with Ermine re 'Godswalk'; and
25. Letter Agreement with Ermine re 'Danzatore'.

BONSHOW LIMITED

26 Enclosed please find a loan agreement dated July 30, 1985
   made by the subject company with Ermine Holdings Limited and
   Company duly signed for your disposal.

Yours faithfully,
DELOITTE HASKINS & SELLS

Anita Cheng (Mrs.)
Secretarial Department Manager

Enclosures

they exist, but they clearly had been in New Zealand at one point. The glaring question for Dickie – where were they now?

Even without the contracts themselves, the list describing them told a pretty easily understood story. Agreement one, for example was listed as "Agreement with Lindsay Park Stud Pty. Ltd. ("Lindsay") re 'Crystal Bright'."

Further down the list, at number 21, was "Agreement with Ermine re 'Crystal Bright'." It didn't take a rocket scientist to work out that Zorasong had purchased Crystal Bright from the Lindsay Park Stud in Australia, and then onsold the horse to the Ermine partnership.

Dickie called them "stage one" and "stage two" contracts.

"You had stage one, Lindsay Park Stud to Zorasong, in respect of the interests in this horse. That's document one. Document twenty-one was the second stage, from Zorasong to Ermine. Zorasong being the middleman.

"Now the other thing that intrigued me," said Dickie, looking around furtively, "is that the last word in the letter is 'enclosures'. So one assumes that the enclosures were with the covering letter. The other thing was that there were ticks down the side of the list, which to me clearly denoted that someone had ticked off that they'd got all the bloody contracts! Well I'll tell you something mate – to this day I still haven't seen one of those fucking stage ones!"

The lawyer wasted no time dragging the tiny photocopier out of its pouch, feeling like a refugee from a Cold War spy thriller, one eye on the door and the other on the document slowly feeding through. Praying that a Russell McVeagh lawyer would not walk through right at this instant.

As it was, he needn't have panicked. Russell McVeagh would later hand over the letter he'd photocopied – although not the stage one contracts it referred to – during the "discovery" process, where both sides in litigation disclose all their documents to their opponents at a pre-trial stage, in the interests of fairness.

Generally speaking, each party discloses documents they currently have in their possession, or documents that they once had, but no longer have, in their possession.

This disclosure is subject to any claims for legal professional privilege, which means that legal advice from a solicitor to a client is not discovered to the other side, although transaction documentation is.

The significance of the letter Dickie had found cannot be overstated. This was an "original" letter – not a copy – addressed to Challenge Corporate Services Ltd for the attention of Chris Kirkham, but it had been found in the possession of Russell McVeagh.

Question: How had it come into the lawfirm's possession?

Answer: We don't know. But Paul Carran was the solicitor for Challenge Corporate Services. Paul Carran was the solicitor for the Ermine partnership. Paul Carran was the solicitor for Chris Kirkham on some other matters.

Clearly, the stage one contracts, recording sales by the studs to Zorasong, had been in New Zealand at some point in 1985. Not only had they been here, but they had been sent across to Deloittes in Hong Kong who returned them to New Zealand on September 23, 1985.

Russell McVeagh, according to the Ermine prospectus, was doing all the legal work for the partnership, which would ordinarily include contractual documentation. Either the contracts had been in the possession of Challenge Corporate Services, or in the hands of the lawfirm.

But not one of the defendants or their agents ever "coughed", however, to the existence of the contracts described in the letter.

As we've just spelt out, normally if a party to a lawsuit once had a document but no longer has it, it is required to state that as part of the discovery process. That didn't happen.

"It wasn't 'we don't have them'," complained Dickie. "It's been a case of 'we don't know where they are, we can't explain'. The damn documents have never been discovered. I realised then that we were in an incredibly serious situation. The original Ermine contracts had disappeared. They'd been here but they'd gone. What else might be missing?"

CHAPTER 11

The Black Stump

"Twenty-six Russian tax collectors were killed in the course
of their work last year, 74 were injured, six were kidnapped
and 41 had their homes burned."

– REUTERS, 1997

Chris Dickie angrily paced Tony Molloy's chambers, grimacing every so often as he glimpsed the offices of Russell McVeagh McKenzie Bartleet & Co in the black building with the mirror glass across the road. They'd dubbed the Shortland Street edifice "The Black Stump".

"Bloody Carran's behind this – I can feel it," he growled.

Dickie was now suspecting a concealment or deception – civil fraud. Quite apart from that view, however, he also had a major gripe over the fees Carran had charged the partnerships.

Paul Carran would, during the course of the legal battle, be accused of usury by angry investors. The Ermine Statement of Claim, for example, alleges that "the legal work involved was straightforward, involved nothing unique or innovative, and would justify legal fees of approximately $10,000.

"Russell McVeagh was to receive. . .fees of at least $50,000 for each of this and any subsequent scheme. . . [which would be charged] to the partnership, which would pay from the funds to come to hand from the subscribers.

"The excess over approximately $10,000 was an entrepreneurial reward for the part Russell McVeagh was to play in the creation, promotion and management of the scheme."

Accused of all that, Carran had managed to get up Dickie's nose again, this time by charging him twenty-five dollars for the supply of some photocopied documents. It had not been a wise move by Carran to add insult to injury.

And it wasn't just Dickie who got annoyed by Paul Carran's charging regime.

"What was a 40 cent stamp suddenly became $8.50, just because the lawyer was licking it," muttered one of the investors, Graeme Hadlee.

But the big question remained unanswered. Who the hell was Zorasong? And what the hell was it doing buying horses from the studs and on-selling them to Ermine?

In a bid to find out, Dickie arranged for the Hong Kong office of Simmons & Simmons, a major London lawfirm, to begin searching for records of

Zorasong in the Hong Kong companies office. They eventually found Zorasong in London, England.

Its registered office was listed as 128 Queen Victoria St, London, and it had an authorised share capital of £100, although only £2 had actually been paid up. Its shareholders were more interesting, however. They were two companies called Becmac Ltd and Camceb Ltd – which Dickie later sussed out was just Becmac spelt backwards – based in Hong Kong. Both companies gave their address as "26F Wing On Centre, 111 Connaught Rd, Hong Kong".

By a happy coincidence, this was also the address of Deloittes in Hong Kong, who also lived on the 26th floor of the Wing On Centre. Except that Dickie didn't believe in coincidences any more.

"The last annual return of [Zorasong] was made up to January 12, 1990," wrote Simmons & Simmons lawyer Juliet Finnigan, "and stated that the amount of indebtedness was US$185,942.05. There are, however, no charges registered against the Company."

What this meant was that Zorasong's creditors were unsecured. None had bothered to register their exposure officially.

"I am arranging for company searches to be made against Becmac Ltd and Camceb Ltd," continued Finnigan, "and will forward the results to you as soon as possible."

The directors of Zorasong, according to the initial search, were companies rather than individuals: Hanwin Ltd and Rayfull Ltd, both of the 14th floor of the Hua Chiao Commercial Building, 88 Des Voeux Road, Hong Kong.

"I have also been informed," wrote Finnigan, "that one of the partners at Chau and Cheng, the solicitors whose offices are at 14/F, Hua Chiao Commercial Building, has a brother who is a partner at Deloittes. Although this may be wholly irrelevant, I thought you might like to know at least."

The plot, as they say, was thickening.

In official documents, Hanwin's business was described as "to provide company secretarial services. That is, Hanwin can act as a secretary, director, nominee, trustee or agent for companies incorporated in Hong Kong or else-where and has all the powers and duties necessary to perform such capacities."

This was a strong sign that whoever was behind Zorasong wanted their identity kept hidden. If you probe a company set up in New Zealand, you will usually find that the directors are real people living at real residential addresses. But in tax havens, like Hong Kong or the Cook Islands, the directors of a shell company can be shell companies in their own right. Searching for the true owners can often be an exercise in playing with corporate Russian dolls. Even if you find a real human further down the food chain, that person is probably only a nominee human.

This was certainly the case with Hanwin, which had four Chinese directors all based on the 14th floor of the Hua Chiao building, but a check of their names against a list of partners in the Chan and Cheng lawfirm turned up zilch.

"It can only be presumed that they are either non-legal staff in the firm or not employed at the firm," wrote Finnigan in another letter to Chris Dickie.

What she did find was that Hanwin, Rayfull and Becmac – all linked to Zorasong – were also involved with a company called Bonshow. Bonshow had provided loan finance to the Ermine syndicate totalling half a million US dollars – nearly NZ$1 million – except, as Dickie would later allege in court, it was a fake loan.

You will come across explanations of these kind of loans later in this book, because they bear repeating, but here's how they work:

In any business, if you can inflate your on-paper costs you are decreasing the amount of tax you will have to pay because those costs are deductible expenses.

Normally, in a business sense, such expenditure must be paid for with real money, which means that the profit of the company will be lower. But the tax avoidance industry worked a little differently.

If you could inflate the amount of the costs, without actually spending any extra real money, then you were in effect increasing your profit. In some investment schemes, investors taking advantage of such mechanisms could actually earn two or three times their investment by using the jacked-up tax losses.

But how do you increase your on-paper costs without actually having to spend real money? Easy: if you jack-up the costs on one side of the ledger, then you create a paper loan on the other side of the ledger to "pay" for the fictitious expenditure.

The prices of one group of Ermine horses had been jacked-up by almost a million New Zealand dollars. Just coincidentally, Ermine had taken out a loan from Bonshow for roughly the same amount.

Dickie had first stumbled across Bonshow during an early analysis of Ermine's audited accounts for the 1985/86 year. Dickie had spent two and a half weeks cooped up in the offices of accounting firm Arthur Young, going through fourteen cartons of documents.

One of Ermine's auditors had made what the lawyer regarded as "an extraordinary note", questioning the Ermine accountant as to "why there appears to have been an unusual form of resolution in relation to the uplifting of the Bonshow loan."

Despite the note, no further action appeared to have been taken by the audit team, and the auditor's note quoted Ermine's accountant as saying "the answer is too deep." What the hell did *that* mean? Dickie wondered.

He went upstairs to raise the matter with one of Arthur Young's senior accountants. "Oh, don't worry about it Chris. It's just one of those jack-up loans," he answered.

"You're joking?" said a dumbstruck Dickie.

"No," sighed the accountant. "It's a tax arrangement. It doesn't have to be repaid."

Several years later, Bonshow took on a new relevance.

By then Dickie was investigating Bonshow's links to Zorasong. Unfortunately, the auditor's documents on Ermine, the common denominator, had since been destroyed. There was nothing untoward about this. It was just a case of making space – all accountants have a documentation storage/destruction policy.

The documents had been destroyed in accordance with Arthur Young's policy, but it proved an issue of lasting annoyance to Dickie who considers the documents should have been kept given that the litigation was now well underway.

The company search provided by Juliet Finnigan at the Hong Kong lawfirm showed Bonshow had been created on April 23, 1985, around the same time that Ermine was being set up. Zorasong's date of birth as a company was June 4, 1985.

Documents had gone missing in New Zealand, Dickie already knew this. Now Finnigan's search revealed Bonshow had been voluntarily liquidated. Significantly, its shareholders had just voted to destroy its records.

This was despite the fact that Ermine was clearly involved in New Zealand litigation and the process of document discovery was underway.

That decision to destroy the files had been taken on August 30, 1990 at a meeting in Hong Kong, but hadn't been filed with the Companies Office until three weeks later. The books were to be shredded within three months – the end of November. Time wasn't running out, it was sprinting.

The McVeagh Fleming team moved into the legal equivalent of hyperdrive. In a series of late night phone calls and faxes, they brainstormed with their Hong Kong attorneys. "Is there a way of stopping the document destruction?"

Juliet Finnigan didn't think so.

"The Official Receiver will usually only prevent the destruction of the books of a company being wound up if the applicant can show that the documents are required for the purposes of litigation, and that the person has a sufficient interest in proceedings.

"I am not sure, however, that he will interfere where the litigation has not yet commenced, or where the litigation is to take place in New Zealand."

"Shit!" cursed Dickie. He could feel the situation spinning slowly out of his control.

Perhaps Finnigan sensed the desperation. "It might be more appropriate to bring an action against Deloittes for an order for discovery," she ventured. Under a 1973 British court case, <u>Norwich Pharmacal Company and Others</u> v <u>Commissioners of Customs and Excise</u>, it was now possible to get a Court order against a person or a company holding documents that disclosed evidence of wrongdoing, even though that person or company may not have been involved in the wrongdoing.

In other words, if a company committing a fraud passed the documents on to a third person for safe keeping, the victims of the fraud could obtain a Norwich Pharmacal order forcing the third person to hand the evidence over.

In the eyes of the law, the third person had become an unwitting accessory.

"It was held that the person against whom discovery was sought had himself been involved in the wrongful acts of another, so as to facilitate a wrong doing, even though through no fault of his own," explained Finnigan in legalese.

"In those circumstances he will be under a duty to assist the person who has been wronged by giving him full information. The particular matter in which you are involved seems to be very similar in the circumstances, and this may be the best option available."

As to the problem of flinging fraud accusations at legal and accounting firms in the tax havens, Finnigan had some suggestions there, too.

"You may also be aware of the 1989 case, Agip (Africa) Ltd v Barry Kingslay Jackson & ors. In that particular case, an Isle of Man firm of accountants was found guilty of assisting in a fraud where they acted for a number of nominee companies involved in a conspiracy.

"Even though the firm of accountants had not knowingly assisted in the fraud, they were guilty of wilful and reckless failure to make the enquiries which an honest man would have made in order to satisfy themselves that they were not acting in furtherance of a fraud, and were held liable to account."

As they began to analyse the chances of a successful Norwich Pharmacal application, Dickie surged forward on a new front: a letter to the Minister of Revenue, Wyatt Creech, which has since been tabled at the Winebox Inquiry. In it, Chris Dickie spelt out his concerns.

"For the past two years the writer has been acting for several hundred members of the public who, in 1985-1987, invested huge sums of money in bloodstock syndicates which were then the subject of very favourable tax treatment.

"Most of these syndicates have failed badly, and the disputes are generally as between the syndicates, on the one hand, and the financiers demanding from them millions of dollars under loan facilities and guarantees.

"Our investigations on behalf of our clients are revealing a picture of fraudulent practices by promoters: scamming off millions of dollars, both from the investors and also from your department.

"There are distressing indications strongly suggestive that the fraud was formulated, connived at or knowingly and recklessly facilitated by members of some of New Zealand's most prestigious legal and accounting firms.

"We were approached some months ago by [tax] inspectors who had seen newspaper reports of our involvement for the investors in the fraud allegations. It was clear from the ensuing discussions that your department had hit a brick wall because, as we have also discovered, the schemes involve a long chain of companies incorporated in Hong Kong leading up to blind trusts!

"We also have been hitting that wall, although we suspect we may have made more progress than your department in some respects."

So far, so good. Dickie was setting out the background. But now he wanted the Minister's help. "A few days ago, however, we learned of the liquidation of one of the critical companies; on terms which will enable its records to be destroyed by 26 December unless we can show civil cause before then, or unless Mr Charles Sturt, Director of the Serious Fraud Office, with whom we have worked closely, can show cause to enable his Hong Kong counterparts to intervene before possibly critical evidence is destroyed.

"Such destruction undoubtedly would place the fraudsters in a much stronger position to escape detection, to the detriment of your department, as well as of Mr Sturt's office and of our clients."

Warming to the task at hand, Dickie explained that there was possibly a way that he and Molloy, acting as lawyers for the investors, could co-operate in a joint investigation with the IRD and the SFO.

"The proposal involves a request from your department under the exchange of information clause in the tax treaty between New Zealand and the Republic of Ireland; seeking certain invoices and details of transactions involving the sales by a leading Irish stud of certain fractional interests in a list of named bloodstock."

There is an important point here. Chris Dickie is suggesting that the IRD make investigations under its tax treaty with Eire, to obtain the information that his clients needed to fight their case. Normally it would be illegal for the IRD to divulge tax treaty information, but Dickie and Molloy thought they had a way around that.

"Whereas your department normally must never divulge information, it can do so to the extent of disclosing to a taxpayer details of his own file. Since our clients are the syndicates, *they* are the taxpayers onto whose file that information could be placed, and from which it possibly could be divulged to them or to us as their representatives.

"We, in turn, could disclose it (with our clients' permission) to the Serious Fraud Office, which could advance its enquiries in tandem with our own.

"If something along these lines were to be possible, the interests of the fleeced public in recovering money, of the Serious Fraud Office in bringing major white collar criminals to book and of your department in recovering what may be tens of millions of dollars stashed offshore, would be advanced."

The Serious Fraud Office, still at that stage in relative infancy, appeared at this point in its history to be keen to investigate further.

"The Serious Fraud Office is in agreement with us," said Dickie, "that failure to cooperate in the manner suggested would cause the tragic loss of what might be an unrepeatable opportunity. With the Hong Kong deadline now so close, it is imperative that these matters be explored, if at all, within the next few working days."

Dickie closed by saying that he and Molloy "and Mr Sturt or his Deputy, all would be prepared to meet" the Revenue Minister and the Commissioner of Revenue within that timeframe, "if you wish to pursue this suggestion. The Director of the Serious Fraud Office is to see the Attorney-General in the morning and will be raising with him the desirability of this course."

Dickie added that he was sending a copy of the letter to Finance Minister Ruth Richardson as well.

There was no swift reply, and two weeks later Dickie's hopes were dashed with a letter from Revenue Commissioner David Henry.

"The reason for your request," wrote Henry, "is to obtain information for your clients for use in possible proceedings of a non-tax nature."

The Commissioner explained that under the terms of the tax treaty with Eire, he could only disclose such information in specific tax proceedings. "I do not have the legal authority to act in the manner suggested by your letter."

All Molloy and Dickie had wanted was for the department to use that information to clear up the investors' tax liabilities. That was, they argued, perfectly lawful and was central to the statutory obligations of the Inland Revenue Department. But the department didn't see it that way.

So it was back to the drawing board.

Bonshow, a company that had ostensibly "loaned" Ermine US$500,000, had a paid up share capital of only HK$2. That's about fifty New Zealand cents.

Joining the dots, Dickie tried to build the picture as it stood.

The Ermine partnership had been created on July 31, 1985. Private investors, the special partners, had pumped in $1.4 million worth of capital. Equiticorp Holdings Ltd had loaned the partnership, through Equiticorp Hong Kong, the sum of $4 million, and Bonshow Ltd had loaned Ermine the equivalent of almost a million New Zealand dollars – the so-called "Bonshow Loan".

This had given Ermine a working capital of $6.4 million to play with, of which $4.4 million had been spent buying horses.

But where had Bonshow, a HK$2 company, scraped up half a million dollars US? The documents showed it had been loaned this money in the first place by Zorasong. It was what financial investigators call a circular transaction. Self-cancelling. A loan on paper only.

What is even more incredible to a lay observer: Zorasong made this unsecured advance to Bonshow on July 31, 1985 – the very same day that it first commenced business, according to Zorasong's 1986 annual report. Not bad for a company with £2 in paid-up capital. But then again, when you're playing with monopoly money it's not really such a big issue.

After seeing the Deloittes letter showing Zorasong's involvement, Dickie now had good cause to suspect that all of that $4.4 million had gone first to Zorasong, rather than direct to the studs. The question was, had Zorasong been buying the horses at a cheaper rate and flicking them on to Ermine at an inflated rate? The only way to find out was to ask for the receipts. Easier said than done. It took months, and even then, only a handful of receipts were ever discovered.

Dickie was a lawyer who liked giving lectures about the need for hard evidence: getting to the basics in a transaction. One of his favourite lectures was delivered to investors, his legal partners and me at various times in the investigation, it was even recounted at the Winebox Inquiry. The lesson goes like this:

In Dickie's Auckland office sits the figurine of a horse. Taped to the horse is a receipt, and it's been sitting there gathering dust ever since a trip, several years earlier, by Dickie to a local rubbish dump. The receipt tells Dickie that he went to the North Shore tip. It lists the date he went, it confirms that he paid twenty dollars inclusive of GST, and it thanks him for his custom.

"If a bloody rubbish dump can do it," muttered the lawyer, "you'd think one of the world's top bloodstock breeders could do the same."

Alas, no. The studs claimed they had no records on file, and the bloodstock partnership promoters and their lawfirm said they didn't have any receipts either.

At one point during the investigation, Colin Hayes – the man behind Australia's prestigious Lindsay Park Stud – told journalists "this all happened so long ago that all our records have been chucked out."

Dickie couldn't believe it, and made his views widely known to the investors. "Now here am I, a solicitor representing three hundred or so people who've bought literally millions of dollars in bloodstock and no one has got any records of any of the prices, and I am asked to believe that!"

He used to lecture his clients, telling them it was really a very simple issue: the clients needed to know how much they'd paid for the horses they'd bought.

"Suppose you come into my office," he told one investor, "and ask me to fly over to the Gold Coast and buy an apartment for you. You tell me I can spend anywhere up to $400,000 on this apartment.

"So I go over, purchase an apartment for $200,000 but tell you it cost $380,000. But, when you ask me for the receipt and the certificate of title, I tell you to get lost! Do you think that's acceptable behaviour in a commercial transaction?"

While the message from the studs was the same – "we have no records" – Dickie wondered if the studs simply didn't want to get involved with what could be embarrassing litigation.

"I think," mused Dickie, "in Ireland one of the motives undoubtedly was that the studs had such a valued reputation. They proudly talked about relationships with Her Majesty. Any hint of mud sticking was to be avoided at all costs. The mere use of the word 'fraud' sent them running a million miles in the opposite direction.

"I think the second motive, undoubtedly, was that many of the buyers of horses from these studs were using tax haven jurisdictions. Any thought that some lawyers from the South Pacific were climbing into these tax havens would scare the other purchasers witless if they thought that the studs were helping them."

World War III – Saddam Hussein vs The Rest Of The Planet – had begun and ended by the time Chris Dickie finally found himself holding the first horse purchase receipts he would have the good fortune to obtain. It would be three years before he received another set.

They arrived in the mail after yet another approach to Adelaide's Lindsay Park stud.

"The accountants have no invoices in the office in Adelaide relating to Zorasong," wrote Lindsay Park secretary Harry Line. "We have searched all invoice records here from January 1984 to June 1988 and have no invoice to Zorasong, however we have a receipt made out to Zorasong dated 6 August, 1985.

"The receipt is for $525,000 and covers the purchase of:

KEYNETON ROAD, ANGASTON, S.A. 5353   Telephone: (085) 64 2424

Cust. No.   Date 6 - 8 - 85   № 7808
RECEIVED FROM

M _Zorasong_ FX Hong Kong

re. C. KIRCHAM Godswalk & Morris $25,000.00

LINDSAY PARK STUD PTY. LTD.   per.

Moonlight	100,000
Adaptable	100,000
Crystal Bright	100,000
3 *Godswalk* shares	225,000

"Sorry we cannot help you with any more information."

Altogether, the purchase had cost Zorasong NZ$675,000. Those same horses were bought by Ermine investors within a day for NZ$1.4 million.

"I've got you, you miserable little scumsuckers," shrieked Dickie triumphantly. It wasn't many horses, but a horse in the hand was worth two in the bush. Now the game began in earnest. This was no longer a story about contract law. His belief was growing that this was a story of fraud.

The lawyer picked up the phone. It was time to call in the investors.

CHAPTER 12

Horses & Fairies

"Some circumstantial evidence is very strong,
as when you find a trout in the milk."
– HENRY DAVID THOREAU, 1850

The chill of winter had settled on Auckland in a foggy blanket of ice. From his 15th floor roost in the CML building, Chris Dickie could sometimes look out his window and gaze straight out on a cloudbank below the window ledge. This was one of those mornings.

Draining his cup of the last dregs of coffee, he turned to face the day – or the spectre of it that now haunted his in-tray. Three hundred and six investors now relied on him. A hundred and eighty-five in Buckingham as of the latest head-count, eighty-three in Wicklow and now thirty-eight more in Ermine.

He'd kickstarted legal action for Ermine investors on the strength of the Zorasong discovery. What had been the smallest of the partnerships and, frankly, nuisance value as he tackled the bigger problems in Buckingham and Wicklow, now took on the lead significance across all three cases.

What's more, it allowed the court action across all three syndicates to be bundled into one massive court case. Dickie had struck it lucky with Ermine's financiers, Equiticorp. Unlike the DFC and Westpac, Equiticorp's statutory manager agreed to hold off seeking judgment against the Ermine partners pending the outcome of legal action by the partners against the promoters. Equiticorp, Dickie told clients, "confirmed their confidence" in the outcome of that action.

On the Wicklow front, the DFC bank was stalling, and in Buckingham's case Westpac was said to be "in breach of the court order requiring that it file the list of documents in its possession."

"Until now the main focus of attention has been to deal with the Partnerships' financiers, namely Equiticorp, DFC and Westpac, and the avoiding of judgment being entered. We can now shift the main focus to the cause of the damage – namely the promoters.

"It is Dr Molloy's opinion that all partners in each Partnership have strong claims against the promoters for the full losses they have incurred."

In the June 1991 letter to investors, Chris Dickie also revealed for the first time the existence of an IRD investigation into the schemes.

"We are aware that the Department is investigating various bloodstock partnerships including Ermine, Buckingham and Wicklow."

With growing uncertainty over the financial goings-on inside the partnerships, even the auditors were now unwilling to sign-off on any of the accounts.

"It is hardly surprising," wrote Dickie, "that Deloittes will not complete the current tax accounts. It is a mark of the current firm's integrity that it will not do so."

By this time, the McVeagh Fleming legal team had brought in their own squad of forensic accountants from Ross, Melville, Bridgman. It would be their task to review all the available accounting information in a bid to piece together the financial jigsaw. There was some more news for embattled investors: another QC had joined their legal stable.

"Today, at the suggestion of Dr Molloy QC, we are formally instructing Mr Julian Miles QC. The promoters have engaged two Queens Counsel to conduct their case. The total damages being sought in the three partnerships could exceed $30 million. The allegations against the promoters are serious."

Julian Miles' job description was to "tear to bits" the Molloy/Dickie thesis – in other words, look for holes in their case.

Miles is one of the top litigation QC's in the country, a short, slim character with eyes that seem to laugh as though he has seen all your secrets, and whose tongue "slices, dices and juliennes" with all the dexterity of a tepanyaki chef. If anyone was going to tear Dickie and Molloy to bits, Julian Miles was the man to do it.

But as legal action against the promoters began, it was nearing an end against Westpac. For their part Molloy and Dickie had acknowledged that there was no way clients were going to be able to weasel out of liability for everything, which had been one of the thrusts to the early skirmishing with Westpac. But by the same token the lawyers now believed the case was rock-solid for limiting that liability to four-sevenths of the debt, representing the partners' four million dollar share of the seven million dollar capital.

Westpac, already on the back foot after the Court of Appeal ruling the previous year, finally accepted the inevitable and settled out of court. The deal, in mid-1991, prevented summary judgments being entered "against any client and, more importantly, prevents bankruptcy proceedings from being initiated."

For Dickie, this meant Westpac was not going to get almost $21,000 out of him, but instead a much smaller sum and only after a long wait. In addition, whatever sum he had to pay Westpac, he could now take legal action against the other defendants to recover the amount of his loss.

"I was one of 60-odd investors with the smallest holding of ten units: ten thousand dollars. I mean, for some people they were going for bloody squillions. Literally squillions. I was on ten units, we had one person who had 300. Work that figure out! They wanted twenty-one from me.

"There's no question about it, people were just crying. I had people who were really desperate, they were in a state of shock, absolute shock. And don't forget, we hadn't even discovered Zorasong at the stage that Westpac went for us."

It was a chance for the lawyer to reflect on the events of the preceding two and a half years. "Dear Client," he wrote on July 29, 1991. "By the time you receive this letter the writs in Ermine, Buckingham and Wicklow will have been filed and served on the defendants.

"That step is the culmination of events which first started with the partnership's manager Mr Kirkham requesting the Buckingham partners in November 1988 for more injection of capital, and has concluded with the serving of the writs."

The lawyer had been contacted by more than a hundred clients during July, and they had common concerns.

"First and foremost, there has been an increasing anger felt as more and more of the activities of the promoters became uncovered. Not one of us has remained unaffected by what has been found.

"Initial concerns quickly became suspicion and, in turn, a certainty that *not one of our clients would have entered into these investments if the real position had been described in the respective prospectus.*" [Dickie's emphasis]

From the perspective of Graeme and Pat Hadlee, Dickie was right on the button with his observation.

"I don't think we even need to be bothered answering that one," said Pat. "There's no way we would have invested. Graeme and I had never had any money, and we had both been quite religious in our younger days and we had a very high moral/ethical standard.

"It might have eroded a bit through the period of our marriage break-up, but we still have very high standards and there's absolutely no way! As far as I am concerned, money that is made and taxed is just fair-do's.

"You might disagree with the Government of the day at the level of tax, but I don't believe that tax evasion or avoidance is fair game.

"All I can remember of the motivating factors was that there were a lot of people we mixed with at the time who were making a lot of money and saying 'you don't have to pay all this tax, you know, you can find ways around it. Talk to your accountant'.

"So that's really what it was. My whole basis has always been: if other people can do this why can't we? And I would say to accountants 'What the hell are we paying all this stuff for when other people don't?'.

"But if I'd known there was anything scammy or the slightest bit fringy about it we would have just had nothing to do with it!"

These were the kind of opinions that Dickie was picking up from his disgruntled clients as he wrote his memorandum. "We all know that chaotic results flow from misdirected feelings. This has not happened here. Between Dr Molloy, our firm and our clients a very strong team providing mutual support has now culminated in the filing of the three actions."

The last statement may have been true at the time, but the warm fuzzy feelings were not always visible, especially as the ongoing legal bills continued to mount. The Mad Butcher, Peter Leitch, remembered one meeting in particular.

"I know I got pissed off with the lawyers," he recalled. "I'll never forget one day, at one of the meetings, we had this QC called Molloy. Dickie used to get up and say 'I'd like to thank Dr Molloy for being here today' and pissing around like this.

"Anyhow, one day I couldn't stand it any more, so I stood up and said 'Listen! We're paying bloody Molloy. We're paying him friggin' plenty! There's no need to friggin' thank him. It's not a lawyers' benevolent society!' I tell you – everyone stood up and clapped. The people that won out of this are all the lawyers."

Leitch was one of those who finally settled out of court at the beginning of 1996. "I got out of it earlier this year because, mate, it was just going around in bloody circles. The lawyers kept saying 'yeah, yeah, we're going to win, we're going to win,' but mate: they may win but, shit, I might be dead by the time they friggin' win!"

Sitting on the end of a telephone listening to the Butch recount the yarns, I could visualise him screwing up his face in disgust at it all.

"Are you going to write a book on it then?" he asked after a moment.

"Yeah," I told him.

"Well put me on the bloody front page!" he quipped with a chuckle as he hung up the phone.

Tony Molloy remembers the tensions well. "It wore people down. There was a war of attrition going on. People were being slagged, we were being labelled as 'obsessive'.

"I just heard yesterday from an official in a Government department that I was supposed to have charged eight million for my fees in this case. They were feeding this sort of thing to our clients you see, trying to destabilise the group, and it was working. Chris was fighting very hard, for their own sake, to keep them together!"

As Graeme Hadlee recalled, it was a time of white fury.

"The thing that impressed me was the tremendous anger from all the people. They were really angry! It was sort of like a Roman crowd: if Christ had been outside they'd have nailed Him to the Cross there and then! They were all furious with Russell McVeagh."

For Chris Dickie in July 1991, however, there was a need to get the investors' anger tightly focused.

"You would not have entered into the investment if you had been told the truth [about Zorasong's secret markup on the horses]. This is the essential ingredient of your case and accordingly any anger is not only justified, it is now properly directed against those persons who utterly ignored both their moral and legal responsibilities to you.

"The time for frustration is passed. You are now pursuing the real target.

"Shortly after I began investigating Wicklow I was telephoned by one of the defendants. I was informed that if I persisted in the enquiry then they will ensure that my wife and I would be 'financially ruined'. I purposely refrained from informing Tony Molloy of that threat until after the Wicklow proceedings had been filed.

"Two weeks ago Mr Boyt at Westpac admitted to me that Westpac's decision to select me as the target for the summary judgment proceedings was based on the intention of preventing me from being solicitor for any proceedings filed for my Buckingham clients."

There had been another motive behind Westpac's action though. Dickie ran into Glyn Boyt on the street one day. "Why did you single me out?" he asked.

"Well," said Boyt after a moment, "do remember saying if we were going to sue anyone you wanted to be the first to know? We decided to keep our word."

As Dickie would later tell the Winebox Inquiry in response to a question on the issue from European Pacific's QC, Richard Craddock: "To put it colloquially, I was picked out as the fall guy, Mr Craddock."

Big boys' games. Big boys' rules. Dickie outlined a few more nasties in his briefing to clients.

"Again, last July, another defendant threatened me with defamation proceedings. One other defendant made similar threats and a few weeks ago yet another party (not at this stage joined as a defendant) indicated very strong concern as to our enquiries. I must admit that I have found these times very stressful."

"For many clients," he continued, "this case is the first that they have been involved in. I am certain that there is not one client who, two years ago, could have guessed what has been uncovered.

"You are one of a large group of persons representing a cross-section of New Zealand society who have been financially savaged by people you thought you could rely upon. You are now taking the steps to put matters right."

Little did the lawyer know, but the pressure had only just begun.

Across town, Paul Carran, Chris Kirkham and bloodstock adviser Mitchell McLeish were feeling the pressure as well. They held what even they would describe as "clandestine" meetings to discuss Dickie's progress in hunting them down. For them, the issue was complicated because they were using Zorasong as a vehicle to purchase their own private bloodstock interests, aside from the machinations involving the syndicates.

Paul Carran was said to be so concerned about electronic surveillance – "room and phone bugs" – that he insisted the trio meet in the carpark of Kirkham's office building.

"The horses have to be sold," Carran told his colleagues bluntly, referring to their private herd. "The money has to be repaid to the bank, and we should forget we ever owned them!"

McLeish, sensing the rising paranoia levels and feeling a little infected himself, had to vent his anger through clenched teeth to avoid the chance of their voices carrying in the still air.

"There's no way that's going to happen!" he hissed. "It can't be done."

"Look Mitchell," argued Carran, "there are things going on here that you don't understand."

"Well I've got news for you laddie! There's things going on that you don't understand either: for one, the market is weak, we can't just dump our bloodstock and run, it's not going to sell! Secondly, the horses are doing well and we've got a very significant portfolio.

"Thirdly," continued the Irishman, "when you get off your ass and take a lawsuit against Coolmore Stud for the money they owe us, then we'll be in very good shape and able to pay the bank. Besides, we can't sell the horses until the transfer agreements are completed."

Paul Carran stared at McLeish with a disgusted look on his face, then turned to Kirkham, who'd stayed quiet during the exchange.

"For heaven's sake, Chris, talk some sense into him." Carran walked away, a man clearly under stress. And no wonder.

"Dickie did cause a few problems by running around and he caused fear, I think, mostly in Carran," recalled McLeish in an interview with the author. "And it was Carran's inability to act, out of that, I mean the Irish lawyers didn't know whether they were coming or going because instructions were conflicting.

"I couldn't give instructions because there was nothing to say that I was connected at all, apart from a power of attorney to act as an agent for them, so I didn't have any clout and Kirkham didn't have any clout."

It is something that rankled at McLeish throughout. Here was a man in the horse business- who loved horses – finding his own dreams dashed because he'd become embroiled in something bigger.

"In the horse business," he wrote at one point, "one needs a bit of skill and a lot of luck. We certainly had more than our share of luck. Rarely, if ever, has such a small band of horses achieved so much.

"You can understand my disappointment and bitterness at what has happened. I was, and indeed still am, very proud of these horses. However, communication between Securelaunch and myself can best be described as diabolical, to the extent it was nearly non-existent.

"The NZ leg of Paul Carran and C J Kirkham was not much better, and currently neither of them want to admit to the existence of either Zorasong or Securelaunch. (This has to do with a tax investigation being carried out in NZ at the moment.) I was supposed to be made a partner too, but this did not eventuate."

Coolmore Stud, which had refused to transfer the horses from Zorasong to Securelaunch back in 1990 had also stopped paying the trio any income from their private bloodstock breeding venture.

There were several reasons for this, and they included the fact that Coolmore was having problems with two of the New Zealand bloodstock partnerships failing to pay their accounts.

But if Zorasong was finding the going tough, Securelaunch was all but bankrupt. Accounts obtained by the author show Securelaunch was already £115,000 in the red by the end of 1989, and the blood was spilling at an ever increasing rate.

In a June 1990 letter to Chris Kirkham, Channel Islands tax engineer Ed Bendelow had written "you will be able to note, for the information of your clients, that I am not prepared to accept beneficial ownership of the Hong Kong structures until I am convinced of their solvency, and I am sure you will understand the reasons behind this.

"I should advise you that the insolvency practitioner I have consulted in Jersey has confirmed that I can continue to trade for only a further period of 7-10 days, in view of the lack of cash I am currently experiencing.

"He informs me he would have advised immediate administration, but for the $10,000 in transit that I am hoping shortly to disburse to the Irish lawyer we have discussed. It is underline imperative therefore that you transfer the remaining $32,000 to our office immediately, or we still risk this company going into administration fairly shortly."

In addition, Kirkham and McLeish had fallen behind on the lease payments for a stallion they shared, *Don't Forget Me*.

Coolmore was retaliating by refusing to pay money it owed to the Wicklow syndicates and Zorasong Limited.* You could joke that there's only one thing worse than a falling-out among thieves: a falling-out among "horse thieves!" Kirkham and McLeish found Paul Carran's plight a subject of considerable mirth.

Meanwhile, at a meeting to brief clients, Dickie laid out on a whiteboard what had been discovered so far. He and Molloy drew diagrams like there was no tomorrow, linking Zorasong and a series of intermediaries scattered between Hong Kong and the Channel Islands with names like Secretaries Ltd, Becmac and Camceb to the bloodstock deals.

"I had called a meeting of the investors in Ermine, of which about 70 came to my office. We had, by this time, identified Zorasong and were certain of its role. We had identified the round-robin of communications and document-ation, and we had obtained searches of all the companies that were sitting underneath these entities."

This is an important point, because it became fundamental to the film and bloodstock investigations, and the research into the winebox, that you had to "get behind" the front companies. A company like Zorasong may be involved in a deal, but who owned it and in turn who owned its owners? To say it involved smoke and mirrors would be a gross understatement.

"We drew this diagram," remembered Dickie, "and this was an amazing time in the case because you were addressing a roomful of people who had been completely and utterly mislead. You should have seen the looks on their faces when we started to whiteboard where the documentation was going, and they were all sitting there, scratching their heads, saying 'hang on, I wasn't told any of this – this is my investment, what the hell's going on?'.

"This particular afternoon we had drawn Zorasong's wiring diagram of

---

* Buckingham's administrators and Scorten Investments, the company led by investors Bob Wilson and Murray Carter that had purchased some of the bloodstock in a deal with Westpac, ended up taking legal action against Coolmore, and eventually succeeded in forcing the stud to treat all the entities separately, and not set off the debts of one against the assets of another.

interconnecting companies on the board, and when the meeting ended one of the Ermine investors, an Auckland lawyer who eventually opted not to join the legal fight for personal reasons, stayed behind to talk to me. He was very, very upset, and he said 'can I see you in your room?'

"Now, this was a guy who was very much my senior, and a person I regarded as being a pretty switched-on commercial lawyer."

Clearly sensing something was wrong, Dickie escorted the solicitor to his office, grabbing some beer from the McVeagh Fleming partners' fridge on the way. The Ermine investor took a long draught of the cool liquid, and neither man spoke as the dust eddies swirled in the sunlight bathing Dickie's desk. His horse statue, with the receipt still attached to its neck, cast a long shadow.

Regaining his composure, the lawyer broke his silence as he ripped the tab off a second beer.

"Listen, Chris, this is bloody important! I've seen all these companies before, and it's nothing to do with bloodstock. The Inland Revenue are investigating them. I've got the details in my office, if you'd like to come and see me tomorrow."

Dickie got such a shock he almost spat his ale all over the desk.

"Shit! You're joking!"

"No. I was an investor in the movie *Merry Christmas Mr Lawrence*, and the revenue were going to prosecute every single investor, including me, because they considered that we had been involved in a tax fraud. They had written to each one of us asking us to show reason why we should not each be prosecuted."

Dickie poured himself another beer. This was going to be interesting.

CHAPTER 13

Making Movies

"Ha ha ha, hee hee hee, I'm the laughing gnome
and you can't catch me!"
– DAVID BOWIE, *LAUGHING GNOME*, 1972

Once upon a time, New Zealand had a fledgling film industry. Its modern history probably had its roots in the mid to late 1970's, with the release of movies like *Sleeping Dogs* and *Solo*.

The former was the vehicle that catapulted a little-known actor named Sam Neill into the consciousness of the New Zealand public, the man who later starred opposite Merryl Streep in the Azaria Chamberlain dingo-drama *Evil Angels* and Nicole Kidman in *Dead Calm*. Neill is perhaps best known to world moviegoers however for starring opposite T. Rex in *Jurassic Park*. But if it hadn't been for a four hundred thousand dollar movie about a fugitive on the run from a totalitarian NZ Government, Sam Neill's career might have taken a different route.

Those early movies were funded largely by generous and possibly naÔve investors, who had faith that NZ films could make a profit. In the cultural cringe of the day it was more common for local audiences to rubbish any NZ productions, as New Zealand still hadn't gained the confidence to believe that it could produce anything of value other than meat, wool and dairy products.

In the book *Film in Aotearoa New Zealand*, movie producer Geoff Murphy described *Sleeping Dogs* as the most impressive of the Kiwi films released at the time.

"It was the strongest at the box office, taking nearly half a million of which maybe $150,000 returned to the producer after costs. Despite some foreign and television sales, it must have lost quite a bit."

There had to be a better way.

In an effort to unify the fledging movie industry, the Film Commission was established to organise funding and provide logistical assistance, particularly in sales and marketing. Not that Murphy found the Commission easy to deal with, even with what would become the box-office smash *Goodbye Pork Pie*.

"The Commission, who have never suffered from the delusion that they could tell a good script if they fell over it, were less than enthusiastic. After consideration and assessment, they reluctantly decided to grant development funds, but only if I listened to a couple of the commissioners who had strong views on how the script should be developed: it needed to be softened; and it needed to be tougher. I came away from all this greatly confused."

Nevertheless, with an eventual budget of $320,000, *Pork Pie* went on to gross more than $1.5 million at the box office, and it changed the way New Zealanders looked at themselves.

With those sort of returns, the film crews who'd been working up until then mainly for the love of it began to tire of making sacrifices: they wanted to get paid a decent wage for the work, and given more reasonable budgets to work from. Private investment was needed and, according to Murphy, the lightning rod in its procurement was the Film Commission's Executive Director, Don Blakeney – an accountant with what Geoff Murphy called "a fair understanding" of tax law.

"It was probably inevitable that he would begin to examine the possibility of a tax loophole for investors. Tax shelter had been used and abused in many other countries.

"Instead of investing directly in a film, the Commission would lend its money to an investor, who would match the amount with his own money and invest the total amount in the film. This enabled the investor to show a liability for twice the amount he had invested and avoid tax for that amount."

This, of course, was the precursor to the bloodstock dodges, and the principle was exactly the same. Whereas the bloodstock investors were using loan money from banks to boost the amount of capital invested and therefore boost the tax write-offs on the horses, movie investors were using loan money from the Film Commission to achieve the same result.

"Sixty-six percent was the tax rate at the time," writes Murphy, so [the investor] could get a write-off of $132 for every $100 he invested. He made a profit of over thirty percent before the film even began production. If the film died at the box office, he was fine. If it made a lot of money, his investment paid dividends. He then paid tax on profits and couldn't lose."

But there was trouble brewing. The nouveau riche were getting wind of the opportunities. Among them, Michael Fay.

"Away from the property scene," write Morrison, Haden and Cubis in *Michael Fay – On A Reach For The Ultimate*, "Michael Fay discovered another exciting field of investment that he couldn't resist. It was film-making. At the time, investment in films was encouraged by huge tax incentives. That was a big enough attraction in itself.

"In 1979 Michael Fay and David Richwhite contributed out of their own pockets a third of the one million dollar budget for the movie '*Beyond Reasonable Doubt*'. They had considered a number of scripts before that, but Fay had knocked them all back, feeling they lacked international appeal.

"However, when producer John Barnett brought them the screenplay for David Yallop's bestseller about the conviction of Arthur Allan Thomas for murder, they immediately saw its potential. " 'I read it and thought, wow!' says Fay. 'The impact was stunning. You just couldn't put it down.'

"Thomas was still in jail when Fay and Richwhite made their decision to back the project. When he was pardoned, they feared for a time that people might no longer be interested, but the fears quickly proved groundless. Soon after filming was finished, a Royal Commission of Inquiry was set up, and Fay saw this as a chance to move the film into the international arena.

"He was to recall later: 'We made only two stipulations – that the movie be finished on time, and that it stay within budget. The rest was up to Barnett. We didn't have anything to do with the picking of actors or crew. We just found the money, then kept right out of it.'"

The opening titles of the movie note the financial support of Fay Richwhite, Brierley Investments and Bob Jones, in association with Endeavour Productions.

It was another hit movie and, as Geoff Murphy noted, it was a loud advertisement for the new tax engineering.

"The Film Commission urged producers to be discreet about it and use it with restraint. Once John Barnett applied it to *Beyond Reasonable Doubt* the cat was out of the bag. David Hemmings, who had a lead in the film, was a partner in Hemdale, an American company, and could recognise a good thing when he saw it.

"Within a year he was directing *Race For The Yankee Zephyr* in Queenstown. It was not long before other foreign interests were on the case and the floodgates were opened."

Funnily enough, familiar faces could be seen in the *Yankee Zephyr* financing as well. "What appealed most to Michael Fay," write his three biographers, "was the glamour associated with the industry. He linked up with the moguls of Hollywood and put together the financial package for the international release movie, *The Race For The Yankee Zephyr*."

Having stumbled on a tax lodestone, the gnomes of Queen Street mined it for all it was worth.

"If you could create a liability for an investor with Commission money," explained Murphy, "then why not with [deferred expenses]? You could buy a script for $20,000, promising the writer another $100,000 when the film was in profit.

"This meant that the producer would owe the writer $100,000 unless there were never any profits, in which case he would owe him nothing. However, on the books it showed as a liability.

"There are ways of transferring this liability to an investor, who could double it as he would with Commission money. Thus, the producer would receive $100,000 of real money from the investor as his part of the investment.

"If that worked, then why not make the script more expensive – say a deferral of $500,000. Suddenly, by the use of tax shelter funny money in the form of often bogus liabilities, you could raise millions."

There were other mechanisms for falsely inflating the costs of a movie too. Russell McVeagh tax lawyer Geoff Clews gave one example of "limited recourse" funding to the Winebox Inquiry in 1996.

He explained how a New Zealand group making a movie might raise $50 to pay for a film director, but the director comes in from overseas and says he wants $100, because that's what he got paid for his last film. But $100 represents the total budget for making the movie. Quelle horreur! To pay the director what he wants means there's no money left to make the film.

The director, said Clews, turns out to be a generous person who really does want to make this movie in New Zealand so, sensing the New Zealand group's sadness, he charges them a hundred dollars, but immediately lends back fifty dollars of it to the group so they can meet their other expenses and stay within budget.

"What about repayment?" the New Zealanders ask.

"Oh, don't worry, you don't have to repay me until the film makes $1,000 in profits," says the generous director, who walks away with fifty dollars in the hand, and an IOU from the New Zealanders for another fifty dollars that will probably never be repaid, because the film won't make that much money.

On the film company's books, however, it has used a limited recourse loan of fifty dollars, and is carrying a deferred obligation to pay that director fifty dollars. It has inflated its costs to $150 for tax purposes, but stayed within a production budget of $100.

"Once the original scepticism had been swept aside by greed, every yuppie in the country rushed to invest his profits from a bull stockmarket in New Zealand films," continued Geoff Murphy. "And, according to high-powered, expensive advisers, it was perfectly legal."

Well, maybe not all the lawyers were prepared to say it was legal. Tony Molloy had been dubious about the schemes from the beginning.

"A barrister who was involved in the case later on reminded me that I had sent him away with a flea in his ear some years before," remarked the QC, "when he'd come to me from a small firm with a film deal that was just like these ones. He explained it to me, and I just told him he'd go to jail if he did it and not to have a bar of it. I'd forgotten that, but this lawyer remembered that and reminded me how I'd kicked him out. He said he thought I was going to explode when he put it to me!"

Molloy talked also of another lawyer who, at the time, had been a junior partner in a major Auckland lawfirm.

"One of his senior partners had said to him 'look, we want to do this for a big American client. You set it up!'

"He had huge misgivings, and didn't want to set it up because he thought it wasn't kosher, but it was made clear to him that if he wanted to have any sort of future in the firm, the firm had to get involved in these things because that was the new wave and they had to be competitive.

"So he did it, and he told me he then had many sleepless nights – really agonising over the bloody thing. Funnily enough, another person involved in the same deal was a client of McVeagh Fleming's, and I'd been asked to consult on it. I had told him it wouldn't work, so the scheme got kyboshed in the end.

"But this lawyer told me he was very grateful that I'd done that, because he was really worried he might end up in jail."

It wasn't long before Molloy's feelings became widely known in the legal fraternity, and the word seemed to go around that the QC was to be avoided.

"People like [Rudd Watts & Stone partner] Paul Darvell briefed me on odd matters, where they were doing these circular funding deals, and again I just scotched them. I remember Darvell, there was one brilliant scheme he had, a marvellous intellectual thing, and I could see it was very important for the firm because they were putting a lot on it, but I had to say 'look, this is tax avoidance, you can't run it.'

"I got the impression not long after that that people were saying 'shit, don't go to him because he won't play ball!'.

The Jiminy Cricket conscience twinges within the legal profession were few and far between however. There was money to be made and it was every rat for himself.

"Suddenly it was boom time," wrote Murphy, "a boom which all but destroyed the New Zealand film industry. Tax shelter was a form of legalised fraud. It enabled the rich to avoid taxes. It was the Robin Hood syndrome in reverse.

"We robbed the poor (who of course did not have high-powered lawyers) to pay the rich so that we could make films. The deals were very complex, often requiring the setting up of offshore companies and complex legal papers to hide behind should anything go wrong.

"They were outside the scope of most film makers. A new breed of producer appeared to exploit this circumstance. He was usually an ex-lawyer or financier with little or no understanding of film, and often very little interest in it. Deal making became more important than film making."

And out of the woodwork came every kind of movie imaginable. Take this *Metro* interview in the mid 1980's with film maker Michael Firth – the man behind *Off The Edge*, *Sylvia*, *Heart Of The Stag* and *The Leading Edge*.

"New Zealand is just filled with wonderful, really talented people and I've got together with a few of them. We all live in a big house together, it's just down the road, and it's like being in a rock'n'roll band!

"We get up in the morning and start talking about the film around the breakfast table, and suddenly we come up with this great scene – a simply terrific scene – and we leap up from the table saying 'Let's film it', and we do! We film it almost immediately! And it's just spontaneous and marvellous.

"It's really like Woody Allen," he confides to *Metro*'s James Allan. "We use our own living room in the film, just like he does in his. We use our friends and our friends' houses, just like Woody does.

"It's a team effort, it's so energising and great and just the way I've always dreamed film making could be!"

Firth described how *The Leading Edge*, a ski movie, came about as a result of a phone conversation with Greg Taylor, brother of round-the-world yacht racer Digby Taylor.

"I'm chatting to Greg on the phone, and we get talking about film scenarios, and I start creating, on the spur of the moment, an *On The Road* sort of film, set in New Zealand, taking in all the great scenery, lots of sporting action and some real New Zealand characters.

"In that one phone call I practically mapped out the entire script.

"The next week I typed it up into a five page synopsis which I took into Fay Richwhite and they said, 'Hey, sounds great, here's a million dollars! Go make your film!'

"Just like that!" gushed Firth.

"Michael had his script written," wrote James Allan, "his money in his hot little hands, and all he needed was a hero. Once again his extended family network saved the day.

"His cousin in Hamilton called up and said 'I've found you a star', which is how he met Mathurin Molgat, a real hunk-in-a-million, who just happened to be living with some girls in Te Awamutu.

"He's HOT, he can ski, and he's French-Canadian, which means he shouldn't need to be dubbed when the film is released in the US. So what if his name sounds like a new antibiotic?" concluded Allan.

Fay Richwhite's services to New Zealand culture through the film industry continued for several more years, with the merchant bank teaming with film and television producer John Barnett to arrange the financing of *Footrot Flats: A Dog's Tale*.

It is important to note, at this point, that while the tax breaks in the movie industry became a rort of enormous magnitude, there were nevertheless some flow-on benefits for the country. These came in the form of technical training. The vast number of movies in production meant our directors, actors and film crews were gaining valuable experience, experience that would later show its worth in films like Jane Campion's *The Piano* or Peter Jackson's *Heavenly Creatures*.

But back in the early 1980s, the movies being made were, frankly, appalling in a critical sense.

In one case, American actor Tatum O'Neal was brought down to New Zealand for several months to star in a movie called *Prisoners*. The film was so bad, according to staff at the Film Commission some years later, that it was never commercially released. *Prisoners* would eventually achieve its fifteen minutes of fame courtesy of revelations at the long-running Winebox Inquiry in 1995 and 96 – but more on that later in this book.

The movie that Chris Dickie was interested in at this point was called *Merry Christmas Mr Lawrence*. It starred 35 year old British rock icon David Bowie and was directed by Japan's Nagisha Oshima.

The beauty of the Japanese language is probably lost in the translation somewhere but, in English, Oshima's film credits included such notables as *Night and Fog in Japan* (1960), *The Pleasures Of The Flesh* (1965), *A Treatise Of Japanese Bawdy Song* (1967) and the 1968 cinematic experience *Three Resurrected Drunkards*.

He had a fan, in the form of British movie critic Ian Cameron writing in *The Second Wave* in London.

"Japanese cinema in the 1960's has produced a battery of young talent, but none as serious, precise or versatile as Oshima. Arguably, he is the first Japanese director who seems to be functioning within a totally modern world.

"He has rejected the period film and grappled with the agonising forces compelling Japan to choose between its traditions and modernity. Much of his early work is still unknown in the West, but his subject matter indicates the new, post-war, consciousness.

"*The Sun's Burial* is a picture of a seething slum community. *The Naked Catch* deals with a Negro soldier taken prisoner during the war. But it was in 1968 that Oshima made his decisive impact with *Death By Hanging* and *Diary Of A Shinjuku Thief*.

"The first is the story of the execution of a young Korean who had raped and killed two Japanese girls. It has the icy clarity of composition, scraped clean of direct emotional associations, and with it the first evidence of Oshima's almost surrealistic eye for the ritual workings of Japanese society."

As for *Shinjuku Thief*, Cameron described it as "animal self-expression. . .in brutal confrontation with social moves and the codes of Japanese living.

"Oshima is effortlessly shocking but always chaste, watching the vivid sexual performance of his characters as if they were insects.

"But his masterpiece," enthused Ian Cameron, "is *The Ceremony*, a bleak but luminous picture of how domestic ritual destroys or perverts the life force in a family.

"Once again, the stinging touch of a Bunuel is evident in the scenes like that in which the young mistress is discovered bound to a tree, dead, and as the camera circles the sword is drawn out of her body and an arc of blood jumps out behind it.

"Oshima looks like one of those relatively young men, like Bertolucci, Rohmer and Hellman, who could be proved in the next ten years as major figures in cinema history."

It depends, probably, on one's definition of young when it comes to describing movie directors. By the time he worked on *Mr Lawrence*, Oshima had turned 50.

Every movie needs a distributor – someone who can market the film and get it into as many cinemas as possible. For *Mr Lawrence* this was Terry Glinwood, a 48 year old Brit who'd been in the business since joining Columbia Pictures in 1960.

Glinwood's background was accounting, and he was the numbers man on movies as diverse as *Lolita* and Roman Polanski's *Repulsion*. He spent the 1970's working under entertainment magnate Robert Stigwood – the man behind The Bee Gees in their *Saturday Night Fever* days, and when Stigwood moved his base from Britain to the USA in 1977, Glinwood quit to set up his own business, Osprey Films, as a distribution agent.

Producer Jeremy Thomas's credits included directing the movie *Sinbad's Golden Voyage*, and producing a string of British films – perhaps the best known of which is *The Great Rock'n'Roll Swindle*, starring The Sex Pistols.

When the great movie tax schemes began with *Beyond Reasonable Doubt* back in 1979, it hadn't taken long for the Inland Revenue Department to start sniffing out the 11 secret herbs and spices that constituted the tax dodge recipe.

Prime Minister Robert Muldoon's Government finally took the axe to the perceived loophole on Budget Night, August 5, 1982, but they left an escape hatch: movies already in production would have a further two years' grace.

"Inland Revenue," noted author and political columnist Bruce Jesson in his book, *Behind The Mirror Glass*, "immediately received fifty-three spur-of-the-moment scripts. All of the tax avoidance money that had previously been going into kiwifruit and agriculture now went into films. And the tax avoidance films continued at a greater rate than before.

"These films were financed by special partnerships, which allowed the individual investors to claim a tax benefit while participating in a corporate enterprise.

"The tax angle would be worked out by the film producer. And a merchant bank would act as intermediary between the producer and the investors, collecting a promoter's fee and a management fee.

"Challenge Corporate Services – an investment bank owned by Fletcher Challenge – was responsible for arranging the finance for many of these films."

And it was Challenge, through its subsidiary Broadbank, that was behind *Merry Christmas Mr Lawrence*.

Although the budget had knocked the movie rorts on the head, *Mr Lawrence* was one of the 53 already in production – scripting work had begun in June and filming was underway by August. The IRD even kindly sent the producers a letter confirming the movie was "pre-budget" for tax purposes.

"Yippee!" shouted Queen Street's gnomes in unison.

In a letter dated December 23, 1982, Broadbank's film finance manager, Chris Kirkham invited potential investors to send him their cash. Specifically, he wanted $3.42 million.

"Partners' contributions of capital will be required by means of a cheque post-dated to 8 February 1983. Cheques should be made payable to Mr Lawrence Productions Ltd."

Just as Buckingham Enterprises Ltd. had been the general partner in the Buckingham Enterprises Ltd and Company special bloodstock partnership, Mr Lawrence Productions filled the same role in the *Mr Lawrence* partnership.

It is a one hundred dollar company established as the launch vehicle for the David Bowie film.

In his letter, Kirkham spells out the benefits to investors.

"The production cost of $11.77 million will be spent in the year ending 31 March 1983, and the Partnership will thus suffer a trading loss of $11.77 million for the first year."

It is of critical importance to note, at this point, the amount that Kirkham claims the movie is costing to produce: $11.77 million. It would later be alleged that the real cost of the movie was only $4 million. But, as far as the investors knew, they were investing in a $12 million movie.

"Each partner," continued Kirkham, "deducts his share of this loss, giving a deduction of $3.44 for each $1 of capital contributed to the film. That is, at the average marginal tax rate of 63 cents, partners will save tax of $2.17 for each $1 of capital."

As for the merits of the movie itself, Kirkham's December 1982 proposal waxed eloquent. "The distributor of *Merry Christmas Mr Lawrence* is of the opinion that the quality of the film is such that it has a strong prospect of winning an award at Cannes.

"*Merry Christmas Mr Lawrence* is a New Zealand feature film set in a Second World War Japanese prisoner-of-war camp in Java, with flashbacks to New Zealand. The film was shot on location in New Zealand and the Cook Islands and drew upon a cast including more than 100 New Zealanders.

"The film is based on the book *The Seed And The Sower* by the South African author, Lawrence Van der Post, and depicts the violent clash of cultures between a group of prisoners-of-war and their Japanese masters.

"The prisoners are led by a young New Zealander, Celliers (played by David Bowie), who becomes the hope of the allied prisoners as daily they face the harsh realities of physical and mental degradation at the hands of the Japanese.

"Seen through the eyes of an English officer, the story encompasses the brutalities of life and death in a camp in South East Asia. This is the most powerful film on the subject since *Bridge On The River Kwai*.

"Filming was completed in October 1982, after a period of eight weeks. Post production work is currently underway and the film is scheduled to be ready by January 1983.

"The lead actor, David Bowie, is one of the most successful recording artists in the world. Bowie established himself as a leading actor in the Broadway stage production of *Elephant Man*.

"He subsequently starred in some highly successful BBC television plays and created a worldwide impression when he featured in the films *Gigolo*, *The Man Who Fell To Earth* and, most recently, the German film *Christine F. Wir Kinder Von Bahnhof Zoo*.

"Bowie is backed by co-stars Tom Conti and Jack Thompson, and a New Zealand/Japanese supporting cast."

Documents tabled in Parliament show movie stars and rock icons were well looked-after in 1982. Bowie was to receive US$2,000 per week just in living expenses during his time on the movie, along with first class air travel for himself and a woman named Corine Schwab "from New York or Switzerland to any place or places in New Zealand at which David Bowie may be required to render his services."

Bowie was also charging the movie-makers a further weekly living allowance for Corine, and US$500 a week to pay for his personal chauffeur/bodyguard. *Metro* magazine quaintly referred to the rock star as "Mr Bowie" in a small article on the movie in its January 1983 issue.

Every last detail of the movie, even down to the size of the type font used in the end credits, had been legally nailed down.

CINEVENTURE & RECORDED PICTURE COMPANY   50%
  Presents
A FILM BY NAGISA OSHIMA   35%

"MERRY CHRISTMAS MR LAWRENCE"   100%

DAVID BOWIE   75%
TOM CONTI   75%
RYOICHI SAKAMOTO   75%
BEAT TAKESHI   75%
JACK THOMPSON   75%

Well, the pre-publicity and the hype was out there already. Now all Chris Kirkham had to do was sell the idea to investors.

While the crack-down on dodgy film partnerships was announced in the August 1982 Budget, Kirkham and his Film Financing Division team at Broadbank had been tipped off at least a month earlier.

In a June 1982 analysis, tabled in Parliament by the then rebel National MP Winston Peters ten years later, Chris Kirkham writes of his discovery.

"From now on the financing of films made in New Zealand will be dependant on the new legislation which is expected to be announced in the Budget.

"However a draft copy of the legislation, requested by the NZ Film Commission, which I have, places the emphasis on commerciality of films."

Tax-driven movie deals, described as "Category A" and "Category B" films, would find their futures limited.

"In Australia," noted Kirkham, "where similar legislation has been in place for two years, investment in Category A and B films has been running at $10 million per annum, while investment in other. . .films has amounted to $42 million per annum. The latter category of film is normally much more commercial and with greater chances of income and, as such, has attracted the entrepreneur investor."

Significantly, Kirkham also listed the proposed budgets for five movies under consideration by Broadbank. They included Tatum O'Neal's *Prisoners*, at a cost of $2.9 million, *Mr Lawrence* at $4 million, *James Barry* at $3.2 million, *Finding Katie* at a cost of $1.4 million, and a car chase movie called *Shaker Run*, starring American teen singing idol Leif Garrett, with a budget of $2 million.

All up, said Kirkham, Broadbank needed to find $13.5 million to actually make these movies, with $5 million of that coming from private investors and $8.3 million coming from corporate investors. The budgets for *Mr Lawrence* and *Prisoners* were a lot smaller here than the inflated figures presented to the IRD further down the track.

Broadbank's expertise, noted Kirkham, included the arrangement of funding facilities "ex Netherlands" and the use of a "Hong Kong company".

Prisoners, of course, was never released commercially. It was a victim of what Geoff Murphy had called "the new breed" of film producers.

"Because the investor made his profit as he made the deal," said Murphy in describing the general situation, "there was no interest in the film. It didn't have to be any good. It didn't have to make a profit, or even any money. It didn't even have to be released. A few of the films, perhaps mercifully, never were.

"Standards plummeted. Some good films were still produced, but they were outnumbered by the many more poor ones.

"Because tax shelter money could be raised relatively easily, financial institutions and producers began charging large fees for their services. Crews were not slow to notice this. Anyone who worked cheaply was a fool.

"Wages skyrocketed and everyone demanded an assistant. After tax shelter was declared illegal, wages did not fall or crews get smaller. It is hard to run history backward."

The sole purpose of the business, he claims, became to make producers and investors rich. The films got progressively worse in quality as the crews lost interest in what they were doing, but the NZ film industry's "Good News" machine kept cranking out the hype, claiming each movie was fantastic.

"Film producers and the industry generally were discredited, being regarded as little better than thieves – a view that was not entirely inaccurate and had an interesting historical resonance.

"On the list that grades integrity, we were placed somewhere below used car salesmen and just above child molesters and politicians."

While most countries making movies for commercial reasons could churn out one a year per million citizens, New Zealand was making up to four times that many – 10 or 12 a year.

"The industry had to expand to accommodate this and the standard of talent in all aspects of the industry could not be sustained. Part of the reason that crews got so much larger was that individuals were capable of so much less," said Murphy scathingly.

"The effects of tax shelter were predicted and we all saw it happening. Some of us pursued the tax money with ill-disguised greed, others went along with it as a necessary evil. Few complained. There was a conspiracy of silence.

"None of us who participated can claim innocence. Many of its most aggressive supporters deny any blame. I was one of New Zealand's foremost directors through this period, and I did nothing to stop it."

Borrowing an analogy from the bloodstock partnerships, the horse was not only out the gate – it was bolting down the road at speed.

CHAPTER 14

Celluloid Dreams

"The populace cannot understand the bureaucracy:
it can only worship national idols."
– GEORGE BERNARD SHAW, 1856–1950, *MAXIMS FOR REVOLUTIONISTS*

The boys at Broadbank did their best to have a Merry Christmas at the end of 1982, because they knew their David Bowie movie was well and truly in the can.

Marketing began in January 1983, with a number of distributors invited to Tokyo to view a preliminary copy of the movie. They came from the United States, France, Britain, Australia and Europe. After Tokyo, *Mr Lawrence* distributor Terry Glinwood took it on a travelling roadshow to Europe and the US.

"By the time of the Cannes Film Festival in May," wrote Broadbank in a report to investors, "most countries had in fact seen the film and had purchased it. "There were, however, notable exceptions, in particular Germany and the US. Many major distributors from the US had made offers in the lead up to the Cannes Festival, but these were refused by Glinwood in order to delay the decision until the full impact of the marketing campaign at the Cannes Festival was apparent.

"When the film was accepted as one of the 12 entries in the Grand Prix, Palm d'Or, the producer, sales agent and ourselves decided to carry out an intensive advertising and public relations campaign in Cannes to create an even higher level of awareness of the film, aimed at generating demand in the unsold territories and increasing the chances of winning the Palm d'Or award."

What followed was probably an object lesson about the dangers of believing your own publicity.

"The film was consistently rumoured as that most likely to win the Grand Prix. In the final analysis, it won neither the Grand Prix nor the second prize."

Naturally, the producer and director were disappointed at the end result, but Glinwood was a happy distributor. He finally scored a sale to a previously "indifferent" German agent, and "by the end of the Festival, Glinwood had accepted an offer from Universal Studios for the US and Canadian market and had completely sold ever other foreign territory."

While Universal had been planning a limited release, its internal market research indicated the movie might have a wider appeal than anticipated and, in October 1983, it moved into 200 US cinemas.

In Britain, *Merry Christmas Mr Lawrence* was running a close third to the James Bond movie Octopussy.

"In France, 89 prints have been released; in Amsterdam the film is in its 17th week having done the best of all films over the summertime heat wave."

It was a similar hit in Belgium, Holland and even Australia where it broke box office records on its first weekend in Sydney and Melbourne.

"In Japan," advised the Broadbank team, "it is about to be re-released and this will make the box office receipts from that country the second-highest ever recorded after E.T.

"In the initial release in Japan, reports were that people were paying for seats when there was standing room only."

Not surprisingly, Broadbank and the distributor, Glinwood Films, were rubbing their gnomish hands together in glee. Not only was the venture going to claim an inflated $11.77 million dollar loss for its first financial year, giving investors a massive tax break, but the movie was now an international hit, with expected "worldwide gross receipts of between US$30-40 million, about half of which will be derived from the US.

"On the basis of these figures, we would estimate that New Zealand investors should receive between one and two times their capital in the form of income from the film over the next three to four years."

But were the investors really going to make that much money? Not according to the Inland Revenue Department.

Documents released at the Winebox Inquiry show that by 1987 the IRD was already well and truly on the tail of the people behind the David Bowie movie, for suspected tax evasion.

Readers will recall that the scheme's promoters had inflated the movie's alleged costs from four million dollars to $11.77 million, and they planned to declare those costs as a loss in the first financial year so as to maximise the tax break for investors.

According to IRD records, the partnership claimed a loss of $11.2 million in the year to March 31, 1983. At this point, of course, the movie had not been commercially released and so had not earned any money.

Mr Lawrence Productions Ltd, the general partner in the special partnership scheme, had been incorporated on July 16, 1982 and the owners of a hundred dollars worth of shares included Broadbank Corporation with 99 shares, and Broadbank Nominees Ltd with one share.

Ominously, the IRD review paper, dated March 30, 1987 and written by senior inspectors Denese Latimer, Alan May and S Bayford, noted that "the review was initially restricted to an analysis of the legal documentation and the funding of the non-recourse loans. However, because of the resulting discrepancies, the 'offshore' review was extended up to the year ended 31 March 1985."

While the general partner, or manager, of the scheme had been set up back in July 1982, it wasn't until February 1983 that the special partnership itself came into existence.

"The initial contributors to this Partnership were Messrs R L [Robin] Congreve and P C [Paul] Carran of the legal firm of Russell, McVeagh, McKenzie, Bartleet & Co. of Auckland," wrote the IRD investigators. "The capital was initially one thousand dollars and further subscribers increased this to $3,335,000.

"The special partnership was formed for the purpose of carrying on in common the business of film production, distribution and dealing in films."

Apart from the capital provided by investors of $3.3 million, the IRD noted also a series of loans made to the partnership by various entities. A company called Charlesbay Ltd, and based in the Channel Islands, had lent just over US$3.3 million.

The money had been handed over on July 29, 1982, and it was what's called a "full recourse" loan. In other words, it's a loan that must be repaid. The conditions were that repayment would take place in the year 2002. But something funny was going on. The IRD discovered that the conditions of the loan had been altered on March 31, 1983, soon after the special partnership was formed.

"The second agreement superseded the first and this was for a non-recourse loan of US$3.335 million."

A "non-recourse" loan is the kind that every homeowner or credit-card holder would love to have: it does not have to be repaid unless certain events take place. Such events might include, for argument's sake, the taking over of the planet by sentient apes, or perhaps an even tougher test, such as the discovery of intelligent life in any parliament.

In the case of *Merry Christmas Mr Lawrence* the event that triggered repayment would be the movie earning the partnership more than US$10 million.

Now, given that even under the most optimistic projections the promoters were suggesting investors would make only one or two times the amount of their NZ$3.3 million capital, it was pretty clear the chances of Charlesbay ever being repaid were diddly-squat to zip.

So what kind of company just gives away US$3.3 million?

Good question – more on that later.

The IRD's agents also found that Broadbank Corporation had loaned the partnership US$5.5 million as a stand-by loan facility for "30 months to assist in financing. Part of this was repayable from the subscribed capital of the special partnership with charges secured over future film revenue and a letter of credit held with a bank in Holland."

By March 31, 1983, Broadbank had obviously been paid back a substantial sum, because the outstanding balance was now only US$2.4 million.

There was a third loan. A Hong Kong-based company called Bonningdale was named in loan documents as providing up to US$2.9 million in March 1984, "being repayable only from film receipts after the borrower [the partnership] has retained US$10 million and also the loan from Charlesbay Ltd has been repaid.

"According to the annual accounts, only US$1,759,739 has actually been uplifted. This transaction took place offshore."

So, if the chances of Charlesbay being repaid were already zip, then the chances of Bonningdale being repaid were zip to the power of 10.

Now, it's important to remember at this point that the actual cost of making the movie appears to have been around $4 million, yet the inflated cost claimed for tax purposes was more than $11 million. It figures that if the special partners invested real money of $3.335 million, then most of the loan money provided to the partnership on top of that was probably as fictitious as the inflated expenses it was being used to allegedly pay for.

In short, if you are going to have "paper costs", you need "paper money" to pay them. The tax department kept digging, looking next at who was going to benefit financially from the sale of the movie into the world's cinemas.

Under the heading "Distribution and Potential Income", the original offer document to investors was clear on where the money would go.

"On completion, the film is to be sold to Glinwood Films Limited, England, in return for a share of the net receipts from the distribution of the film.

"Under the film sale agreement with Glinwood Films the New Zealand partnership will receive 80% of receipts from England and France, and 40% of receipts from all other territories, the balance going to sales agents.

"This is after the distribution fees, which should be approx. US$3 million. When the New Zealand partners have recouped NZ$3.42 million, their share of receipts is reduced by 50% (the balance going to producers and principal artists in accordance with normal industry practice)."

That was how it was supposed to work – in theory.

"The establishing as to whom the film was ultimately sold," reported the IRD, "took some time as quite a few overseas companies were supposed to be the recipient of this honour.

"For instance, in the prospectus, the film is supposed to be sold to Glinwood Films of England for a share of the net receipts. In the Charlesbay Loan Agreements, mention is made that the film has been sold to the Recorded Picture Company of London, and in the second Loan Agreement the film has been sold to the Saudi Channel Islands Capital Corporation Ltd of the Channel Islands."

Confused? It gets better!

"According to the accountants for the special partnership, (Lawrence, Anderson, Buddle), the agreements to these companies were not executed and the film was actually sold to Bonningdale Ltd (Hong Kong).

"This agreement," notes the IRD, "is dated 6.9.84 and states that the film is sold for the 'divisible receipts', which is varying percentages from the exploitation of the film from various areas of the world but excludes Japan altogether. The 'divisible receipts' becoming operative after Bonningdale has retained US$2.9 million."

In other words, Bonningdale bought the rights to the movie in 1984, a year after the movie's mainstream world release. So who had been pocketing all the earnings up until then? The IRD analysis doesn't say.

The actors and producers of the movie obviously had to be paid for their work on the film, and the IRD says the main vehicle to bring those people "into the fold appears to be a company called Woodline Ltd, registered in Jersey, Channel Islands."

In an agreement dated July 30, 1982, and for a fee of $US1,925,000, "Woodline has agreed to procure certain goods, loans and services required for the production of the film. The source of funds for the special partnership to pay this fee was from the loan from Charlesbay Ltd."

Recapping, the Charlesbay loan was for US$3.3375 million. According to the accounts books, US$1.3375 million of that was credited to the account of Hill-Samuel & Co merchant bank in the Channel Islands tax haven to be used as a part-payment to Woodline. The balance of the $1.9 million fee was paid to Woodline via an account at the State Street Bank in New York. The IRD was curious to know whether all the money was legitimate.

Woodline spent the US$1,337,500 deposited in the Channel Islands as follows:

- Procuration of script writing services of Oshima & Myersberg   US$400,000
- Partial satisfaction of procuring services of Oshima   US$100,000
- Partial satisfaction of procuring services of Hara   US$37,500
- Partial satisfaction of procuring services of Glinwood   US$37,500
- Procuring loan of US$3.3 million   US$325,000
- Procuring services of J Thomas   US$400,000
- Alfaro Communications for procuring J Thomas   US$37,500

"As Woodline Ltd is registered in a tax haven," complained the IRD, "it could not be checked further whether the remittances were actually made, or the above was simply 'circle money'. Based on experience from the investigation of other film ventures, it is more than probable that it falls into the latter category."

What about the remaining funds that had been channelled through New York's State Street Bank? The IRD listed payments through it:

Recipient	To Bank At	$US
Oshima-Magisa Prodns	Japan	175,000
M Hara	Japan	37,500
David Bowie	Switzerland	250,000
T Glinwood	Channel Islands	37,500
Jeremy Thomas	Cyprus	100,000
		$600,000

"Again, because of international barriers, it would be impossible to authenticate payments to recipients – or follow through later disbursements – because of the use of tax havens. However, as the State Street Bank is the main overseas clearing bank for Broadbank Corporation Ltd, it lends to the view that these are 'genuine' transactions."

Making a movie is a complex business. First of all, someone owned the copyright to the movie. That someone was Oshima Productions Ltd, owned by the director of *Merry Christmas Mr Lawrence*. As copyright holder, Oshima had granted exclusive licence to Woodline Ltd to actually make the film, and Woodline subsequently onsold its rights to the New Zealand special partnership, for the princely sum of £1.00.

While Oshima owned the copyright, Mr Lawrence Productions Ltd & Co (the special partnership) owned the use of it.

The next task for the IRD team was to discover who was behind these mysterious tax haven companies. Charlesbay Ltd – the company that had loaned the partnership US$3.3 million with little expectation of repayment -had been registered in Jersey, in the British Channel Islands, on July 16, 1982. Its shareholders were listed as Messrs David Fisher Le Quesne, Peter Michael Ward-Tetley and a Vella Holmes, all of 23 Pier Road, Jersey.

Woodline Ltd, the company representing the producers and actors, was also registered in Jersey, on June 6, 1982. Its shareholders were also Le Quesne, Ward-Tetley and Holmes.

Bonningdale Ltd was registered in Hong Kong on November 12, 1982. Its shareholders were companies called Becmac Ltd and Camceb Ltd, both of Hong Kong. Both Becmac and Camceb featured extensively in the bloodstock deals as well, as the nominee owners of Zorasong.

"Searches were made of these further Hong Kong companies," reported IRD investigators, "and control eventually established as being that of the nominee company of Deloitte, Haskins and Sells of Hong Kong, or individual partners in this accounting firm."

But there was another mystery player in this three-ring circus, a Hong Kong company called Benidorm Ltd, and registered on January 22, 1982. IRD investigations for this 1987 report revealed two interesting pieces of information. Firstly, its shareholders on registration were New Zealand companies: Broadbank Investments Ltd and Broadbank Nominees Ltd. Secondly, on December 31, 1985, those shareholders had changed to Challenge Corporate Services Ltd, Group Nominees Ltd, and Cook Islands Trust Corporation Ltd.

The latter company, at one point half-owned by Challenge Corporate Services Ltd, was the forerunner of European Pacific – the banking and tax haven conglomerate at the centre of the Winebox Inquiry.

By this stage, the IRD team was pretty certain it had found something fishy going on, but it wasn't sure what kind of fish was on the end of the line. They knew, for example, that the partnership had returned a loss of $11.2 million in the year to March 1983, but they could only find evidence of $3.3 million of real expenditure. The difference of $7.9 million was noted in a portion of the report headed "Discrepancies Ascertained".

In the 1984 financial year, however, the partnership had listed a loss of only half a million dollars, but the IRD had evidence that the real loss was more than $3.8 million. In the year to March 1985, the partnership declared a profit of almost six hundred thousand dollars, but the IRD believed its real profit should have been returned as $5.7 million.

Was this a case of massive tax evasion? The IRD began to wonder.

"Information requested through the special partners' accountants was very slow in forthcoming," the investigators complained.

"What information that was received required considerable analysis as various agreements kept mentioning different parties. Questions had also been asked as to the ownership of the shares in the offshore companies, but no one appears to know who owns them.

"Background papers were also requested in the hope that this would explain how and why the structure had evolved as it had. These have never been forthcoming."

Brick walls were being hit, and the New Zealand Inland Revenue Department decided to try and chance its luck through the tax havens. The IRD filed company searches in the various havens, but "this came to no avail as all shares are registered as being held by nominees."

Straw-men. Paper cut-outs. Nominees – shareholders in name only. Not the real owners. With nowhere left to turn, the IRD investigators played their last card.

"Information was sought from Broadbank Corporation Ltd, as funding facilities had been made available to the film venture with the hope that background information would be held. What happened can only be described as extremely fortuitous!

"Broadbank Corporation Ltd (BCL) had just recently been purchased by Government Life and, as they didn't know what records they could hold, we were given free access to their record store."

Like pack-rats in a camping equipment shop, the IRD team was in tax inspector heaven. Not only had they gained access to the vast records held in Broadbank's archives, but in them they also found significant clues about what had really taken place.

CHAPTER 15

An Orchestrated Litany. . .

"I hope I shall never be deterred from detecting what
I think a cheat, by the menaces of a ruffian."
– SAMUEL JOHNSON, 1709–1784

To say that the IRD had stumbled on a goldmine would be a cliché. It would also be true. It turned out that BCL had been worried about the security of their money when they agreed to provide loan facilities to the boys behind *Mr Lawrence*, and they'd kept an awful lot of records reflecting that concern.

"This information," the tabled IRD report continued, "was contained in the Minutes of the Credit Review Committee that monitors the position of large funds loaned to other companies.

"If it wasn't for this concern it is doubtful whether this information would ever have surfaced."

And what was this information? Well, for a start, it showed that the Channel Islands company Charlesbay Ltd hadn't made that US$3.3 million loan on its own behalf. A flow chart found in the records vault showed that "the loan advanced to the special partnership had been primarily funded by Japanese investors. Charlesbay Ltd appears to be simply a vehicle to hide the identity of offshore investors. This had never been disclosed before."

The next question the IRD asked was whether this was a passive, straightforward loan from some Japanese investors on the terms expressed in the Loan Agreement, or whether there might be other hidden benefits involved.

Sure enough, there were.

All the proceeds from the movie worldwide were being sent to the UK Film Distribution Trust, also known as the National Film Trustee Company. This was an organisation established by the British Government. It had been described in the original offer document to investors as "a Government-controlled body [which] provides an ideal independent party of absolute integrity to ensure the New Zealand partnership's interests are protected."

There is no question of any slur on the integrity of the NFTC. It is a reputable organisation which collects film earnings and then redistributes the money to those who are entitled to it. What the IRD found were the instructions that had been given to the NFTC on where the money should go.

For every dollar received by the NFTC, nine cents would go to Glinwood

Sales Agency. Five cents would go to the actors and producers. Five cents would go to the director, and one cent would stay with the NFTC as its handling fee.

That left 80 cents to distribute.

If the original dollar had come from a Japanese movie theatre, then the 80 cents left was to be paid by the NFTC directly to the Japanese investors as a profit, not as a loan repayment.

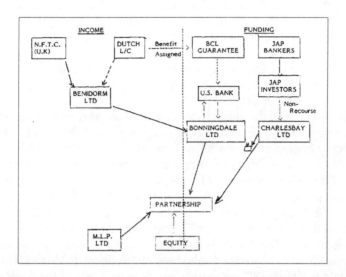

If the original dollar had come from a British or French cinema, then the remaining 80 cents was to be paid to Benidorm Ltd, the Hong Kong company owned by Broadbank.

If the original dollar had come from a movie ticket booth anywhere else in the world, the NFTC was to split the 80 cents down the middle, paying 40 cents to Benidorm and 40 cents to the Japanese investors – again as a return of profits, not as a repayment of the loan.

From a New Zealand point of view, which is what the IRD was interested in, Benidorm was the "bag man" for the cash destined for this country. As Benidorm's purse filled, it was to pay up to US$2.7 million to Bonningdale Ltd so that Bonningdale could repay loans from the US bank.

The next US$10 million in receipts earned by Benidorm was to be paid to the special partners who'd invested in the movie project. The next US$18 million after that was to be used to repay the Japanese loan to Charlesbay Ltd.

"This information," said the IRD team, "clearly establishes that the Japanese investors are not there purely as passive loan funders. They enjoy defined percentages from the exploitation of the film which clearly portrays a participative role."

From the IRD's perspective, this meant that the Charlesbay loan to the partnership – NZ$4.6 million – was essentially bogus, and therefore the expenses that it allegedly funded shouldn't be tax deductible.

The IRD also believed that $3.8 million dollars of film income had been disguised as loan funds, and not declared for tax purposes. This was money routed through Bonningdale.

"This company has advanced loan funds in other film ventures and, to try and understand its role, questions had been asked (accepting on face value that this is a bona fide commercially run company) as to why large sums of money were being lent on extremely uncommercial terms.

"The response has usually been that this is an internal matter of that company to which the promoters etc. are not privy. In other words, as the company is offshore, it is not anyone else's business.

"The flow chart (previously portrayed) would explain why a company would advance funds on these terms. The possession of third party guarantees negates the risk factor altogether.

"The existence of this third party guarantee had never been disclosed to the department probably, one of the reasons being, as it would invite further questions as to the ownership of these offshore companies registered in tax havens."

Ownership was a big issue in determining where the organ-grinder might be. The IRD was sick of interviewing his monkeys. As an example, the IRD knew Bonningdale was nominally owned by companies called Becmac Ltd and Camceb Ltd of Hong Kong, but who was the real owner? No one claimed to know.

Not until a document emerged in Broadbank's file vault, which described Bonningdale as "a Hong Kong based finance company which is a subsidiary of Benidorm Ltd, a wholly owned subsidiary of Broadbank Investments Ltd."

According to the IRD reconstruction of events, some of the film's income, held in an account at the State Street Bank in New York under Broadbank's control, was funnelled through Bonningdale to Mr Lawrence Productions Ltd disguised as a limited recourse loan, so that MLP could repay some of its outstanding debt to Broadbank Corporation.

Correspondence between Bonningdale and Broadbank on February 18, 1983 discussed the financing issues.

"The original loan was to MLP, with repayment first from partners' equity [of] $3 million [and] secondly from proceeds of film income. As the latter would have been taxable in partners' hands, the loan is to be raised in Hong Kong by a [Broadbank Investments Ltd] subsidiary, to be repaid out of film receipts in Hong Kong tax free – thus avoiding NZ tax.

"Meanwhile, income will flow to Benidorm and be deposited in an account at the US Bank in the name of Broadbank Corporation Ltd and Bonningdale, to be operated by Broadbank Corporation Ltd."

The tax department noted that "the Benidorm link may not have been used. No explanation for this omission is known, but the fact that this company has the New Zealand ownership actually registered is a possible explanation."

From the evidence available to the IRD, the film proceeds in the State Street Bank had been sitting there untouched for more than a year "and may not have been able to be utilised until the appropriate legal documentation had been drawn up and duly executed.

"Another reason for delay could have been in respect of the letter of credit. Apparently the Hollandsche Bank wouldn't honour the letter of credit on the basis of some type of fraudulent misrepresentation."

Serious allegations, but the IRD believed it went some way to explaining why Mr Lawrence Productions Ltd still hadn't repaid all of its debts to Broadbank at the end of the day.

In support of their contention that the Bonningdale loan was really disguised film income, the tax team unearthed previously secret memoranda and Minutes from Broadbank Corporation's Credit Review Committee.

One document was a letter from Broadbank director D F Botting to Broadbank General Manager T J Haydon, dated March 7, 1983.

"I asked [Broadbank Investments Ltd] to let me know more about the structure of the film," wrote Botting, "and John Gow arranged a meeting with Graham and a lawyer. This was three weeks ago, and it was at this meeting I formed the impression that nobody outside Russell McVeagh understood the structure or the facts.

"I learned for the first time of the intention to route the film through a tax haven."

What he said next should earn Botting an MBE for services to business ethics.

"My misgivings on it are," he said, "I agreed to divide the ethical tax aspect from the credit considerations. If approved on credit, I would write to the Board that I consider Boards of Fletcher Challenge companies should not support such blatant tax avoidance schemes from which no good returns to New Zealand."

In a March 28 memo, Botting continued his theme.

"It is my opinion that the Boards of [Broadbank Investments Ltd] and BDG [another subsidiary] should not have been parties to a device to route film income to offshore tax havens to pay offshore banks in lieu of limited recourse loans to New Zealand from these sources, knowing that the film expenditure from these loans will be deducted for tax purposes in New Zealand."

On August 31, 1984, MLP was due to repay the Broadbank loan, of which US$3.1 million was still outstanding. Total funds held at the State Street Bank to offset to bill were only US$1.7 million, although "Mr Kirkham assures. . .that he has a further USD 200,000.

"It seems that Mr Kirkham expects sufficient revenue from the sale to theatres, video and to television to finally repay this facility before 31 May 1985."

Explanations for the problems in repaying the loan were found in Minutes of a meeting held on September 7, 1984. Present were three Broadbank executives, along with Russell McVeagh's Paul Carran and movie partnership promoters Chris Kirkham and Graham Perrin.

The Minutes record that the men from MLP had originally estimated that they would get US$2.9 million in film receipts. Instead, despite all the hype and talk of *Merry Christmas Mr Lawrence* being a US$40 million worldwide hit, only

US$1.45 million had been received by Bonningdale, "which has on lent by limited recourse to MLP, who in turn has paid this to Broadbank Corporation Ltd in State Street, New York.

Armed with all of this knowledge in March 1987, the IRD team drew up a list of questions they wanted to ask, starting with Graham Perrin. There were 169 questions, covering three main areas, which included:

1. That Charlesbay Ltd was a front for Japanese investors.
2. That Bonningdale was under the control of Broadbank Investments Ltd and used to perpetrate a 'sham'.
3. That film income had been routed offshore to avoid NZ income tax.

The IRD recorded Perrin's memory as being hazy about events "five years ago". Perrin had been the Managing Director of Broadbank Investments Ltd, and its successor Challenge Corporate Services Ltd. He eventually purchased the latter company for himself, and transferred the management function of the movie to Strada Holdings Ltd, another of his corporate vehicles.

The IRD also wanted to find out whether Strada still held any background papers on the movie deal.

"I am not sure," answered Perrin, "but Broadbank would have some while the remainder would be held by Glinwood and Nethercott."

Terry Glinwood was, of course, the distributor and Nethercott was one of his colleagues who travelled with him to New Zealand when they were seeking finance for the film package.

The IRD claimed that previous requests for documentation had also been met with the "go ask Glinwood" response, which was all very well but Glinwood was out of the tax department's reach.

"It appears obvious," concluded the tax investigators, "that although the structure may originate from overseas, the promoters are aware of the global structure and this is simply not being supplied."

Although, by March 1987, Mr Lawrence Productions Ltd was now owned by NZI Corporation, Perrin remained a director, and of course there was still the ongoing management agreement between MLP and his own company, Strada Holdings Ltd.

"The background papers should then have been under his control or knowledge and been made available for inspection," wrote the IRD team, Alan May, Denese Latimer and S Bayford.

"It appears that these papers, most probably, have simply been destroyed. As an aside to this, there is the suspicion that background details could be held in the offices of Russell McVeagh – solicitors of Auckland – but attempts with other film ventures to obtain background details have been frustrated by the 'legal privilege' sections of the Act.

"This has not been able to be taken any further as, in many cases, we have no idea as to the content – if any – of the background information. The solicitors will not condone fishing expeditions."

The investigators hauled two other men in for questioning about the movie deal, but made little progress there either. At the end of their 22 page report, they were scathing.

"During the course of this investigation, the Department's requests for information have been met with an orchestrated litany of obstruction (no disrespect meant to the late Mr Justice Mahon) and information received having been clearly 'vetted' before despatch.

"As an aside, the inspection team involved with this review understand that the promoters concerned had agreed amongst themselves to delay replying to requests for as long as possible (as a result, many requests were only answered after a Section 17 letter [a formal demand to produce information] had been issued), and at the same time, complain to the media/make representations to MP's with the hope that the decision would be made to stop the reviews.

"The result of this particular review raises the question of culpability. Obviously the majority of the investors would not be aware of the fine details of the arrangement, but someone must eventually accept/acknowledge responsibility."

Now the IRD trio were ready for their king hit.

"To this end, one of the recommendations is to be that <u>every</u> individual investor is to be asked for a written explanation as to why the discrepancies arose.

"The reason being that the following investors, based on the weight of evidence obtained, appear to be parties to the deception. These are: Mr C G P [and] Mr C J K, ex Broadbank Investments Ltd, [and] Mr P C C [and] Dr R L C, [of] Russell McVeagh."

Bending over backwards to be fair, the investigators didn't want to zero in on just four investors and later be accused of picking on them. Instead, the IRD opted for a blunderbuss approach, knowing that the targeted birds would be hit in the process.*

"It is realised that this will be a major exercise, but the Department cannot be seen as pre-judging," they explained.

As for the companies involved, explanations were to be requested from MLP about its role as manager of the special partnership, from Broadbank Investments Ltd for "aiding the committing of an offence," from Broadbank Corporation Ltd for "aiding the committing of these offences," and from Challenge Corporate Services Ltd for "aiding the committing of an offence."

Within 24 hours of delivering their report to the IRD's Auckland Regional Controller, the dream team had their answer: all recommendations were approved.

---

* The blunderbuss backfired. When ordinary partners protested their innocence, as Latimer & May knew they would, the IRD staff reassured them that the accusations weren't directed at them. The partners passed this on to Russell McVeagh, who assumed the IRD wasn't serious about any of the allegations. So, tax lawyer Geoff Clews subsequently told the Winebox Inquiry that Latimer and May had "hastily withdrawn. . .assertions of possible dishonesty".

Denese Latimer sat down to draft a very provocative letter to all of the investors in *Merry Christmas Mr Lawrence*, including the four that she was really after.

It would become one of the most controversial letters she ever wrote, and it would have an impact on the careers of her colleagues in years to come.

CHAPTER 16

Treasure Islands

"When you can fall for chains of silver, you can fall for chains of gold,
You can fall for pretty strangers, and the promises they hold.
You promised me everything, you promised me thick and thin,
Now you just say 'oh Romeo, yeah, you know I used to have
a scene with him'."

– MARK KNOPFLER, *ROMEO AND JULIET*, FROM THE DIRE STRAITS ALBUM *MAKING MOVIES*

It had been just 18 hours since the worried lawyer had approached Chris Dickie after the investors' meeting and told him the names he'd unearthed in the bloodstock case were also involved in film deals. Eighteen hours since they'd shared a beer and discussed the ramifications.

Now Dickie was in the other lawyer's office, and the world of film was about to open up on him. The reason for this: while Dickie and Molloy were specifically litigating the bloodstock issues, the new information that would come to light on the movie deals would be important to their case.

Central to that case was the issue of establishing beneficial ownership or control of the secret tax haven companies that had turned up in the horse partnership deals. Getting hold of that information was proving extremely difficult.

The documentation on the movies, however, would become relevant under what is known in legal terms as "similar fact" evidence. If Dickie and Molloy could examine other deals involving Carran and Kirkham, or which had been set up by Russell McVeagh, and find evidence of similar tax haven operations, they could use that as circumstantial evidence in the bloodstock litigation: "See, your Honour, the defendants did this in the movie deal, here's the proof, and we allege this is the kind of mechanism they used in the horse deal."

That's a simplistic explanation of why similar fact evidence is relevant, but it captures the general principles. Indeed, the same principle was applied to the film and bloodstock transactions at the Winebox Inquiry.

While they were not winebox deals and therefore not within the inquiry's terms of reference, the film and bloodstock deals were relevant as "similar fact" when Sir Ronald wanted to compare the IRD and SFO performance on those deals with their performance on the winebox investigation.

"So this is the letter?" said Chris Dickie, still staring at the two sheets of paper in his hand that had been sent to the lawyer as one of the investors in *Merry Christmas Mr Lawrence*.

"Yeah," said the other lawyer, gazing intently at the McVeagh Fleming partner. "I'm telling you Chris, it's the same crowd that are behind the bloodstock."

Dated April 7, 1987, it spelt out in simple terms that $4.6 million of expenditure claimed by the partnership in its first year was being struck out.

"The loan from Charlesbay Ltd is considered to be a sham," Denese Latimer had written, "and the purported payments thereto are to be disregarded accordingly."

The letter also advised that a sum of $3,876,077 "purportedly borrowed from Bonningdale" and a further amount of $2,431,718 were being re-classified as assessable income in the March 31, 1985 income year.

"Finally," Latimer concluded, "in view of the discrepancies disclosed, it appears that an offence against Section 416 of the Income Tax Act 1976 may have been committed. Please let me have, in writing, your personal explanation of the discrepancies and any reason why you consider that penal action should not be taken against you."

Dickie was fixated by Latimer's name. Latimer. "I know this Denese Latimer," he said after a moment. "She came to my office when we started checking out the bloodstock. If I remember correctly, she was asking me what I knew about some people called Mildred Li and Anita Cheng."

"That's not all," sighed the other lawyer as he opened a folder on his desk. He passed a wiring diagram to Dickie.

"God, how I hate wiring diagrams," Dickie muttered. But this one was special. It related to a children's fairytale TV series, called *The Adventures Of The Little Prince*, and in the middle was a company called Chary Holdings Ltd. He also spotted the involvement of Charlesbay Ltd, which he noted was also interlinked with *Mr Lawrence*.

The diagram also spelt out the owners of some of the exotic companies: the shareholders were listed as Becmac Ltd and Camceb Ltd, of Hong Kong.

The same companies involved in the bloodstock deals, now at the centre of movie investigations as well.

For Dickie, it was the dawning of a realisation that the picture was a lot bigger than he'd realised. "The bloodstock was just the pimple on the pumpkin," he noted wryly. This wasn't just about bloodstock, now it was about movies and TV programmes as well.

The other lawyer, ironically a former partner in Russell McVeagh, had kept a series of documents, many of them relating to the Bowie film. Dickie found them a useful stepping stone into a new offensive position against his foes.

Sensing that the IRD was months ahead of his own investigation, Dickie rattled the cages of his investors, collecting as much of the film documentation as he could lay his hands on in order to further understand what the hell had been going on.

One letter from the IRD to investors raised the issue of the Bonningdale loan to the partnership of US$2.9 million. According to IRD analysis of the loan documentation this loan was only repayable from film receipts "after the borrower [the partnership] has retained US$10 million and also the loan from Charlesbay has been repaid."

But the IRD letter Dickie was looking at suggested an amount of some $2.9 million had disappeared – never made it to the partnership. Dickie also knew that Britain's National Film Trustee Company had been acting as the international clearing house for the film's earnings.

In the investment offer to investors back in 1982, the promoters had stated that "the receipts. . .will be paid directly to the National Film Trustee Company Ltd who will be charged with the duty of collecting receipts, correctly accounting for the same and remitting the New Zealand partnership's share direct to it."

Dickie remembered those words in particular: "direct to it."

"This company will undertake all audit functions worldwide to ensure that the New Zealand partnership receives its entitlement to the income produced from the distribution of the film."

Well, thought Dickie, if anyone knows where the $2.9 million went, it should be the NFTC in Britain.

"We had an incredibly good piece of luck," he remembered later. "We rang Simmons & Simmons in London, and we got them to go, on a Friday afternoon, to the National Film Trustee Co.

"We had a letter introducing ourselves, and our London lawyer said 'Look, I'm acting for some New Zealand investors, we just want to identify where these funds have gone – can you assist us with this?'

"Well, they gave the lawyer, David Sandy, four or five documents – this was on a Friday afternoon – and David faxed them to us. It was a bloody goldmine. The money had gone into a Channel Islands bank account – two accounts in fact – and when we looked at these two bank accounts the amount stated was precisely the sum, to the damned cent, that the IRD said had disappeared. Here it was in these Channel Islands bank accounts!"

Included in the fax from London was another document, a telex from one Edmund Lionel Bendelow, listing himself as a director of Charlesbay Ltd, and giving his address as Pirouet House, St Helier, Jersey.

Dated January 22, 1987, the teletype message was addressed to the NFTC and advises the film trustee company that Charlesbay is the duly appointed agent of Bonningdale, which apparently is due to receive US$2,920,000 from the NFTC.

"We understand that you are currently in the process of remitting monies to the account of Bonningdale Ltd at the Chase Bank and Trust Company (C.I.) Ltd, Jersey, Channel Islands.

"Please note that due to a change in Chase Bank's computer system, the account number of Bonningdale Ltd has been changed from 7921987017 to 7921990151."

There was also a letter from Bonningdale to the NFTC, which referred to a hitherto secret arrangement between Bonningdale and Mr Lawrence Productions Ltd, that had been made on March 23, 1984.

According to this January 1987 letter to the NFTC, Mr Lawrence Productions had "assigned to us, Bonningdale Limited, *our previously undisclosed beneficial interest* in the first US$2,920,000. [author's emphasis]"

Dickie's mouth hung open. He was speechless, but not for long. "What the hell is this?"

The loan documentation had been crystal clear: Bonningdale was not to receive a bean until the investors had first received US$10 million and, secondly, Charlesbay Ltd was to have been next in line for payment. Bonningdale was supposed to be last. Who had authorised this queue-jump? Why had the men running Mr Lawrence Productions signed away the investors rights to the first US$10 million?

Dickie began to suspect a straight theft from the investors by Mr Lawrence Productions, and by virtue of that a fraud on the revenue. This was US$2.9 million in taxable income that had been diverted.

"We hereby authorise and instruct you," continued Bonningdale in the letter to the NFTC, "to pay all moneys held by you on our behalf pursuant to such assignment of previously undeclared beneficial interest of ourselves in such moneys to our bank account."

One of Dickie's first moves was to call Denese Latimer at the IRD's South Auckland office. "Mrs Latimer, I've got some evidence that I think you'd quite like," he told her down the phone. A short time later, he was physically in her office. Also present was Alan May.

"Remember that letter you sent to all the investors in *Merry Christmas*?" smirked the lawyer, as he handed her a copy of her 1987 missive. Denese just smiled.

"Then how would you like this?" he grinned as he slapped the "previously undisclosed interest" letter down on Latimer's desk. The senior tax investigator couldn't believe it. "She literally started to dance a jig. The poor soul had good reason to be ecstatic, because they had spent so much time trying to get underneath it and there it was. Bang! Sitting there. I left it with her. My obligations were discharged, it was up to the department to resolve it."

Dickie believes the IRD Auckland office had every intention of hammering the movie promoters with the new evidence.

"I was left in the clearest impression that they now had the evidence they needed to prosecute, and planned to do so." But it never happened.

At the same time, disgruntled *Merry Christmas* investors were asking Dickie whether they could fight the IRD's tax evasion allegations, on the basis of what the investors had originally been told by the movie's promoters.

The McVeagh Fleming solicitor got his first hint that the IRD's Auckland office might have trouble taking the *Mr Lawrence* investigation any further, at a meeting on July 31, 1991 with *Mr Lawrence* promoter John Gow and Russell McVeagh tax partner Geoff Clews.

The Russell McVeagh partner had requested the meeting after learning that Dickie and Molloy were now investigating the *Merry Christmas* deal on behalf of some of the investors.

Clews, an urbane and sophisticated man with dark hair and a neatly trimmed beard, evidently knows no other game than hardball. And he made it clear to Dickie and Molloy that he was taking no prisoners. At least, that's what Dickie told the Winebox Inquiry in 1996.

Clews, he said, was concerned that Dickie and Molloy's foray into *Merry Christmas Mr Lawrence* on behalf of some investors could prejudice negotiations the Russell McVeagh partner was having with the Inland Revenue Department on behalf of all investors.

Dickie's view was that you couldn't negotiate a settlement with the IRD: either the transaction was kosher and the investors got every cent of the deduction they were claiming, or it wasn't kosher and they had to pay all of the extra tax. As far as he saw it, the tax laws were black and white.

But Clews and Gow appeared most concerned at the sudden appearance of Dickie and Molloy and their litigious group of *Merry Christmas* investors on the scene, for reasons that soon became clear.

"Mr Clews informed us that he would not deal with the investigating officers at Otahuhu, including Mrs Latimer, but would only deal with the head office of the Inland Revenue Department at Wellington.

"He further informed us that he was endeavouring to obtain a settlement in not only *Merry Christmas* but also in a number of other film partnerships. I do not know the names of the other partnerships, but it was plain from that meeting that the settlement proposals which Mr Clews was undertaking certainly included more than just *Merry Christmas*."

Lawyer Bruce Squire QC, acting for the Inland Revenue Department, told the Winebox Inquiry in 1995 of the background to the department's film investigations.

"More than 100 partnerships representing some five thousand investors were investigated by the Department, and the investigations, Sir, were complex – lasting in some cases over nine years.

"Most were settled and many millions of dollars in back taxes were assessed."

Clews was secretly negotiating with the IRD to settle a group of 16 disputed films out of court, but Dickie didn't know this in July 1991.

"Mr Clews stated that one of his reasons for his dealing with head office was that he was not prepared to enter into a discussion with Mrs Latimer concerning the merits of the review findings, and he appeared confident that he would not discuss the merits with the IRD head office either," he told the inquiry.

Translated into English, this meant that Geoff Clews was allegedly not prepared to even discuss whether his clients were legally in the right or whether they'd broken the law and should pay more tax. According to Dickie, as far as Clews was concerned, the merits of the case were firmly off the agenda – he had another weapon.

"He intended to advise head office," testified Dickie, "that unless a settlement was reached, he would tie up the Department's resources over the next three years with a separate case. . .for every investor. In *Merry Christmas* alone, that would involve over 300 cases."

Tony Molloy, by this time, was dumbfounded, and argued that the courts would not allow such a timewasting approach to litigation.

"Mr Clews' response," said Dickie ominously, "was to say words to the effect: 'We have got something on a certain senior tax inspector, which would be of embarrassment to the Department,' and that he intended to raise that issue with head office.

"Mr Clews appeared assured that raising that issue would assist in securing a settlement with head office officials."

Dickie said that after the meeting he immediately alerted either Alan May or Denese Latimer of the Russell McVeagh lawyer's plans. What happened next became the centrepiece testimony in one of the most dramatic episodes of the two and a half year Winebox Inquiry.

CHAPTER 17

Indiana Nash & The Taxmen Of Doom

"What emerges is a fully documented, often bizarre tale of sheer
incompetence and conspiratorial malfeasance. It affords the kind
of insight into how the government actually works for which
historians generally wait a century or more but which
thinking citizens need to know now."

– THEODORE DRAPER, *A VERY THIN LINE: THE IRAN-CONTRA AFFAIRS*, 1991

Geoff Clews was, indeed, making his presence felt at IRD head office and it
wasn't just over whether prosecution should be dropped in the *Mr Lawrence*
case.

He had approached the department with a list of 17 films that he wanted to
settle with the IRD out of court. The list was later cut to 16. He did have a secret
weapon: the IRD's own senior investigator, John Nash, and it related to
something Nash had done on a wintry Wellington afternoon three years earlier.

On June 2, 1988, Nash and a team of tax investigators raided the Oriental
Bay offices of a company called Endeavour Productions Ltd. Endeavour was a
film company run by John Barnett, who's now the managing director of TVNZ
subsidiary South Pacific Pictures.

It was just after 2.30pm when the raid commenced, but Barnett was
oblivious – he had travelled to Auckland on business. The first he knew of the
IRD's move came in a phone call at 2.40pm from Endeavour's Wellington office
manager, Rosalie Lai.

"John, we've got a problem down here. Some men from the Inland Revenue
Department have come into the office. They've got a letter and they want to
examine and take away some of our documents. What should I do?"*

The letter was a formal IRD Section 17 notice to the occupier of the

* The following conversations have been reconstructed by the author from paraphrased
comments contained in affidavits sworn by those involved about the events of that day and
tabled at the Winebox Inquiry. They capture the tenor and the main factual points of the
conversations, but they are not a verbatim reproduction of what was said, as no verbatim notes
exist.

premises, requiring the hand-over of "any books and documents (including correspondence, telex messages, facsimile messages and working papers) relating in any way whatsoever to films and television series produced, managed, promoted or packaged by John Daniel Barnett in any way whatsoever." The tax department was playing for keeps, and Barnett was the bunny in the cross-hairs.

"Who's the head guy from the IRD there? Can you put me on to him Rosalie?"

In the Endeavour office, Lai handed John Nash the phone.

"Listen," said a worried Barnett down the line, "I'm not happy about you people just walking in and demanding to examine or review our files. Why didn't you give us prior notice?"

The conversation quickly became heated. "What the hell are you after anyway?" queried Barnett.

"Everything," Nash allegedly replied. "We never get anything from you, and we're going to get it this time!"

"You can't just waltz in and take everything! We've got a business to run – you can't just walk in and take all our documents."

"Listen to me, Mr Barnett – I have the authority to take anything I want. And you had better understand that."

"Not as far as I'm concerned, you don't," sputtered Barnett in disbelief.

"I must warn you that you are obstructing me in the performance of my duty," said Nash ominously.

"Well, I'm standing by what I've said already. I'm perfectly happy to meet you tomorrow when I return to Wellington, and we can discuss this, but I'm not prepared to let you remove documentation from the office in my absence."

"What you are doing is criminal obstruction," warned Nash again.

"I'm not obstructing you, for heaven's sake. I'm more than happy to co-operate, within reason. Look, I'll be back in Wellington this evening, why don't we meet and discuss this then?"

"I may still be here," muttered the tax department's rising star.

"Look," sighed Barnett, "I'm not prepared to let you or your team to stay alone on the premises without a member of my staff present. In the meantime, I want to ascertain my legal rights in these circumstances. I'm going to ring my lawyer and I'll call you back as soon as I've done so."

"How long?" asked Nash.

Barnett glanced at his watch. "Give me 20 to 30 minutes. I'll call you back." He hung up the phone. "Bloody hell!" he cursed.

On a desk in the Black Stump, a phone was ringing. Russell McVeagh partner Paul Carran reached for it. "Carran speaking."

"Paul, it's John Barnett. The bloody IRD's raided my office in Wellington while I'm up here in Auckland. They're waving a letter around and claiming they've got authority to take away all our records on the film productions. John Nash is behind it."

Like all lawyers faced with a challenge, Carran felt the adrenalin beginning to kick in. "Get your office to fax me a copy of the IRD letter, if you will, please John. I can't really advise you until I see what it is they're up to. I'll get Geoff Clews in here too – he's one of the tax partners and very experienced in litigation."

John Barnett phoned his office back just before 3.00pm. "What are they doing?" he asked Rosalie Lai.

"They're waiting," she responded, "but Mr Nash wants to know how long you'll be."

"Well give them coffee and a video to watch, or something, please Rosalie. Anything to keep them occupied and away from the documents until I can get this thing sorted out. Tell them I'll be back to them in about 20 minutes."

Barnett didn't keep his word. He had a pre-arranged meeting to attend at three, and didn't clear it until 3.30pm. It was 3.45pm before he reached Geoff Clews on the phone and briefed him on what had taken place. By the time Clews phoned Endeavour Productions and spoke to Rosalie Lai, the IRD team had gone, taking with them numerous files.

Unfortunately for Nash, some of the files he and his team had taken did not come within the terms of the document production order. One box, for example, was tantalisingly titled "Fraud – Legal/Agreements".

"*Fraud*," said Barnett in an affidavit sworn later in the case, "is the title of a book for which I had acquired the film production rights. Those rights have now lapsed. Those files do not relate in any way whatsoever to films or television series produced, managed, promoted or packaged by me in any way whatsoever."

It was a similar story with several other files, files that Barnett argued were crucial for the day to day running of his business.

The IRD had also seized files which he said were legally privileged – meaning they were communications between the company and its lawyers which the IRD was not entitled to ask for or hold.

Barnett told the Court that his company had co-operated with the IRD in the past, allowing the IRD access to inspect files for three days the previous year. The raid, he complained, amounted to "deceitful conduct" on John Nash's part.

"The Defendant's conduct is a flagrant abuse of the liberties of the Plaintiffs and I respectfully pray this Honourable Court to order the return to the Plaintiffs of the materials seized from them, and other relief appropriate to meet the circumstances."

The night of the raid, an incensed Barnett won round one. Justice McGechan of the High Court at Wellington granted an ex-parte injunction, restraining the IRD from referring to or using the documents, and ordering the department to deliver them into the custody of the Court.

A full-on lawsuit began, with Barnett alleging "deceit, misfeasance in a public office, trespass and conversion."

As is always the case with litigation, the lawsuit dragged on interminably earning the lawyers large fees, undoubtedly, and costing everyone else large sums of money and time.

It was still a live issue when Geoff Clews began discussing with the IRD the prospect of settling 16 films out of court. As Clews told the Winebox Inquiry in 1996, documents relating to three of those 16 films had been seized in the 1988 Endeavour swoop. The three handled by Endeavour included the films *Dead Kids*, *Race For The Yankee Zephyr* and the unreleased Tatum O'Neal classic, *Prisoners*.

John Nash, meanwhile, had realised he was on a hiding to nothing for exceeding his authority. For failing to dot his i's and cross his t's. Which was a shame, because the Winebox Inquiry heard evidence that Nash had estimated $50 million in tax could be recoverable from the Endeavour movies, and that was before the possible imposition of the triple-tax-penalty for evasion, if it was later determined that fraud was involved.

In a July 1990 analysis of the position that he'd placed the department in, Nash wrote "The Barnett case requires settlement." He listed six points counting against the IRD, including "we cannot show non-cooperation from Mr Barnett or Russell McVeagh. If we lose, we may also lose the 'spot audit' power."

Spot audits are, of course, a major weapon in the IRD arsenal.

Nash conceded that there were missing links in the evidence needed to fight Barnett, and that a continuation of the struggle would be a waste of "time and valuable resources."

Tellingly, he noted that "Master Williams [of the High Court] has ordered full disclosure of our hand (220 Eastlight files) – the deficiencies in all our cases will be revealed should this order not be overturned by the Court of Appeal."

The same principles, he argued, could now be applied in many of the other film deals under investigation.

"Our strategy up until now has been built around winning the first one or two court cases and then having all the other film objections disappearing into thin air on account of these initial successes.

"The reality is that it is now July 1990 and we have not yet been to Court on a substantive issue. There will also be delays should cases go to the Court of Appeal or through to the Privy Council.

"What if we don't win the first cases? What if the best cases are conceded by the other side out of court?

"The cases are now all very old, and there is still no end in sight. There is currently a wait of about three years for Auckland High Court cases. . .Opposing counsel can and will delay matters further through lengthy interlocutory procedures (for example, the Barnett case)."

Nash, once so gung-ho, was now advocating rapprochement, the politics of ordinary, rather than gunboat, diplomacy.

"The Department is not a business, but that is not to say that we should not take some of the most useful business techniques and apply them to the goals of being efficient and effective in the use of investigation and litigation resources. Negotiation is a fundamental business technique."

The IRD would have been aware by now of just how litigious the promoters using Russell McVeagh were – if their own experiences with the film investigations wasn't bad enough, they only had to look across to Chris Dickie's legal action in the bloodstock partnerships to see how expensive justice can be to obtain.

"The court system is already dogged," wrote Nash, "without having to take numerous unnecessary film cases – our top inspectors and legal counsel have better things to do than 'flog dead horses'."

It was probably an unintended pun, in the circumstances.

Far better, argued Nash, to jettison the films where too much work was required to nail down alleged irregularities and illegalities, and instead concentrate on the films known to be prosecutable, the so-called "Black" cases.

"Maximum publicity of good film case wins will follow. Prosecution and penal tax action, although remote, remains a possibility for black cases fast-tracked to Court over the next six months.

"We are not 'phased' [fazed?] should we have to litigate the black cases (ie., conclusive circles, knowledge of beneficial ownership of tax haven entities, simple concepts easily put before a judge, obstruction apparent, etc), and moreover we will be able to manage these cases."

John Nash was also displaying a conciliatory streak as far as the big lawfirms were concerned.

"Regardless of perceived misdemeanours on the part of certain advisers (notably Russell McVeagh and Bell Gully), we, as a Department, do have an ongoing relationship with them."

If the IRD had evidence of misdemeanours involving the major lawfirms, albeit "perceived", then why didn't it take action against those firms?

It seems IRD head office was ready and willing to take John Nash's advice, because the Auckland investigators headed by Denese Latimer received a memo from director of taxpayer audit, Tony Bouzaid at head office a short time later.

"The Department has invested many years into the investigation of the film industry. Throughout the investigation we have had to make decisions based on the facts available at the time. Obviously we made mistakes. At this stage we still do not have a case in court.

"The Commissioner and 8th floor management at head office have been extremely worried about the film investigations," continued Bouzaid ominously.

"As you know, some of the ventures started in 1981 – almost ten years ago. If the litigation process were to proceed with many of the cases it would be years before we could conclude cases."

So this is how, it appears to me, you beat the tax system: you snatch the tax benefit, and then you wear down the IRD with interminable obfuscation and legal delaying tactics until the department loses what little stomach it had for a fight.

Russell McVeagh lawyer Geoff Clews claimed "some officers dealing with film related matters seemed to be going through the motions and there was a lethargic, almost resigned air about them as they asked questions relating especially to overseas elements of the transactions."

In his memo, Tony Bouzaid acknowledged that the investigators may have cases where they strongly suspect "that certain parties own Hong Kong companies. If we cannot prove it, then that must be taken into account in the negotiation."

The IRD would soon get strong evidence to support such allegations, but never used it.

In the first sign of a difference of opinion within the department, Bouzaid announced that he was appointing John Nash as Chief Negotiator in bringing the film settlements to a close, and warned the Auckland staff "I am therefore asking for your cooperation in this exercise. There must be no display by our department that we are split on this process.

"We cannot unjustifiably seek to gain the impossible. If we cannot prove the discrepancy then that must be taken into account."

The man who had led a dashing but doomed raid on the nerve centre of some of the alleged tax-dodge films was now doing penance by shutting the investigations down into everything but the so-called black cases.

They had battled 10 years to get the hard evidence, fighting every delaying tactic thrown at them, but now with victory arguably within their grasp, the IRD was running up the white flag.

While the IRD's Otahuhu investigation centre found itself blanketed in a depressive cloud of frustration and discontent, McVeagh Fleming lawyers Chris Dickie and Peter Edwards were celebrating their good fortune over getting the goods on *Mr Lawrence* with Tony Molloy. Little did they know what was to follow.

CHAPTER 18

The Adventures Of The Little Prince

"There can be no whitewash at the White House."
– RICHARD NIXON, 1973

Imagine, if you will, the city of Hollywood, Los Angeles, California, in 1940. Forget the 1990's version, with homeless drunks sleeping on the sidewalk, and drug-crazed misfits trying to rob tourists at the Hollywood Burger King. Forget the sense of age and decay that now clings to a run-down neighbourhood, and transport yourself back in time.

The pastels of the Spanish-influenced architecture capture and hold the California sun like they were made for each other, and the movie business drives this city like a heartbeat.

Charlie Chaplin is taking an afternoon stroll along Hollywood Boulevard, still remembered and respected from the demise of the silent era a decade earlier, and about to star in a talkie – *The Great Dictator*. A young Norma-Jean Mortenson has just turned 14. Within a few years she'll be married and divorced, before posing nude for calendar shots in the back streets behind Sunset. It will be several years before she emerges as Marilyn Monroe.

War has broken out in Europe, but on the west coast of California it is nothing but a page five foreign story in the Times.

With the late afternoon sun streaming in a window, two men are enjoying a cigar and a brandy across a desk.

"Damn it, Jim, you cracked it boy! Disney loves it. We're made." The older man is Rudy Eising, a partner in what had been a failing movie support studio, specialising in cartoon animation.

While the stars like Jean Harlow and Greta Garbo captured the hearts of young men across America on the silver screen, their younger brothers and sisters were growing up to a new phenomenon. Cartoons.

Walt Disney had broken new ground with *Steamboat Willie*, starring one Mickey Mouse, in the early thirties, but other studios, like Eising's, had quickly caught up. He and Disney were slugging it out, producing cartoons for the big distributors to handle. But then Rudy hit the rocks.

Only a few months earlier he'd been forced to let most of his staff go, after losing the lucrative Metro Goldwyn Meyer contract. It had been tough, and new work had not eventuated. There'd been scraps, enough for young writer and animator Jameson Brewer to nibble on, but little more. Little, that is, until Brewer had an idea.

"Rudy, you've got practically no one left here but me. Why don't you go to Walt Disney and ask if he won't give you one of the things he's got in the works? He's got a hundred things there, they can't possibly handle them all?"

It was a suggestion that stuck in the craw for Eising. Not only had he lost work contracts to his arch-rival, but Walt Disney had also hired most of Eising's staff in the process.

"He owes you one," pushed Jameson Brewer.

"Yeah, maybe you're right," Eising had conceded at the time. The gamble had paid off, big-time.

"Sure Rudy," came the voice of Walt Disney down the phone, "I'll give you one of my pictures to do. I'll send the files across tomorrow."

A truckload of material duly turned up, but Jameson Brewer couldn't make any sense of it. "It was just a mish-mash of rough sketches and drawings, and nobody seemed to know where they were going with it." Brewer sighed and went to see his boss.

"Rudy, this stuff is rubbish. Why don't you just let me take the whole thing and throw it out, and I'll start from scratch and we'll just do an original picture."

Eising felt his guts churning, but he had little option. "Ah, what the hell. You go ahead Jim. Do what you have to."

Brewer worked fast. Within a month he'd plotted out the story, and drawn rough sketches to go with it. By the time he'd produced the storyboard, Eising was increasing the stakes of his gamble by hiring some of his old studio hands back to join the production team.

"Within three months," remembered Jameson Brewer five decades later, "we had the whole picture made, and sent to Disney. He was flabbergasted. They opened it at the Chinese Theatre at a big premiere, and it got more attention than the feature picture. As a matter of fact, it was up for the Emmy Award that year."

Disney was utterly stunned, and he bailed up Rudy Eising. "We couldn't lick this thing! For two years we had it in here – who did it over there?"

Eising told of the talented young animator and writer who'd nursed the cartoon back to health. Within a week of his celebratory drink with Eising, Jameson Brewer had been hired by Walt Disney to join his cartoon production team.

For Brewer, it was to be a lot more than 15 minutes of fame.

"You have carte blanche," explained Disney as he escorted Brewer around the Disney studios, "to take anything we've got in the works here and do it."

"At that time," remembered Brewer in his 1996 interview with the author, "they had only done one feature, which was *Snow White*. They had in the works one called *Bambi* – they were starting on that – and they were talking about *Pinocchio*, but that's as far as that had gotten."

"But I saw them in one department, working on a thing called Mickey Mouse that was to be an extra-long short subject called *The Sorceror's Apprentice*. I said 'hey, this is something else!' "

Brewer called Walt aside. "I think you've got a bigger idea here than just a short subject, with Mickey Mouse, in *Sorceror's Apprentice*. Why don't you do a whole symphony feature, a concert feature?"

Disney was momentarily shocked at the idea – not least because he had no knowledge of music, but then the potential dawned on him.

"I convinced him of it," says Brewer, "and he was enough of an entrepreneur to sense when something was different and worth doing."

"Well, I gave you carte blanche already, what do you need?" queried Disney.

What Brewer wanted was what he got: the top music programmer in the country, Deems Taylor from New York, and the conductor of the Philadelphia Philharmonic, Leopold Stokowski, to compose and arrange the score.

"Within a week Walt had them both out there for me, and I was meeting with them, and it was down to work."

The end result of Jameson Brewer's work was a movie that won honours at the Academy Awards, a movie called *Fantasia*. A movie that Jameson Brewer wrote.

Brewer is still in the movie business, but over the years he's seen technology improve and techniques change. Back when he started out, animators would painstakingly draw a sketch for each of the 24 frames that make one second of film on screen. A one minute sequence would contain more than 1,400 individual pages of art.

Now, video technology makes it possible to halve that, producing only eight or ten sketches per second, without any drop in animation quality. Even so, he says, some of the old work still stacks up.

"The Disney studio has really done some remarkable things, and I think that technologically today they are really superior to anyone else. But there were some very good things being done thirty, forty, even fifty years ago, that haven't really been improved on that much.

"I would say it is the entire picture that has changed. Where it used to be that you were just intrigued by the fact that drawings were moving, now you have to have story, you have to have characters that are appealing, you've got to have songs that are hit songs – there are so many more elements now that come into play."

When Jameson Brewer first toured the production house with Walt Disney all those decades ago, and saw them planning for *Pinocchio*, little could he have imagined that his own life would later resemble a scene from the childrens' classic.

In 1985, Brewer was led astray by what he came to regard as two sly and worldly-wise critters from a place called New Zealand: Paul Carran and Chris Kirkham. But to understand how this came about, one first has to leap from 1940 to 1977, where Jameson Brewer is still actively involved as a senior figure in the animation industry.

Since the early 1970's, Japanese TV producers had been trying to sell their animated cartoon shows to the rest of the world and, in particular, the United States where the prices are highest.

"Their technical work was always excellent," says Brewer, referring to issues of design, staging, characters and camera effects, "but their concepts, or stories, were completely incomprehensible to the rest of the world. They attempted to dub in English voices over their pictures, but the result was still the same – their pictures made no sense conceptually and were rejected by all TV outlets worldwide."

This was the background, then, when Jameson Brewer was approached in 1977 by an American financier, Sandy Frank, who'd bought the rights to a series of animated Japanese films. He wanted Brewer to dub in the English voices.

"I'd be wasting my time and your money," drawled the former Disney animator. "The Japanese culture is completely different – even the pictures speak a different language. If you put English voices in without changing the sequence of the pictures, you'll still be left with a series that's complete gibberish to non-orientals."

Sandy Frank scratched his head, now wondering if the difference between a "bargain" and a "lemon" was purely dependent on which side of the deal you were on.

"Look," continued Brewer after a moment, sensing the producer's distress, "I can turn this into something that you can market worldwide, if you're prepared to spend some money doing it properly."

Frank nodded, waiting for the bad news.

"I would totally restructure the various episodes," Brewer explained, "creating new personalities for the characters, devising new storylines which would fit the filmed action but in no way relate to the Japanese concepts.

"I would record a new and impressive music score and sound effects track, edit out the unacceptable violence which the Japanese always employ lavishly, switch scenes and episodes from one picture to another, add a few new scenes and completely re-edit everything.

"The animation, which is the most expensive element in cartoon production, would remain but overall the series would be completely new, exciting and, like I said, marketable throughout the world."

"Great," smiled Sandy Frank weakly, thinking he was staring at certain bankruptcy. But he gave the go-ahead.

Jameson Brewer beavered away for the first nine months of 1978, turning what he'd been given into 85 episodes. The series premiered on US television on a syndicate of 100 channels that September, under the title *Battle Of The Planets*.

It immediately became the number one children's programme on US TV, and Sandy Frank made US$15 million from that first run alone.

For the next two years, Battle Of The Planets continued to decimate the opposition on US television, and Frank was a millionaire many more times over. Rival companies were buying up the rights to whatever Japan could produce but, according to Brewer, they hadn't figured out how to decode the Japanese productions for Western consumption.

Then, in 1983, one of those companies knocked on Brewer's door. "Can you do for us what you did for *Battle*?" they pleaded.

So for the first nine months of 1984, Brewer again found himself chained to an animator's desk, completing 104 episodes of a new series called *Voltron*.

"This series immediately became the number one rated children's programme on TV, replacing *Battle* which went to second place."

It was the start of a trend that created such shows as *Transformers* and *Gargoyles*, a trend that continues today. But for Brewer, the next stop was a series called *The Little Prince*.

"I knew I could reshape this one into a delightful, charming fantasy and I agreed to do a pilot film for Joseph Tandet, an attorney in New York city who had acquired the rights to 26 episodes."

They took the series pilot to the Cannes Film Festival in France, and immediately secured a number of orders from international markets. But there was a harbinger of things to come.

"They sold it to about 15 or 20 foreign countries, and they [the distributors hired by Tandet] picked up all this advance money. They came back but they blew all this money on something – I don't know what but it wasn't the production.

"I was in the middle of doing the second picture for them when they went broke and said 'we can't go any further'. So the man in New York who they were doing it for, Joseph Tandet, called me in and he said 'look, will you take this over and finish it? These guys have violated their contract.' I said I would, but he wasn't prepared to finance it."

Tandet signed across the production and distribution rights to Brewer, contingent on Brewer financing the series. Such was his belief in the series that Brewer sank US$300,000 of his own money into it.

"I quickly produced 18 episodes and secured an impressive US release on all the principal ABC stations in New York, Los Angeles, San Francisco, Detroit, Boston and others. These contracts," Brewer pointed out, "were secured on my promise to deliver 26 episodes.

"The series quickly became the number one children's programme in all its time slots, and was number one of *all* children's shows in New York and other major cities."

With the series a hit, but only 18 episodes completed, Brewer needed to produce the final eight episodes before he could collect a cheque from the various TV companies he'd sold it to. He'd run out of cash after funding the first 18, and was now looking for outside finance.

His first step was to sign an independent distributor, Tom Horton, to look after international sales of *The Little Prince*.

"I'm not equipped to deal with the US syndication market," explained Horton as they discussed the fine detail of their deal on the afternoon of June 12, 1985. "But, I do know some people down in New Zealand that I've dealt with before in terms of distribution. I might be able to persuade them to finance the last eight for you."

When Horton phoned in August to say that the New Zealanders were definitely interested, Brewer was rapt. Horton explained that the foreigners were coming across to LA to negotiate a deal. Brewer was not invited to those discussions.

It appears that Horton had been a busy boy behind the scenes. He'd written to the directors of a company called Primula Holdings Ltd in New Zealand on May 25, 1985.

Primula was the special partnership being promoted by Challenge Corporate Services for investors wanting to plug their cash into TV programmes.

"We have also been marketing the childrens animated series titled *The Little Prince*. To date the first nineteen episodes of the series have been broadcast in five test USA markets for syndication sales and broadcast or sold in various foreign markets.

"To date the series has been sold and/or we are waiting to receive contracts from recent offers in Canada, Cyprus, Greece, Ireland, Italy, Middle East, New Zealand, South America and UK cable."

From the foreign deals, Horton was expecting to receive almost US$300,000, which he estimated "represent about 20 percent of the total market for first-run broadcast rights.

"Based on the above sales figures to date for the first nineteen episodes, it is reasonable to expect total worldwide sales for these programmes to exceed. . .US$1,800,000 for a total of twenty episodes."

In the letter, which was included in the prospectus sent to Primula investors in the first week of July 1985, Horton concluded with the belief that he actually expected the series to do even better – US$2.7 million.

The prospectus spelt out the background to *The Little Prince* project.

"The Little Prince, an extraordinary small person from the planet B-612, has captured the love and admiration of many millions of children and adults around the world. He visits Earth in each episode of the half-hour animated TV series, *The Adventures of the Little Prince*.

"Antoine de Saint-Exupery's literary classic, *The Little Prince*, has sold over 5,000,000 copies since 1943 and still sells over 200,000. . .each year. It has been translated into over 50 languages.

"The Little Prince lives on a tiny planet barely large enough to support his small castle. He is devoted to his Flower, a rose of unmatched beauty but overbearing pride. It is her pride that often drives the Little Prince to seek other friends on other planets. In his travels he discovers great truths about faith, courage, friendship and caring."

Of the producer/writer Jameson Brewer, the promoters wrote: "Perhaps best known for his scripting of Disney's enduring classic, 'Fantasia', Jameson Brewer . . .is currently represented on theatre screens as writer of the lavish animated musical production 'Heidi's Song', produced by Hanna-Barbera.

"Since his collaboration with Disney, Jameson Brewer has written in excess of 2,000 TV programs, over 50 theatrical feature films and more than 250 animated pictures, including the creation of several animated series currently appearing on the major TV networks of the United States.

"Several of Brewer's theatrical features have won major awards, and theatrical shorts such as those he did for Robert Benchley and Pete Smith won Oscars. Brewer has written for such stars as Fred Astaire, Jimmy Stewart, Bette Davis, Greer Garson and producer/director Alfred Hitchcock, winning numerous awards."

The prospectus also pointed out the luminaries who made up the voice cast of the cartoon series.

Julie Dees played the voice of the Little Prince. "The voice she created for this role is irresistibly appealing. She claims she patterned it after her own small son.

"She has appeared in such films as '*Bugsy Malone*' for Paramount and '*Can't Stop The Music*' for MGM."

Her TV credits included roles in *Happy Days* and *Taxi*, *Hollywood Squares* and the *Rich Little Show*.

"She is not new to animation, having done many voices on '*The Flintstones*' and she was the voice of Casper on the popular animated show, '*Casper the Ghost*'.

Also in the voice stable for the programme being made by New Zealand's Primula Holdings was Janet Waldo. Who, you ask? Janet was the teenage daughter in The Jetsons, and also played 'Penelope Pitstop' and 80 year old motorcycle freak 'Granny Sweet' in the cartoon series *The Wacky Racers*. Her voice was that of Morticia in *The Addams Family*, and she was Josie in *Josie and the Pussycats*.

Enough pop-culture nostalgia yet? I think not! Another top talent brought in to enliven *The Little Prince* was Hal Smith. "Although a man of a thousand voices," exclaimed the prospectus, "Hal Smith is seen almost as often as he is heard on TV and in motion pictures. He will long be remembered for the eight years he appeared on the *Andy Griffith Show* as 'Otis, the old town tosspot'.

"He has also been seen on '*Fantasy Island*', '*The Dukes of Hazzard*' and hundreds of educational shows and specials.

"In cartoons, Hal has been the voices of Jiminy Cricket and Goofy for Disney."

For the record, Smith also appeared in *The Flintstones*, *The Jetsons* and *The Smurfs*, and was the voice of *Winnie the Pooh* in the Disney movie classic.

It is worth taking a look at what the Primula prospectus was telling potential investors about the production schedule.

"Nineteen half-hour episodes have already been produced and are currently being exhibited in the USA and distributed further afield.

"A further twenty half-hour episodes are currently being produced to which the partnership will acquire rights when completed."

Excuse me? A further twenty episodes? Not according to Jameson Brewer! But then, he was only the guy actually making the programmes and, from the evidence available, no one had asked him at this stage or told him anything about the final eight suddenly becoming a further 20.

But the prospectus continued. "Production towards the double head fine cut stage of production is well advanced with most of the animation having been completed. The Distributor will contract to have these episodes to the double head fine cut stage of production by 30 September 1985."

Which was fine, except the distributor didn't even tell Brewer that there was a deal in the offing until a phone call at 8.00am, on the morning of September 24, 1985. Brewer's diary records what happened.

"8.00am – urgent call from Horton to meet NZ investors at 10.00am! Simon Taub [Brewer's attorney] can't make it to represent and advise me."

Horton explained that the meeting was to take place in the offices of major Los Angeles lawfirm O'Melveny & Myers, a practice with nearly 120 partners. One of them, Stephen Scharf, was Tom Horton's lawyer and he was hosting the gathering.

Brewer's diary again: "10.00am – met in law offices of O'Melveny and Myers. Present were Tom Horton, his legal rep, Scharf, and Chris Kirkham and Paul Carran, the New Zealand investors. We signed contracts for financing final eight episodes of *Prince*, and also signed new contract with Horton for distribution."

That last point is important, because the documentary evidence shows that, for reasons unknown, the US attorney involved, Stephen Scharf, required Brewer to sign a document which contained variations to the existing contract. It was backdated to June 12, 1985. This was the date of the original contract between Horton and Brewer.

Brewer picks up the story. "Mr Kirkham and Mr Carran, the New Zealand investors, I was introduced to for the first time. It was my understanding then that both these gentlemen were prospective investors. I learned later in the meeting that Mr Carran was an attorney representing Mr Kirkham and his interests."

Kirkham handed Brewer a business card, showing he was the "Manager, Film Financing, of Challenge Corporate Services Ltd, investment bankers of Auckland, New Zealand." Reading the card, Brewer assumed Challenge Corporation was the organisation that would be funding him.

The previous day he'd been sent a copy of the new contract, some 25 pages long, in close-set body type and full of legalese. One sentence alone was 116 words between fullstops. And that wasn't uncommon.

Brewer's lawyer, Simon Taub, had been tied up in a court case and unable to read the document. Brewer, an elderly artist whose career had been spent creating animated cartoons, had had neither the time to read it nor, on first glance, the ability to understand it.

He was given a copy of the contract at the meeting as well, and while skimming through it noticed that the company funding him was not Challenge Corporation, but an outfit called Chary Holdings Ltd, of Jersey, in the Channel Islands.

"I queried the New Zealand gentlemen about this and they explained that

Chary Holdings was a subsidiary of Challenge and the two companies were synonymous."

As an added spur, Horton and his lawyer reminded Jameson Brewer that Kirkham and Carran would be flying back to New Zealand and that matters had to be wrapped up quickly.

"I was informed that the New Zealand people had to leave by noon," noted the cartoonist.

According to Brewer, he signed two contracts: one a funding agreement with Chary Holdings and the other a distribution agreement with Tom Horton, backdated to June 12. The men from New Zealand wanted the documents signed before they discussed the deal. Foolishly, without a lawyer present, and little hope of understanding the bulky contracts in the short time available, Brewer signed.

"Those present. . .hurried and pressured me into signing the two documents as the New Zealand men had to leave momentarily to return home. If not signed now, the deal was off. I later learned that Kirkham and Carran were still in Los Angeles several days later."

So what were Kirkham and Carran up to? Why the hurry? Well, there's now strong evidence that the entity they represented, Primula Holdings, planned to use the signed and complex agreements in what would be alleged in the Royal Court of Jersey was similar fact evidence of a rort against the New Zealand Inland Revenue Department and investors.

Under NZ tax law, a transaction can be struck down as a "sham" if the parties to the deal do something different to the way it is set out in official documentation, such as signed agreements.

If Brewer had read the agreements he'd been given, he would have discovered that he had, in fact, promised to produce those twenty extra episodes, as well as giving up the money from the 18 he'd already made.

Brewer didn't discover this, because once he'd signed the papers the New Zealanders began discussing the deal with Brewer, and the deal they were talking about was the one he'd asked for: funding for the final eight episodes.

"We next discussed the cost of producing the eight additional episodes. I said I would require US$5,000 per episode for my writing, directing and producing services.

"There would be new music scores, new voices and sound effects and considerable editing. Plus final dubbing and prints. I estimated another $7,000 for all these elements for a total of $12,000 per episode, or a funding of approximately $100,000 for the eight episodes.

"Kirkham and Carran said the money would be funded to Thomas Horton, since they had done much business with him previously, trusted and respected him and their stockholders would feel more secure with his supervision and distribution of production costs. I agreed to this."

On October 18, 1985, Jameson Brewer received the US$40,000 he'd asked for as compensation "for my personal efforts on the eight episodes at $5,000 per episode." He immediately started work on restructuring the cartoons, billing

Thomas Horton directly for the other production expenses and receiving reimbursement.

It is significant that Brewer's signed agreement with Chary Holdings does not refer to any specific funding per episode.

It would appear, then, that there were two kinds of agreement in existence relating to *The Adventures Of The Little Prince*. On the one hand, there are written contracts – capable of being shown to the IRD or a Court – which state one thing, and on the other hand a verbal agreement which appears to have been the real agreement.

To this day, Jameson Brewer is adamant that the written agreements were shams.

"The basic terms, according to our verbal understanding and agreement at that meeting, were that Kirkham (and whatever company he was representing) would finance 8 additional episodes. They would share in the revenue of these eight new episodes, but not in the revenue of the 18 already completed and sold.

"There could never have been a discussion of more than 26 episodes since that is all the segments that the Japanese had produced. If additional new episodes were to be produced, starting from scratch, that would have called for an entirely different funding agreement, since the production of totally new films would have cost six or seven times the amount I was asking for to restructure the eight Japanese episodes.

"It is inconceivable," writes a very annoyed Brewer, "that I would assign my rights and revenue in the 18 episodes I had already completed to Kirkham/ Chary Holdings, since that would negate any profits I would receive from doing an additional eight episodes to bring my total to 26. In such a case I would do best to continue with my 18 pictures and realize what profit I might from a limited series."

It is probably also significant that the New Zealand prospectus for the Primula partnership, which was funding this venture, contained information that was not true.

That prospectus was issued back in July 1985 but contained the claims that nineteen (not eighteen) episodes had already been made, and that a further 20 were in production. In July 1985, when the promoters made those claims, they certainly did not have the signature of Jameson Brewer on any agreement stating that! Those agreements, even though one was backdated to June 1985, weren't signed until September 24, 1985.

Arguably, the New Zealand prospectus for Primula is a fraudulent misrepresentation, containing statements the promoters knew – or should have known – at the time of its issue were not true.

There was one other factor that niggled at Brewer: when the contracts had been passed around to sign, "it was my impression that Kirkham had signed the document in my presence." Yet when he finally received the contract in the mail, it had been signed by one "E.L. Bendelow" as a director of Chary Holdings.

"It is puzzling to me how Bendelow's signature comes to appear on this document only two days after our meeting at O'Melveny & Myers, when he was not present at that meeting or even in this country.

"This entire scenario begins to resemble more '*The Prince*' by Machiavelli, rather than '*Adventures of the Little Prince*' by Saint-Exupery."

As Brewer came to rue the day he'd ever set eyes on Kirkham and Carran, his path would inevitably cross that of another New Zealander, Chris Dickie.

"Chris Dickie was in touch with me for months, in fact he even flew over and met with me. I even talked with some woman there who was in your Internal Revenue Service.

"But anyhow, Chris Dickie was hunting them down and finally found them somewhere in the Channel Islands. He said 'well, we're moving in now, I've got the papers that'll allow me to get in to look at all their records and go over everything. We've got em nailed now!' And that's the last I ever heard of Chris Dickie, I never heard another word."

CHAPTER 19

Colombian Marching Dust

"You are sitting in the director's chair given to you by Fay
Richwhite. And sitting at the outside table given to you by Fay
Richwhite. Drinking juice from a Fay Richwhite jug in Fay
Richwhite glasses, wondering and worrying whether you
should write this book."

– THE LATE BRUCE GOODING, *INSIDE STORIES OF FEAR AND LOATHING*

As 1991 sped to a close, Chris Dickie felt like an arrow heading for a bullseye.
The key to the bloodstock and film investigations, he believed, lay in
establishing who owned or controlled the various tax haven companies
involved, in Hong Kong and Jersey.

If control or ownership could be pegged back to any of the promoters or
their legal advisers, it would be a lot easier to prove deception/fraud and other
allegations, such as the taking of secret commissions.

But proving the ownership and control would be a very difficult task.
Denese Latimer and Alan May had, he knew, been shown the door by Deloittes
in Hong Kong when they tried to visit there and obtain information for the
Inland Revenue investigation.

But, even as Dickie and Peter Edwards prepared their battle plans, another
event was unfolding in Hollywood that would, four years later, have a
tremendous impact on their investigation. It involved a company called
European Pacific, and a takeover bid for the giant MGM studios.

In the world of high finance and big business, gossip about the sensational
and dangerous is often disguised in allegory, or anonymous faxes that fly
between offices.

One such amusing conspiracy story was written by a lawyer in a tax haven
jurisdiction, a man involved in the scandal. Entitled *The Pauper's Tale (scripted
for the family audience)* it went like this:

"Once upon a time, in Rotterdam actually, a worthy Dutch burgher named
Slavenberg started a bank and, being unadventurous, the bank survived, stodgy
but sound, and gave Meester Slavenberg's family a good living.

"Meanwhile, down the road, the French bankers spent their time and francs
going bust, being nationalised, socialised, reconstructed, destructed and
generally re-stuffed like a mattress for the pleasure of the politicians of the day.

"Just then, a socialist called Mitterand, who had bankrupted the country, decided it would be a totally brill idea to flog off all the banks which he had nicked in the first place – tax free of course.

"And, this being the cunning part, he would charge the banks and their new shareholders a whopping fee so that the banks could actually do business outside France with all those weird and rather uncouth people who were not French, but who did have the redeeming feature of having quite a lot of money which he – meaning France – could sort of swap and trade and screw around with in Europe – particularly when he was already taking the Brits to the cleaners on the Common Agricultural Policy.

"The froggie bankers were full of passion and delight at going cross-border and rushed off to see the cheeseheads in Amsterdam who told them to stuff it. Which was a bit upsetting.

"They nagged and nagged the cheeseheads. Meantime, in mid-nag, back at Slavenberg bank a policy decision or two was being carried out thus:

1. take in more deposits (so what?)
2. write more assets (so what?) and
3. be in the Dutch Sandwich business in a big way (meaning what?)

"Well, everybody knows that corporate America and most of Europe fiddled their interest-taxes by rinky-dink, you-beaut, brass-plates in Curacao, Netherlands Antilles, not unadjacent to Colombia, linked up to form what the tax wallahs call a Dutch Sandwich.

"In a moment of completely accidental and total lapse of memory, inadvertent closure of eyelids and deafening temporary loss-of-hearing (not to mention marbles) the Dutch Sandwich was seasoned with condiments from Colombia and artistically wrapped in celluloid – I mean cellophane – no I don't.

"Just then, Cannon Pictures was making absolute tons, and a lot of films too; until Yoram wanted to buy the Great British Saturday Afternoon, being cinemas, and what with one thing (British Safety Council standards) and another (an urgent personal need for approximately US$200 million) Cannon Pictures conked out. Slavenberg was, by complete coincidence, short of US$200 million and also, by complete coincidence, was no longer called Slavenberg but Credit Lyonnaise Bank Nederland N.V. (CLBN).

"This change of wrapping paper around a bomb was delivered courtesy of the central cheesehead bankers who were utterly sick of being nagged by the frogs.

"CLBN's Afman – stayer that he is – is extremely knowledgeable about films and tax structures, so much so that he was shown the door last month: I mean, condiments are happenstance, US$200 million is coincidence, but US$1.5 billion is a bit thick. Especially when the berks like Parretti that you've set up to asset-strip MGM and refloat the logo through a cash box called PentaAmerica decide to stiff their friends (Golan and Sunna) on paying for the last round of companies (Cannon and Comfinance).

"Besides, Parretti's in the market for a Boeing 747 so that his holidays to Morocco and the Azores – well known international banking centres – are a little less stressful, after the coppers in designer slip-ons let down the Gulfstream's tyres at Rome airport.

"Sunna accidentally has his passport arrested. . .so there was nothing for it but to swipe a half-bar from the waiter's till and slope off to Uruguay (US/ European visa-free passports legit. already for US$25,000 no commission), to reflect on what might-have-been as a has-been.

"Anyway, somebody at the bank loses the ciggie-packet on which Parretti has written down 'IOU $1.5 bill' and then the fan was turned up to maximum speed, what with Christmas and balance date coming and all.

"The refloat is still OK, so arms don't wave around too much, until the creditors hire some streetfighters to start razoring MGM, and Parretti's senior partner Fiorini opens his trap to announce the refloat for US$2 bill and then retires hurt. So the refloat is a dud and Yoram hands in a doctor's certificate to be excused from games for a while.

"A thermonuclear device is meantime inserted in the bank's underwear by, allo allo, Mitterand's man on the cash desk, Berogovoy – Finance Minister, sole-shareholder-for-the-State of the bank, and long time bad-mouther of Parretti who, meantime, has been declared by the bank to have been responsible for the Gulf War as well.

"MGM starts to disappear from sight – rather as Merrill ('the undersigned acted as advisers to MGM/UA') Lynch did as soon as the streetfighters made the bankruptcy petition stick, and the Beverly Hills air turned blue with writs.

"Well, the bank has come and gone a long way from the gentle days of Meester Slavenberg, but I guess that a couple of billion can be covered in new and even more imaginative ways than ever thought possible."

So that's the unofficial version of the events behind the MGM takeover bid. But what it didn't tell readers was the crucial involvement of a company called Century Insurance, a Cook Islands-registered company set up from the European Pacific building in Rarotonga. It was catapulted to prominence by a front page story in the *Los Angeles Times* on April 10, 1991.

"RAROTONGA, Cook Islands – In the frantic final days leading up to his acquisition of MGM/UA Communications Corp., Italian financier Giancarlo Parretti signed an agreement trading 10 million shares of studio stock he didn't yet own for an insurance bond that allowed him to close the deal, according to documents filed here in support of a lawsuit.

"Parretti assigned the MGM/UA shares to Cook Islands-based Century Insurance Ltd. on Oct. 29, three days before the studio purchase was consummated, according to an agreement signed by Parretti and contained in the court record. The MGM/UA stock was valued at $17.50 a share, the same price that Parretti later paid investor Kirk Kerkorian and other stockholders.

"Parretti was chairman of Pathe Communications Co. at the time, the company that later merged with MGM/UA. In a letter to Century that has been introduced as court evidence, he wrote: "Pathe declares that it owns clear and unencumbered title to the stock and is capable of making this assignment and of delivering scrip for the stock hereunder."

"If Parretti completed financing for the faded MGM studio with shares he didn't own, as the suit implies, there may have been irregularities in the deal. The case also suggests that Credit Lyonnais Bank Nederland, Parretti's chief lender for the MGM/UA deal, may have financed the final part of the acquisition with an unsecured loan.

"Parretti has denied any wrongdoing in the case. The Century Insurance plan was one of several he allegedly devised to obtain the last block of money needed for the $1.4-billion buyout. The Cook Islands court case suggests that Parretti attempted to put together a series of last-minute deals to complete the purchase as the clock wound down on the payment deadline.

"The file is rife with puzzling references to mysterious European money men, international financing plans and the high-stakes legal manoeuvres of Washington lawyers hired to facilitate matters. Behind the scenes, the agreement with Century unravelled weeks after the acquisition occurred. It appears to have become a key problem in Parretti's continuing struggle to hold the studio together.

"The court file indicates that Parretti met Donald A. Davies, Century's chief executive, in October. The two men struck a deal shortly afterward in which Davies would issue a $175 million insurance bond in return for a $1.75 million fee, according to filings.

"Davies charges that Parretti also agreed to sign over 30 million shares of stock in various companies he owned as collateral, including the 10 million MGM/UA shares, which are interchangeably referred to as MGM-Pathe Communications Co. stock in court documents.

"The insurance bond was issued just before Parretti acquired MGM/UA in November, according to Davies. He contends that Parretti subsequently broke his agreement to pay the $1.75 million fee and that Credit Lyonnais refused to release the shares pledged to Davies.

"Davies sued Credit Lyonnais over the disputed stocks Jan. 15, maintaining that the European banking giant is illegally holding the Parretti shares in an escrow account. The insurer also charges that the stock gives his firm ownership of as much as 35% of MGM-Pathe.

"An MGM-Pathe spokeswoman has called Century's claim "bogus." The studio maintains that Century never posted a legitimate bond on its behalf. In a letter included in the court file, an attorney for Parretti says that there is no valid bond because Century didn't provide satisfactory financial statements, bank references or guarantees from its parent company.

"But the Cook Islands court record contains numerous letters and documents that allude to the bond and the Parretti-controlled shares that allegedly were put up as collateral.

"In a Dec. 24 letter to Davies, Credit Lyonnais Bank Nederland executive Dallis Radamaker wrote that he had "sent an urgent fax to Mr Parretti to obtain an explanation of non-payment of the premium due to Century for the guarantee bond."

"Concurrently, in a letter characterised as "extremely urgent," Radamaker told Parretti that failure to pay the premium "may result in immediate cancellation" of the policy.

"Credit Lyonnais has challenged the jurisdiction of the Cook Islands court to hear the case. And the bank has told Davies that his dispute is properly with Parretti. Patrick Bastin, head of entertainment lending for the Rotterdam-based bank, has declined to comment on the suit.

"Chief Justice Clinton Roper of the Cook Islands, a group of small islands 2,000 miles northeast of New Zealand, has put a restraining order on the shares pending movement in the case.

"Meanwhile, Parretti – who triumphantly declared that he would make the famous MGM lion roar again when he acquired MGM after several delays last fall – finds himself surrounded by hungry predators. Century is seeking delivery of the 30 million total shares in Parretti companies that it says it owns, about $120,000 in damages, court costs and any further relief the judge deems appropriate in the Cook Islands case.

"At the same time, a group of creditors including Century is trying to force Parretti's MGM-Pathe into involuntary bankruptcy in Los Angeles federal court. The petitioners say they are owed more than $10 million. MGM-Pathe has disputed the validity of some of the claims but reportedly is engaged in discussions that could result in an out-of-court settlement.

"A long-delayed 10K annual report from MGM-Pathe, now scheduled to be filed Monday with the Securities and Exchange Commission, also should shed new light on studio finances.

"In his Cook Islands affidavit, Davies maintains that Parretti contacted him about the insurance bond in the final days before the deal was set to close. There is no explanation of how Parretti came to Davies, but people close to the two men say that they met in New York.

"Davies said his company had never written a completion guarantee for a takeover bid, even though it had "substantial experience in insurance."

"People familiar with the deal have said Credit Lyonnais, which already had hundreds of millions of dollars in loans committed to Parretti on the MGM/UA deal, was reluctant to loan any more to Parretti without an insurance bond. The bond was to guarantee sales of future television and movie rights negotiated with various companies.

"Time was very short to complete the deal, Davies' affidavit states. Parretti had to close it by the end of October or "lose the whole deal and many millions already spent." Davies said Century agreed to write the bond in return for three blocks of stock that were to be held in lieu of payment. Parretti also promised him a lot more insurance business, Davies said.

"An agreement letter in the court file, dated Oct. 29, identifies the Parretti blocks of stock assigned to Century as 10 million Pathe Communications Co. shares, valued at $50 million; 10 million shares of Melia International NV, a Dutch travel company, with a value of $60 million, and the 10 million shares of MGM/UA, valued at $175 million. A notation on the letter said MGM/UA's name would be changed to MGM-Pathe Communications Co. after the merger.

"Parretti executed three separate agreements signing the stock over to Century as "tangible security," according to Davies. The insurance man said the deal was completed on Oct. 29, while he was staying at Parretti's Beverly Hills home.

"Davies said he became worried when he didn't receive his promised fee after the MGM/UA deal closed, especially since Century faced a possible liability of $175 million. Davies said Credit Lyonnais eventually told him it was launching its own investigation of Parretti's finances.

"In February, after repeated conversations with Credit Lyonnais proved fruitless, Davies contacted Continental Transfer Co., the registrar for the shares, and said he had serious doubts as to the validity of the Pathe share certificates, the court record shows.

" 'From my personal observation of Parretti, I am convinced that he has little regard for regulators or legal procedures if they stand in his way,' Davies said in his affidavit. 'The bank has an unscrupulous customer in Parretti who is a practiced if not talented liar. . .He has a primitive approach to documents, which he does not like. He shreds them and did so in my presence at his Los Angeles home, to my amazement.'

"Michael Cieply reported from Rarotonga and Alan Citron from Los Angeles."

The scrap was attracting the attention of a New Zealand barrister living in Hong Kong, David Gunson, who had at one time been Century's Hong Kong legal adviser. Now Gunson had become an investigator, and would later provide crucial assistance to Chris Dickie as the two men joined forces to attack what was rapidly becoming a global manhunt.

Century Insurance had been established by Australian insurance salesman Donald Andrew Davies in 1990. According to investigative work by award-winning journalist Frances O'Sullivan, writing in the *National Business Review*, "those who have dealt with Mr Davies. . .say he is nothing but a coldblooded fraud artist."

"When Brisbane-based Don Davies wanted a company to sell so-called tax free insurance bonds," she wrote, "European Pacific dusted off one of its numerous shelf companies for him and renamed it Century Insurance.

"A pro-forma balance sheet was constructed to satisfy the Cook Islands Monetary Board that Century Insurance had the necessary US$100,000 in assets to register as an offshore insurance company based in the tax-haven.

"But the US$100,000 in assets were clearly duds. And even before Century Insurance had got its Cook Islands licence, a financial planner was on the road among the farming communities north-east of Perth peddling insurance policies based on a glossy but baseless false brochure."

Century offered investment policies to ordinary Australians, sucking them in with an offer of a 30% return in the first year. But when Century collapsed in 1991 in the wake of the MGM deal, it took with it the life-savings of 65 small investors who'd plugged A$2.2 million into the company.

Those investors began legal action, and David Gunson was one of the lawyers on the case.

As O'Sullivan writes, investigators quickly found Century was involved in a lot more than insurance fraud.

"Don Davies had bigger pretensions for Century Insurance than simply that of issuing small-time insurance bonds. On a trip to the United States later in 1990 he met up with members of the fabled Knights Of Malta and investigated a proposal to finance the society's New York headquarters."

O'Sullivan talked of Davies "hobnobbing" with the Knights, and staying "care of Prince Arnaldo Petrucci Di Siena". The US$80 million property financing plan raised some eyebrows back in New Zealand where prestigious insurance companies linked to the Century scandal, and acting "as custodian of the company's assets", were seeking more information about the deal.

"We would. . .wish to have further assurances on the bona-fide's and connection of the bondholder to the Knights Of St John," wrote the NZ company executive. "The only connection I can see, so far, is a letter from the bondholder in his capacity as a Grand Master of the Knights Of Malta, the letter being addressed to Century Insurance.

"The letterhead has the name Knights Of Malta but there does not seem to be an address. From what address is the Grand Master writing? Without wishing to tar all princes with the same brush, the last one I dealt with turned out to be a crook."

"Through the Knights Of Malta," continues O'Sullivan, "he met Italian financier Giancarlo Parretti who was having trouble financing his US$1.3 billion buyout of Metro-Goldwyn-Meyer from US billionaire Kirk Kerkorian.

"The Italian businessman had managed to secure most of his funding from French bank Credit Lyonnaise but ran into problems getting the full amount, which was outside the bank's lending limits.

"Mr Davies had a solution. He and his lawyer structured a creative financing deal with Credit Lyonnais to get around Mr Parretti's cash needs and keep the full exposure off the bank's balance sheet. *

"Century Insurance, which had paid-up capital of only US$1, issued a performance guarantee bond to Credit Lyonnaise for US$225 million. Mr Parretti got his cash and the bank held on to some MGM stock as security.

"Century Insurance later dipped out on promised fees when Credit Lyonnaise seized control of MGM. Mr Parretti is now facing criminal charges in the US."

All of this was happening contemporaneously with Chris Dickie's bloodstock and film investigations, and appeared to be unconnected. Indeed, if

---

* There have been allegations that a similar technique was used in NZ in 1989 when Fay Richwhite purportedly took its borrowing from the Government controlled Bank Of New Zealand over the billion dollar mark. To hide the exposure from Reserve Bank officials, the BNZ insisted that $400 million worth of loans to the Fay Richwhite group – for use in a series of tax deals – went through a series of front companies nominally controlled by lawfirm Kensington Swan.

Dickie saw any news coverage of the MGM scandal at the time it would have washed right over him like drops in a rainstorm.

And yet, years down the track as he began to close in, the events taking place in Hollywood, France and the Cook Islands would come to affect him too. More to the point, his subsequent involvement in the MGM/Century insurance maelstrom would eventually provide him with the most crucial breakthrough in his entire investigation.

CHAPTER 20

Blackmailing The IRD

"Two households, both alike in dignity,
In fair Verona where we lay our scene,
From ancient grudge break to new mutiny,
Where civil blood makes civil hands unclean."
– WILLIAM SHAKESPEARE, 1564–1616, *ROMEO AND JULIET*

It was now getting close to Christmas, 1991, and at the Inland Revenue Department's Auckland investigation centre the mood couldn't have been any gloomier if the Grim Reaper himself was stalking the corridors.

The news that Paul Carran had just quit Russell McVeagh didn't engender more than a brief flutter of interest. In almost the twinkling of an eye, Carran departed. Friday, September 27, 1991. News of that had nevertheless travelled fast, with Chris Dickie labelling it "a most significant development".

"Russell McVeagh got rid of Paul Carran very early on," recalled bloodstock investor Pat Hadlee. "When he disappeared I thought that Russell McVeagh was conceding there was something there by letting him go – I couldn't understand why people didn't pick up on that then.

"Our press are so frigging useless in this country! If he'd been anywhere else where there was any sort of a live press, they would have said 'hang on, why have Russell McVeagh got rid of this protagonist of the bloodstock schemes?'"

Carran himself appeared to be cracking under the strain in the lead-up to his departure.

He had called another clandestine meeting with Chris Kirkham and Mitchell McLeish, this time in his car. The glory days for Russell McVeagh's former golden boy were clearly over. To McLeish, he looked like a wreck, and terrified.

"Things have become really serious," he told the two men. "My partners have been grilling me for hours. They've forbidden me from talking to Ed Bendelow in the Channel Islands." He paused for a moment, looking away. When he met their gaze again McLeish could discern a haunted look in Carran's eyes. "I've also been forbidden from speaking to either of you."

"For Christ's sake, man!" said McLeish, "there's got to be a way through this funny business with Coolmore Stud. Horses don't just bloody disappear!"

After the meeting, McLeish took matters into his own hands and briefed a lawyer, Paul Davison – son of winebox commissioner Sir Ronald Davison.

Davison had taken up Mitchell McLeish's concerns with Russell McVeagh.

Whatever events were now taking place within the mega-firm at the end of 1991, it was serious.

Serious enough for two senior Russell McVeagh lawyers, Laurie Mayne and Chris Browne, to fly to Christchurch and meet Mitchell McLeish at his half-million dollar mansion. They took a tape recorder with them.

McLeish felt he owed loyalty to Russell McVeagh in their battle with Chris Dickie because of his work for them over the years, and told Mayne and Browne probably even more than he'd told his own lawyer.

He told them of the problems Zorasong was having with the transfer of bloodstock from Coolmore, and couldn't believe "that a million pound company is being thrown away like this!"

His annoyance was heightened by the fact that Coolmore had taken two of Securelaunch's best mares and sold them to some of the stud's associates for what Chris Kirkham had described as "very low prices contrived by Coolmore.

"Coolmore retained the funds against expenses. It still refused to transfer the stallion shares or pay any cash which it was holding from those shares to Securelaunch Ltd.

"The two mares," said Kirkham in a memo, "went on to leave foals which made millions at the sales, in which Zorasong Ltd/Securelaunch Ltd would have shared."

But, as he reeled off Zorasong and Securelaunch's woes, McLeish didn't know who now had control of Zorasong's affairs. For some time he'd been trying to persuade Russell McVeagh partner Paul Carran to sue Coolmore stud. In McLeish's eyes, Zorasong was a client of Russell McVeagh's, but for some reason he couldn't find the magic switch that would make the lawfirm take instructions from him regarding Zorasong. Nobody seemed to be paying any attention, as Zorasong became a pawn in a larger game.

Russell McVeagh partners did not know about the private dealings of Kirkham, Carran and McLeish until late September 1991. When they found out, as a result of McLeish alerting them, it is his opinion that they took control of Zorasong and Securelaunch.

Meanwhile, Tony Molloy was sniffing around the tax haven bank accounts and lawyers' offices of Jersey, in the Channel Islands. He'd detoured whilst en route to exhibit his St. Nesbit wine in Germany, and his scouting mission in relation to *Merry Christmas Mr Lawrence* was creating waves.

Back in Auckland at the time, the nightmare was getting worse for Carran. Not only was he still licking his wounds after his departure from Russell McVeagh, but now he received a communication at his home, telling him where Molloy was.

In a fax tabled at the Winebox Inquiry, dated October 10, 1991, Carran's Jersey agent, Edmund Bendelow revealed all was not well in the tax haven.

"I was telephoned today by Nigel Harris who is an English solicitor in practice in Jersey. Mr Harris confirmed to me that he is retained by a number of individuals who have lost a tremendous amount of money 'due to your activities'. He also informed me that you had been sacked from your firm last Friday."

The slap in the face delivered, Bendelow continued.

"Mr Harris then invited me to attend a meeting at his offices at which a New Zealand barrister [Molloy] would be present, and I would exchange information which would be to both our advantage, and may well be useful to me in recouping the large amount of money that ANZ Grindlays Trust Corporation is owed."

If that paragraph didn't send Paul Carran reaching for the migraine pills, the next few lines should have.

"It was clear to me that Mr Harris was on an initial 'fishing' expedition and I feel fairly certain that the partners in New Zealand may well seek the assistance of the Jersey Courts.

"As we have discussed in the past in relation to these particular clients, it is possible for the Jersey Courts to convene a Commission Rogatoire at which I can be required to give evidence under oath to a pre-agreed series of questions.

"Alternatively, we have our Evidencing [sic] Foreign Proceedings Law, which can lead to a Jersey resident being cross-examined in the Royal Court as part of a foreign proceeding."

The final sting came in the tail, however. Bendelow's trust operation was now owed serious cash for its work administering Securelaunch and Zorasong, money that those companies couldn't pay because Coolmore Stud wasn't paying out the dividends it should have on the bloodstock Zorasong and Securelaunch owned.

Bendelow made it clear to Carran that this overdue payment issue was top of his mind as he decided which way to jump.

"I would be grateful if you would, as a matter of urgency, liaise with the client and obtain definitive advice as to whether I can cooperate with any further enquiries for information in the absence of a Court order, or [whether] it may be possible to settle all outstanding financial matters in Jersey and possibly transfer the administration of the relevant entities."

Evidently somebody found a way to reassure Bendelow, because he would still be playing hard to get when Chris Dickie went hunting him a year later.

On all sides of the investigation, people were digging in to their respective offensive and defensive positions, and information on the offshore companies remained as scarce as hen's teeth. What Dickie didn't know, wasn't going to hurt. Well, not yet.

Little did anyone know that within less than a year Dickie would stumble across a treasure trove, and allege in the High Court that Russell McVeagh had compounded the fraud by withholding documents.

The discussions between McLeish and Mayne and Browne from Russell McVeagh were frequent. The wily Irish breeder noted early on that the two lawyers appeared to squirm whenever Zorasong or Securelaunch were mentioned. It amused McLeish no end to mention them "as often as possible".

The carrot for McLeish to cooperate with the lawfirm was a promise that they would help him with his Zorasong problem with Coolmore after the NZ bloodstock cases ended. It would prove to be an illusory carrot.

But, in the IRD's Auckland office, it was movies, not bloodstock, that occupied their attention. As the Winebox Inquiry learnt, Assistant Controller, Investigations, Denese Latimer was coming under pressure to do a deal on the movies from her superior at head office, Tony Bouzaid, as she recorded in a diary note.

"He considers Clews' 25 percent offer reasonable."

Latimer pointed out to Bouzaid that two of the films involved income that had not been declared, four involved circular funding arrangements or what she described as "round robin" evidence, two were on an IRD black list and "one had been ascertained to be fraud."

Bouzaid replied that despite all of that, he "still thought a package deal would be best for the department."

One of the big discoveries by the Auckland tax unit was that one of the documents in the *Merry Christmas Mr Lawrence* case appeared to be fraudulent.

With information supplied to her a few months earlier by Dickie that indicated up to US$2.9 million had been funnelled into a Channel Islands bank account, Latimer had taken the issue up directly with tax lawyer Geoff Clews.

Confronted with the claims that millions of dollars in film income had not been declared, the Russell McVeagh partner had presented a document to the IRD indicating the money didn't belong to the special partners and therefore didn't need to be declared.

It was a document post-dating the investors' original subscription which signed away their rights to the income. If the investors weren't entitled to the money legally, it could hardly be taxable income in their hands.

With this new piece of late evidence being offered by Clews, the IRD had no choice but to accept it and ignore the undeclared income issue when it came to continuing the settlement discussions. But Denese Latimer and her team remained suspicious.

The tax unit sent the document presented by Clews to leading forensic document examiner John West, and received a shock. "His preliminary response," testified Latimer, "was that it couldn't have been written in 1982 because of the print." It was a preliminary response because West needed more time to access police forensic databases.

West's evidence and further inquiries by the IRD established not only that the document appeared dodgy forensically, but that the person who allegedly witnessed the signatures didn't even work for the organisation concerned at the time, and wasn't even in the country on the date of signing.

Head office administrator Tony Bouzaid dismissed West's evidence, telling Latimer in a November 22 phone call it was "a pity Mr West couldn't have been more helpful".

The allegedly forged document purported to assign away rights to income from *Merry Christmas Mr Lawrence*. John Nash had relied on this document to knock aside Latimer's assertions about undeclared income. Don't forget, this is also the document that allegedly signs away the investors' rights to the money too.

"Mr Nash advised me," said Bouzaid, "that there had been an assignment of rights and that that income didn't belong to the special partnership.

"The advice I was receiving from Mr Nash was that Mrs Latimer and Mr May were not interpreting the documents correctly, as the rights had been assigned and accordingly the partnership had no entitlement to the receipts in question."

Unlike her bosses, Latimer had the nous to be suspicious of a document that conveniently turned up just in the nick of time with all the right answers. It's the ability to think laterally and maintain a healthy scepticism that differentiates good investigators from average ones.

As for Bouzaid, he went on to tell the inquiry that he took some comfort when he heard Geoff Clews dismissing West's initial forensic findings.

"The position is," suggested Latimer's lawyer John Haigh QC, "that Mrs Latimer raised concerns, including the West tentative views. Mr Clews, representing the partnership, had told you there was nothing in it, and so you went ahead with the settlement concluding the *Mr Lawrence* transaction. Is that a fair summary?"

"He had conveyed that. . .yes."

But in my opinion Bouzaid should have been on notice to the possibility of fraud, because Denese Latimer spelt out just how weak Geoff Clews' case was in a memo to Bouzaid on November 20, 1991.

"An interim reply from Mr West," she wrote, "indicates that his best guess is that the document [dated 1983] could not have been prepared prior to 1985 based on the print type.

"By way of a note, *Mr Clews confirmed* [author's emphasis] at the meeting on the 8/11/91 *that the document was prepared by his firm in 1983*, but this appears unlikely as the type setting bears no resemblance to similar dated documents prepared in their office."

When Latimer wanted to chase up the undeclared income issue further, Bouzaid allegedly said he wasn't prepared to wait any longer.

"I told him we had just received information that Charlesbay was the agent for Bonningdale, which brought it [responsibility] back to Carran in Russell McVeagh," her diary records.

"He said that it wouldn't make any difference – we wouldn't get behind the nominee companies and he didn't think that McVeagh Fleming would be successful anyway, as no one ever was. . .the legal firms would be very upset if they thought that these nominee companies could be got behind."*

Well, Tony Bouzaid may have been prepared to lie on his back and wave his

---

* In what in my opinion is a major scandal, the inquiry later heard that at the time Bouzaid was saying this, the IRD head office was already holding a tax haven document linking Paul Carran to a range of offshore entities. Bouzaid had enough evidence to justify further investigation into possible Inland Revenue Act offences, but he was telling Latimer to drop it.

legs in the air in a gesture of submission, but history would show he was very wrong in his assessment of McVeagh Fleming's – and others – abilities to root out information about who really controlled the tax-haven nominee companies.

Take this document, now in the possession of the author, backgrounding the collapse of Zorasong and Securelaunch in 1990-91.

"The successful operation of the venture relied heavily on the stallion income," wrote the document's author. "This income was dependable and not subject to auction fluctuations.

"The stallion selection for our mares was based on this income, so that when Coolmore withheld this income from Securelaunch, on the grounds that it was not rightfully theirs, it put the company in an impossible position.

"We had mares not being bred at all. We could not pay our bankers or any of our running costs, resulting in the loss of a mare by way of a lien. We have subsequently lost all income from the mares and stallions plus all potential and future income.

"All of this could and should have been avoided, had Deloittes in Hong Kong [the nominal owners] instructed [lawyers] to pursue Coolmore. Deloittes could not do this as they had not received instructions from New Zealand. Carran was, I'm sure, still a partner of Russell McVeagh through all of this."

Another document was just as explicit:

"I do not recall discussing which company would hold the [blood] stock as this was part of Paul [Carran's] job. For example, I found out quite recently that the partnership's first purchase – 30 percent of the mare *Catopetl* – was originally held in a company called Chary Holdings Ltd, which has some connection with Securelaunch Ltd or Kanasawa Ltd.

"I did know that our stock was to be held in an offshore company and that Paul Carran would be in control of it, and at some time in 1986 Zorasong became 'the vehicle'. It just seemed to happen."

If Bouzaid wanted documentary evidence as to the state of mind of the participants and their knowledge of New Zealand control, he only had to know where to dig. Which is precisely what Tony Molloy and Chris Dickie were meanwhile doing, on location, in Britain, Ireland and Jersey.

Molloy, one of the Commonwealth's pre-eminent tax lawyers, knew how the Channel Islands tax haven worked first-hand. Over the years he'd done quite a bit of work for wealthy English gentry moving their money around, particularly when some of them retired to live in New Zealand. As part of marrying the tax requirements of different jurisdictions, Molloy had worked alongside Jersey entities more than once.

"Because of that, I got to know some Jersey lawyers. We knew bloody well that since they were running offshore companies which we'd tracked down to Jersey and Hong Kong, I knew how they operated and I knew that they would have extensive files, so we basically just started snooping.

"We found out who their lawyers were, we got it from an English company search. Once we knew the name of Zorasong we managed to get a company search which led us to those Jersey solicitors."

But there was another clue that helped Molloy and Dickie pinpoint the identity of Ed Bendelow's Jersey lawfirm Ogier & Le Cornu, which was being used by Paul Carran to set up the various shell companies and blind trusts masking the various deals.

Carran knew how to charge! And to substantiate his hefty bills he sometimes produced itemised lists of out of pocket expenses: things like toll calls and faxes. I say "sometimes", because on other occasions Carran wrote: "You have requested our estimate of the allocation of our fee to the establishment of the special partnership, Buckingham Enterprises Ltd & Company and the prospectus for it.

"Although we kept no separate time records between this and the transactions for acquisition of bloodstock and general advice, we estimate that a correct apportionment would be say $10,000."

During the process of legal discovery, McVeagh Fleming was given some of Carran's charge sheets. "Russell McVeagh had huge disbursement charges in their computer printouts relating to this Jersey lawfirm, and many, many international toll calls which again turned out to be the fax number of this Jersey lawfirm, so that's how we started off," explained Molloy.

"So I just went over there to snoop initially, and to see what available mechanisms there were for us to get orders that might help us to prise the thing open.

"It was a funny kind of community, really basically involved in international money-laundering and so on, although the people who were there doing the legal work were people you would regard as quite 'upright' people. They were making the assumption, of course, that everything coming through there was legitimate, investment stuff.

"The international drug trade has of course really only ballooned recently, so I'm sure that in the early days much of what went through Jersey was pretty much legitimate.

"But if you look at what was going on here in New Zealand, with these rorts that were tax avoidance schemes – if you like – just insofar as the New Zealand onshore component was concerned, but what made them into tax evasion in my view was the offshore loop which hid it from the revenue authorities.

"They must know that there's a vast amount of that going on, but they take the attitude that they will treat everyone as a gentleman unless they've got reason to believe otherwise. And I suppose, when you're dealing with clients, it would be very hard to run a practice here, if you thought prima facie that every client was a crook, so I've got sympathy for them."

After meeting Jersey solicitor Nigel Harris to discuss his options, and giving Paul Carran and Ed Bendelow no small fright in the process, Molloy slipped out of Jersey and back to England.

"I went straight back to London, to Lincoln's Inn. They're very good to me there, they let me use their library – I think it dates back to the reign of Henry II, a lovely old place – and I went in there, bought some legal stationery and spent a couple of days in the Lincoln's Inn library just drafting up the Order for Justice, which is what they call the initial pleading in Jersey."

Across town, in a City of London law office, solicitors at Simmons & Simmons, hired by McVeagh Fleming to dig hard and fast, were coming up with the goods.

"The original shareholders of Securelaunch Ltd were Olec One Ltd and Olec Two Ltd. However, we have not been able to determine the identity of the shareholders of Olec One Ltd and Olec Two Ltd because both companies are registered in Jersey."

Both were, in fact, shelf companies set up by Ed Bendelow's lawfirm, Ogier & Le Cornu. Olec.

Back in Auckland, Denese Latimer told Tony Bouzaid she too could go digging in Britain, by arranging for a company office search in London, to reinforce the evidence that Chris Dickie had provided, but Bouzaid was blunt. "No! Settle."

But it wasn't just *Merry Christmas Mr Lawrence* that significant evidence was emerging about.

On the Primula partnership, and the mystery involving the unproduced episodes of *The Adventures Of The Little Prince*, Bouzaid revealed what I consider to be utter IRD naivety regarding the elements of deceptive conduct.

"There was something like, say, 20 videos to be made," recalled Bouzaid at the Winebox Inquiry. "And they never made – they never completed the series. Mrs Latimer was worried about the situation. She said, well, I've got some, I think, hearsay evidence from the United States, that they weren't all made. And I think it might have been – let's say 15 had been made."

Let's stop Bouzaid there for a moment. Firstly, you can see he's not briefed on the detail regarding *The Little Prince*. Secondly, the IRD's Auckland office had spoken directly to Jameson Brewer, the man making the videos. His evidence saying the extra episodes were never made was hardly "hearsay".

"The advice I received from Mr Nash," continued Bouzaid, "which brought me back to real attention, was: so what if they haven't all been made? This is an arms-length transaction.

"This is like going and buying a lot of timber from a timber merchant and then you find that they don't actually deliver it all to you. There might be a civil thing, but it is not a tax issue.

"If someone enters into a bad deal and they have signed a contract which says that they incur all of that expenditure well, then, that's the law. That's the deduction they get."

Which ignores the fact that the bad deal was not the failure of Brewer to deliver, but that Carran and Kirkham had presented a contract to the investors and the IRD which it appears they knew did not reflect the true deal or the true monies involved.

But despite Bouzaid's haziness on the witness stand, he had been briefed, once.

A memo from Denese Latimer to Bouzaid on November 20, 1991, sets out her concerns in Primula.

"It is clear from his letter that Mr Clews does not wish the department to continue with its enquiries," wrote Latimer, "but has acknowledged a recognition of documentary shortcomings."

This acknowledgment, she said, was reflected by Clews no longer demanding only a 25% disallowance of the claimed expenses, but generously agreeing to let the IRD disallow 33.33%.

"The documentary shortcomings," she continued, "can be described as follows:

- A purchase of rights agreement clearly states that 20 completed episodes in the TV series *The Little Prince* would be purchased by the partnership from Dawn Hill Ltd* (Hong Kong). However, this agreement does not give the names of the episodes.

- The distribution agreement between the partnership and Thomas Horton Ltd (USA) includes a list showing the names of the 20 episodes purchased.

- It has been confirmed. . .through Mr Clews that only 8 episodes were in fact purchased, and they provided a list of these. Only two of the eight were included on the list in the Distribution Agreement, so the question becomes as to how the partnership acquired the other six episodes and why the two agreements both refer to the purchase of 20 episodes.

"As a result of information supplied to us by the US producer," said Latimer, "the following has been revealed:

- Only 26 episodes in total were ever made by the producer.

- 18 of these episodes were never sold to the NZ interests.

- Only 8 episodes were sold to a supposedly NZ party.

- The rights in these 8 episodes were sold by the producer to Chary Holdings Ltd, a Channel Islands company, who was represented during discussions by Paul Carran and Chris Kirkham.

- The producer thought that Chary Holdings Ltd represented the NZ parties. He has not heard of Primula.

- Of the 20 named episodes listed in the Distribution Agreement 18 had already been produced and marketed prior to the formation of the NZ special partnership and were not for sale.

- When signing the sale agreement with Chary Holdings Ltd Paul Carran was the person representing that party.

- The 18 episodes plus the 8 episodes sold to Chary Holdings Ltd equal the total of the episodes made.

- The maximum received by the producer for each of the eight episodes was US$5,000.

---

* A company the inquiry heard was linked to Paul Carran.

"Mr Kirkham was interviewed and he confirmed that he and Paul Carran had discussions with both the producer and Thomas Horton regarding the series.

"He was under the impression that he was acting for the partnership but as he was only involved in the signing of the Distribution Agreement he assumes that Paul Carran is the only person who can explain how Primula acquired the 6 episodes from Chary Holdings Ltd and why the other two agreements refer to episodes that were not available for sale.

"At this point of time Mr Paul Carran has not been interviewed.

"The total NRL [non-recourse loan] was for US$1,300,000 and it was used towards paying for the series, the total cost of which was US$1,380,000.

"*The balance of US$80,000* was paid from the investors contributions and *would appear to be the actual amount paid*, including costs, as borne out by the information provided by the producer. [author's emphasis]

"There has to be a link," continued Denese Latimer, "between the Channel Islands company Chary Holdings Ltd and the Hong Kong company Dawn Hill Ltd, and the common denominator appears to be Paul Carran who is, in fact, Russell McVeagh.

"Mr Clews is also part of Russell McVeagh and therefore he is wanting to negotiate himself (his firm) out of having to provide information in relation to enquiries that have not at this point of time been completed by the department. . .one can only ask why?"

So that was the weight of the evidence confronting Bouzaid when he closed down investigations into Primula as well.

In a conversation with IRD head office solicitor, Angela Satterthwaite, Latimer mentioned the action that Dickie was taking in the Channel Islands and that it might be useful to the IRD "because Chary Holdings was a common factor" in several of the film deals. Latimer's diary records that Satterthwaite "bit my head off and told me not to talk to McVeagh Fleming or else the Commissioner would get into a lot of trouble."

A few days later Latimer found herself being ordered to sign an agreement not to prosecute partners in the lawfirm Russell McVeagh, and not to investigate them further.

The full story of what took place has only emerged as a result of the Winebox Inquiry which, in 1995, was rocked by the following revelations.

On November 27, 1991, Geoff Clews wrote to Latimer, with a draft of the proposed settlement offer. At issue was the amount of expenditure involved in making the movies which the IRD was prepared to allow as a deductible expense. In the IRD's eyes much of the claimed expenditure was bogus, existing only on paper and funded only by paper loans.

Section three of the Clews letter specified that this would be a "full and final settlement of the tax affairs of [special] partners arising from their participation in any one or more of the Partnerships."

He then set out the specific terms. Rather than a full investigation to determine exactly whether avoidance or evasion was involved, and to calculate the exact amount of the tax owing, the IRD and Clews had effectively tossed a coin – reach a negotiated settlement based on guesstimates. It might have been that 90 or even a hundred percent of the claimed expenditure was bogus, but the agreement was nowhere near that tough.

Of the 16 films involved, the IRD disallowed only 25 percent* of the claimed expenditure on five of them, 30 percent on six films, 33 percent on three movies, and disallowed 45 percent of the expense claims on one movie. On the last, involving a partnership called Five Miles High, the department disallowed the full 100 percent of expense claims.

The disputed expenditure on these movies totalled some $38 million, but only $12 million would actually be disallowed under this agreement. A further $59 million went untouched.

Clause 3.2 of Clews' draft contained a condition that directly impacted on the *Merry Christmas Mr Lawrence* investigation. Chris Dickie had already, of course, passed on to Latimer and May the information about the missing millions sitting in the Channel Islands, but clause 3.2 prevented any further scrutiny of that issue.

"The [IRD] Commissioner acknowledges that for the purpose of settling the tax affairs of the partners in those partnerships which he has suggested derived income which has not been returned, he is no longer pursuing such suggestion."

In other words: even if the IRD thought tax fraud was involved – ie. income had been hidden – it would no longer follow such avenues of inquiry. But there was an even bigger sting in the document.

Clause 4.5 provided a special deal that was only available to members of the Russell McVeagh lawfirm who had invested in the movie *Prisoners*. The special offer was not available to the other investors in the movie, and Clews was demanding that the great deal given his Russell McVeagh colleagues was not to be disclosed to the other investors.

"The agreement for settlement with partners in *Prisoners* is limited. The offer is to be extended by the Commissioner only to those persons whose names are set out on the list attached as schedule 2.

"The terms of the offer are to be relayed in a way which makes it clear that the offer should remain confidential from other partners in *Prisoners*."

And why should it remain confidential from other partners in the same movie? Because the Russell McVeagh lawyers were getting a financial advantage from the IRD not offered to other investors in the same movie.

This deal was being offered by the IRD to the Russell McVeagh partners "in consideration of those persons [the Russell McVeagh lawyers] not financially supporting or supporting further (as the case may be) the litigation" in the *Endeavour* proceedings.

---

* Technically, the IRD was actually disallowing percentages of the non-recourse loans used to pay for the alleged expenditure, rather than disallowing the expense claims themselves. But for all intents and purposes, they are the same thing.

According to one IRD document tabled at the inquiry, Clews was acting for nine colleagues from within his lawfirm and promoter John Gow.

"When asked the reason for linking this specific film settlement with the [*Endeavour*] case," Latimer wrote in the memo, "he advised that it was a means of additional leverage."

She also noted that the *Endeavour* case "has nothing to do with the individual partners" represented by Clews.

Denese Latimer was in no doubt about what was taking place when she read the proposed settlement document. She called it "blackmail".

"I had been told by Clews," testified Latimer, "that Russell McVeagh was funding it – that they pulled the strings.

"Clews was blackmailing us, by saying if you want out of [*Endeavour*] you will give in on [*Prisoners*]." *

The Russell McVeagh lawyers were prepared to bankroll John Barnett in his litigation against the IRD, even though they were not parties to the litigation, if they didn't get a sweet deal of their own from the tax department.

The Tatum O'Neal movie had already been settled, or the IRD thought it had, with a substantial 60 percent of expense claims disallowed by the tax inspectors. Most of the investors in *Prisoners* had accepted the 60 percent penalty, but not the Russell McVeagh partners who'd invested in it. They wanted something better and Clews was the boy to get it for them.

In the list of movies settled, the well-connected and deep-pocketed Russell McVeagh partners in *Prisoners* only had 45 percent of their expenses disallowed, compared with the 60 percent everyone else had paid.

But it was a promise not to prosecute certain parties that raised the most controversy about the agreement.

Clause 4.11 of the deal between the IRD and Geoff Clews is arguably illegal and unenforceable, but nevertheless, it was part of the deal they struck.

"No partner accepting the Commissioner [of Revenue's] offer to settle that partner's tax liability arising from participation in one or more of the partnerships shall be subject to any impost of penal tax or to prosecution.

"This agreement shall apply notwithstanding any request by the Commissioner of that partner for a personal explanation of any alleged discrepancy or any advice to that partner that his case is to be considered under the penal provisions of the Income Tax Act 1976 or otherwise."

To Denese Latimer and other observers, it was staggering. A special financial deal for a small group of lawyers, an amnesty from penal tax or prosecution, and a promise by the IRD never to re-open the investigations.

---

* Clews also allegedly threatened to go over Latimer's head if she didn't agree to his terms. "If we were not prepared to continue the discussions," she testified, "he would have to go to a higher power. . .the Commissioner, the Minister of Revenue and the Minister of Finance." Clews denied making such a blatant threat. In a form of damage control, Fay Richwhite's lawyers tried to get Latimer to agree that it wasn't blackmail, merely "negotiating leverage".

Latimer knew she could not sign this agreement. She sought advice from senior IRD solicitor Michael Scott.

"I advised her that in the circumstances she should not sign the agreement because I also believed it was inappropriate," said Scott as he became the first IRD officer to break ranks and testify against head office at the Winebox Inquiry. "The settlement appeared far too low, and purported to benefit unnamed persons.

"Mrs Latimer had been requested three times to sign the settlement letter by Messrs [John] Nash, Bouzaid and [IRD lawyer Angela] Satterthwaite and refused to do so.

"Eventually, as I understand it, Mr Bouzaid signed the settlement letter agreement on behalf of the Inland Revenue Department."

When Latimer refused to sign the final version of the agreement on December 4, 1991, she had been rung by Satterthwaite, who told her to get on with it.

Later the same day John Nash – the man who'd blown the *Endeavour* investigation in the first place – phoned and told Latimer that she wasn't aware of the background circumstances, and that she should "put the past in the past".

On December 6, Geoff Clews rang and wanted to know what was happening, and that was followed by a phone call from Tony Bouzaid.

"By this stage," Latimer told the Winebox Inquiry, "there had been quite a deal of aggravation between myself and Messrs Bouzaid, Nash and Ms Satterthwaite over the settlement letter. I was still refusing to sign it.

"When Mr Bouzaid rang, I told him that I had given the matter a great deal of thought and refused to sign the letter. Mr Bouzaid said that he supposed he would have to sign it, which I accepted."

The IRD's Assistant Controller of Investigations said she felt the deal was unduly favourable to the taxpayers concerned, but spelt out other reasons for her disquiet as well.

"I accepted the reasons for settlement in relation to films in general, ie. logistic problems – so many films, so many taxpayers, insufficient resources – and accepted that the individual taxpayers gained a tax advantage. But they [the individuals] were, in the main, unaware of the structuring of the schemes. I believed that the promoters were, however, in a different category.

"The settlement gave the promoters, and other interested parties, both known and unknown, an amnesty from investigation, up until 1990. I considered this to be quite improper and even more so bearing in mind that the majority of films reviewed fell within the 1980-1986 period."

The Inland Revenue Department boasts "It's our job to be fair", but critics have argued that the special deal breached not only ethics but the law. A 1966 court ruling was quoted at the inquiry to reinforce the point.

"It is of the highest public importance," opined Justice Turner, "that in the administration of such statutes, every taxpayer shall be treated exactly alike. No concession being made to one to which another is not equally entitled."

Justice Turner noted that in cases where the particular statute gave the

Commissioner of Revenue express powers of discretion, obviously he could exercise that discretion, but not in any other circumstance.

"He must, with Olympian impartiality hold the scales between taxpayer and Crown, giving to no one any latitude not given to others."

Denese Latimer told the inquiry that those were the principles the IRD should have been operating under.

"Do you believe that the [film] settlement reflects that principle?" asked Brian Henry, the lawyer for Winston Peters.

"No, I don't," replied the witness. She explained that, as she saw it, the IRD had been prepared to overlook possible fraud involving the promoters of the movies, in return for the IRD's own misdemeanours in the *Endeavour* litigation being overlooked. In essence, the IRD was trying to make a right out of two wrongs.

As the inquiry learnt, Bouzaid's position was plain. His reasons for settling included that:

- the films dated back to the early 1980's
- the department had pumped "many person-years" into these investigations without a final result
- the IRD's resources couldn't cope with a court fight over the 16 films
- you can fool all of the public some of the time, or, in IRD-speak: "The public believe the Commissioner succeeded on these film cases because it is well known that investors did not get their deductions allowed – the original news is more important than news a long time later whereby some people will hear that people [actually] did get a fair amount of their deduction"
- "as an organisation we must get out of the film investigations. . .there are other, bigger discrepancies awaiting our detection"
- "you two [Latimer and May] both need a break – you have worked on these cases for something like six years"
- "These film cases were complex, made extensive use of tax havens, were difficult to investigate because of the non-availability of records and lack of assistance provided by promoters and advisers. I am confident that both of you have done very well, along with John, on what was a difficult exercise in terms of our knowledge of industry and our lack of legal resources throughout the enquiry"
- "The recent resignation of Mr Paul Carran, from Russell McVeagh, is also successful [for the IRD] in that he now disappears from that firm, which restricts that firm's ability to promote similar types of schemes and one assumes that has not been good for that firm's goodwill"
- "The Minister has asked for a report – there could be a damaging element here, as all the good work that has been done could be adequately portrayed in a brief report"
- "Further, in relation to the Minister, the department is under scrutiny as

regards section 17 and our inquiry powers, hence any issue relating to criticism of the department's use of powers. . .could exacerbate an already unfortunate situation" *

In addition, Bouzaid had worked out that the ongoing film investigations were costing almost $1,500 an hour – equivalent to the cost of keeping a commercial helicopter in the air eight hours a day, five days a week, for however long it took. Time, said Bouzaid, to cut and run.

Denese Latimer, on the other hand, regarded the demand for her to sign the agreement as "very serious".

"The Department attitude," probed Brian Henry, "that they just simply wanted it signed, over your objections, is that a common occurrence in the Department?"

"I have never been in that situation before," agreed Latimer, pointing out she'd been with the IRD for 30 years. And it wasn't as if Denese Latimer was some wet-behind-the-ears IRD flunkey. She had a staff of forty tax inspectors reporting to her.

So why was the IRD head office ignoring the expertise of its own front line tax investigation chief – the woman in charge of investigations in New Zealand's largest city, and apparently caving in to demands from Russell McVeagh? Denese Latimer had one theory.

"When somebody from Russell McVeagh was mentioned, it always seemed to take on more importance than if it was somebody from another legal firm. I felt that they treated Russell McVeagh with a certain type of reverence that they didn't treat others."

As for Geoff Clews, he was to tell the Winebox Inquiry five years later "I reject absolutely any suggestion that the outcome of the negotiations was the product of undue influence, blackmail, intimidation or any of the other colourful words which have been employed in and outside hearings of this Commission to describe these events.

"This was a careful, professional negotiation, not a crude shakedown of the IRD. The only influence I or my firm has had in relation to the IRD has been the influence of experience, the influence of argument and the influence of logic.

"That is what our clients expect of us and that is what I brought to bear on these negotiations. That and nothing more."

Whatever the reasons and the influences, it was Tony Bouzaid's signature that appeared on a secret deal not to prosecute a small group of Russell

---

* The reference to the Minister seeking a briefing on the film cases is significant. For years, the Government has maintained that Revenue Ministers are not permitted to intercede in individual cases, and yet the evidence presented to the inquiry suggests that Ministers did take an interest in specific cases, and also that Ministers discussed such matters with corporate parties. The Minister had, of course, referred Dickie's 1990 letter on the bloodstock deals straight to the IRD.

McVeagh lawyers, who were also to receive a special, favourable deal not available to other taxpayers who'd invested in the same movie.

Within weeks of the December 1991 settlement, a whispering campaign would begin, fuelled by an allegorical newspaper tale, which would come to have an explosive impact on New Zealand's future. Tony Bouzaid unwittingly became the man who lit the fuse that became the Winebox Inquiry.

CHAPTER 21

Tales Of The Arabian Nights

"Well there are winners and outlaws and leaders and lovers,
behind every man in the news, and one thing I know is behind every one
there's a boy who had nothing to lose. Behind every man who has
something to say there's a boy who had nothin' to prove,
Every hero was once, every villain was once,
Just a boy with a bad attitude."

– MEATLOAF, *BAD ATTITUDE*, 1985

Christmas, 1991, may have brought peace to all men but goodwill was missing by the bucketload within the bloodstock and film partnership circles. Somebody knew about the settlement deal, and somebody decided to leak innuendo about it to the business media.

When the storm finally broke, it came in the form of a Valentine's Day present, gift-wrapped in allegory and ticking furiously from within.

"Once upon a time, in a land far, far away...", the article, published in the *National Business Review* and since tabled at the inquiry, began:

"New Zealand used to be a country where one could never fix a parking ticket. Graft and corruption were almost unknown – outside Trade & Industry and the Customs Department.

"Then along came the Labour era. Dealing the old-fashioned backhander in coins of the realm demode. Better, cheaper and ever so much more seemly to reward the faithful for services rendered or about to be rendered with dongs than dollars. (Shades of Lloyd George).

"News of such carry-on reaching Shoeshine's ears could, of course, never be relayed to you, dear readers, this country's disgraceful libel laws being what they are.

"Better to black to boots of success than ask whose soul dangles from its watch chain, which would be embarrassing for both parties.

"In the real world, mum's the motto. But there's little harm in tooling off on a fantastic voyage to the mythical island republic of Southern Wogistan. Were there any such place, Wogistani public affairs would be carried out in a manner not altogether dissimilar to those in this green and pleasant isle. Readers will please keep in mind, as a patriotic article of faith, the fact that Kiwi officials are, and forever shall be, incorruptible.

"In Wogistan dwelt Ali Baba, a man well-known among the republic's pleaders. Ali

and his band had friends in high places – in particular a leading legal Vasir ever so grateful to Ali for his help in filling pre-election coffers.

"Ali was a particularly adept tax lawyer – so apt [sic] he could, it was said, get bulldust – if not camel dung – through the eye of a regulatory needle.

"Before the sharemarket crash reduced the Southern Wogistani stock exchange to rubble, dozens of well-heeled merchants trod the dusty path to Ali's door in search of a bit of income protection. Ali and his band devised schemes so cunning they did baffle the fiscal fiend until, one fateful day, Ali and his band overstepped the bounds of what we self-righteous Kiwis would call moral rectitude and, in a rash moment, not only dodged the taxman but defrauded their clients as well.

"There was, it seems, a way to dodge the fiscal fiend's greedy fingers. As was the fashion of the time, Ali's colleagues were in the habit of forming special partnerships for favoured clients and often steered such people towards bloodstock – not ordinary bloodstock, mind, but racing camel bloodstock.

"But Ali wasn't especially fond of horses. An urbane and sophisticated man, he liked movies – and here Ali saw an opportunity for his clients. Not on-screen, of course. Their complex tax problems meant the better-heeled among Ali's clients preferred to slink in the shadows. But Ali figured they could be flicked into special film partnerships not unlike those bloodstock schemes so favoured by his colleagues.

"So it came to pass that dozens of Wogistani punters were pulled into film partnerships, including one starring the Thin White Duke, who was making part of the movie in Southern Wogistan.

"But unbeknown to the special partners, Ali and his colleagues had persuaded the film commission in a neighbouring country to sink money into the enterprise.

"Ali was loathe to trouble his clients with this small detail. Their worries, after all, were great enough as it was. It would be so much simpler just to park the money – several million shekels, it is understood – into his firm's trust account in a tiny tax haven far from the shores of Southern Wogistan. Ali's partners agreed. It was better all round that investors and clients didn't hear of the film commission's generosity.

"But as the years passed it became crystal clear to the Wogistani counterpoint of our fiscal fiend that mischief was afoot. Within his department was a man with more balls than political reticence, who vowed to take Ali and his band to the cleaners.

"Quietly he began to probe – firstly the partnership itself, and then the partners' trust account tucked away in that far-off tax haven. The harder he probed, the more excited he became.

"Ali and his partners had been to the best schools. They had friends in high places and dined with the most powerful of the vasirs, from whence many favours came. The man from infernal revenue was also growing fearful. How would the Wogistani establishment react to fraud charges against its favourite sons?

"But as it came to pass he worried in vain. It reached the ears of one of the top – and, as it happened, one of the silliest – vasirs that Ali and his band were under investigation. Naturally, the Vasir wasn't pleased. A scandal, especially within the patrician classes, was the last thing he needed. A by-election was nigh, and who was to say how the common herd might react and, even more frightening, who could say where his probing might lead?

"*There was nothing for it, the Vasir decided. The man from infernal revenue must be stopped. And so, using loyal lackeys so it could never be traced to him, the Vasir nipped the investigation in the bud.*

"*Such are the politics of Southern Wogistan. It could never happen in New Zealand.*"

Whoever was responsible may as well have hauled in kegs of gunpowder and set them alight under parliament buildings. Certainly that was the effect that the article had both within Government and within the Inland Revenue Department.

One Inland Revenue employee to feel the fallout was the IRD's Regional Manager, Taxpayer Audit, for the northern region, Norman Latimer. He was Denese Latimer's husband, and second-in-command of the IRD's Auckland-based outpost. He had 1200 staff underneath him.

"In my view," he told the Winebox Inquiry in 1995, "there has been a certain amount of paranoia from head office that there was somebody from within the department who had been leaking information to the press since February 1992. At times I have felt that I may have been suspected of leaking the information.

"The [Wogistani] article was supposedly about various strange dealings in a mythical foreign land involving tax-dodging schemes in bloodstock and films. It implied links between politicians or Inland Revenue officials, and lawyers involved in designing tax effective investment schemes.

"Among the inferences and innuendos in the article, are inferences concerning dealings connected with the Commissioner of Inland Revenue in this supposed mythical foreign land, and relationships between either the Minister of Inland Revenue or other politicians and partners of a large legal firm.

"Some time after this article," Norman Latimer noted, "there were a number of odd inquiries from the then Commissioner, David Henry, as to whether I had had any contact with Chris Dickie."

David Henry had, in fact, written to the *National Business Review* fairly swiftly to "reassure" readers that it really was just a fairytale.

"The Shoeshine column of February 14," wrote Henry, "was fairly obscure. However, even though I am a simple bureaucrat, after several readings I came to an unpleasant conclusion: perhaps some of your readers might interpret the story of Wogistan as an allegory of New Zealand.

"They might infer that things similar to those depicted in the Shoeshine column happen here. If that is the case, I must move to reassure your readers that investigations into the affairs of taxpayers in this country are a matter for the Commissioner of Inland Revenue.

"They are carried out without external influences being exerted on the process. The Commissioner carries out the statutory function in accordance with the law. While investigations might be 'nipped in the bud' for nefarious purposes in Wogistan, that is not so in New Zealand."

Henry had good reason to feel the heat: his department had just signed a piece of paper essentially agreeing, in my opinion, to cover up a possible crime.

In addition, it was an agreement which even lawyers for the Serious Fraud Office acknowledged at the Winebox Inquiry was probably unenforceable in law.

The National Government evidently began to feel the pressure too. Justice Minister Doug Graham took the unusual step of commenting on NBR's fairytale in a letter to the editor.

"Shoeshine's column of February 14, 1992, describing events that occurred in Wogistan, by innuendo at least, implies some improper coercion during Labour's era. I am happy to be able to reassure your readers that to the best of my knowledge no such action, if it ever occurred at all, has been repeated since the election of the National Government."

These denials were enough to set tongues wagging in political circles, and it was only a matter of weeks before dozens of questions appeared on the parliamentary order paper from Labour MP's wanting to know what it was all about.

But, as with most titanic power struggles and matters of intrigue in New Zealand, most of the skirmishing and manoeuvring was taking place behind closed doors. It was certainly outside the public gaze.

Among those entranced by the Wogistan story was Winston Peters, the then-National MP for Tauranga.

"It was both curious and illuminating," Peters told the Winebox Inquiry, "and I discussed the matter with my counsel, Mr Henry, who told me he had received a note from an informant suggesting that I should look into the article and take it seriously.

"Mr Henry told me that his source recommended contact with Mr Larry Johnson, a potential informant regarding the Bank of New Zealand. I instructed Mr Henry to contact Mr Johnson and to follow up on the Wogistani article.

"Now, the rumour within the National Party at the time was that the allegorical personalities included Russell McVeagh McKenzie Bartleet & Co, the Honourable Doug Graham and Robin Congreve.

"If the article was, in fact, meritorious, the matter deserved investigation and I decided to investigate.

"Mr Henry provided me with a number of documents relating to a film called *Merry Christmas Mr Lawrence*. He advised me that these documents disclosed a prima facie case of fraud on the New Zealand revenue. It was explained to me that the film's financing was not bona fide, but rather a pretence.

"More specifically, I was advised that the true producers and promoters of this venture were individuals who had facilitated a tax reducing scheme on a film that had made a profit, encouraging the shareholders to declare tax losses whilst denying the shareholders a share in the actual profits.

"The advice I received was that there was prima facie evidence that the Inland Revenue Department had been defrauded. Now, that information gave the Wogistani article new meaning. That would make the article no longer allegorical. I continued to try to obtain information.

"It is important to remember that during this period, Mr Henry was defence counsel representing an ex-Equiticorp director [successfully] in High Court proceedings brought by the Serious Fraud Office and was thoroughly conversant with the law pertaining to criminal fraud. I relied on Mr Henry's expertise and advice throughout."

So, Winston Peters was on the hunt, the Inland Revenue Department's head office was seething, and Chris Dickie was in the dark.

The first Dickie knew of the article came in a phone call from the IRD's Norman Latimer, a few days after its publication. He outlined the conversation to the Winebox Inquiry.

"He advised me that it was causing serious concern at the Inland Revenue Department head office. As I recall, Mr Latimer said words to the effect that 'all hell had been let loose'.

"He then advised me that the IRD head office considered that I had written the article or had caused it to be written. I told Mr Latimer that I had not been responsible and that I did not even know who was the writer behind the Shoeshine column in the paper. I was shocked and dismayed at Mr Latimer's advice, and told him so.

"I recall that later Mrs Latimer or Mr May also informed me that their head office thought I was responsible for the article."

Annoyed that the article was hurting their relationship with the IRD and others, Dickie and Molloy stuck to the task at hand, furiously analysing the information that they'd managed to assemble so far on the tax haven companies involved in the film and bloodstock deals, looking for similar fact evidence on who owned and who controlled them.

Central to the analysis was a recently completed investigation by Auckland-based forensic accountancy firm Ross Melville Bridgman & Co. In a four page review on the bloodstock side of the equation, John Bridgman spelt out what he'd gleaned from the various company searches Dickie and Molloy had located on Zorasong, Securelaunch and Ermine Holdings Ltd and Company.

Molloy, drawing on his extensive experience working with non-resident United Kingdom companies had rightly concluded that Zorasong and Securelaunch would have to file accounts with authorities in England. It had simply been a matter of tracking those accounts down.

"Zorasong was a private limited company," wrote Bridgman, "incorporated on the 4th day of June 1985. The ordinary share capital of the company was GBP 100, divided into 100 shares of £1 each. At the time of incorporation two ordinary shares of £1 each were issued to subscribers for cash at par.

"The business affairs of the company and all acts in relation thereto were to be controlled and managed exclusively outside the United Kingdom. Becmac Ltd and Camceb Ltd of Hong Kong were shareholders for a short period prior to the transfer of the shares to Hanwin Ltd and Rayfull Ltd."

The ownership change had taken place on July 25, 1985, and at the same time Hanwin and Rayfull also became directors of Zorasong, and Hanwin Ltd took over as company secretary for Zorasong as well. In tax havens it is common for companies, not individuals, to fill director and secretarial roles. This shields individuals from scrutiny.

Hanwin and Rayfull, noted Bridgman, were registered at a Hong Kong address belonging to Chan and Cheng, solicitors.

On the day of the Zorasong ownership change, its registered office became the London address of giant accounting firm Deloitte Haskins & Sells. On October 21, 1986, Zorasong called an extraordinary general meeting of its members, to alter its official objectives to include:

"To carry on business as dealers in, importers, exporters, breeders and proprietors, whether as principal or agent, of bloodstock horses and other live-stock and animals."

As for Olec Secretaries Ltd's involvement with Zorasong? As far as Bridgman could see, the subsidiary of Ed Bendelow's Jersey lawfirm, Ogier & le Cornu, had taken over as Zorasong company secretary from the latter part of 1990.

Now, in fact, that secretarial change reflected some major turmoil within Zorasong. At the start of 1990, a year into Dickie's investigation, it is clear that attempts were being made to cash up Zorasong and close it down. But those plans got fouled when the sale of bloodstock assets to Securelaunch went awry thanks to Coolmore Stud refusing to recognise the transfer.

By late 1990 Zorasong's feud with Coolmore, and the latter's refusal to pay out any money, was really beginning to cause a cash squeeze. As the creditors closed in, Deloittes in Hong Kong was attempting to get someone in a position of responsibility in New Zealand to explain what the hell was going on, and to get the company into a position where the final accounts could be signed off.

On December 12, 1990, Chris Kirkham had written back to Deloittes, saying "I have further considered your request. Whilst I am not now and never have been in control of Zorasong Ltd, I sympathise with you in the difficulties you face in relation to finalising these accounts.

"I will do what I can to assist, particularly as I am well aware that there are pressures this end on NZ investment partnerships that dealt with Zorasong."

There is probably no bigger nightmare for a user of tax havens, than to find that when you need to close down a tax haven entity and run, you can't. And all the time the investigators are getting closer. It must be akin to stalling your car on a railroad crossing.

"I think I may be able to get someone here to sign the return," continued Kirkham, but I'll need more background before I can push this through.

"At least some of the time I can still get Paul Carran to respond to me, although I understand he's 'off the air' to you."

It was too much for Deloittes, and the accounting giant spat the dummy. On December 19, 1990, Deloittes accountant, Kar Kui Yu, wrote to Chris Kirkham.

"It is unacceptable for us to represent an unknown client and, after lengthy consideration of all aspects of this case including our ongoing efforts to resolve its difficulty, we have decided that we must now withdraw all our services to this company.

"We intend withdrawing our services and to instruct the existing nominee directors and secretary to resign on December 31, 1990. Kindly also let me know to whom and of which address I should send the company's books, records and old documents."

When even the tax havens are closing their doors to you, you just know you must have done something pretty significant to annoy them. So that's how Zorasong ended up shifting allegiance from Hong Kong to the Channel Islands.

The Bridgman report to Dickie wasn't privy to that background at the time, but it continued with an analysis of Zorasong's financial accounts for the year ending March 1986.

"There was a deficit in working capital of $579,396. A company in this condition would be expected to be experiencing cash flow problems due to its lack of working capital."

Zorasong had an unsecured loan payable of half a million US dollars, and an unsecured loan receivable of half a million US dollars. To the tax department, this would be a clear signal of a circular funding arrangement – a paper loan.

"I have also observed that the unsecured loan receivable. . .of US$500,000 is the exact same amount as the Bonshow loan recorded as a liability within the Ermine Holdings Ltd and Company financial statements," said Bridgman, in a piece of financial detective work.

Bonshow was a two dollar company that had "advanced" Ermine a massive "loan" to buy horses at inflated prices. Bonshow had been lent that money in the first place by Zorasong, itself only marginally financial.

By the 1987 financial year, Zorasong had lodged a warning in its accounts that it looked unlikely to recover a US$499,999 "doubtful debt". The Bonshow loan, that investigators figured would never be repaid because it didn't have to be, apparently wasn't going to be repaid.

As for Securelaunch, a British registered company, Bridgman gleaned from its December 1989 financial statements that "the Auditors have been unable to verify the company has title to the bloodstock or stallion shares. This indicates a possible impropriety with the purchase transaction."

Olec Secretaries Ltd had acted as company secretary since February 1988.

Under his closing comments, Bridgman concluded "there are a number of 'clone-like' similarities in the set-up and operational structure of Zorasong and Securelaunch."

They included:

- capital structure (minimal nominal, issued and paid capital)
- nature of business being bloodstock traders
- large unsecured liabilities implying related party funding and transactions
- nominee shareholders and directors
- the company shell structure with no employees other than the directors
- Olec Secretaries Ltd acting as secretary

Surveying this information, Chris Dickie and Peter Edwards had also become aware that Securelaunch now appeared to be owned by an outfit called British & Commonwealth Merchant Bank Plc. What they didn't know was that the bank had seized control of Securelaunch because of outstanding debts caused by the Zorasong/Coolmore crisis.

Carran, Kirkham and McLeish had lost control of everything.

Meanwhile, the more that Dickie, Edwards and Molloy dug in early 1992, the dirtier they became. Another discovery was a movie called *Hamburger*, which involved an outfit called Komanti.

An IRD analysis of the Komanti project was disclosed at the Winebox Inquiry, and showed that production of *Hamburger – The Motion Picture* began on May 29, 1985.

"Production costs were funded by the Busterburger Limited Partnership (38 investors) as to US$2,700,000. As at 2 May 1986, total production costs were reported as being US$2,529,023."

Once the movie was completed, a chain of tax haven transactions would see rights to the film traded for huge sums of money. The chain began in the Channel Islands, where Dickie's old friend Chary Holdings Ltd of Jersey sold "certain limited rights" in Hamburger to a Hong Kong company called Komanti Investment Ltd for US$9,270,000.

Komanti – a company with one dollar in paid-up capital – had actually been set up for a totally different reason by Auckland fashion retailer Murray Carter, the owner of Shanton Apparel, but Russell McVeagh's Paul Carran had offered to buy it from him.

Komanti's massive investment had been largely funded by a US$7 million limited recourse loan.

Komanti onsold its rights to a consortium of New Zealand companies that included Shanton Apparel and Emphatic Enterprises Ltd – a 100 dollar New Zealand company that just happened to issue US$7 million worth of shares to a Hong Kong company called Redwell.

"These additional shares," wrote John Nash in the IRD position paper, "were held upon trust by Durham Nominees Ltd, a nominee company of Russell McVeagh McKenzie Bartleet & Co."

Emphatic, which now had seven million dollars sitting in it – on paper – spent that money buying shares in the rest of the consortium, so that they – on paper – would have enough dosh to buy the film rights from Komanti.

One of the wonderful twists in the Komanti story discovered by Dickie and Molloy was that a Hong Kong bank statement showing $2.3 million in deposits had been used to fool people about the company's financial state, because the column showing $2.3 million in withdrawals had not been disclosed. Most of the deposits and withdrawals had actually been simultaneous.

Like Winnie the Pooh dropping deflated rubber balloons into an empty hunny-pot and taking them out again, someone had stood at the counter of the bank depositing and taking out the same $500,000 over and over again. So that's what we pay expensive tax lawyers to dream up!

The IRD's John Nash took a dim view of the Komanti project, especially after consulting "a person who is an expert in film industry matters. This expert has had many years of experience in the production, financing and marketing of

35mm gauge full-length feature films, including such films produced in the United States.

"The expert has advised that SPS [the Shanton Apparel subsidiary] and the other three New Zealand companies must have expected a box office gross of truly blockbuster proportions, since even at a box office of US$125 million, the returns would have realised no more than US$2,353,310 in aggregate – nearly US$7 million short of the sum said to have been invested.

"In comparison," said Nash, "the top grossing 1985 release of *Cocoon* and the top grossing 1986 release of *Top Gun* took just US$40 million and US$82 million respectively in actual gross receipts.

"Whilst a bigger budget for a film does not necessarily mean a greater chance of success (and indeed there have always been some big-budget flops each year as well as low-budget breakthroughs) it can be a guide to the quality of the resulting film, particularly in the exploitation market which relies upon some 'marquee value' to pull in an audience.

"According to the expert, *Hamburger* had no marquee value at all in that there were no star names amongst the cast or creative principals."

Apart from the totally unrealistic profit levels needed, Nash and the expert also noted that the New Zealand companies investing had bought in at a stage of production when the "quality and general audience appeal of the picture is readily apparent."

In other words, they should have known that this film was a turkey that was never going to make triple the amount that *Cocoon* pulled in.

"The expert considers that the company or its representatives should have been able to make judgments as to the likely market outcome before investing in a share of the rights.

"The total investment by all four New Zealand companies could have almost fully funded the production, as opposed to purchasing only a very diluted share of the potential income stream with no share of copyright or equity participation."

The IRD moved to strike down the tax losses claimed by Shanton Apparel as a result of its movie investment, pegging back the movie's cost from the claimed US$9.29 million to the "real cost of the film", US$2.29 million – basically disallowing the US$7 million money run-around in the middle.

The McVeagh Fleming team were entranced by the bank statement paper-folding: that was definitely one to watch out for in their future investigations, they decided.

The legal bill to McVeagh Fleming's clients now totalled more than $1 million.

Chapter 22

The Edge Of Darkness

> "Money laundering can be defined as the hiding and processing of
> illicit proceeds, through banks, otherwise legitimate businesses or
> complicated networks of offshore shell companies, into
> untraceable investments."
>
> – Bryan Burrough, *Vendetta*, 1992

One of the big problems Dickie and his team faced in early 1992 was an inability to get any sense out of Kirkham as to what the financial state of the three bloodstock partnerships, Ermine, Buckingham and Wicklow was. While everyone knew the syndicates were in a horrific state, nobody had the exact figures and the final accounts still had not been prepared.

"Dealing with Mr Kirkham through his legal advisers," complained Dickie in a letter to investors, "in endeavouring to obtain a finalisation of the partnership's accounts for the tax returns has been quite impossible."

He added that he'd "been presented with a series of quite unacceptable excuses as to why Mr Kirkham is unable to complete the accounts.

"One explanation which Mr Kirkham gives is the extreme difficulty in obtaining a reconciliation of accounts between the three partnerships with the Coolmore Stud in Ireland. He states that only he can deal with Coolmore Stud and is capable of understanding and resolving the various claims being made by that stud."

Kirkham was telling the truth. How could he possibly get any help from Coolmore when the stud had hung Zorasong and Securelaunch out to dry? And yet the fortunes of Zorasong and the three bloodstock partnerships were inextricably intertwined from the view of the various studs, as one of Kirkham's own memo's showed.

In a letter to Harry Line at the Lindsay Park Stud in Australia, Kirkham wrote,

"Lindsay Park showed a credit balance of $14,788.36 for Ermine as at end of August. Upon enquiring of its whereabouts we were advised that $12,268.38 had been used to pay the Zorasong account.

"We have requested this amount to be transferred back to Ermine as these two entities are totally separate and that the Zorasong account will be paid separately.

"Buckingham and Wicklow are also separate entities and funds from Ermine cannot be used to pay these accounts. Please confirm that the amount of $12,268.38 will be returned to the Ermine account."

There was also the issue of who the hell owned and controlled the secret company, Zorasong? Was it Paul Carran and/or Chris Kirkham? Or was it someone else, yet to be discovered?

Kirkham had told Deloittes in Hong Kong "I know that I was not a beneficial owner of Zorasong Ltd. Indeed, I have never known who that beneficial owner was. If you can advise me who, or what entity is that beneficial owner, I will attempt to have them instruct you as to these records, so we can all put the matter properly to rest."

So here you had Carran and Kirkham intimately involved but apparently unaware of who was behind it. And what role did McLeish play? It became a "Holy Grail" quest.

"Chris always had the Holy Grail," laughed Molloy years later, "and it was always a different Holy Grail. The Wicklow certificates were one, and the Anzon cheques were another. I mean, he still rings me: I had a call two days ago where he'd found another Holy Grail. He's still finding them."

But perhaps the biggest Grail of all was the mystery of Zorasong. From an examination of the evidence they'd managed to accumulate, Dickie and Molloy could see that there were links between Zorasong, Chary Holdings, Charlesbay, Dawn Hill and Komanti, but they couldn't see who was yanking the chain.

And then there was the Westpac litigation. Although largely on hold since mid-1991, Westpac – as a defendant in the partnership action – had suddenly come up with some documents as part of the discovery process that had never been previously disclosed. When Dickie saw them he was furious.

The documents, which he later mailed to his clients, indicated that Westpac had known since the very beginning that the capital of Buckingham might actually be what the investors were claiming it was.

On April 7, 1992, Dickie wrote to the investors in a letter, sub-headed "Non-disclosure of critical evidence".*

"We have now found from an inspection of Westpac's documents further material which shows that the bank had knowledge in September 1986 which we consider proves that the capital of Buckingham was $7 million, and not $4 million as it has continued to maintain since the date of its demand in April 1989.

"Not only did Westpac receive written advice from the Statutory Supervisor that 7,000 units had been allotted, but the bank itself, by way of an internal memorandum headed 'Confirmation of Proper Allotment' again recorded that the capital was $7 million.

---

* It is appropriate to point out that Westpac didn't view the documents as relevant, which is why they were not disclosed earlier. Obviously this was where the bank and the plaintiffs had a pretty fundamental disagreement on that judgment call.

"The same memorandum," wrote Dickie testily, "referred to the Wicklow subscription describing it as the 'extra partnership units'.

"We view the bank's non-disclosure of this most material evidence with the utmost seriousness. It is quite clear that the bank had possession of this material at the time the Buckingham Committee was negotiating with Westpac to obtain a settlement of its demand in April 1989.

"The manager of Westpac had informed the writer that he 'was not interested' in the documents which we wished to show to him to demonstrate the capital of Buckingham. Then, when the Summary Judgment proceedings were issued, Westpac failed in its duty, as laid out in the High Court rules, to fully disclose all material documentation.

"We have written evidence which shows that the manager concerned specifically considered the Statutory Supervisor's letter yet did not disclose it in his affidavit. Neither was the evidence disclosed by the bank at the Court of Appeal hearing.

"The non-disclosure is significant from both a practical and legal viewpoint. On the practical side each Buckingham partner has paid interest since April 1989 when, had the bank been open, no interest may have been payable (ie, the capital issue could have been settled and a proper demand issued and met)."

Dickie calculated that investors with a minimum ten unit holding had incurred an interest debt of $4,346. "However, the demand was approximately twice that amount and its non-payment has resulted in an interest charge of $10,866."

"If you are looking at the Westpac affidavits," an angry Dickie later told one of his clients, "what is significant in my view is what they didn't tell the court. That was serious. That was about two years work and an incredible shit fight. The question of the prices of the horses hadn't even arisen at this point. Nobody suspected anything. I was just fighting a rearguard action because many were going to go bankrupt. I had wives on the phone balling their eyes out. The things that bank put people through, and they bloody well knew about Buckingham's capital all along!"

It's at this point that an interesting diversion arises for the reader. It is often assumed by commentators and radio talkback hosts that Joe Punter should not rely on dictionary definitions when trying to debate legal issues. "Don't be daft!" is the comment heard from talk hosts as they tell Mavis Gruntfuttock of Beachaven to put the Concise Oxford away and ignore its interpretation of the word "evasion".

"These matters," say the commentators knowledgably, "are incredibly complex. You can't just race off to the dictionary and play scrabble with the law."

Oh yeah? Wanna bet? They've referred to dictionary definitions at the Winebox Inquiry more than once, and it turns out Westpac had scurried off to the dictionary as it searched for a non-existent escape route from the four sevenths mess, seeking a definition of the word "subscription".

Whatever the bank found in the dictionary, it didn't alter the end result of the case.

When McVeagh Fleming partner and Dickie's co-investigator Peter Edwards finally got the documents, one of his clients remembered Dickie telling him "I just cried my eyes out. It was too much to take. Too much crap that we'd been put through."

But it was time to put others through it as well. They knew that the Inland Revenue Department and Serious Fraud Office were keen to find out what had been going on in the section of the investigation dealing with the offshore companies.

"It was about this time that we had what became known as the vineyard meeting out at Tony's farmhouse," remembered Dickie. "There has been so much misconception talked about the purpose of that meeting, and the thing that's caused a huge stink was the presence of Alan May of the IRD, who was invited as a guest to come and listen.

"He wasn't invited to come and make a contribution, and we didn't want him to. He knew a hell of a lot more than us, but we felt he would benefit from listening to what we were uncovering in *Merry Christmas*, Primula and in the bloodstock.

"That meeting was a real eye-opener for us, listening to what Winston Peters and his solicitors were investigating. The Serious Fraud Office sat there and listened, the IRD made no disclosures at all, and the main people that spoke were Peters, Tony and myself."

So, as they cleared away the remains of lunch in Molloy's farmhouse kitchen on April 22, 1992, and sipped on piping hot cups of coffee, it was hard to imagine the repercussions that would flow from the discussions that day.

"I have become aware," Dickie told the Winebox Inquiry, "of both Inland Revenue Department head office and media interest and speculation as to what occurred at that meeting.

"Such interest and speculation is unwarranted. It was merely one of hundreds of meetings that Dr Molloy and/or myself were to have over a seven year period with other potential witnesses – advisers, professional and business people, Government officials and anyone else whom we considered could assist in clarifying the extent of the use of hidden offshore transactions, the lines of communication, or the identity of those who controlled the same.

"Neither the SFO nor IRD representatives proffered any specific document-ation or advice. I remember that Mr May said very little."

Under cross-examination by IRD lawyers at the inquiry over his relationship with Denese Latimer and Alan May, Dickie denied that he was trying to get information out of the IRD staff in breach of their responsibilities.

"I do not accept that. Initially, Mrs Latimer came to my office and she made it extremely clear to me within a few moments that she was very conversant with two people in Hong Kong who I had identified [Anita Cheng and Mildred Li] in my own investigations [and who] were in some way central to the control of the company that I was endeavouring to get underneath.

"Mrs Latimer made it very clear to me that she was looking for me to assist the department. And I would like to state that she made it very clear, both at that meeting and at subsequent meetings, that communication in respect of any evidence that we obtained would be, to use her own words, a one way street."

The lawyer added that his firm had then been slapped with one of the IRD's section 17 notices – the kind misused by John Nash in the raid on John Barnett's Endeavour Productions Ltd. Such notices require people to deliver to the IRD information and documentation that it may need for investigative purposes.

"I think that the involvement with the Inland Revenue Department also then obtained an additional flavour. It was clear that the investigating officers at Otahuhu were targeting the same objective, but of course from a different angle.

"I was a solicitor, acting in civil proceedings, and I had received a notice from the Department. In turn, they were endeavouring to understand the operation – as far as I was concerned – with Hong Kong entities. As I obtained information which I thought was of assistance, I provided it to either Mr May or to Mrs Latimer.

"I should also state," added Dickie, "that this was the first time that I had become involved in what I identified as circular funding transactions and in particular limited recourse and non-recourse loans.

"Both the officers that I referred to had, quite clearly, infinitely more experience than I did, and I found their comments to be a useful sounding board in my discussions with Dr Molloy, who was primarily involved in providing taxation advice to my clients."

IRD lawyer Bruce Squire QC implied there was some sort of cosy, mutual back-slapping going on between Dickie and the two tax investigators.

"Is it fair to suggest," he asked, "that you would have perceived that they were not unsympathetic to the kind of allegations you were making about Russell McVeagh?"

"I think that would be fair."

"Was it the kind of sympathetic response that you were getting from those quarters which later led you to invite or consider inviting Mr May to the vineyard meeting which took place on the 14th of February 1992?" pounced Squire triumphantly, not realising he'd mixed up the date of the April 22 meeting with the date of the Wogistan article.

Clearly, there was real sensitivity within the IRD about Alan May's attendance at the vineyard meeting, especially given the presence at the meeting of Winston Peters.

"Can I ask you please," continued Squire, "why it was thought necessary to invite Mr Peters to that meeting and for what purpose?"

"Mr Peters and people who were associated with him – in particular Mr Brian Henry – was one of a very large number of people who provided knowledge or introduction of critical evidence. Indeed, if it was not for Mr Henry I would not have obtained the confirmation that I needed at that time of. . .the lines of communication."

But Squire seemed to be fishing for information that might put Alan May in the frame in a more serious way. He wanted to know "at the meeting – was there any criticism of the Commissioner of Inland Revenue?"

"There was a concern," answered Dickie, "as to the perception as to what was evasion and what was avoidance – the form and substance issue."

"Yes," said Squire eagerly, "and were the members present at that meeting critical of the views. . .of the Commissioner of Inland Revenue about that issue?"

Sensing where this was heading, Dickie told Squire that only he and Molloy, and probably Winston Peters, had expressed such concerns. "Certainly I can confirm that there was no criticism from Alan May."

So far, the most complete version of what took place at the meeting has been provided by Winston Peters in his testimony to the inquiry.

"In April, 1992, Mr Henry arranged a meeting with Mr Christopher Dickie, partner of McVeagh Fleming, and Dr Molloy QC. Mr Henry wished the Serious Fraud Office and the Inland Revenue Department to be present to ensure that no one could level any untoward allegations at me as a Member of Parliament."

Peters flew to Auckland specifically to attend the vineyard rendezvous.

"Dr Molloy recounted a detailed narrative of how tax fraud was deliberately and systematically perpetrated by certain Russell McVeagh McKenzie Bartleet & Co tax partners. I understand these schemes were the work of a small clique within that lawfirm and not known to the wider partnership.

"It is unfortunate, indeed, that the remaining Russell McVeagh partners have not since seen fit to expose the perpetrators."

During a break in the meeting, Brian Henry took Winston Peters aside, reinforcing Molloy's credentials as a meticulous tax lawyer with a reputation for thoroughness.

Dickie and Molloy took the opportunity to meet the politician and bring him up to speed, although Dickie, of course, had already met Peters earlier that year when he met Paul Darvell to discuss how tax haven companies were controlled.

One of the lawyers' major concerns was the alleged threat by Russell McVeagh tax partner Geoff Clews that had taken place in that heated meeting almost a year earlier in July 1991, and it was this incident, coupled with the Wogistan article, that fuelled Peters' suspicions of corruption within the IRD.

"Their story of this meeting," Peters told the inquiry, "strongly suggested something was seriously amiss in the [Inland Revenue] department. It appeared that Mr Clews was in a position to obtain a settlement from the head office of the department of Inland Revenue, irrespective of its merits and unavailable to others.

"It is strongly suggested that departmental officials, in particular the Commissioner of Inland Revenue, were not merely incompetent but were conducting themselves in an improper manner contrary to the taxation statutes. These were tax schemes that the Commissioner alone supervises, without any person or agent scrutinising his decision to prosecute or otherwise.

"The meeting satisfied me that the Wogistani article was beginning to unravel. I wished to talk to the source of the article, but was advised by Mr Henry that I had already met the person [who] didn't wish his identity to be disclosed.

"The result of the vineyard meeting was that both Serious Fraud Office and Inland Revenue Department personnel had heard Dr Molloy's statement of both fact and opinion, including a compelling suggestion that the Inland Revenue Department was being manipulated and improperly influenced by Russell McVeagh McKenzie Bartleet & Co.

"Shortly after that meeting," Peters concluded, "I spoke with the Honourable Wyatt Creech, the then Minister of Inland Revenue, and gave him a personal warning regarding these matters and he assured me he knew nothing of such events."

For Dickie and Molloy, it really had been just another meeting, just another briefing. The only difference being that it was Government officials and a politician being briefed, not clients.

But the bunsen burner was, coincidentally, being turned up underneath one Tony Bouzaid at this time. On May 6, 1992, he rang Denese Latimer to discuss the controversial film settlement deal.

"He said that he was in the hot seat over [*Prisoners*]," she told the Winebox Inquiry. "Mr [IRD Commissioner David] Henry had asked him some questions and caught him on the hop, and that he had to reply to him on the Friday, and could I refresh his memory?"

After discussing what Latimer called the blackmail issue, she told him that he "would have to wear the repercussions" if there were any.

"He then went on about Lawrence Anderson Buddle also helping to fund the case, and that was part of the reason for his decision. I asked him where he got that notion from as I had been told by Clews that Russell McVeagh was funding it, that they pulled the strings and that that was part of my concern over his attitude to [*Prisoners*].

"He remembered that John [Nash] had told him and I commented that John was always repeating grapevine gossip."

Latimer told the inquiry that Bouzaid now seemed to be doubting his own decision.

A week later, Bouzaid wrote to David Henry with an explanation. He set out the department's weaknesses thanks to the Endeavour case, where "John Nash and a number of investigators had 'removed and retained' " Endeavour's records.

The fact that 11 investors* in a totally separate case, most of them Russell McVeagh lawyers, had agreed to put money into the kitty to bankroll the Endeavour litigation if they didn't get a sweetheart deal on the movie they'd invested in – *Prisoners* – added to the IRD woes, he explained.

The cost of the deal, he told Henry, was only $38,000 to the department, compared with the cost of fighting Endeavour and losing.

Incidentally, Bouzaid refused to categorise it as a "special deal". The colourful adjective is the author's.

---

* The figure has been variously referred to at the Winebox Inquiry as 10, 11 or 12 investors. Any other bids?

On May 27 Henry contacted Bouzaid and told him his explanation was accepted.

On the lawsuit front, it was time for Dickie to again bring his 300 clients up to speed. "From the outset," he wrote on June 17, 1992, "the Ermine investigation and proceedings have centred around the method by which the bloodstock was purchased, and the non disclosure to you by the promoters of material transactions and information, including the lifting of prices of bloodstock through the undisclosed offshore entity, Zorasong Ltd.

"In the Buckingham and Wicklow proceedings, the initial concerns were directed more to the claims against you by the financiers and it was only subsequently that we became aware of Buckingham's apparent insolvency from its first day of operation, and the acquisition of bloodstock again through the undisclosed company, Zorasong Ltd."

Dickie pointed out that Russell McVeagh had now listed a number of relevant documents in their possession, which included "references to many of the offshore companies which we had already identified, as well as other organisations such as a Channel Islands law firm and a Hong Kong accounting firm."

Much of the work in recent months, he explained, was centred on discovering "the true nature of Zorasong's activities and that of the other offshore entities.

"The difficulty was that these offshore company schemes are constructed with concealment as the uppermost objective. Obtaining evidence to present to the court was proving near impossible, so we found it necessary to work laterally, seeking evidence of other offshore companies promoted by the same people and investigating their activities to see whether what we could learn of these offshore companies could shed light on those with which you are vitally concerned.

"It has become apparent," the lawyer explained, "that the activities of those other offshore companies had a striking resemblance to what has apparently occurred in Ermine.

"Prices and expenses show in the accounts sent to the members of the various partnerships reflect a very different position from what appears to have occurred in practice.

Chris Dickie used one of the new film partnerships he'd stumbled across during a search for similar fact evidence as an example: the *Smiling Buddha* partnership.

"We found evidence of directors' fees being 'lifted' well beyond the fee disclosed as having been charged to the partnership, and the excess paid out by the partnership through an advance by a Hong Kong company.

"That transaction bears a striking resemblance to the price 'hydraulicking' in Ermine, in which four horses were charged to the partnership at about $1 million more than their purchase price, with that extra 'cost' being met by way of an advance of $1 million to the Ermine partners by another offshore entity, Bonshow Ltd.

"We have interviewed the film director involved in *Smiling Buddha*, a New Zealander who, as a result of her own initiative and concern as to the true intentions of the directors of the promoter [Smiling Buddha Ltd], kept an extraordinary record of handwritten diagrams provided to her by the New Zealand promoters."

Not only that, but the suspicious film director on the project became so concerned that she not only made notes after conversations with executives from the promoter, she even recorded their conversations on tape in some cases.

Briefing the clients on his investigations into *Merry Christmas Mr Lawrence*, Dickie wrote "the prospectus [offering memorandum] clearly stated that the film income was to be paid to the New Zealand investors through a legitimate UK company.

"However, again without disclosure to the investors, the promoters appear to have diverted the income receipts through their offshore Hong Kong company, again not disclosed to investors, to bank accounts held in the Channel Islands.

"We have also obtained documents suggesting that that film cost $4 million, whereas the investors were told that it had cost, and they were charged, $11.77 million."

And as for *The Adventures Of The Little Prince*: "A variation of the technique was revealed through our examination of the Primula special partnership, in which the promoters stated in the prospectus, the partnership accounts, and in correspondence to the investors, that the investors had acquired 20 episodes of a TV series.

"However, we have established, following lengthy discussions and correspondence with a Los Angeles attorney and the producer, that only eight episodes were made and available for sale to the partnership. Twenty episodes were never available, so the investors were being charged for 12 non-existent films."

Dickie told his clients he was satisfied that the legal team had established "a serious case of fraud" against investors by the promoters in the bloodstock deals but added that, with two exceptions, he didn't yet know who had "pocketed the money" at the end of the day.

"It is not necessary for you to establish the latter in your proceedings, which are civil proceedings and not criminal prosecutions," he explained. "It is necessary only for you to establish that you were not informed in the prospectus of what were clearly material transactions; that reasonable investors would not have got themselves into the deals had they known them to be fraudulent; and that the legal advisers were in breach of their fiduciary duty to you by concealing and the allowing the use of these offshore entities."

SFO director Charles Sturt had recently featured in Wellington's *Evening Post* newspaper, and Dickie quoted one of Sturt's major points about investigating corporate fraud.

"In many cases," Sturt had said, "there has to be massive reconstruction to establish the main trail and indeed, the whole train of evidence."

The past eight months, said Dickie, had been spent massively reconstructing what took place. It had not been helped, he added, by the disappearance of key documents.

"We have always believed that there must be some written documentary material relating to the sale of the bloodstock from the original vendors in Ireland and Australia to the Hong Kong intermediary Zorasong Ltd.

"We were told by Mr Kirkham that no such documents existed and our own enquiries revealed only very little such material. That material related to the lifting of the bloodstock prices with the Australian bloodstock.

"Mitchell McLeish, the horse buyer for the partnerships, had reported to us a telephone conversation he'd had with David Nagle (Barronstown Stud) at the time of the purchase of the bloodstock for Buckingham on 31st July 1986.

"Mr Nagle said to Mr McLeish that he was 'up to my arse in paper'. Although this colourful description sounded genuine we had constantly been told that there were no contracts."

Indeed, some contracts did exist, but Dickie wouldn't get hold of them until 1993.

As for Paul Carran, Dickie believed they now had evidence to contradict testimony on oath from the former Russell McVeagh partner.

In an affidavit sworn on June 11, 1990, Carran had testified: "Each of the statements of claim against [Russell McVeagh] mis-states the nature and the extent of the legal work undertaken by my firm to Buckingham Enterprises Ltd and Anzon Capital Ltd. . .it is unnecessary to detail the respects in which these allegations are incorrect, *except to deny that I ever participated in the management and decision making functions of Buckingham Enterprises Ltd.*" [author's emphasis]

"We have found," said Dickie, "ample evidence to refute this sworn testimony, and by way of example attach copies of certain telexes and secondly a signing authority for Buckingham accounts in Hong Kong.

"You will note that Mr Carran deflects enquiries to Zorasong in Hong Kong and then that Zorasong has to obtain Mr Carran's instructions as to how it should reply to the deflected enquiries."

Dickie had gone so far in his sworn evidence to the High Court at Auckland as to suggest Carran was perjuring himself, and reprinted the paragraph from his affidavit in the letter to clients.

He firstly set out three telexes from Carran to various overseas studs, dated between February and April 1986, which tell the studs to stop asking him questions and instead direct their inquiries to Zorasong in Hong Kong.

Dickie's reprinted affidavit then records "that the impression given in [those] documents is a lie appears from document 3557, a telex from Mildred Li. . .to Carran at the Russell McVeagh telex number."

The telex, document 3557, is headed "Zorasong" and reads, "Today, again receive a TLX from Coolmore Stud to urge reply by May 21, 1986 morning their time on request for payment re 'Careleon' [sic] [and] 'Danzatore'. PLEASE ADVISE WHAT ACTION WE SHOULD TAKE."

In fact, there was plenty more evidence nailing Carran firmly to

Buckingham. Such as this letter from Carran to Anzon Capital Ltd on May 20, 1987:

"We refer to our account. . .to you in the amount of $40,000. The $40,000 fee can be broken down to $10,000 for the establishment of the special partnership and the prospectus.

"The balance of the fee, namely, $30,000 has been estimated by us as allocatable towards the running of the business of the partnership, namely, the acquisition of the bloodstock and the subsequent work effected relating thereto. This includes the writer's attendance at board meetings, consultations and the such like."

So that was what the clients were being told, but in McVeagh Fleming's Buckingham Palace the hard work continued around the clock, interrupted only occasionally by news reports on the case, which was beginning to filter into the public consciousness in the wake of the Wogistan furore.

"Out of pocket investors who took a punt on bloodstock are taking the country's biggest lawfirm, Russell McVeagh McKenzie Bartleet & Co to court, accusing it of concealment, misrepresentation and taking a secret commission," ran a front page story in the *Sunday Star* on July 5.

"The allegations revolve around a series of bloodstock partnerships set up by Russell McVeagh. The investors include dozens of prominent Auckland doctors and dentists who lost millions when the Ermine, Buckingham and Wicklow partnerships went bust.

"Russell McVeagh managing partner John Lusk* says his firm will 'vigorously defend' the allegations.

" 'Our advisers regard the claims as being without merit. We are very positive about it and are starting to roll our side of the story. They (the plaintiffs) seem to forget that the world bloodstock market collapsed and we see no reason why the other side should be cashing in on that.'

"For the first time, the plaintiffs have spelled out how the three partnerships allegedly fit together – a link denied by Russell McVeagh.

"As one partnership reached the brink of bankruptcy, funds were solicited from the public to form a new syndicate, it is claimed.

"But instead of being invested in this new entity, the money was used, unbeknown to investors, to 'rescue' its predecessor."

For Molloy and Dickie, it was an unwelcome spotlight, especially as what they were about to do had to be cloaked in the utmost secrecy. Since arriving back from the Channel Islands at the end of 1991, Tony Molloy had been "kicking around" the draft Order for Justice that he'd begun on stationery at the Lincoln's Inn library. It was time to knock it into shape and, with it, an affidavit for Chris Dickie to take over to the Channel Islands the size of two large telephone books.

They were going after the Norwich Pharmacal order against Ed Bendelow's

---

* Cousin of Attorney-General and SFO Minister Paul East.

lawfirm, Ogier & Le Cornu: they figured the documents there relating to *Merry Christmas Mr Lawrence*, *The Adventures of the Little Prince* and the bloodstock deals would be crucial in unravelling the mystery.

Mindful of the need for absolute stealth in the venture, Chris Dickie even refused to tell his wife, Sue, where he was going or how long he would be away for. Nor did his partners or friends know. As far as the world was concerned, Chris Dickie merely went to work one day, and vanished.

Dickie didn't realise what he was getting himself into.

CHAPTER 23

Eye Of The Storm

"I was gambling in Havana, and I took a little risk,
Send lawyers, guns and money, and get me out of this,
I'm the innocent bystander, but somehow I got stuck,
Between a rock and a hard place, and I'm down on my luck."
– WARREN ZEVON, *LAWYERS, GUNS & MONEY*, 1978

It was the lights that attracted his attention first. Strobing and weaving in the distance, buffeted in the chill autumn winds that were teasing up whitecaps in the bay. But these lights were not seaborne.

Chris Dickie paused at the head of the aircraft steps to gaze back into the murky dusk swiftly enveloping this forlorn rock in the middle of the English Channel. Row upon row of lights – at least 11 sets that he could see – all of them attached to incoming aircraft, wide-bodied international jets on final approach, all of them coming here. The buffeting gave way to a good solid thumping as each airliner passed over the cliffs, their wings shuddering in the strong updraft.

The lawyer rubbed his eyes, partly to ease the discomfort of 24 hours of travel, but mostly in incredulity. Jersey, a tiny tax haven, with an air traffic problem to rival Chicago's.

Off to the left, only metres away, the scream of a turbine and unmistakable "thwop" of helicopter blades. It was the largest chopper Dickie had ever seen, and as black as a nightmare.

Even straining his eyes, it was hard to pick out where the shadowy form of the helicopter ended and the rapidly encroaching darkness began, so when a door opened in the craft spilling a warm glow of orange light onto the tarmac, it was as if someone had carved a hole in the night itself. From within emerged six Asian men, all dressed identically in black and each carrying an identical black briefcase.

The lawyer paused before descending the steps to the tarmac, half expecting to see the bowler-hatted Chinese assassin who gave James Bond such a hard time in Goldfinger.

The attorney grimaced as he wondered whether it was just nerves or something worse that had caused the reaction. Somewhere inside his head a wry voice laughed bitterly, "welcome to the big smoke, Dickie! This is where it all happens."

Tony Molloy, who'd been there almost a year earlier, had a similar reaction to Jersey.

"Oh, it's a creepy place! I suppose it's a beautiful place in its own way. It's quite nice and very agreeable sitting outside the L'Horizon Hotel on St. Brelard's Bay, looking out at a fairly bleak beach but when the clouds break you can see the coast of France. But I found it a creepy place, and very in-bred.

"Unless you're Jersey-born you can't live there. Unless you can buy your way in. British Airways had an inflight magazine with an article on tax havens, and I think the comment was made that if you had about £20 million sterling to invest, you could probably get residential rights in Jersey, but short of that you didn't have a hope."

The boy from Auckland suddenly realised he was a long, long way from home.

The sublime, however, has ways of quickly sliding into the ridiculous. A giant sign at the airport, featuring British TV actor John Nettles waving his hand, welcomed visitors to "Bergerac Country" – a reference to the hit television series that made the Channel Islands a household name in many countries around the world.

Nettles actually went to the trouble of writing a book about Jersey, and included an analysis of why the island was chosen for the setting of a police crime series by TV producer Robert Banks-Stewart.

"His unswerving instinct for commercial potential decided him to set his next series in Jersey," wrote Nettles, "on the grounds that it was an extremely various island, exotic to a degree, apparently very rich with upwards of eighty millionaires amongst its eighty thousand or so inhabitants.

"While it was in some ways exactly like mainland Britain in others it was entirely different. In short, he saw it as a potent mix of the familiar and the strange, where crimes of passion and crimes of greed might believably be committed.

"Was it not likely that criminal elements might gravitate towards Jersey, attracted by its status as an offshore tax haven? Might not drug barons from across the world launder their ill-gotten gains through the Jersey banks? Might not international arms-dealers ply their unseemly low-profile trade from somewhere relatively quiet like Jersey? Might it not be that all kinds of undesirables flourish and prosper in this beautiful isle?"

Certainly those issues have placed Jersey under increasing international and media scrutiny, but the island's legislators say they're on top of it.

"Whenever the laundering of the drug money through a Jersey bank is identified," Senator Reg Jeune was quoted, "every reasonable assistance is given to other enforcement agencies to bring those concerned to account.

"There are a number of ways in which this support is presently provided. The island's success in this endeavour is perhaps best summed up by quoting from a letter written recently to the Attorney-General by the legal attaché at the US Embassy in London: 'You may rest assured that the FBI considers Jersey among our closest allies in combating illegal activities.' "

But John Nettles felt the problem remained. "At the heart of Jersey's difficulties is this dilemma: how can the island's financial institutions allow investigative bodies access to their books without compromising that confidentiality which is an absolute condition of their continued, profitable existence?"

It was this very dilemma that New Zealand lawyer Chris Dickie would force Jersey to face on this visit, and in doing so make world legal history.

First occupied by cave-people eighty thousand years ago, the Channel Islands have had a turbulent history. When Britain's infamous King John lost control of Normandy in neighbouring France in 1204, he lost the Channel Islands as well, which set up their own form of self-government in loose association with the British Crown. Two centuries later the islands fell briefly into French hands, and in 1643 the English Civil War led to eight years under siege for the inhabitants.

But it was the American War of Independence that led to one of the oddest battles in Jersey history. When France joined the American revolutionaries, it also declared war on Britain's Channel Island outposts. Taking advantage of the hostilities, pirates operating from Jersey led raids on French shipping in the Channel.

Deciding in 1781 to teach the pirates and Jersey's protectors a lesson, the French tried to invade the territory using a force of one thousand mercenaries, who were to be guided in under cover of darkness by a Jersey harbour pilot who'd been bribed.

The reefs and a falling tide at La Rocque, the chosen landing point, played havoc with the operation however and some of the troopships couldn't discharge their armed cargo onto the shore. The French commander, Baron de Rullecourt, was left with only six hundred soldiers on Jersey soil, compared to the island's defence forces of a thousand troops plus three thousand militiamen.

Nevertheless, a sneak attack on the capital, St. Helier, caught the island's Lieutenant-Governor napping, and forced to surrender in his bed.

Only a few miles away Major Francis Peirson, the commander of Jersey's 95th Foot, caught wind of the invasion and led a combined force of Highlanders and militiamen to take back the capital.

"The main thrust of the counter-attack," writes Nettles in *Bergerac's Jersey*, "came along what is now Broad Street and Library Place. Peirson himself led a third detachment up the present King Street precinct and through the Place named after him into the square.

"The Battle of Jersey lasted all of ten minutes. The French, realising they were hopelessly outnumbered, surrendered quickly, though not before both commanders, de Rullecourt and Peirson, were killed.

"In the parish church a somewhat prosaic monument records that Major Francis Peirson 'died in the flower of youth and in the moment of victory on the sixth day of January 1781 aged 24',"

An 1822 *Gazetteer of the Most Remarkable Places in the World* records the fate of the French invaders who "were all killed, drowned or taken prisoners".

The only significant invasion since then was the Nazi occupation during World War II, and the scars from that are still etched in the hearts and even the rocks of Jersey.

Arriving in St. Helier that first evening from the airport, the Auckland lawyer checked into his hotel, a tiny establishment called The Yacht Club, which was right on the port, overlooking the water.

Grabbing his coat, he ventured out to find the restaurant recommended by the hotel concierge. Across the causeway he could see the shadowed castle guarding the harbour entrance. Originally named the "Castle Fort Isabella Bellissima" which translates as "Most Beautiful Elizabeth" by the then Governor of Jersey, Sir Walter Raleigh, his choice of title was shortened to "Le Chasteau Elizabeth", which eventually became Elizabeth Castle. Despite the chill Dickie was enjoying his walk along the wharf in search of dinner, although he soon realised he didn't have a clue where to find the eatery.

Help, in the form of a young woman loading fishing nets into a car, was at hand.

"Sure," she said, "I know where it is. Hop in and I'll drive you there. That is, if you don't mind the smell of crabs," she grinned.

Dickie suppressed a smirk, but by journey's end a couple of blocks later had to admit there was a strong odour of fish.

"Come on, I'll show you," offered the woman, opening up the boot of the car. Inside were the largest crabs Dickie had ever seen. Shanker crabs, a local delicacy. They were still moving and had massive pincers, but the lawyer noticed none of the pincers were closing.

"It's kind of cruel," said the woman, "but we have to break the lower pincer as soon as we catch them, otherwise they're strong enough to take our fingers off."

Chris Dickie's first impression of the island was one of extreme wealth. It was very French, very small, and the vehicles, mansions and pleasurecraft in the harbour oozed ostentation.

"One of the lawyers I was dealing with had his own aircraft, his own farm, and a boat that I couldn't hope to own or acquire in several lifetimes."

Dickie had hired a local barrister, Peter Mourant of Mourant du Feu & Jeune, to help prepare the case for document seizure, and some of that work was done in the comfort of Mourant's own boat. The level of wealth in Jersey made Auckland look cheap, and Dickie recalls being "blown away" by it on a daily basis.

In his mad dash to Auckland airport to make the flight to London earlier that week, he realised he'd left behind his umbrella. Unfortunately the only umbrellas left at the Auckland airport store were All Blacks souvenir ones, commemorating New Zealand's national rugby team. He bought one, shoved it in his briefcase and raced for the plane.

Mourant had, earlier in their first day of fulltime work on the case, re-stressed to Dickie the need to tell no-one where he was from. "There's no way anyone was to know I was from New Zealand, because we wanted to do all the preparation, go straight to court, get the order, get the documents. Once we got the documents they could do what the hell they liked."

At the end of that day, Dickie was walking back to his lodgings when it began to rain. Not just rain – it bucketed down. In fact the downpour was so severe that Jersey's newspaper revealed the next morning that half the island's roads had been washed out.

Dickie, sheltering under the eaves of an old stone building, remembered his good fortune in having an umbrella, took it out of his briefcase and briskly walked through the puddles to the scungy hotel he was staying at.

It wasn't until he arrived there, five minutes later, and was shaking the water off the brolly, that he realised what he'd just done.

"Christ, if ever Dickie wanted to advertise that he was in Jersey," he recalled later, "here was this short little bloke with this bloody umbrella with the New Zealand All Blacks and silver fern logo emblazoned all over it!"

Because of the torrid legal workload and long hours of preparation, Mourant asked Dickie to leave his hotel and come and stay at the Mourant residence.

"We'd been going flat out all week, Saturday morning had arrived and Peter had a migraine so was staying in bed.

"I sat down and had breakfast with his lovely wife Anne. She told me her grandmother had been on the island during the war, and there's no question that the Jersey people were deeply affected by the war and what the Germans did. It's something that we New Zealanders don't understand at all."

Anne Mourant, over croissants and coffee, took Dickie on a journey back in time, to Monday, July 1, 1940. "Gran was in the garden digging," recalled Anne, "what turned out to be the last crop of Jersey Royal new potatoes for supper.

"As she dug she heard the noise of aircraft, knowing that it could only be a German plane and that in the past few days they had been strafing the sea front and had dropped bombs – first at La Rocque and then several on the outskirts of town.

"In her haste to get out of the exposed vegetable garden she quickly threw the long, sharp-pronged potato fork into the ground. The two outer prongs went through her shoe into her left foot."

Thinking it wasn't serious, Mourant's grandmother washed the wound and then continued with her work. A few days later her foot swelled up and she was admitted to the Jersey hospital with tetanus.

"What happened?" asked a curious Dickie.

"My grandmother lost her life because the Germans withheld tetanus serum from the island doctor at the hospital."

The 49 year old died on July 19, 1940. Her death certificate reads "Cause of death: Tetanus Poisoning."

Anne Mourant took Chris Dickie to a place on the coast, a lookout built by the Nazis. It was a beautiful view, with the morning sun streaming in and the sound of birdsong in the meadows nearby, but cemented into the walls of the lookout were the bodies of Polish prisoners who'd been brought in as forced labour by the Germans to build the massive fortifications.

"I don't know whether the Jersey people leave the German structures there on purpose, but the island on one hand is a very beautiful place, on the other it is also hideously ugly," muttered Dickie as he recalled his visit to the lookout.

"The battlements that the Germans built are just absolutely hideous. I mean, they're hideous for what they represent, they're hideous because they are just bloody hideous!, and in this radio room that looks out to the French coast are the remains of prisoners who, if they didn't perform, were just thrown into the foundations as they were pouring the concrete. It was very melancholy."

But melancholia was not something that either Chris Dickie or Peter Mourant would have a lot of time for. From virtually the first minute they met it had been all hands to the pumps, and Dickie discovered the tall skinny lawyer with the serious expression and very English mannerisms had a "wicked sense of humour". They would both need it over the coming week.

Dickie had brought with him a four kilogram affidavit with documents attached as exhibits of evidence to support his case. But going for a Norwich Pharmacal order in a tax haven jurisdiction was almost a contradiction in terms, and it would need more than a weighty affidavit to swing it Dickie's way.

For a start, there was a thorny issue involving conflicts of interest within the Jersey lawfirm. Mourant du Feu et Jeune was one of the territory's oldest firms. With a hundred and seventy staff, it provided legal and offshore trust services to clients throughout the world, including a bank called ANZ Grindlays – a division of the ANZ banking group. ANZ Grindlays was represented by none other than Edmund Bendelow from Ogier & Le Cornu, and had been deeply involved in Dickie's investigation and his affidavit tracked money flows through the bank. It caused major friction within Mourant du Feu et Jeune.

Peter Mourant knew that by taking Dickie's case he was setting himself against Jersey's very raison d"tre, and he knew he was going to be in difficulty with his fellow legal partners.

"Their office had a very large trust department," said Dickie, "and Peter was being asked to attack the trust department of another major lawfirm on the island, certain individuals and a bank, ANZ Grindlays. Within a day and a half other partners became aware of what was going on, and there developed some real tension."

Heavy partners' sessions were held behind closed doors as the lawfirm thrashed out whether it could handle our case or whether it had a conflict of interest, but Mourant fought hard. "It's a proper application, it's going to be heard and I'm going to deal with it!"

It may have been a tax and banking haven, and he may have been a tax and banking haven solicitor, but Peter Mourant was proud of his code of ethics and took it seriously. Obviously his colleagues recognised this, because soon afterwards he became President of the Jersey Law Society.

As a New Zealand lawyer, Chris Dickie was not permitted to have a speaking role in the Royal Court of Jersey, which would be hearing his application. As a consequence, Peter Mourant had to fully acquaint himself with the several thousand page affidavit, and all of its points. It had taken Dickie and Molloy nine months and several hundred thousand dollars to assemble the information for the affidavit and collect it together in one place. Dickie and Mourant had just four days to get it right. Every day, Chris Dickie found himself being cross-examined by Mourant.

"Why do you say that? Where's the evidence for this? How can you say this?" he would ask, constantly testing Dickie and looking for weaknesses in his argument or his evidence.

It reached the point where Dickie would be violently ill in his hotel room each morning, sick with fear about the absolute grilling he knew he was in for. He had come so far, spent so much, and put everything on the line. If he stuffed it up here, Dickie knew he may as well take what was left of his expense cheque, go and find a quiet desert island somewhere and curl up and die.

Everything in the previous four years came down to getting this court order.

The whole thrust of a Norwich Pharmacal order is to obtain documents or information from an innocent third party where there is a suspicion that those documents may contain evidence of a fraud by another party.

The fraud being alleged here was of course centred on the civil issue of concealment/deception. Dickie and Mourant didn't need to prove that a fraud had taken place. They only had to prove that in the documents they already had there was prima facie evidence identifying people in the Jersey lawfirm Ogier & Le Cornu who could add to whether or not a fraud had occurred.

And that was the constant theme of Dickie's questioning at Mourant's hands.

"Show me the people at Ogier & Le Cornu who you say are involved. Show me what documents you have to prove their involvement, and tell me why you think they can provide information that may relate to a fraud."

Mourant was certain they had a viable case. He believed that from the mark-ups on the horses, the way the loans were structured, and the flow of documents and money through the Channel Islands and Hong Kong, relating to both the bloodstock and also the film productions *Merry Christmas Mr Lawrence* and *The Adventures of the Little Prince*, that enough questionable dealing was going on to justify suspicion.

Ed Bendelow had blown the whistle to Paul Carran when Molloy first visited the island nearly a year earlier. Now Dickie had Bendelow in his sights and his finger on the trigger – legally speaking.

Friday morning, the day of the Court hearing, dawned with Dickie making his regular trip to the bathroom to throw up. Something else was also niggling at him: a feeling that the Judge was going to find one crucial paragraph in the massive affidavit difficult to understand. "Blast," thought Dickie, "we should have explained it better." He re-read the paragraph, and wrote notes on his hand about it.

When he finally arrived, pale and wretched, at the door of the Royal Court he drank in the aura of antiquity and elegance that cloaked the place. Although the building in its current guise was completed in 1887 it is Jacobean in style, with tremendous timber panelled walls and a silver mace presented to the island by Charles II soon after the Civil War.

The judge enters the chamber with two lay people, all of them dressed in red cloaks, and proceedings begin with a recitation of The Lord's Prayer in French.

Chris Dickie spent most of the morning watching fascinated as the daily parade of Jersey court business rolled out in front of him. Minor offences, mainly, such as charges under the Housing Act. These included being caught living on the island without a permit, and living in a house when you don't own the house. Jersey is a tight-knit community that guards its borders jealously. Only the incredibly wealthy or the sought-after can generally get approval to stay on the island as residents, and even then there are no guarantees.

When the time came for his own case to be heard, in the judge's chambers, the New Zealand lawyer was quivering with fear and anticipation. Chief Justice Sir Peter Crill fixed his gaze on Dickie from behind the massive desk.

"Mr Dickie, you've come a long way and this has taken a long time."

"Yes sir, it's taken since 1989 for me to get here," replied the lawyer, with more bonhomie than he actually felt at that moment.

The New Zealander's Norwich Pharmacal application was global in scale, in the sense that he was after everything he could get. The application listed some 53 entities and any document they'd come across that mentioned the Channel Islands. Dickie, Edwards and Molloy were after anything that would reveal who owned and controlled the tax haven companies.

Sir Peter glanced back down at the 30 centimetre thick affidavit, then peered across at Peter Mourant. "Are you satisfied, Mr Mourant, that all the exhibits that are attached here are referred to specifically in the body of the affidavit?"

Mourant looked calm and composed. He could afford to – he knew how the Jersey system worked, and he sensed this was going to work just fine. "Yes, I've spent the whole week cross examining Mr Dickie, and I'm satisfied that all the allegations that are made in the affidavit are supported by the documentation and the exhibits."

And then there was silence. The tick of the clock, and the muffled sound of an occasional car outside, the only noise in the room for the next half hour, as Sir Peter read through the massive document. Then came a question, as the Chief Justice asked Mourant for an explanation on one of the allegations. Mourant was having difficulty sorting it out.

Mindful that he wasn't permitted to speak, Dickie sat on his hands and breathed through his nose, getting more distressed by the second. Finally, unable to resist it any longer, he whispered in Mourant's ear. "I have the answer if that would be of any assistance."

The Judge looked across at the New Zealander. "Can you help us, Mr Dickie?"

"It's paragraph 35, second clause, your honour!"

The Judge flicked to the relevant page, and then looked quizzically back at Dickie. "Thank you very much. How, on earth, did you know that?"

"Your Lordship, I've spent nine months working on that document, and I actually thought you might ask me that question, so I've written it on my hand," Dickie explained, waving his paw in the air.

Former SFO director Charles Sturt at the Winebox Inquiry, 1997.

Chris Dickie (in white shirt) and Peter Mourant discussing the case in Jersey, 1991.

ABOVE: *Mont Orgueil Castle, Jersey.*

LEFT: *Shanker crab, Jersey. The pincers are broken by fishermen, as they are powerful enough to inflict very serious injuries.*

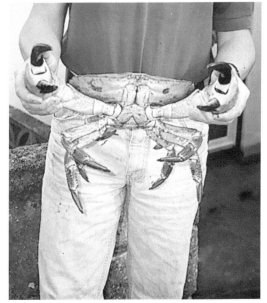

TOP AND CENTRE: *The Royal Court of Jersey.* COURTESY *THE JERSEY EVENING POST*

LEFT: *Pirouet House, Jersey, containing the Ogier & Le Cornu lawfirm and tax haven operation.* COURTESY *PETER MOURANT*

The bloodstock: Rustic Lace *(above) and* Hard To Tell *(below).*

Bloodstock consultant Mitchell McLeith.

Bloodstock and film promoter Chris Kirkham.

Brian Henry, counsel to Winston Peters at the Winebox Inquiry.

Sir Ronald Davison, Winebox Inquiry commissioner.

The National Bank
of New Zealand Limited

JEAN BATTEN PLACE
AUCKLAND

CHEQUE
DUTY
PAID

31/7 19 86

Pay Buckingham Enterprises Limited and Company

the sum of Two Hundred and Fifty Thousand

Dollars

$ 250,000

or Bearer

ANZON CAPITAL LIMITED

⑈431581⑈ ⑈060101⑈ 060113⑈000 ⑈

*One of the Wicklow cheques for subscription in the Buckingham partnership,
written but never banked.*

Sir Peter Crill's austere features burst, first into a grin and then a long, rolling laugh. "Look, this weighty tome of yours needs some consideration, so I've decided to cancel the rest of my afternoon sitting to deal with it. I'll give you a decision at 4.30pm."

The next few hours were tough on Dickie, but he felt the tide had turned. The body language had been good. "I was confident we were going to get the order. I was confident we had it. It was an ex parte application so there were no defendants present, it was just a question of satisfying the court.

"Basically we were trying to satisfy the Jersey court that their jurisdiction was being used for laundering, and there were people who could assist in establishing whether or not a fraud had occurred."

The phone call from the court to Peter Mourant's office duly came at 4.30pm. "The order has been made and will be ready to pick up and serve on the defendants straight away," confirmed the registrar.

"Thank Christ," exclaimed Dickie. It was time to swing into action. Mourant dialled up Ogier & Le Cornu's phone number and asked for Ed Bendelow. Dickie was grinning like a Cheshire cat in the corner, and Mourant didn't bother hiding a smirk either.

"I'm sorry," replied the receptionist. "Mr Bendelow is leaving for Iceland tonight."

Dickie's eyebrows levitated several centimetres. "Oh yeah?" he muttered. "Not anymore he's not."

"Well," continued Mourant, "please be advised that we're putting you on notice that a court order will be served in the next ten minutes." And it was.

Tony Molloy was clearly impressed that Jersey regarded its own reputation as a tax haven to be more important than protecting some of its less salubrious clients.

"Once we were able to indicate that we had a strong case of fraud, the Jersey Courts were very anxious, they made it quite clear 'we will not be knowing instruments of fraud, and that's that. The islands' reputation will be buggered if that happened', so they didn't raise any obstacles to us. It's always hard to show fraud — it's hard here — but once we'd shown it to their satisfaction the Jersey Courts didn't fudge it."

Bendelow left for Iceland knowing he now had a major problem on his hands, but Dickie and Mourant chose to relieve the stress with a boating excursion. They sailed across to the neighbouring island of Guernsey.

"The air is pure and the soil rich and fertile," records the 1822 *Gazetteer*. "A lake at the north part of the island affords excellent carp. Game and poultry are plentiful. The island is defended by a ridge of rocks, from one of which emery is collected.

"Wine is imported from France in great quantities, and is the usual drink of the richer inhabitants; but elder, of which many hogsheads are annually made, is the common drink of the inferior classes.

"The staple manufacture is knit stockings, and Port St. Pierre is the chief town."

Exactly 170 years after those words were recorded for posterity by some long-dead traveller, another traveller would get the chance to form his own impression of Guernsey.

"It was very early autumn there. The tourists had left and the weather was nice. Beautiful rolling countryside, mighty small of course, but a very pretty place.

"The thing that amazed me was the tides. The tides are 40 feet! The second-highest tides in the world."

As they motored up in Mourant's cruiser to the port entrance, all Dickie could see was a massive sea wall towering above them. "There's a water race across the top of the wall, and you wait for the tide to come in so you can take the huge launch through it. And you literally wait under this huge wall for the tide to lift you and carry you through."

Having gained entrance to the harbour, visiting craft anchor and wait for the Customs launch to arrive. Beyond, Dickie could see the historic old village with its cobbled streets climbing up the hills behind. But as for the "inferior classes", there's not a trace left of the peasants or their hogsheads of elderberry.

"No, they're not ordinary country folk. The wealth is beyond belief. You go down into the marina and you see the boats – we can be proud of Westhaven and say we've got big boats, but the boats in Guernsey and Jersey were just mega-cruisers, massively expensive beyond belief."

In the Channel Islands, even the peasants are millionaires.

"There was a guy who was a baker, and that was his job: baking bloody bread! But he was also a secretary for a whole lot of these so-called offshore companies and he had to sign documents. He was a secretary for about 500 companies, and signing off documents he earned money for each document.

"Talk about making bread! The money was phenomenal.

"As for the Mercedes Benz cars and the Porsches, it's a joke! They've only got one road, and they've got one straight – they call it the five mile straight but it's only three-quarters of a mile long – and it's narrow, but it's absolutely ridiculous. They have all these incredible cars, but you can't use them.

"Everyone drives around in these unbelievable cars, but there's nowhere to go. It's weird. There are so many cars in Jersey, incidentally, that if you lined them up from the port they would stretch all the way up to Bristol, in England. Peter Mourant had five vehicles."

So after a weekend of sailing and drooling, Dickie was suitably revved up for a Monday morning showdown with Ogiers. Escorted into a room at the lawfirm's Jersey office, Dickie and Mourant found themselves facing a line of lawyers on the other side of the table with absolutely stony faces. If looks could kill, Dickie suspected he would have been incinerated on the spot.

The discussions did not go smoothly.

"Look," explained an exasperated Mourant at one point, "life would be a lot easier for all of us if you just admit who you are representing!"

But the protestations of innocence continued, accompanied by what Dickie called "the glazed look of a stunned mullet".

"It's very unfortunate," explained one of the Ogier team, "but Mr Bendelow does have to leave for Iceland straight away, and he won't be back for three weeks."

"No problem," soothed Mourant. "You make your files available and we can flick through them here, because we're only looking, in the end. All we need is the papers that show the beneficial ownership and control of Zorasong, Chary Holdings and Komanti."

The atmosphere began to become quite nasty. Ogiers were clearly very, very tense, because of the client privilege issue, that an order had been made against them to cough up the documents, and they made it very clear that this was putting the lawfirm out considerably. They certainly weren't prepared to let Mourant and Dickie sift through their files looking for evidence.

"Mr Bendelow is the person handling this case. He is going to be away, I suggest we talk again in three weeks on his return," said an Ogiers representative.

Dickie and Mourant tried to work off the tension by taking a drive to the other side of the tiny island that evening. The lights at the base of Mont Orgueil Castle cast brilliant pools of yellow on the centuries-old stone walls and, in turn, spectacular shadows as the two men walked beneath it in the darkness.

Further below them, the fishing village at Gorey Harbour, and the fleet of fishing boats wallowing in the tide's ebb.

"What are our chances of getting anything useful out of this?" Dickie wondered aloud.

"I should think the odds are pretty bloody good, actually," replied the Jersey lawyer. "You see, Chris, while our clients might destroy records back in their own jurisdictions, you'll find tax haven trust companies and lawyers keep copies of everything. It's our only safeguard, especially if the client turns out to be involved in something illegal which we could be held responsible for.

"Ogiers won't have destroyed anything, they'll have it all."

So Dickie flew home, knowing that he'd won the court case requiring Ogiers to produce the documents, and being assured of that firm's "cooperation".

The next three weeks were like a very long Christmas Eve for the New Zealand lawyer. Murphy's Law decreed that something would have to go wrong: the Holy Grail would have to remain unattainable, although Ogiers had again confirmed to Peter Mourant that they would fully comply with the court order to hand over all the documents.

Fresh from round one success in the Channel Islands, however, Chris Dickie thought he would try his luck in Hong Kong while he waited to return to Jersey.

He made arrangements through his London lawyers, Simmons & Simmons, to meet up with a representative from their Hong Kong office, Colin Leaver, to discuss the possibility of a Norwich Pharmacal order in Hong Kong against Deloittes.

In a Hong Kong office tower late one July afternoon, Dickie sat with Leaver showing him the material he'd managed to dig up and detailing the nature of proceedings in Jersey.

"Chris," said Leaver after a while, "don't even try. Don't even think about it."

"But Colin," protested the New Zealander, "we've got the evidence, it should be easy to go for an order here!"

"If you try," said Leaver, staring directly at Dickie, "you will be bumped off. You will not get to Kai Tak airport tonight."

The New Zealander didn't believe him. "Don't be so melodramatic, Colin, nothing's going to happen."

"Don't be so bloody naïve, Chris! This is Hong Kong. Don't you realise what goes on here? Let me spell it out for you: if you go to see one of the big legal or accounting firms here, you don't know who will be listening to your conversation, and you will have no control, because what you are after will instantly be known to everyone."

"Then why don't I take this to the Hong Kong Serious Fraud Office, or whatever it is that you have here," said Dickie. "They can investigate, they've got the power to deal with these people."

Leaver felt like smacking his forehead with the palm of his hand in a gesture of exasperation.

"I obviously haven't explained this properly. This is Hong Kong. Organised crime runs this city, and they run the law enforcement agencies too. You cannot trust any of them. If you go to a law enforcement agency with this information, you will be dead before you reach the airport to leave."*

It may sound over the top, but the threat was very real. In an interview with the author, a former top fraud investigator for the Hong Kong Government confirmed the extent of corruption within the colony's law enforcement agencies.

"I was a victim of my own success, Ian," he said. "I kept digging into the bad guys, and I found that the money laundering, gun running and drug trafficking was intertwined with some of the major corporates here, Government officials and even the British security services.

"When I wouldn't stop investigating, they let me keep my title, but gave me a desk without an in-tray. I was given nothing more to investigate. The Hong Kong police force is run by the Triads.

"That's one of the reasons that you now have Asian organised crime in New Zealand," he added. "When the Labour Government opened up immigration in the late 1980's, it naively thought it could screen the immigrants and weed out the undesirables. Even more naively, your Government was allowing Hong Kong Government agencies to do the vetting, and Hong Kong's got the best agencies money can buy."

---

* There is no suggestion, nor should the reader draw any inference, that any parties to the NZ film and bloodstock issues would in any way be involved in such threats. As will be explained in this book, the danger to Dickie was from unrelated parties in Hong Kong who may have become aware of his investigations into some of the colony's companies involved in tax haven work. It was suggested that such parties would shoot first rather than waste time asking questions to ascertain whether the New Zealander posed a real threat or not.

The full enormity of his plight was beginning to dawn on Dickie, but what he couldn't figure out was the reason for such sensitivity.

"Why? Why should they care about some pisspot little bloodstock and film deals running out of New Zealand?"

"They don't," replied Leaver bluntly, "but you are digging into the Hong Kong nominee companies behind those entities, and you will find those companies are not just providing nominee services to New Zealand, they're providing them to a whole range of clients – the kind of clients who take decisive action if they think someone is trying to investigate them.

"They will not tolerate such an investigation in their jurisdiction."

Dickie slumped back in his chair, gazing out over the hazy skyline. "We're fucked," he sighed. "Absolutely and utterly fucked."

"You know," he said, turning to look at the Hong Kong lawyer, "this is all beginning to get very big – too big. I just want to go home."

But he wouldn't be home for long. Dickie was due back in Jersey, but he wasn't expecting the shock that awaited him there, either.

"Ogiers amassed an incredible amount of time and expense collating all these documents. We got a bill for nearly $300,000. They had a number of partners and staff who'd been working week after week collating this stuff, and they presented us with this bill we had to pay because Ogiers were quite 'innocent' and we had to provide security for costs."

Dickie felt like he'd been set up. He and Mourant had offered to sit with Ogiers and search the files themselves, but that offer had been turned down. Now he was having to pay at maximum legal rates. He wondered now whether this was where Paul Carran had picked up his bad habits when it came to charging. Still, Dickie could see he was getting quite a bit of bang for his buck, as the Ogier lawyer explained to him.

"Look, you've never believed us, you've never trusted us, but we want you to know that we are to be trusted and we've done everything the way we felt it had to be done.

"We can assure you that we have got all the documents that you requested. In fact, I have to tell you that there are so many documents that the biggest problem you've got is how on earth you're going to get them back to New Zealand."

The Jersey solicitor looked at Dickie intently. "I'm not kidding. You're going to need a jumbo jet to take them back. There are that many documents."

But Chris Dickie had no intention of using a jumbo jet, or taking them back to New Zealand. After his Hong Kong fright, the last thing he wanted was to be caught with a planeload of top-secret tax haven documents in New Zealand – especially after the threats that he and others like Dorothy Coates had already received. For the first time in the investigation, the lawyer began to fear for his life.

No, there was no way these documents were going to New Zealand. A call to a friend of a friend in France led him to a fishing trawler captain.

Just as the ill-fated French incursion of 1781, the 1992 plan would see the

French fishing boat slipping in under cover of darkness to take a cargo of documents. Destination unknown, as far as any Jersey officials were aware.

In fact, Dickie made arrangements to offload the treasure on the Brittany coast of France. But it wasn't to be. Russell McVeagh had been tipped off after an unfortunate coincidence, and applied to stop the transfer of the documents.

The chain of events that brought Russell McVeagh across to Jersey is still fresh in the mind of Mitchell McLeish.

"When Securelaunch was being investigated by Dickie, we found out in a very odd manner. I was trying to deal with Bendelow in Jersey on the same issues, and he wouldn't take any calls from me, you see.

"But you know, when you ring these offices, that these guys are always around. He was always out, and it appeared to be my name, so I got Tracey to ring up and she said 'Hi, it's Tracey from Canterbury' and of course he assumed she meant England and he immediately took the call, which she passed to me.

"But he said he was in all kinds of trouble over this thing and wasn't allowed to talk about it. So that's how we knew that Dickie was there, so of course we rang Russell McVeagh who immediately sent two fellows up in a plane and spoiled his fun.

"That's how serious Dickie was," chuckled McLeish. "He was stoppable, always, you know."

There was a screaming match in the courtroom, and in the midst of the uproar Dickie managed to get the costs of accessing the documents dropped to less than a third of the original figure. Russell McVeagh fought against their release on the grounds some of the documents might be legally privileged on behalf of their clients, although the lawfirm didn't specify who its clients were.

So the documents went not to a fishing trawler stinking of haddock and cod, but into the custody of the Jersey court. Ogiers bowed out, leaving Russell McVeagh and McVeagh Fleming to continue their titanic struggle in an ancient court room in a medieval fiefdom 18,000 kilometres from home.

As the Ermine Statement of Claim later pointed out, the Jersey treasure trove was a major discovery. The statement alleges that Russell McVeagh's process of discovery left a hell of a lot to be desired, especially when the plaintiffs had to travel halfway around the world to find "63 boxes of relevant documents" that had been referred to in one *paragraph* by Russell McVeagh which said "Other relevant documents the existence of which are known to Russell McVeagh but which are in the possession of other persons. . .overseas financial institutions referred to in the pleadings and in this list. . .Ogier & Le Cornu and related entities."

Licking his wounds, Dickie flew home, only to leap from a frying pan into the fire. *

---

* The legal battle in Jersey was never resolved. With the element of surprise lost and a lengthy and expensive struggle ahead, the Channel Islands litigation dwindled in importance as Dickie and Molloy found new evidence in other locations. The documents remain in Jersey, merely waiting for someone with enough money and powerful lawyers to uplift them.

CHAPTER 24

Winston's War

"If thou be of the Table Round, quoth Tarquin speedily,
Both thee, and all thy fellowship, I utterly defy."
– SIR THOMAS MALORY, *LE MORTE D'ARTHUR*, 1470

Chris Dickie's neighbour was there at Auckland's Jean Batten International Airport to collect the lawyer from his flight. "Gidday mate," the man grinned, "did you hear the news this morning?"

A weary Dickie gazed out the window of the car at the strange mix of industry and farmland that bracketed the main road from the airport to the city.

"No," he sighed, "why?"

"Winston Peters," said the driver as if he was delivering a punch-line. Dickie could feel his guts tightening. "There's a *Herald* in the back seat there somewhere, it's the lead on page 3," continued his neighbour.

Dickie was already grabbing for it. "Peters alleges tax fraud in movie funding" yelled the headline across the page.

"Mr Winston Peters yesterday launched a new attack on the Bank of New Zealand sale," began Andrew Stone's article, "accusing two of its Fay Richwhite Ltd directors of tax fraud in a 10 year old film financing arrangement.

"His allegations, denied last night by the directors – the BNZ deputy chairman, Dr Robin Congreve, and Mr Geoff Ricketts – once more were made under parliamentary privilege where MPs are protected from libel action.

"Mr Peters also accused the Inland Revenue Department of failing to act in the matter, which he described as 'massive criminal fraudulent activity'."

"Shit!" exclaimed Dickie out loud. "Shit."

"The MP asked in Parliament: 'What immunity from prosecution do these perpetrators of fraud have?'

"He said that earlier yesterday he gave the file to the Serious Fraud Office. The Commissioner of Inland Revenue, Mr David Henry, said last night: 'Any suggestion there has been inactivity by the Inland Revenue Department is completely wrong.'"

In Parliament, Peters had honed in on the involvement of Congreve and Ricketts as investors in *Merry Christmas Mr Lawrence*, spelling out that for every dollar they had invested they'd received tax benefits of $2.44. He estimated that Congreve – who'd sunk $10,000 into the venture – was responsible for "defrauding New Zealand Revenue personally of $34,400" and Ricketts, who'd invested $35,000, was guilty of "defrauding New Zealand Revenue of $120,400 and, as we all know in this country, both Robin Congreve and Geoff Ricketts are directors of the Bank of New Zealand."

This was of special significance to Winston Peters: it was the Bank of New Zealand bailout that he was really concerned about, and which he desired an inquiry into. The Government had steadfastly refused an inquiry, and Peters was looking around for anything he could throw that was likely to stick. Allegations of tax evasion against two BNZ directors would do nicely, thank you.

Not that Peters was leaving their Russell McVeagh colleague, Paul Carran, out of the loop. "The third person is Paul Carran, who invested $15,000, thereby defrauding New Zealand Revenue of $51,600."

The MP added that in addition to the straight tax rort, there was also the rort on the investors involving the hidden profits in the Channel Islands. He attacked the letter from Ed Bendelow, while he was wearing the hat titled Bonningdale Ltd, which asked Britain's National Film Trustee Company for a "previously undisclosed fee" of US$2.9 million.

"The promoters and their advisers," Peters told Parliament on August 4, 1992, "have a clearly established scheme for how the money is to be controlled, and the documents prove it in the form of a memorandum showing the intended cash flow. Clearly, the purpose of Bonningdale in the chain is to take all of the money due to the special partnership.

"This structure is an absolute fraud; the moneys that the genuine investors expected they would receive are being taken by Bonningdale."

Peters tabled documents relating to the movie deal, including the April 7, 1987 letter from the IRD warning investors they were facing prosecution. Former Prime Minister David Lange swung in behind Peters, telling Parliament "I commend him for bringing the issue forward to the House in that detail. .there is a very clear body of evidence that indicates a clear conspiracy amongst those people to produce from the taxpayer more than they ever hoped to get from artistic endeavour in the cinematographic area.

"They ought to be brought to book in relation to those gains; whether they be called civil or criminal evasions, or whatever, they are, it seems to me and it is my submission, returnable to the taxpayer."

But Chris Dickie was still wallowing in the detail of the *Herald* report on the drive back to the city. "Last night," continued the article, "a senior Russell McVeagh partner issued a statement describing the Peters allegations as grossly inaccurate, wildly extravagant and simply untrue.

"Mr John King said the firm had total confidence in the partners named by Mr Peters. Dr Congreve and Mr Ricketts, he said, had been singled out because they were BNZ directors. Their involvement arose because the firm advised the promoters and they, like other Russell McVeagh partners, invested in the film.

"Mr King said *Merry Christmas Mr Lawrence* had been fully investigated by Inland Revenue 'and no allegations of fraud have been made by the department against the investors or promoters.'

"He added that the Inland Revenue Department letter alleging the funding was a sham was later withdrawn by the department. The lawfirm, he said, categorically denied that it or any partners were involved in a fraud on the department or film investors."

Of course, as we now all know, the withdrawal of sham allegations over *Merry Christmas* remained a highly contentious issue amid feelings that the IRD had been blackmailed into backing down by Russell McVeagh. Certainly John King's confident assertion that the film had been fully investigated has been shown by history to be incorrect – Tony Bouzaid had ordered the investigation closed despite the appearance of fresh new leads and information.

The IRD's Denese Latimer told the inquiry she still stands by the original sham allegation. But of course, no one really knew this back then.

In the Inland Revenue Department's head office, however, the paranoia had reached epidemic proportions. They believed either that someone within the IRD's Auckland office was leaking information to Winston Peters, or that Dickie and Molloy were supplying information to Peters, or that their staff were leaking to Dickie and Molloy who passed on the information to Peters.

On Wednesday, August 5, IRD Commissioner David Henry phoned up Denese Latimer at 9.00am. "Have the media been in touch with you about *Merry Christmas Mr Lawrence*?"

Latimer was taken aback by the Commissioner's sudden interest in her activities, but confirmed to him that she'd had no media contact and if she had any inquiries she would refer them to head office.

The inquiry documents also show David Henry wanted to know what had taken place in the settlement of *Merry Christmas*, and Latimer explained that Geoff Clews had managed to obtain the settlement through the use of what was alleged to be a forged document. She also told Henry how Bouzaid had forbade her from inquiring further into the allegation that US$2.9 million in movie profits had been hidden in the Channel Islands. Henry's response to the news was blunt.

"Tony made that decision, and that's enough for me."

Henry, having already told the media there was nothing in the allegations made by Peters, appears in the eyes of the author to have shot first and asked questions too late, judging by his next questions to Denese Latimer.

"Was there a fraud against the investors?"

"Yes," answered Latimer.

"What about us?" asked Henry who, by rights, should have been sweating by now.

"By accepting Mr Clews document without properly finalising our inquiries," said Latimer, "we were virtually saying no."

"Well," said Henry remembering his comments to the media a few hours earlier, "we withdrew the sham and fraud claims."

"Actually, we didn't," said Latimer. "The settlement chose not to deal with these aspects, but the end result, in effect, was yes."

"The department isn't concerned with who got the money," continued Henry.

"Under the settlement, we agreed not to look at anyone associated with the film and therefore that wasn't looked at," explained Latimer. "McVeagh Fleming provided us with the information, so they will be aware of the position."

"If the Serious Fraud Office contact you," he concluded, "you are not to give them any records, and you are to contact me."

"I'll do that," promised Latimer.

David Henry phoned back later the same day. He wanted to know whether the additional information would have resulted in a different decision on *Merry Christmas Mr Lawrence*.

"Given the circumstances of the settlement [presumably meaning the IRD's desperation to settle and avoid being hammered over the Endeavour raid]," said Latimer to the inquiry in 1995, "I didn't think so. He said a judgment decision had been made and, assuming it was correct, the data added nothing."

David Henry and Tony Bouzaid had, of course, already discussed the "judgment decision" back in May 1992 in some depth, and agreed on the course of action taken.

On Friday, August 7, 1992, three days after the Peters speech, another bomb went off underneath IRD Commissioner Henry, this time in a letter from Barclays Bank NZ. Barclays had promoted six feature films, including *Shaker Run* starring teen pop idol Leif Garrett.

The bank wanted to know why its partnerships had been treated harshly by the department, when others seemed to be getting special deals.

"By way of response, we were informed by your officers that each partnership had been subject to independent analysis by your legal staff, and that the department's unwillingness to compromise was the product of the strength and merits of the department's case on the evidence available to it.

"Given the essential similarity in the structures employed," continued the bank, "these general explanations were hardly satisfying at the time. They have become even less satisfactory, however, as the result of inquiries we have conducted since the failure of settlement discussions.

"As a result of the further information now available to us. . .we have concluded that the explanation for the differential treatment must lie in considerations other than those of which we have been advised.

"That situation is satisfactory to neither ourselves nor partners. We, and they, find it difficult to accept that the department has acted in an even-handed and consistent manner across the range of film partnerships.

"We request a meeting at which we would have the opportunity to reiterate our and our partners' concerns at the apparent lack of consistent treatment between taxpayers whose position is, on the basis of our inquiries, in all material respects the same."

What made the spat particularly interesting was that all of the Barclays partnerships had been categorised by the IRD as "black" cases.

On the same day, August 7, the Deputy Commissioner of Inland Revenue, Robin Adair, sent a memo to Northern Region's second-in-command, Norman Latimer.

"Given that the investigation into the film special partnership relating to *Merry Christmas Mr Lawrence* has concluded and the investigation into the bloodstock industry has been stopped, I do not wish there to be any further contact or discussion between our people and Mr A P Molloy QC or Mr C A Dickie or anyone acting on their behalf.

"The only exception to this would be if these people wished to post to us material they wish us to have. Can you please ensure that all of your staff are told of this decision."

Latimer was concerned at the directive, and especially the suggestion that the bloodstock investigation was being "stopped" as well. On August 11 he fired back his own memo to Adair.

"I feel obliged to raise with you some important background matters, and to respectfully question the desirability of the action that you have instructed.

"I note that the investigation into the bloodstock industry has never been 'stopped', as such, but has been held in suspension pending the outcome of a civil action brought by some of the bloodstock partners against the legal firm of Russell McVeagh McKenzie Bartleet & Co and others.

"As a result of a pending trial, the department finds itself in the position of being 'the meat in the sandwich' between Russell McVeagh and the promoters and various investors of the relevant special partnerships, represented respectively by Messrs Dickie and Molloy.

"Because of the well-publicised Parliamentary intervention of Mr Winston Peters MP, the matter is now clearly in the political arena, and is unlikely to be removed from that arena for some time to come."

Latimer agreed with Adair that the IRD needed to stay independent of either side in the bloodstock scrap, but said that Dickie had already been told this some months earlier and had been "most understanding". As a result, Dickie was now dealing directly with Norman Latimer, rather than the investigators Alan May or Denese Latimer.

"Such contact has involved unprompted approaches by Mr Dickie to update me about what has been happening with the above-mentioned litigation against Russell McVeagh and others, and to provide the department with documents in relation thereto.

"It should be remembered here," warned Latimer, "that in the interview held in your office with Messrs Molloy and Dickie in December 1990, they each agreed to hand all information in respect of these matters to the department."

Hell, the IRD had even slapped a section 17 notice on Dickie ordering him on pain of punishment to keep handing information over!

Latimer was also mindful of the practicalities of limiting contact to mailbox only. "A number of the papers provided by Mr Dickie have been highly sensitive and confidential and have, in my opinion, been properly handed directly to me. In addition. . .the physical bulk of some of the documents has rendered it to some degree impractical to use post or fax facilities – all the more so since Mr Dickie's office is only a short walk from my own.

"I am unclear why the department is now suggesting that contact with

Messrs Molloy and Dickie should be curtailed except through the medium of post."

Norman Latimer added that the two lawyers had done everything asked of them so far, and "carried out their part of the arrangement without impropriety."

In a section of his memo headed "My Concerns", Latimer wrote: "One of the points that Mr Peters makes under Parliamentary privilege is that there has been some kind of cover-up. While I naturally do not subscribe to this theory, it is important for the department to ensure that its actions do not give apparent substance to his allegations."

Latimer was opening fire on his head office now, with tact and diplomacy perhaps, but his barbs were like bullets wrapped in velvet: soft to the touch but still deadly. "I note with concern in this regard," he wrote, "that subsequent to Mr Peters' disclosures in Parliament, the department has been in communication with Messrs Russell McVeagh in respect of the matter.

"I am extremely concerned that the department's actions in communicating with Russell McVeagh, while at the same time limiting communication with Messrs Molloy and Dickie and suggesting that the bloodstock investigations have been 'stopped', might wrongly be construed by an independent third party, acting upon inquiry, as being evidential of not only a cover-up, but also of a conspiracy between the department and certain taxpayers or their representatives."

Forget the independent third party – within three years of that memo the IRD's own staff would be in the witness box at the Winebox Inquiry making the gravest allegations ever levelled at the IRD by senior employees.

But Norman Latimer wasn't finished yet. "Mr Dickie has openly admitted to me that Mr Peters has had contact with him. He has, however, denied providing any documents to Mr Peters. It is very likely that if he is advised of the restriction that you propose, he will immediately and adversely communicate with Mr Peters on the subject. This is likely to cause further questions to be raised by Mr Peters."

Latimer finished his memo to Adair by recommending that contact should continue with Dickie and Molloy under the existing arrangement, which had worked well. Should his recommendation be rejected, however, Latimer told Adair he had no intention of being the person to explain it to the two men.

"Common courtesy would require your office to make that communication direct with Messrs Molloy and Dickie, as they would no doubt require reasons for the department's position, which I am not personally in a position to provide."

Translated into a more direct form: do your own dirty work.

Adair apparently didn't have the intestinal fortitude to deliver the fatal blow personally. He wrote back to Latimer and confirmed the ban on contact would stay, and that it was Latimer's job to tell the two lawyers.

"There should not be further communication with Messrs Molloy or Dickie. They may continue to send us material if they wish.

"Please acknowledge this message and confirm your acceptance of my instructions."

By chance, Chris Dickie rang Norm Latimer later that afternoon. Latimer took a diary note of the conversation.

"I informed him of the situation and invited him to make further contacts and provision of items by mail. He did not wish me to talk to Mr Molloy and undertook to speak to him himself as he had a meeting arranged with him.

"The reaction of Mr Dickie was one of surprise and he indicated that he was appalled. On the other hand he indicated that he accepted the instruction and would abide by it.

"He also stated that he would deal with the issue in his own time. He stated that he thinks the Commissioner may have some problems but did not elucidate further. He then terminated the call."

The following day, August 13, 1992, Dickie wrote to the Commissioner of Revenue demanding an explanation and clarification of the bizarre order "in writing, immediately". He sent the letter via Norman Latimer's office.

Deputy Commissioner Adair wrote back confirming the order. Adair also wrote to Norman Latimer to chew him out over the memo he'd written taking the department to task.

Adair demanded "a list of all contact (including Otahuhu Inspectors) with Mr Dickie together with copies of notes of interview. Where notes had not been kept a summary of matters discussed and information supplied should be made.

"I am pleased to note that you do not subscribe to the theory that there has been some kind of cover-up," sizzled the words on Adair's page. "However, the fact that you have chosen to burst into print with your concerns about the department's actions in communicating with Russell McVeagh is unfortunate.

"We did receive a copy of the Russell McVeagh media release and sent them a copy of ours. We also asked for a copy of a letter sent to investors and as you know this was sent to the Otahuhu Inspectors for confirmation of the percentage figure used.

"Mention of 'cover-up' and 'conspiracy' from a senior officer only casts doubt about the department's actions when there are absolutely no grounds for any doubt."

Well, that was the head office opinion perhaps, but others saw it differently.

"Because of your close involvement," Adair continued, "you know that the film investigations were conducted under standard procedures and were consistent with the tax legislation.

"Independent legal advice was taken where necessary. I understand that you personally agree with the outcome of the investigations.* Your memo is subject to discovery in the event of any proceedings and frankly does not help at all."

It was the beginning of the end for Norman Latimer's long IRD career, as he, his wife Denese and senior investigator Alan May found themselves in the gunsights of head office. But there was other strangeness afoot.

---

* Latimer told the inquiry that whilst he agreed in principle with settling the almost 100 resource-hungry film investigations, he was not happy with some of the settlements at issue.

CHAPTER 25

Incompetent? Or Corrupt?

"A certain laird in Fife, well known for his parsimonious habits. .
.his weekly contribution to the church collection never exceeded
the sum of one penny. One day, however, by mistake, he dropped
into the plate at the door a five shilling piece, but discovering his
error before he was seated in the pew, hurried back, and was about
to replace the dollar by his customary penny when the elder in
attendance cried out, 'Stop, laird, ye may put in what ye like, but
ye maun tak naething out!' The laird, finding his explanations went
for nothing, at last said, 'A weel, I suppose I'll get credit for it in
heaven.' 'Na, na, laird,' said the elder, 'ye'll only get credit for
the penny.' "

– DEAN RAMSAY, *SCOTTISH LIFE & CHARACTER*, 1862

When Winston Peters made his controversial August 4 speech about Merry Christmas Mr Lawrence, he also laid a complaint with the Serious Fraud Office, asking director Charles Sturt to investigate possible corruption involving IRD Commissioner David Henry over the film settlement deal.

In a letter dated August 7, Peters stated "my complaints are:

1. It is clear from the documents that a significant conspiracy to defraud exists.
2. Mr King, a senior partner in the law firm Russell McVeagh McKenzie Bartleet & Co has publicly stated that the Inland Revenue complaint of 7 April 1987 has been withdrawn.
3. Mr Henry, Commissioner of the Inland Revenue Department, has publicly stated that this matter was fully investigated and completed in December 1991.
4. Early next week I will send you Mr Henry's response which can be read from the Minister's responses to Parliamentary questions from the Honourable David Caygill, which questions arise from an article in the NBR of early this year.
5. I understand that the great majority of investors in the film *Merry Christmas Mr Lawrence* are being required to repay the money deducted in reliance on the investment.

"This can only be the case if the Department of Inland Revenue's view, as expressed in the 7 April 1987 note to investors, remains unchanged and an improper deduction has been made.

"I believe the perpetrators named in my speech in the House have reached an agreement with the Commissioner of Inland Revenue, which is recorded in writing and includes an agreement not to prosecute.

"I believe such an agreement is unlawful and that a serious criminal conspiracy has been wrongfully covered up in circumstances where the Commissioner of Inland Revenue had, and still has, a duty to initiate a prosecution."

Now, what Peters didn't have in his hot little hand was the actual settlement agreement signed by Tony Bouzaid after Denese Latimer's refusal to do so. As can be seen from Peters' letter to Sturt, the politician suspected that such a written agreement existed, and he wanted the SFO to go looking for it.

"I asked them to investigate an agreement between a civil servant and a so-called taxpayer that was unlawful," Peters later told the Winebox Inquiry, "and, more importantly, to find the document which I believed was in existence."

Peters, meanwhile, was upping the ante. On August 19, 1992, he again attacked Russell McVeagh and the Inland Revenue Department.

"The fact that I want to point out to the news media and to certain people in this country who think the deal was OK is that *the film made money*. [author's emphasis] As with the Watergate scandal, we have to follow the money to find out where the fraudulent behaviour is. The film made millions.

"Yet, after the promise was made to the investors that they would acquire a share in those profits, and after the promise was made to the Inland Revenue Department that, if profits were made, those profits would be deductible [taxable, sic], the money did not come back to New Zealand. It did not come to the investors, or to the Inland Revenue Department.

"For four years the Inland Revenue Department had the view that this was a sham. I want to know what happened to change the mind of the Commissioner of Inland Revenue. Why, for four years, did he assert that there had been a sham: fraudulent behaviour, in fact criminal behaviour?

"If he could substantiate that allegation, why for four years did he keep up that assertion, then suddenly in December 1991 change his mind?"

Peters wanted to know how "Russell McVeagh McKenzie Bartleet, or partners in it, is able to obtain a no-prosecution arrangement?"

Within two hours of Peters' new speech, David Henry was on the phone to Denese Latimer. He asked if it was possible that Chris Dickie might have known the information that was released in the House, and where he might have obtained the information from. Latimer told him she had no idea.

Given that even the number two official in the IRD's massive Northern Region office had recognised that the non-prosecution agreement might raise issues of corruption and conspiracy, was it at all unreasonable for Winston Peters to seriously believe that the IRD and the SFO might actually be corrupt, given the events that were about to follow? Because what followed, in my view, was absolutely unconscionable.

As you will discover, later in this book, the Serious Fraud Office did not investigate Peters' complaint, despite claiming publicly to have done so.

Instead, on August 21, 1992, Sturt issued a media release at 11.50am.

"There is no information before me that would lead me to conclude that Mr Henry has been involved in any way in a cover-up of a criminal conspiracy."

Winston Peters couldn't believe his ears, because the previous evening he'd found David Henry telling the media "when the Serious Fraud Office agrees to discuss it with me, I will be happy to do so."

"I drew the inference," Peters told the Winebox Inquiry in 1996, "that the Director of the Serious Fraud Office had made little or no inquiry, and certainly not of the Commissioner."

Which begs the question: how could the SFO know whether there was any evidence if it never went looking for it? Again, what inference would a reasonable person draw from such a situation?

Having heard the outcome of his complaint on the radio, Peters wasn't officially informed until three days later, on August 24.

"I apologise for the administrative oversight in not acknowledging your complaint of 7 August 1992," wrote Sturt.

"You may not have been aware that the *investigation* [author's emphasis] into the allegations surrounding the film partnership *Merry Christmas Mr Lawrence* and other film and bloodstock partnerships were commenced by this office in 1991."

And then came a bare-faced lie from the director of the Serious Fraud Office.*

"Furthermore, the *investigation* of the allegations relating to Mr Henry, Commissioner of the Inland Revenue Department, were likewise commenced and completed many months ago.

"The findings of our *investigation* satisfied me completely that the allegation of any criminal wrong-doing by Mr Henry was groundless. As would be expected, this was treated in the strictest of confidence.

"The matters to which you referred recently in Parliament and the material you forwarded to this office were already well known and did not alter in any way the conclusion I had already arrived at some time ago."

SFO senior counsel, Willie Young, outlined to Peters the extent of the SFO's inquiries.

"Following the publication of the Wogistan article, the existence of possible corruption in relation to the IRD was discussed within the Serious Fraud Office.

"The investigators dealing with the films investigations were asked to keep an eye out for any evidence that supported that allegation."

Young explained that "keeping an eye out" included attending the vineyard meeting, but the officers who attended learnt "nothing new".

"Now, the SFO will say that the allegations of corruption against Mr Henry

---

* Sturt was once asked at the Winebox Inquiry by Colin Carruthers QC: "Do you think it is ever acceptable for a law enforcement agency to make statements which are misleading?" Sturt's reply: "In particular circumstances, they may be justified."

were seen in the light of the inability of anyone ever to produce anything concrete."

"Mr Young," snapped Peters in response. "Did your client ever ask the Inland Revenue Department for that agreement? Did they ever ask Inland Revenue for this agreement which sets out clearly an agreement not to prosecute and other favourable privileged matters?

"One simple question by Mr Sturt to Inland Revenue would have found all the evidence that you, or anybody else, required!"

"Mr Peters," snarled Willie Young back, "you are not here to ask me questions!"

"Mr Young. . .a Member of Parliament is making serious allegations about a non-prosecution agreement. 'Mr Henry, does such an agreement exist?' Simple question. The most rudimentary of questions and procedures to follow, and it appears to me your client didn't bother to take that very minor step."

On August 26, *New Zealand Herald* journalist Denise McNabb quoted Sturt as saying his office could find no evidence of serious fraud in a number of bloodstock syndicates also involving Russell McVeagh and the subject of class action before the High Court.

The veracity of Sturt's claims would depend, I believe, on one's definition of the word "investigation", a word Sturt had major trouble with at the Winebox Inquiry. Certainly, it is now known that the SFO made no inquiries of the IRD in relation to the settling of the film deals, and certainly did not speak to Henry or Denese Latimer about it. To suggest that the SFO had "investigated" the matter is nothing short of a lie by the director of the Serious Fraud Office, in my view.

Certainly, even Willie Young acknowledged that the film settlement deal was dodgy in the eyes of the law.

"I agree that there may well be a real issue as to the enforceability of an agreement not to prosecute in this context and no one from [the SFO] is going to suggest anything else.

"For the position of the SFO, we understand the argument that an agreement not to prosecute is, at the very least, highly likely to be regarded as unenforceable."

Again, what inference could a reasonable person draw from the SFO's behaviour at this point? History shows that an arguably illegal non-prosecution agreement did exist, for which the IRD head office was responsible. History shows that a complaint was laid with the Serious Fraud Office, which then failed to investigate the specific complaint, but said publicly that it had and found nothing.

At best, it was sophistry.

Not only that, but after making no attempt to obtain the "secret, non-prosecution agreement" that Peters had been rabbiting on about for all this time, the SFO then admits, having been shown it by Peters at the inquiry, that the deal is unenforceable.

Is it any wonder that within legal and media circles associated with the film, bloodstock and soon-to-be winebox investigations, commentators began to discuss whether there was merit in Peters' parliamentary allegations?

It is important to take a look at whether an agreement not to prosecute is even lawful. If such an agreement is not lawful, then in my opinion the logical conclusion must be that the IRD staff and lawyers who agreed to it must have either deliberately ignored the law, or are careless for having failed to investigate further.

But the evidence would show that the IRD lawyers were not incompetent. Because Tony Bouzaid had asked IRD senior counsel Angela Satterthwaite the specific question.

"The advice I received," he said, "is that if fraud is detected later on, well fraud unravels the agreement."

But fraud was never going to be detected, because no further investigation was done. Bouzaid's response also appeared to be at odds with an earlier statement he'd made at the time of the settlement.

"What we are guaranteeing here," he told his staff, "is that we will not take any further action in any way on any person in relation to these specific films.

"It will therefore mean that if, for example, we found that there was no film in the camera in Primula, it's tough bickie."*

So the burning question must be: why didn't the IRD immediately re-open its investigations into *Merry Christmas Mr Lawrence* or any of the other suspicious movies, and throw the gauntlet down to Clews on the basis of Satterthwaite's advice?

But they didn't, despite knowing they had the power to do so and despite having enough circumstantial and forensic evidence in my opinion to justify it.

Why didn't Satterthwaite, or other members of the IRD legal team, override the IRD staff involved in the settlement and stridently point out that any issue of possible fraud *must* be investigated?

The IRD's overall failure to do so is, in my view, deplorable. The IRD must have deliberately ignored the law.

Still, as Willie Young QC pointed out, just because the settlement was dodgy didn't automatically prove corruption.

"Mr Peters, it is one thing to say this is an agreement that is a pretty good deal for the Russell McVeagh boys. This is an agreement that contains a non-prosecution agreement that, I think, should not be entered into by a Government department. That is one view. No one is disputing or challenging your right to say that.

"A very different view is to say that anyone who enters into that agreement is corrupt, guilty of a criminal conspiracy and appropriately the subject of all the other florid epithets you used."

---

* In my humble opinion, Bouzaid is displaying incredible naivete. I find it utterly incomprehensible that any competent New Zealand judge would accept such an analysis without taking a long hard look at dishonest intent first.

"Mr Young," replied an angry Peters, "your first statement is unmitigated drivel. It is a disgrace in a modern society."

It was too much for Sir Ronald Davison at this point, and the winebox commissioner stepped into the ring.

"Mr Peters, I am not going to have those statements made of the counsel."

All of this in just one 20 minute session of the inquiry. There were many others like it.

It is also important to bear in mind the other major events bubbling to the surface in late 1992, and upon which the MP was crystallising his views. Winston Peters was in full BNZ inquiry mode, the first winebox documents were beginning to surface in legal circles and would soon end up in the media's hands, and a computer dealer named Paul White who'd been meeting Winston Peters to discuss alleged corruption was about to get killed in a car accident.*

Back at the Inland Revenue Department, meanwhile, the witch-sniffers were out in force.

By the end of August, David Henry had demanded from the two Latimers and May details of all contact that they had had with the Serious Fraud Office. They all replied to the request, but the message came back from head office solicitor Angela Satterthwaite that May was to re-word his reply.

"Mr May's reply was considered by Angela to be facetious and she felt he should use more appropriate language, when replying to the Commissioner," Denese Latimer told the inquiry. It was clear that head office was looking for something to pin on someone.

On September 17, 1992, Denese Latimer, Alan May and Norman Latimer were summoned to Wellington for a meeting, "supposedly because of a complaint that Mr May had made about certain things," Denese Latimer told the inquiry. Except that the trio knew the subject had to be bogus, because "Mr May hadn't made any complaint to anybody."

There was small talk about the film deals, and then suddenly Commissioner of Revenue David Henry strode into the room. It was then that the real point of the meeting became crystal clear: he wanted to know about the vineyard meeting.

"The questions were," said Norman Latimer, "Have you spoken to Winston Peters? Have you spoken to Brian Henry? Were you invited to attend a meeting with Dr Molloy at his vineyard?"

Denese Latimer later recalled Henry's demeanour as "very serious. . .very uptight. . .and very accusing.

"I was actually stunned at what he was even suggesting, and I found the whole thing quite abhorrent."

Both Norman and Denese Latimer answered "no" to each question. In what May would later admit was a major error of judgment, he too answered "no" to all questions.

---

* See *The Paradise Conspiracy* for details of these other matters.

David Henry was looking directly at May. "I have information that indicates you may not be telling the truth. If that's right, you are going to be in serious trouble, Mr May." And then Henry turned and left.

Denese Latimer felt vulnerable. She said it was clear that head office suspected all three staff of leaking information to Peters.

"I had been a dissenter and had not signed that settlement letter, so obviously I wasn't completely and utterly in favour of everything that had occurred within the department."

Not that Latimer was entirely blameless: due to simple human error information obtained by the IRD had ended up in Dickie's hands and was later included in an affidavit filed in the lawsuit against Russell McVeagh and the bloodstock promoters. To make matters worse, that affidavit ended up being tabled in Parliament by Winston Peters.

"It was a pure accident," Latimer told the inquiry during cross examination from IRD lawyers.

"But this lapse on your part," asked Graeme Panckhurst QC for the IRD, "isn't it an example of the dangers that existed and the fact that you weren't necessarily equipped to handle yourself in those dealings?"

"That is your opinion," she replied.

Norman Latimer viewed Henry's Wellington meeting as a snare, "what I term as entrapment. They knew some answers to some questions, namely that Mr May had been to Dr Molloy's vineyard and that they were actually trying to find out if myself and Denese, in particular, had either been invited and declined, or something along those lines.

"In other words, I believe that we were under deep suspicion for some reason or other."

Latimer also took issue with the way head office raised the matter by ambush, given the set procedures in employment law and contracts to deal with such alleged misdemeanours.

"There is nothing more serious, from the department's view, than breach of secrecy, which can result in dismissal. It can actually result in a prison sentence.

"If you are talking about breach of secrecy, you are required to put such things to people concerned. You are required to give them the opportunity to have legal advice."

The Winebox Inquiry also heard that the head office team demanded the hand-over by Northern of any copies of Bouzaid's secret settlement document that remained in their possession.

"Did [IRD lawyer Angela Satterthwaite] say when she got all the documents back that she was going to shred them?" May's lawyer, Paul Cavanagh QC, asked Bouzaid during cross-examination.

"I certainly don't recall her saying that," said Bouzaid.

"Again," said Cavanagh, "evidence can be given that she said that – are you able to refute it?"

"Well, no" said the tax official, reiterating that he couldn't remember what had been said.

As for Alan May, head office didn't come back with a direct accusation immediately, but they worked feverishly behind the scenes to gather the evidence. May's job was going to be on the line.

There was still ongoing paranoia at head office level about Chris Dickie's alleged role in the Wogistan article, and Norman Latimer said Deputy Commissioner Robin Adair again warned him it would be dangerous to keep talking to Dickie.

Someone else, meanwhile, was also finding it dangerous to talk to Dickie. Businessman Stephen Lunn – the man who originally had European Pacific's winebox – had once worked for Challenge Corporate Services, the original company involved in the film and bloodstock deals. Lunn crossed my path in October 1992 while I was working as a news and current affairs journalist at TV3's *3 National News*. I had only recently been introduced to Chris Dickie myself.*

I brought both men together in a clandestine meeting. Dickie ended up having further discussions with Lunn but received a panicked phone call from him one night just after Lunn had been served by helicopter with an injunction ordering him to hand over the winebox to European Pacific.

A short time after the writ had been served, a woman phoned Lunn at his Waiheke Island home and warned that if he didn't cooperate "we will arrange for your boys to fall off the harbour bridge", and his own kneecaps would be broken.

Lunn ended up that night with armed protection, and Dickie's house was used as a police liaison point. All of which added to the lawyer's already grave fears for his own safety.

Chris Dickie was about to make a shocking decision.

---

* This incident is recounted in greater detail in *The Paradise Conspiracy*.

CHAPTER 26

Lawyers, Guns & Money

"What did the former Prime Minister's son actually do and how did
he accumulate his vast wealth? Business deals were conducted
through intermediaries, bank accounts were offshore and
shareholdings were held by nominees. Virtually no part of his
commercial affairs was accountable to the public or the regulatory
authorities and so there was no paper trail."

– PAUL HALLORAN & MARK HOLLINGSWORTH, *THATCHER'S GOLD*, 1995

The scrunch of gravel under the tyres told Dickie they were no longer on asphalt
and, judging by the slow, bumpy progress, he guessed it was a long driveway.
The car coasted to a stop.

"OK mate, follow me," came the voice. Dickie's eyes were still finding it
difficult to adjust to the darkness. He had no idea where he was, except that it
was a courtyard.

He followed his guide into the old house, and up some rickety stairs to a
gloomy attic. All he could see in the dim light was blankets all over the room.
And then the man pulled one of the blankets aside. Dickie's jaw dropped to the
floor.

Weapons. Dozens of guns. One of the largest arsenals the lawyer had ever
seen in his life, and that included during his time in the Army. Growing up after
the war, Dickie had been one of hundreds of thousands of children to undergo
compulsory military training at high school – in his case, Kings College.

Dickie had shown a proficiency for weaponry, to the point where he was
sent on a specialist weapons training course with the Army. At school, he was
in charge of the machine gun team, which hadn't been without its own dramas,
as he later recounted in a speech to his old school.

On one occasion, he'd been in charge of supervising the machine gun during
a parade of several hundred students at the college. The gun had been loaded
with what were supposed to have been blanks, but Dickie discovered to his
horror, as he looked down the sights at the passing students, that the
ammunition magazine was full of live rounds, and there was a real bullet in the
barrel already.

His next move was to have been to squeeze the trigger as part of the exercise,
but it was only the student's quick thinking that prevented a disaster.

The firing of "blanks", had it taken place that day, would have resulted in an incident that would have grabbed world, let alone New Zealand, headlines.

It transpired that after a live firing exercise the previous week with the students, the Army had mistakenly moved a full ammunition box into the dummy ammo pile. No one had discovered the error until Dickie checked before pulling the trigger.

Dickie's weapons training included the use of Bren guns, Sten guns and even mortars. He'd actually managed to blow up a sizeable tree with the latter during one school exercise. As part of the training, students learnt to lock off the mortar barrel before the rockets were dropped in.

Unfortunately for Dickie, his partner dropped the rocket in before Dickie had secured the barrel, and the high explosive charge went off as Dickie was holding the launcher. The force of the explosion kicked the barrel from his hands, sending the rocket careering into a tree with devastating effect. Luckily, no one was hurt.

More blankets were pulled away in the Auckland attic.

"This is a little large to conceal, isn't it?" Dickie said, picking up a handgun with a longer, chunkier barrel than he'd expected. The other man reached across and began twisting the barrel.

"That's because that's a silencer on the end," he explained as he unscrewed it. "What do you want? Straight or silenced? I'd recommend straight in your case, you're only using this in self-defence."

Dickie glanced around the attic, marvelling at the row after row of guns. Not just semi-automatics: some were fully automatic weapons. Enough hardware to start a medium sized war, sitting here in suburban Auckland city.

The lawyer was shown a semi-automatic pistol and shoulder holster. Light, easy to hide. Lethal. He remembered the advice from the friend in law enforcement: "two shots – the first into your attacker's chest, the second into the ceiling."

"Why the ceiling?" the lawyer had asked.

"Because when you've killed someone," explained the man, "and the cops come around to investigate, all they need to see is two shots. You will tell them you fired a warning shot into the ceiling but he kept coming, so you had to shoot him. You will be acting in self-defence.

"Remember, two shots. Kill the intruder first, then fire a warning shot."

Dickie would dine out on that advice for a while. At a social function he found himself surrounded by young accountants, and discussing methods of protecting one's clients. One of Dickie's staff solicitors, with a mischievous look in her eye, couldn't resist temptation. She brought a couple of the accountants up to him for a chat.

"Chris, I've just been telling these people the advice you would give for protecting clients with a firearm."

"Well," said Dickie, enjoying the moment and the smile on his female colleague's lips, "you always fire two shots."

The accountant stood there expectantly, eyes like saucers, as Dickie continued.

"The first shot you fire straight into the guts, because then you know you're going to hit something."

By this time the young bean-counter had gone white, but Dickie was relishing it now. "You fire the second shot through the roof, because when the cops come you can say you fired a warning shot and the bastard kept coming."

News of the pistol-packing lawyer's black humour spread like wildfire through the big accounting firm, which amused Dickie no end.

But had it become laughter without mirth? A grim reflection from a darkening soul. The lawyer was now feeling the pressure as never before. The class action lawsuit was moving incredibly slowly through the court system, and the 18 hour days were taking a horrible toll.

During one of the court hearings, the dark mood had been relieved briefly when the Court Registrar called Dickie's case aloud.

"Will the prisoner please stand," quipped one of the other lawyers in the room. The entire court, including Dickie and the judge, cracked a grin.

It wasn't just bloodstock or even film attracting comment anymore. Other unconnected events could not escape scrutiny either. It was the Bank of New Zealand, it was the winebox, it was the death of Paul White, it was rumours of senior politicians being involved in illegal tax haven deals in the Caribbean involving forestry, it was birthday parties for senior Russell McVeagh partners attended by Attorney-General Paul East and judges.

As former SFO Senior Prosecutor Susan Pilgrim would testify at the Winebox Inquiry in 1997, "I was invited by Dr Congreve to a party he was jointly hosting with another person. Before going to that party, I told [SFO director Charles Sturt] that I would be attending the party and although I didn't know who was going to be present that there could be prominent members of the business community present at the party."

"And after the party," asked Counsel assisting the Commission, Colin Carruthers QC, "did you take the opportunity to say anything to the director?"

"I said something to the effect: it was a great party. And to be light-hearted about the director's concerns I said 'You have no worries, it was not at all partisan. . .I danced alternatively with David Richwhite and Paul East."

The behind-the-scenes tango for Dickie and Molloy included a senior cabinet minister – not Paul East I hasten to add – phoning up one of the legal beagles on the McVeagh Fleming team and chewing his ear for some considerable time, saying "but these people are my friends!"*

By this time Dickie's nerves were utterly shattered. Tony Molloy could sense the pressures his colleague was under, but didn't realise Dickie was armed and dangerous. "I didn't know that, I don't know if I'd have let the little bugger into my chambers if I'd known that!" Molloy laughed. "He's so volatile, having a gun would be a nightmare. My God! I never knew that.

---

* It must be stressed that the senior politicians linked to tax haven dealings did not include East.

"Yeah, well you see we were getting those pressures, and Lunn was getting those threats. It never happened to me. I just can't say I was ever terribly worried. I think one policeman did actually warn me, I remember, that I should take some precautions and watch my back. But really, I wouldn't have known where to start, so I didn't."

But in the meantime, life continued and so did the legal battle. In Jersey, Russell McVeagh McKenzie Bartleet & Co had wheeled in Geoff Clews to swear an affidavit in an attempt to stop Dickie getting his hands on the jumbo-jet load of documents.

In a quaint little section of the affidavit, Clews scoffs at suggestions that investors in *Merry Christmas Mr Lawrence* were swindled out of profits, via the non-recourse loans used to inflate the costs of the movie.

"This fraud theory is apparently that the loans were intended to be repaid, that repayment would be required from film proceeds, and that investors were thereby to be denied proceeds to which they were entitled. It is manifestly unsound."

This was very helpful to Dickie and Molloy, because in fact one of their arguments had been that the non-recourse loans were bogus in the first place. Now Clews was confirming it in his testimony to the Royal Court of Jersey.

"The Charlesbay loan was lawful and effective as a loan for New Zealand tax purposes at the time. . .[but] the events of repayment were remote and would have required the film to perform exceptionally at the box office before repayment was required.

"The film would have had to earn more than US$120 million worldwide for the loan to be repayable."

Which would have required the movie to be a blockbuster on the scale of Star Wars. Incidentally, the latter movie also showed just how gullible New Zealand's taxation authorities and courts would be if they accepted at face value the claimed production cost of $11.77 million for *Merry Christmas*. The force that created Luke, Leia and the Wookie spent only $13 million to achieve it, and that included paying for a whopping 363 special effects shots – a record at that time for any movie.

As for explaining away the US$2.9 million salted away in Bonningdale's Channel Islands bank accounts, which Molloy and Dickie argued should have gone to the investors, Clews argued that it was there because of a contractual cock-up.

He admitted that the offering memorandum to investors had never mentioned the Bonningdale arrangements, but claimed they were a legitimate payment to Bonningdale because another part of the movie's funding arrangements had gone sour and the contracts had to be changed after the investors had already subscribed for shares.

It's always interesting to watch lawyers, particularly tax lawyers, who say the devil is in the detail, try and explain things away when clearly the detail has turned to fudge and the whole situation is rapidly going down the gurgler. In Clews' case, he was telling the Jersey court that even though the end result differed from the legal contracts and what the investors had been told, it was still legitimate.

Clews then boasted a little about the success of his settlement negotiations with the IRD over the movie.

"It is pertinent to note that, even after the comparatively small tax payments which were required under the settlement, for every dollar they contributed as partnership capital, special partners (on a top tax rate at the time of 66%) received a tax saving of $1.91.

"In addition they enjoyed the benefit of, in some cases, an eight year deferral (without penalty) of the comparatively small amount of tax which had to be paid as a result of the settlement."

Clews added that, leaving aside the contractual irregularities, he thought the investors were in roughly the same economic position now, after the generous settlement, as they would have been if they'd actually received the movie profits and been taxed on them. Ergo, where's the problem? And who cares if US$2.9 million went to someone else?

Summing up, Clews told the Jersey court "In broad terms the allegations of fraud concerning the film are that: the cost of the film was inflated to the detriment of investors, and that Bonningdale has fraudulently taken funds due to investors.

"Both allegations are baseless. The first allegation assumes that limited recourse loan moneys must be repaid. That is not the case. The second allegation ignores completely the fact that proceeds from the film can be reconciled and have been applied for the benefit of investors in repaying a debt originally raised to produce the film."

Contrast what Clews was saying here, in the Royal Court of Jersey in 1992, with a question he was asked by Winston Peters' lawyer, Brian Henry, at the Winebox Inquiry in 1996.

"Is it fair comment that these thresholds were such that, as a matter of fact, an assumption that the loans were going to be repaid just didn't get off the ground?"

"That's not the proposition I would accept, Sir," answered Clews. "I think it is certainly possible, with the benefit of hindsight, to say that the events of repayment were remote, that payment might, in some circumstances, have been unlikely. But I certainly can't attest to a position at the time the loans were entered into."

As Basil Fawlty's Spanish waiter Manuel might say: "Que?"

Clews said that he stood by his Jersey affidavit. "If one looked at the financial performance that was required of the film in 1982, the events of repayment were remote, but I would certainly not accept that they were impossible."

Yeah, and the chances of a three million dollar movie about an old POW incident, shot in the Auckland Town Hall and on a Cook Islands beach, being a hit on the scale of *Star Wars* were only slightly higher than the odds of aliens landing on the roof of The Black Stump and requesting legal advice from Russell McVeagh. Not impossible, just almost impossible.

But there's another dimension to this phoney loan business, and it comes in the form of what Dickie liked to describe as "hard evidence". Taking the example of *Mr Lawrence*, if this had been a real loan that the investors were required to repay, why didn't it feature as a liability in the partnership's accounts? It just wasn't there!

A similar thing happened with the Ermine bloodstock partnership and the paper loan provided between Zorasong, Bonshow and Ermine to fund the horse mark-ups. In Zorasong's accounts, the "money" it had lent to Bonshow was listed in 1986 as an "unsecured loan receivable" of US$500,000 under the assets section.

But in 1987, the massive loan had been written down in value to only US$1,000, and the remaining US$499,000 was now listed as a "doubtful debt". Clearly, Zorasong never expected its paper loan of half a million dollars to be repaid by Bonshow.

Curiously, even though Zorasong had clearly written off any likelihood of repayment by Bonshow, Bonshow never passed the favour on to Ermine investors. You can't have your cake and eat it: either the Bonshow loan was a paper deal that no one had to repay, or it was a real loan that should have been repaid all around. Who would have pocketed the US$500,000 if Ermine had actually handed over real money in repayment?

There were other curiosities in the Zorasong accounts that are yet to be explained, such as how a company with no employees could rack up nearly US$1 million in "administrative expenses" in the 1987 financial year.

A report from Deloittes, who acted as Zorasong's auditors, noted "In common with many businesses of similar size and organisation, the company's system of control is dependant upon the close involvement of the directors.

"Where independent confirmation of the completeness of the accounting records was therefore not available, we have accepted assurances from the directors that all the company's transactions have been reflected in the records.

"Subject to the foregoing, in our opinion the financial statements give a true and fair view. . ."

It should be noted that the directors referred to are of course the nominee companies Hanwin Ltd and Rayfull Ltd, rather than named individuals.

On Guy Fawkes Day, November 5, 1992, Tony Molloy delivered some explosive to Dickie's Auckland office, and urged him to take it down to Wellington and leave it in the Inland Revenue Department's head office.

The explosive took the form of a few pages of documentation relating to Cook Islands tax deals.

"Dr Molloy requested that I deliver the same to Mr Robin Adair," Dickie told the inquiry, "and to say to Mr Adair that it was Dr Molloy's opinion that the transaction, as described in the document, was apparently of a highly criminal nature."

The documents, although Dickie and Molloy didn't realise it, had originated from within the winebox, which Dickie had helped Stephen Lunn dump on the Serious Fraud Office doorstep a week earlier.

The lawyer was flying to Wellington the next day, and took the tax haven files to the IRD. The lawyer was also anxious to reassure the IRD head office that Dickie had not been involved in the Wogistan article. Apart from Adair, Tony Bouzaid was also at the meeting, taking copious notes.

The deal that Dickie handed over related to Lion Corporation and a bond deal through the Cooks using European Pacific. An injunction banning further distribution of the documents had been granted a week earlier in the High Court, but Dickie says he was unaware of the link between the papers he'd been given by Molloy and the winebox. Molloy had had them for several weeks before passing them to Dickie, but he had not seen the contents of the winebox either.

Every week, Chris Dickie's nightmare was becoming a little darker. A report in the *National Business Review* later in November revealed his role in handing the papers to the IRD.

"The Inland Revenue Department is studying an alleged 'bond washing' deal carried out by Lion Nathan which MP Winston Peters claimed in Parliament was used by the company to 'cheat New Zealand tax laws'," the article began.

"IRD deputy commissioner Robin Adair and official Tony Bouzaid were given files on the alleged bond washing deal several days before the MP made his parliamentary allegations.

"Auckland lawyer Chris Dickie confirmed he had provided a set of the documents to the IRD. Mr Dickie said they had not come from any of the defendants to a case being brought by two European Pacific companies in the Auckland High Court seeking suppression of EP document details. He was not prepared to comment further."

The article ran for several more paragraphs, but what you've just read was enough to provoke furious phone calls and a letter advising that a major corporate was reserving the right to sue Dickie as a result of handing the files to the IRD.

Dickie made one more phone call.

"Yes, is that TV3? Can you put me through to Ian Wishart please."

"Wishart speaking."

"Ian, it's Chris. I have to tell you that although we're working together on all this, I'm cutting contact with the media because of last Friday's *NBR* story. One of the companies is threatening to sue. It's not your fault, but I felt that you should know."

"Sorry to hear that mate. I'll leave you in peace for a while."

Back in the office, Dickie was also having to hose down worried clients who'd seen all the media coverage of recent weeks, seen the SFO's "clean bill of health" and were worried their lawyers had got it wrong.

"The brief comment by the Director of the Serious Fraud Office, concerning the purported results of their investigation into the Ermine, Buckingham and Wicklow matters, as reported, did not properly record the correct position."

"As has been confirmed to the writer by Mr Denis Pain, the Assistant Director of that office," continued Dickie, "the Serious Fraud Office has never received an official complaint from any bloodstock investor or representative. Only a preliminary inquiry was undertaken by his office which has not been taken any further.

"With respect to the Primula partnership, we understand that two formal complaints have been laid: one by our firm on behalf of a client. Enquiries are continuing.

"We are unaware of any complaint having been laid by a client of our firm with the Serious Fraud Office concerning the film partnership Mr Lawrence Productions Ltd & Company. You will be aware that the press has reported on various allegations made by the Tauranga Member of Parliament, Mr Winston Peters, and that a complaint had been laid by him with the Serious Fraud Office.

"Neither Mr Peters' allegations nor comments purportedly made by the Serious Fraud Office are directly relevant to the evidence which was filed in the court on your behalf on the basis of similar fact evidence."

Sturt's August 26, 1992 media release on the bloodstock issues is unsurprising given his evidence under cross-examination at the Winebox Inquiry. He admitted making suspect, allegedly misleading statements. But at the time this statement was made, the problem for Dickie was that Sturt still had credibility in the eyes of the public.

Dickie had also been horrified to read a few weeks earlier an article in the *Sunday Star* with the headline "**Top law firm accused of role in $13 million conspiracy**" splashed across the front page. Especially as the bulk of the article had been drawn from a 100 page affidavit he'd filed in the High Court back in May and dealing with the similarities between Merry Christmas and the bloodstock deals.

"Approximately three weeks ago," Dickie wrote in the letter to clients, "the writer received a phone call from a person (not a client) who had become aware that a copy of the writer's affidavit. . .had been provided to a journalist. "A few days later, the named journalist rang this firm purportedly on another matter. The opportunity was taken for the writer to request that the affidavit should not be looked at and should be returned to the person who provided it.

"However, the journalist was non-committal and, it would appear, material from the document was used in the *Sunday Star* article.

"It is hardly surprising that your case and matters surrounding it are now becoming public. However, neither Dr Molloy nor our firm will be distracted by the press, politicians or Government departments. We urge you to ignore the publicity."

But there was also betrayal for Dickie. One of the 300 clients was providing key documents and information to Russell McVeagh.

"Sadly, a partner from Russell McVeagh has now acknowledged in a sworn affidavit that he has read a communication sent to our clients. It is commonly understood that communications between a client and solicitor are confidential and privileged. Apart from reporting the matter to the Law Society, there is little that we can do from a practical point of view."

The hunt for the mole would continue unsuccessfully for the three years.

CHAPTER 27

Bankers & Upstarts

"Many foxes grow grey, but few grow good."
– BENJAMIN FRANKLIN, 1706–1790

It was as if war had broken out on numerous fronts in the latter half of 1992. While Dickie and Molloy pursued the "horses and fairies" – the bloodstock and movie syndicates behind programmes like The Little Prince – Winston Peters was lighting fuses under the Bank of New Zealand and the parties behind the winebox deals.

While events surrounding the latter issues are covered in more detail in *The Paradise Conspiracy*, some new information has come to light through the Winebox Inquiry that is directly relevant to the climate that Dickie and others were now operating in.

What follows should arguably be the subject of its own inquiry. As you will see later in the book, the threads will be drawn together.

One of Peters' prime sources on the BNZ affair was Larry Johnson, an American brought in as a troubleshooter after the 1987 sharemarket crash to help cordon off the BNZ's massive overexposure in the property sector.

Johnson had tried to get in contact with computer dealer Paul White – another of Winston Peters' sources – the day before White was killed in a car crash in September 1992.

Larry Johnson was, through me, introduced to Chris Dickie who, in the course of his investigations, had come across another senior BNZ executive who shed some light on alleged banking malpractice.

Johnson's demise after a clash with BNZ director Sir Michael Fay has been well documented, but some of the evidence he provided to the Winebox Inquiry in affidavit form has never been given before.

A former platoon leader in the Vietnam War, he testified that his involvement with the BNZ began just before Christmas, 1988.

At his job interview, Johnson says a senior BNZ executive reached into his shirt pocket and pulled out a piece of paper with "$436 million" scribbled on it.

"Does that scare you?" asked the executive, BNZ treasury manager Errol Hannah. "This is the amount of the loss so far." Evidently Hannah was impressed that Johnson didn't flinch, because he got the job.

The American became a kind of Jiminy Cricket, stalking the bank and cracking down on dodgy property lending deals. He says they used to call him "the bank's property conscience."

In early 1989, Johnson joined senior BNZ managers Peter Travers, Ron Diack and Alan Taylor in what he called a "whirlwind" tour of the main centres to assess for themselves the full extent of the bank's problems.

"The bank was not exempt from the problems that were being experienced by all other New Zealand lending institutions. Even at this early stage, immediately post-crash, the banking industry was in a state of panic.

"The bank was not on the brink of a major crisis. It was already in it. I noted during my trip that all of the account managers visited were in fear of their jobs. It was clear that reporting heavy losses put your job at risk. Cover-up was, even at this time, regarded as the way to protect your job.

"Many of the managers openly wept, admitting they had mis-managed the files."

Some of the managers had "seriously and routinely" exceeded their lending authority, in one case by up to $15 million. But crunch time came at a crisis meeting with the BNZ's Auckland account managers at 7.30am on a Sunday morning.

"Peter Travers initially wanted to see the major accounts and to speak individually to those account managers. It was at that stage that he discovered that those managers were ostensibly running their own bank," Johnson testified.

"Having realised that the senior account members had been advancing large amounts of money without any authority, Peter Travers began to shout, 'Gentlemen, we are here to save our jobs'.

"Some of the account managers burst into tears, and one of the corporate managers was fired on the spot. Two other managers, namely the head of Commercial Lending and the head of Corporate Lending, were dismissed the following week.

"I have considerable knowledge and experience of banks in third world countries," continued Johnson. "None, I stress none, had worse real property banking practices than the BNZ."

Johnson said he had conservatively estimated the bank's property losses at more than $600 million more than had been budgeted for, and his figures were not disputed by the management team.

"Robert McCay, or 'the Chief' as he preferred to be addressed by his staff, at no time disagreed with my severe prognosis of the bank's position. He told me during one of our meetings that he was gravely concerned, but that he simply did not know what to do about the situation.

"He was concerned that there would be a huge public outcry were the bank's position to become public knowledge."

While Johnson and others tried to stem losses at the coalface, the BNZ brought in lawyers from Buddle Findlay to train members of a newly-formed "Recovery Unit", which would travel the country sanitising the files of customers who may have been preparing to sue the bank," he told the inquiry.

"I recall that Buddle Findlay advised us to record any file notes of an adverse or sensitive nature by using yellow Post-It stickers which could be easily cleansed from the bank's files."

When Johnson was asked to tell a meeting of the BNZ's Board of Directors of the full extent of the losses, he was kicked under the table by another member of the executive team who wanted him to stay silent on the grisly detail.

When it finally came time to provide accurate loss provisioning figures for the March 1990 accounts, Johnson teamed up with consultants Booz Allen Hamilton to forecast the real situation. But he testified that the figure used publicly had essentially been made up, after the real loss projection "had been rejected, as too high" by chief executive Lindsay Pyne.

"Lindsay Pyne could not 'sell' that number to the Government. He said they would not accept it and. . .required us to reduce the number.

"Here was a recently appointed chief executive officer with no indepth knowledge of the bank, in cavalier fashion telling us, apparently for political rather than commercial reasons, that the figure was still unacceptable."

Johnson and the consultants basically gave up, after watching the BNZ executive team slash the real figure by up to 30 percent.

"Alan Taylor went up to see Lindsay Pyne again. About 7.30pm he came down and said words to the effect 'they liked that one'. I do not know who 'they' were. The group went off for a drink and a meal and I flew home to Auckland."

Later in his affidavit, Johnson took a swipe at his former colleague Ron Diack, who had earlier testified to the Winebox Inquiry in a session notable more for what he'd forgotten than what he remembered.

"Ronald James Diack was the real brains behind the bank," said Johnson. "It was common comment that Peter Travers would sign off any deal provided Ron Diack told him it was good for the bank.

"Ron Diack has a very good banking knowledge and memory," he said slyly. "He wasn't known as 'sharp as a tack Ron Diack' for nothing. Ron Diack was the wiring diagram expert. One joke in the bank was that he wrote up wiring diagrams and rubbed them off with his sleeve as he wrote.

"This was because he would always meticulously pick up all wiring diagrams and shred the paper or clean the whiteboards himself."

In the affidavit, Johnson made a new serious allegation against former BNZ director Sir Michael Fay. He says Fay told him, at the infamous meeting of February 1990 to discuss a Fay Richwhite property loan application, that his company would make a $7 million profit from its shares in the BNZ for the March 1990 year.

"It indicates," he told the inquiry, "that Sir Michael Fay had prior knowledge of the Fay Richwhite dividend [from the BNZ] at the time of the meeting in February 1990.

"There is no doubt in my mind that had the provisioning numbers not been altered, no profit would have been achieved, the $7 million profit as projected by Sir Michael Fay would have been impossible."

Johnson says he watched from the sidelines as another senior BNZ manager, Dr Brian Perry, was sacked for trying to blow the whistle on Fay Richwhite dealings with the bank in 1989, and he got the message that standing up to either Fay or the bank's top brass was a bad career move.

"I am one of the very few persons in the bank at the time who is able to fully explain what had occurred to the provisioning for 1990. I believe that as I showed I would not walk the company line on the Fay Richwhite loan, they could not leave me credible so they destroyed me.

"The sad part for me is when I applied to the Employment Court for assistance, Judge Travis would not believe the enormity of the misconduct in the BNZ and my file was sealed by a court order.

"To continue suppressing the truth of what the BNZ senior management and senior directors have done is to deny many innocent BNZ customers and investors the opportunity to know the truth and act in their own interests to correct the wrongs they and all New Zealand taxpayers, as owners of the BNZ, have suffered."

In a historical precursor* dripping with irony it was a top Russell McVeagh lawyer, acting as an adviser to the Bank of New Zealand, who during the '96 inquiry told the Bank's president to "on no account" divulge to a hostile MP "which of the BNZ's past directors had supposedly received large loans on inadequate security, thereby placing the bank in jeopardy."

The lawyer, Theophilus Cooper, left the banker clear instructions.

"If you are asked, don't tell them, and let Parliament do its damnedest, but you will get away with it."

Sound familiar? Perhaps, but it's not what it seems. The year was 1896, not 1996. A century ago. Same bank, different scandal. As Alphonse Karr noted in 1849: "Plus ça change, plus c'est la m'me chose" – the more things change the more they remain the same. Theophilus Cooper went on to be rewarded with an appointment as a Supreme Court judge shortly afterward and earned a knighthood to boot.

And now for the bit that makes this part of the book relevant:

"I went to the Serious Fraud Office after my dismissal," continued Johnson. "The office showed no interest in what I said. I terminated the interview."

In 1992 the Serious Fraud Office actually did begin an investigation into alleged wrongdoing within the BNZ, but in 1993, as you will see later in the book, something very serious happened to that investigation.

Meanwhile, a clue to the SFO's general attitude can be found in a phone conversation between the author and SFO director Charles Sturt in late 1992. One of the SFO staff solicitors was a good friend of BNZ and Fay Richwhite director and former Russell McVeagh tax partner Robin Congreve, and had known him since university days. We wanted to know if a potential conflict of interest existed within the SFO.

---

* Recounted in *The Making Of Russell McVeagh*.

When I rang the woman concerned, I got a phone call back from Sturt, which we taped at TV3.

"I will be rubbishing TV3 if this is the scurrilous sort of thing that you're getting involved in," snapped Sturt down the line. "These rumours have been around for some time, emanating from the people, I believe, who've been bringing certain actions in court," he said, referring to the bloodstock litigation.

"We're not dealing with a person like you who wants to bring up such rubbish," he ranted. "And I know in many ways probably whose side you're batting on, so as far as I'm concerned -"

"Mr Sturt," I cut in, "I'm an independent journalist and I'm trying to get to the bottom of things that seem to be very murky."

"Well, as long as you act independently, Mr Wishart!" he warned. "Just make sure that you do and that you're not pushing any particular barrow."

"The only barrow I've got to push is finding the truth," I snarled back. As I started to ask more questions about the SFO's lack of an investigation into certain matters, Sturt got more irascible.

"Look here you little upstart! I'm not here answerable to you!"

"I'm not saying you are, sir"

"Yes. No. Don't you start interrogating me! I'm not taking it from a, from a, from a character like you!"

But the interrogation did continue, with questions to Sturt on the bloodstock, films, BNZ, Larry Johnson and Paul White cases. After initially saying everything was above board, Sturt clarified, saying there were still investigations of sorts into the bloodstock and film deals.

And then, at the end, charming Chas slammed the phone down with the immortal words: "As far as I'm concerned Mr Wishart, you can go and get knotted!"

For the record, we soon afterward ascertained that whilst the SFO staff member was a friend of the Congreve family, she had been careful to avoid placing herself in any conflict situations and everyone involved had acted properly at all times. For us at TV3, it was no longer an issue.

I rang Dickie to alert him to the SFO director's reaction, and the insinuation that rumours about the SFO solicitor's friendship had come from the bloodstock investigation stable.

The Serious Fraud Office rang Dickie to hassle him as well, adding to the pressures he was already under.

CHAPTER 28

When Irish Eyes Are Smiling

"I'm standing in a deep, dark hole. Beneath a sky as black as coal.
It's just a fear of losing control, you know so well."
— NEIL FINN, *IN MY COMMAND*, CROWDED HOUSE

For Chris Dickie the summer of 1992/93 brought with it nightmares, alcohol and paranoia – the price of putting everything you have on the line for your clients. It came at a terrible cost.

He separated from his wife and family, believing they would be safer without him around as a lightning conductor for danger.

Living alone in a disused garage, Dickie would lie awake at night with a gun on the table beside him, wondering if he would survive to see each sunrise. If he slept, the gun slept with him, under the pillow. Chris Dickie's life had strayed into the web of evil that surrounds international money-laundering and tax haven transactions, and he was being consumed by it.

As I have pointed out previously in this book, there is no suggestion that Dickie had anything to fear from any of his opponents in the bloodstock and film proceedings.

Although there had been threats from persons unknown to amputate the limbs of Dorothy Coates' child, or kill Stephen Lunn's children and kneecap him, or attempt to abduct the son of Winston Peters' lawyer, or assault journalist Fran O'Sullivan and break into and ransack her hotel room, or sabotage the brakes on a journalist's car, Dickie did not believe they would have harmed him. But it wasn't the people he knew about who worried him.

It was the people he didn't know, and the possibility that other persons unknown, perhaps with bigger agendas, might not want him raiding the world's tax havens, seizing documents and scaring the locals.

The warnings from Hong Kong had terrified the lawyer. He'd been told New Zealand was small beans, and he could be got at here as easily as if he was in Kowloon. His life was worth nothing. So he took the view that if someone came after him, he wouldn't go down without a fight.

And so it was that he awoke, just after midnight, to the sound of a car approaching up the long driveway to his refuge. Moving to a crouch on his bed, he could see the vehicle had no lights on. It drew to a halt only five metres from the garage.

Dickie's heart was thumping as he reached for the loaded pistol, and unlatched the safety mechanism. He still couldn't see the driver. There was darkness, and silence.

The lawyer crept towards the door, his Army weapons training taking over from any conscious thought now.

"Aim for the chest," he told himself. "Clean kill. Fire into the roof. Two shots," forgetting for a moment as he went into automaton mode that the weapon he was holding was only an air pistol that looked like the real thing – at the last minute in the private arsenal he'd chickened out of carrying a real gun.

Even so, a .177 pellet at close range, in the dark, would not only give an intruder a serious fright: it could, in the right circumstances, do some serious damage too.

The interior light of the car flashed on, and Dickie could now see the driver's silhouette as the car door began to open. He raised the pistol.

The driver was clear of the car now and walking towards the garage. Dickie couldn't see a weapon, but he waited for the knock.

"Who is it?" he asked in a voice strangled by nerves.

"Gidday Chris," came the cheery tones of a friend, "It's me, Moo! We went diving today and I've brought you some scallops."

Dickie slumped against the door for a moment, the adrenalin draining away. He couldn't believe he had almost shot a friend. What had these bastards done to him?

"Hang on," he called to Moo as he stashed the weapon and opened the door. The scallops tasted great.

The start of the new year brought with it a chance to bring all clients totally up to speed with what had been discovered so far in four full years of investigation. Clients arriving back from their Christmas holidays found a 17 page letter from Dickie giving a full round-up of his opinions on the litigation.

The main points included:

- <u>All</u> bloodstock in Ermine has been fraudulently 'price lifted'.
- Bloodstock in Buckingham has been fraudulently 'price lifted'.
- It appears that some of the defendants have pocketed the profits.
- Wicklow bloodstock has been acquired at a price up to 50% higher than market value.
- Ermine was insolvent by the end of its first year of operation.
- Buckingham was totally insolvent on day one – 1st August 1986.
- Westpac knew that the capital of Buckingham was $7 million by, at the latest, 9th September 1986.
- Mr Boyt, (who was not involved in the original financing for Buckingham) knew that, at the time Westpac issued the proceedings in the High Court against you and then in the Court of Appeal, but did not disclose this fact in his affidavits.

- Westpac <u>knew</u> of the interposition of Zorasong.
- Mr Justice Henry stated [in November 1992] that the first five Ermine transactions were fraudulent on the face of it.
- Sir Peter Crill, the Chief Justice in Jersey, has held that there is prima facie evidence of fraud in these transactions and other partnerships created and operated by some of the defendants.
- Fraud in respect of partnerships involving undisclosed use of some of the offshore companies referred to in Russell McVeagh's list of documents in Ermine, Buckingham and Wicklow has been confirmed by affidavit evidence filed by Russell McVeagh in respect of the Channel Islands applications.

It should be stressed, although it should also be obvious, that the allegations of fraud are the *opinion* of Dickie and his legal team. As with all allegations in this book, a conclusive determination could only be made by a Court presented with all the facts.

Having made his points, Dickie then outlined what it meant for clients. Establishing the existence of fraud, he said, would immeasurably strengthen the claims against the various defendants to the class action, and against the financiers. It meant investors could ask the court to restore them to the financial position they would have been in if they'd never invested in the partnerships in the first place. With fraud as an element, clients could also push for a contribution to their legal costs which, by this time, were well over a million dollars spread across 300 investors.

One interesting development was a split in the defendants' camp. Some, like Russell McVeagh, wanted to tough the lawsuit out, allegedly suggesting they would make the plaintiffs "walk on glass for a number of years" until the cost and the pain of continuing became too much to bear.

This was a philosophy outlined in a book called *Bankers and Bastards*, written by Australian senator Paul McLean and a white collar crime expert, lawyer James Renton. The book focused on the so-called "Westpac Letters" controversy of 1991, where an Australian subsidiary of the bank had allegedly been taking foreign exchange gambles with customers' money, passing the losses to the customers and diverting the profits to itself.

According to the authors, the bank's legal advisers, one of Australia's largest lawfirms, suggested that Westpac's "best protection against action by their customers was the complexity of the transactions and the high cost of legal action, so they should string the cases out, making out that they were going to defend each case all the way. But, if a customer seemed like going through to the end, they should settle out of court."

Dickie compared that to Russell McVeagh's approach, and went "snap".

But the McVeagh Fleming team was to have a stroke of good fortune of their own. Other defendants in the case, however, and Dickie didn't name them, had in his opinion "realised that deception was practised on them as well", and had begun to cooperate with the plaintiffs in their fight against the others.

That cooperation included leaking a letter that solicitors acting for Russell McVeagh had sent as a rallying message to their co-defendants.

The letter noted that the defendants in the New Zealand litigation "have a common interest in seeing that this litigation founders as a result of the investors being brought to the realisation that it can achieve nothing of substance for them, other than a rapidly growing interest liability to the financiers and enormous legal costs."

The letter urged the defendants to send letters to the various investors advising them of their folly in continuing to pursue the litigation. Indeed, a group of Dickie's clients subsequently did indeed break away from McVeagh Fleming, as evidenced by a report in the *National Business Review* by Graeme Hunt in July 1993.

"Several investors suing the country's largest lawfirm. . .have changed lawyers after a dispute over tactics in the five year battle.

"The *National Business Review* understands about 18 investors in the failed Wicklow bloodstock partnership switched to Morrison Morpeth after their lawyers, McVeagh Fleming, filed a Statement of Claim alleging Russell McVeagh committed fraud.

"The disgruntled investors are said to oppose the fraud allegations on the grounds they are too strong and will encourage Russell McVeagh to 'fight to the death' rather than settle."

It would appear that Russell McVeagh's war of attrition was having some effect, even if only on 18 investors out of the 300.

"Russell McVeagh partner John King declined to discuss the case with *NBR*," continued Hunt, "but said, 'This is sub-judice. We have made our statement before and we deny everything. No one welcomes these sorts of allegations. They are very strongly denied and we are defending them.' "

In his briefing to clients, however, Dickie was expressing his views on the links between the various defendants and the potential impact that may have had on the whole issue.

"You will recall that early in 1989, particularly before we began to unravel the full story of these partnerships, we sought an accommodation with Westpac which would have finally settled matters, but Mr Boyt was not interested in even discussing the documentary evidence."

Westpac's loan to Buckingham particularly irritated Dickie, because investigations by forensic accountants had shown that Buckingham was broke right from day one, and he felt the bank should never have lent the money to an entity in that condition in the first place. Indeed, one of Westpac's own documents revealed it told Chris Kirkham that keeping to the stated budget was of "fundamental" importance.

Another aspect that continued to get right up Dickie's nose and, indeed, which went to the heart of the whole investigation, was the alleged concealment and/or destruction of documentation.

"Reflect briefly on how you would react if you were wrongly accused of having been fraudulent in a business transaction for which there was considerable documentation which showed that, in truth, you had been honest, straightforward and honourable.

"Would you file affidavits which omitted mention of such important documents? Would you take other steps to ensure that your accusers could not find out about those documents?

"If some of those documents were situated abroad, or were otherwise difficult to obtain, and your accusers were taking steps to obtain them, would you go to enormous trouble and expense to block and fight those steps? The answer is obvious.

"You would bring out the documentation at the earliest opportunity so that all the world could see that your transactions had been as honourable and as straightforward as you claimed they were.

"That is the way any honourable person having nothing to hide or fear would act. He would want the truth established. Fast.

"In these cases, Russell McVeagh's list of documents records that documents relevant to your partnerships are in the possession of:

- The Cook Islands Trust Corporation (European Pacific)
- Fay Richwhite Ltd
- Investment Management Services Ltd, a Cook Islands company
- Komanti Ltd and Dawn Hill Ltd, Hong Kong companies

"Having read the prospectuses and offering documents which contain not a mention of any of these, you might ask what their involvement has been in your investment. We do not know yet, but we are taking steps to find out.

"Certainly the involvement of Zorasong and Bonshow in your investment, about which you were not told either, has cost you hundreds and hundreds of thousands of dollars in extra horse prices. From the accounts of Zorasong, we suspect it is in the millions of dollars."

As for the Channel Islands legal stoush, which by now was no longer a secret, Dickie went over the orders granted by the Jersey court in relation to documents dealing with bloodstock and the Mr Lawrence Productions Ltd and Primula Ltd film partnerships.

"Our advocates in the Channel Islands. . .have been advised that there are 35 boxes of documents which those lawyers and their associated trustee companies in the Channel Islands have found to be directly relevant to your actions and those two film partnerships."

Dickie also tore apart the affidavits that Russell McVeagh had filed in the Royal Court in Jersey during the fight to stop Dickie getting his hands on the documents, saying they confirmed that Carran was involved as a "conduit" in the arranging of marked-up horse prices through Zorasong.

They also confirmed, he said, that investors in *Merry Christmas* were deprived of royalty income from the Japanese market, contrary to what had been stated in the offer memorandum.

But it was Geoff Clews' attempt to justify the missing US$2.4 million that had been parked in the Channel Islands that really got the lawyer going. He said Clews' affidavit confirmed that investors "were told that they had derived no income from the film. It was taken from them under the guise of repaying a 'loan' to Challenge Corporate Services Ltd. That 'loan', however, did not appear anywhere in the books of the partnership. Neither had it been mentioned in the prospectus."

Although it was a different allegation of fraud altogether, Dickie quoted from the criminal case of R v Hawkins – the Equiticorp judgment of Justice Tompkins against Alan Hawkins and others – to ram home his point.

"It was contended (by the Crown)," said the judge, "that the (elaborate offshore company) structure was inherently dishonest, or that its purpose was to conceal from legitimate inquiry transactions known to be dishonest.

"A person who conceals a dishonesty to avoid it being detected has an intent to defraud. An intention to obstruct anyone who might be called upon to investigate a transaction if dishonesty can be shown is itself a fraud."

Justice Tompkins also took up the issue of hiding behind high powered lawyers as a means of protection. "Those responsible for carrying out an operation of dishonest concealment may well regard a firm of reputable solictors as being an admirable front for doing so. Not only are the actions of such a firm less likely to excite curiosity, it has or may be thought to have the added advantage of the confidentiality provided by the solicitor client privilege."

The good judge also took a swipe at those who attempt to justify what happened in the 80s with the excuse that "everybody was doing it".

"Standards of honesty never vary," said Justice Tompkins. "What is dishonest today would be dishonest then. Differing economic or financial conditions can never justify actions that at another time and in other circumstances would be considered dishonest."

Having briefed his clients, made the calls, dealt with the daily drudge, Dickie would return to his lonely garage each night, and wait for the cycle to repeat the next day. And then of course there was his living nightmare.

Dickie was well aware that he was not flavour of the month in Ireland or, for that matter, Hong Kong, so when he left his hideout to drive to work each morning, the lawyer would approach his car in absolute trepidation, wondering whether today was the day the vehicle would explode as he opened the door, or turned the key, listening for the click of the latch or the spark of the starter motor. Wondering.

For what it was worth, he always turned so that he was facing away from the door when he opened it. If he was going to die in an explosion, he'd rather be left with a face than without.

The Irish Republican Army, who'd already shown an interest in bloodstock by kidnapping *Shergar*, had turned car bombs into an art form. But Ireland was where they desperately needed a breakthrough, and in February 1993, that breakthrough came.

Up to this point, Dickie and Molloy had assembled only sketchy evidence about the prices paid for the horses by Zorasong. In fact, the only evidence was one receipt that had come from Lindsay Park Stud in South Australia. That receipt was useful in the Ermine proceedings, but the lawyers wanted similar evidence to be able to present in the Buckingham case.

It was the contracts at the Irish end, involving the Irish studs and the British Bloodstock Agency, that Dickie desperately wanted to see. The studs, however, didn't want to know about Dickie.

"I dealt for a while on the phone with a lovely Irish lawyer who acted for one of the Irish studs. He could talk for hours and I got nowhere. He was a politician par excellence. I would love to sit in a bar with a glass of Guinness, and talk to this guy. It would be fascinating, but you'd get absolutely nowhere.

"The other thing, too, that you need to bear in mind, is that as far as the Republic of Ireland is concerned, the sale of bloodstock is one of its largest industries. There were massive sums of money involved. The studs were owned by people like John Magnier and Robert Sangster – immensely powerful men.

"But there's no question, we just hit an absolute brick wall!"

Chris Dickie, Peter Edwards and Tony Molloy did, however, have a secret weapon: the Norwich Pharmacal order they'd successfully obtained in Jersey.

It was an order that terrified the Irish studs.

Molloy travelled to Ireland to see the lawfirm representing the studs. One of the stud managers had agreed to attend the meeting, but refused point blank to supply the information the New Zealanders were seeking.

"Forget it," he told Molloy, "we're not going to release it to you."

"Fine," replied the New Zealand QC. "Then we'll put you in a courtroom, just like we did with Ogiers in Jersey."

While the stud manager continued to bluster, his lawyer went white. Only three weeks earlier someone had successfully gained a Norwich Pharmacal order in the republic – the first case of its kind in Irish history. Not only had it been a dirty fight, but it had all been conducted in open court, not the gentlemanly closed hearings of the type employed by the Royal Court of Jersey.

Molloy had a copy of the Irish judgment. He let it be known that if the studs were truly worried about negative publicity, they were going to hate the dirty linen that would be hung out to dry if he had to fight them in open court to get the documents he needed.

There was a very "full and frank" discussion that afternoon and, in the end, the studs agreed to start cooperating. It was a slow and painful process, but the biggest development came when the McVeagh Fleming team threw a line in the water and managed to hook the British Bloodstock Agency.

Tony Molloy remembers it well.

"Ireland was funny because Chris' partner, Peter Edwards, was playing that particular fish. We knew there was a bloodstock agency over there, and we thought we might have worked out, from various bits of calligraphy on one of the defendants documents what the mark-ups were on half a dozen horses."

Dickie and Edwards had decided that "instead of trying to gaff a fish that we couldn't see, we would throw out a little bit of bait that we knew the fish would grab at.

"Tony, who is so precise and who wants to cover every point," said Dickie, "had drafted a letter which he wanted us to send to the Irish. Peter and I looked at the letter and said 'no way!' The letter, I think, was about 15 pages, and you could just see the Irish closing their eyes: 'I don't want to know, there's too much detail here, forget it.'

"So we took a punt," said Molloy, "and Peter wrote very low-key letters. His idea was not to go for anything very much, just to go for one very tiny, piddling piece of information to begin with."

The next day they received a reply from the BBA, when a junior clerk there faxed back to confirm what McVeagh Fleming already knew. The fish, as Dickie liked to put it, was sniffing the bait. It was time to jiggle the hook.

"We wrote and said 'look, we're just trying to sort out this partnership, it's in liquidation and we're having trouble tracking down the prices they paid for the bloodstock to the Irish stud. As far as we can ascertain. . .', and we listed our guess of the five prices, and she wrote back and said 'well, you're almost right but you've forgotten to take our commissions into account on a couple of them, so the actual prices are these', and suddenly we had a list of five prices from Ireland. This is the BBA," explained Molloy.

"We must have then asked for just a little bit more information just to clarify something else, and that fitted another part of the jigsaw, and a third low-level one again."

One of the discoveries made by the McVeagh Fleming team was that it appeared even Carran, Kirkham and McLeish had been done like a dinner as a result of their own cleverness.

Tony Molloy placed a call late one night to the BBA's English office to discuss some pricing information that had been provided regarding the sale of horses from the Irish studs to Zorasong.

"There has been armed robbery here!" exclaimed BBA official Joss Collins over the phone as he scanned the price list Molloy had faxed to him only moments earlier. "There's no way those can be the prices!"

At that point Molloy didn't really understand what Collins was getting at, but it transpired that the so called "cheap" prices that Zorasong had purchased the horses for were in fact a lot higher than the BBA thought they should have been.

Dickie came to term it "the double-whammy".

"Clearly, with McLeish wandering around saying he was acting for the subsidiary of the largest company in New Zealand, and he had $10 million to spend – I mean, you can just see him going into an Irish stud and saying 'I've got $10 million to spend', and the Irish rubbing their hands in glee and saying, 'well, today's your lucky day, we just happen to have $10 million worth of horses for sale.' "

It wasn't that Carran, Kirkham or McLeish were bunnies, but probably more to do with the fact that the price of the bloodstock appeared secondary to the issue of making sure the NZ investor got a tax break.

"I started to be left with the feeling," said Dickie, "that these people had simply said 'the punters don't give a tuppence, all they're after is their tax breaks'."

So, according to Dickie, the studs appeared to have overpriced the horses when they first sold them to Zorasong. That was the first "whammy". The second whammy was the markup in price from Zorasong to the partnerships.

The months crept by, but the lawyers didn't want their quarry to get skittish. Finally, it came time to push for the contracts held by the BBA's Ireland office.

"So the letter went off, 'well, you've been very helpful so far, but we've just realised that the simple way around this is if we had copies of the contracts it would save us bothering you all the time, can you send us those?'

"That was met by a get stuffed letter from a lawfirm in Dublin. I think it had gone beyond the range of that clerk. Chris was very despondent, he rang me and said 'they've shut the door on us,' so anyway he faxed the letter to me, and I had a quick look at it, put it in my bag and took it home.

"It was during the weekend, and there was something about that letter that bugged me. I couldn't quite figure out what it was, so I looked at it again, and suddenly I tumbled to it – I'd been visited in 1980, just after we bought the vineyard, by a relative from Ireland I didn't know I had. He'd spent two or three hours with us, had lunch with us, and was a very entertaining guy.

"Suddenly I realised he was a senior partner in this bloody firm! So I rang him up.

"He said, 'yeah, the BBA's our client, they're just around the corner from us here in Lansdowne Rd, by the football ground. . .' He put me on to the young guy in the firm who was dealing with the matter, and we had a bit of a chat, and I explained what we were on about.

"They were concerned, the BBA wanted to protect their studs, who were terribly important customers.

" 'Look,' I said, 'if we can just get these contracts, and any other correspondence that's on your file from New Zealand that sheds light on this, or from Hong Kong, that'll do us, and we'll certainly undertake that we won't raise anything about the studs'."

"He said, 'OK, we can help you' and I went across. I spent a week there in the end, because it got a bit delicate with the toing and froing but finally we worked out an approach and we ended up getting a file on the thing and that included some contracts which John West – the forensic document examiner – considered had been done off the same word processor at the same time as the Russell McVeagh contracts we already had. "The only difference was in the price. So we had them. That was the hard evidence for the first time, and none of that had been discovered to us.

It helped that the New Zealanders were again able to raise the spectre of a Norwich Pharmacal order, although the BBA's cooperation came at a price – $40,000.

Chris Dickie was out of town when the final agreement to supply the documents was struck. It was September 1993, and he had travelled down to Mt Ruapehu's skifields on his own.

"I was stressed out of my brain. One evening I was on rubbish duty, which is a duty I used to quite enjoy, and I was sitting in the rubbish room with a wonderful old coal burner, and as I looked out at the evening sky, at Ruapehu, I started to cry my eyes out.

"Much to my embarrassment a couple of ski club members came in, and it was very hard to explain, but I was completely stressed out because either we were going to get this file with all their records, or we weren't."

Dickie returned to work the following Monday in a mood like a thunderstorm. A really foul mood. As he passed Peter Edwards in the corridor he could see his colleague photocopying something, so he just muttered a grumpy greeting and kept walking. The tension was chewing at every nerve in Dickie's body. And then Peter Edwards walked into Dickie's office, with a grin from ear to ear, and threw a black book at his partner.

Dickie, still recovering from the shock of having the book thrown at him, picked it up off the floor, looked back at the grinning Edwards quizzically, and then down at the book again. And then the letters BBA caught his eye. They had it!

In a scene reminiscent of Denese Latimer's jig-dancing when Dickie gave her the documents she needed on *Merry Christmas*, Dickie and Edwards were "bloody hugging and screaming and shouting. We were like kids! And Peter – the bastard – had been making copies of this thing when I walked past, and he never told me!"

They rang Molloy, who was back in the country by this stage.

"Christ, mate! We've done it! We've got the BBA files."

The trio rendezvoused at a nearby café, which Dickie liked to frequent because the woman who managed the place "had lovely legs".

"We sat in that coffee bar just flicking over the pages and going 'wow!'. The first thing that blew us away was that we had the bloody invoices, sale notes, we had vet reports – and these were the originals! None of the crappy stuff coming out of Hong Kong, this was the fair dinkum oil. I was just over the bloody Moon."

Ironically, the legal team were lucky to get the contracts in more ways than one.

"These contracts are never, ever done in ordinary international bloodstock transactions, they were Paul Carran's idea and they drove BBA and the studs mad," said Molloy. "He seemed to be obsessed with getting documents of title and contracts and so on, and they just found it a bloody nuisance."

So the twist was that in ordinary horse deals, there really were no contracts in most cases, which is what the studs had been claiming all along. And yet Carran had insisted on contracts for his deals and because he was being hunted by lawyers they expected to find contracts, so the denials never washed.

"These were contracts that had been sent over to them by Deacons, solicitors in London and Hong Kong, on behalf of the people Carran was working with and I think what had happened was they must have been signed by the studs at a time when the director of the BBA wasn't there, and I suspect a member of staff thought 'What the hell do we do with these? We'd better take copies for the file'."

"And of course all the other files have disappeared into the maw of one or other Hong Kong law or accounting firms, or the Jersey lawfirms, and the ones back here just disappeared, so these were the only ones we were likely to get hold of.

"If it hadn't been for the boss being away, and the clerk taking a copy just in case, we never would have got them, so it was the luck of the Irish, we were bloody lucky!

"The investors here paid, and borrowed, a large part of $19 million for the bloodstock, and the offshore company paid a hell of a lot less than that, to the tune of several million."

After a cup of coffee, the three lawyers decided to celebrate the discovery of the BBA files in a more traditional manner. At 9.30am, they rolled up to a nearby wine bar, elbowed aside the handful of alcoholics who'd already started to gather, and ordered themselves a bottle of bubbly.

"We walked up to the counter, Tony pulled out a hundred dollar note, bought a bottle of French champagne and we sat there. We were piggies in shit!"

Apart from providing some of the horse contracts for Buckingham, the new evidence from the BBA and the studs provided some important incremental links in the evidential chain.

One telex, from Deloittes Hong Kong accountant Anita Cheng, had been sent to Coolmore Stud with the words "We are puzzled by your reference to a Mr McLeish and a Mr Kirkham. Neither of these two gentlemen have power to bind our company."

What this told Dickie, Molloy and Edwards was that Kirkham and McLeish, while appearing to be intimately involved with Zorasong, obviously didn't have control of the company, which meant someone else did. The question, as always: who?

Another Holy Grail had been attained, but there would be more to chase. The hunt was not over yet.

CHAPTER 29

Charlie's Angels

"Sir, – Reading between the lines of reports of the Winebox Inquiry,
I get the distinct impression that the Inland Revenue Department
might already be privatised. That being so, I want to pay my taxes
directly to Russell McVeagh. After all, they are astute, know how to
look after their clients' money and have a person who answers the
telephone. – Tony Goodwin, Avondale"

– *NZ HERALD*, LETTER TO THE EDITOR 1995

But Dickie wasn't the only one getting a hard time during 1993. At the IRD's Auckland office, Alan May was fighting for his job. Frightened of being caught in the same city – let alone the same room – as Winston Peters at the height of all the IRD paranoia about details of the film settlement leaking out, May had lied when asked a direct question about the vineyard meeting by Revenue Commissioner David Henry in late 1992.

But the IRD head office has ways of finding things out, apparently after talking to the Serious Fraud Office, which also had staff at the vineyard meeting.

Ironically, after suspecting that May had leaked IRD information at the meeting, the IRD investigation would discover that May had said nothing at the meeting, so they tried to hang him for that as well.

"If an accusation is being made [at the meeting] that a Minister has interfered with the process," Tony Bouzaid told the Winebox Inquiry, "and Mr May doesn't respond to that, for some members at that meeting they would take that as tacit agreement as to what has occurred."

A sort of "damned if you do" conundrum for May.

Winston Peters, who was flabbergasted at the lack of coordination between the SFO and the IRD on the winebox, was fascinated that the two departments had apparently managed to work together to track Alan May's movements.

"I was surprised to learn of the Inland Revenue Department's response to the vineyard meeting," Peters told the inquiry.

"In April, 1993, [Peters' lawyer, Brian] Henry telephoned me seeking a waiver of privilege [so] he could swear an affidavit in opposition by an application by the Inland Revenue Department to dismiss Mr May.

"Mr Lockhart QC and Mr May had been to see Mr Henry seeking such an affidavit. The only logical inference I could draw was that the Commissioner of Inland Revenue, David Henry, had been told of the vineyard meeting.

"I hoped not by the Serious Fraud Office, or more specifically by the director of the Serious Fraud Office, Mr Charles Sturt, for the rationale of the director or his office doing such a thing was beyond me.

"The issue in my mind was why did they do it? For I did not think Mr May had potted himself.

"The meeting was essentially an indictment of the Commissioner of Inland Revenue's decision, yet the director of the Serious Fraud Office, rather than investigating the statements of eminent Queen's Counsel, appeared to have tipped off the Inland Revenue Department."

The first the New Zealand public knew of Alan May's predicament came in 1995, when rebel IRD solicitor Michael Scott became the first department employee to publicly testify against his bosses.

Scott had been ostracised by head office in 1994 after suggesting in internal IRD discussion that European Pacific's 'Magnum' transaction was a criminal fraud. "If Magnum is not fraud, then nothing is fraud," he told the inquiry.

He revealed how expressing such an opinion had almost cost him his career within the department, and that his bosses had asked Russell McVeagh's Geoff Clews for advice on whether Scott should be appointed to a senior position in the department. Clews recommended that Scott should not be appointed, because he wasn't as prepared as others to be negotiable on tax matters.

Instead, the job went to a former Russell McVeagh staff solicitor, who'd worked previously for the IRD and also McVeagh Fleming during the blood-stock and film investigations – although he wasn't involved in them. The appointment was subsequently overturned after a number of appeals, and Scott eventually got the job, but only after his appearance at the Winebox Inquiry. But Scott talked also of treatment handed out to others.

"Mr May has told me that from November 1990 onwards he conducted an investigation into the bloodstock partnerships which have been promoted by, amongst others, a major New Zealand law firm.

"In August 1992 he was instructed to cease any further investigations and was later told to return the investigation files to head office in December 1994.

Mr Latimer told me that the department had taken the advice of Mr Grant Pearson who advised there was no fraud involved."

For the record, Grant Pearson was the same barrister who had singlehand-edly advised that the Magnum deal was not criminal either, despite conflicting views from more senior tax QC's. Even judges in the Court of Appeal have noted the possible criminality of the transaction.

"Mr May explained to me," continued Scott, "that in his view there were very good grounds for the department to continue its investigation to determine whether tax evasion had occurred."

When the vineyard meeting issue blew up, Scott says the IRD considered dismissing May, but in the end he "was given a final warning, put on weekly report, and remains on weekly report to this day.

"Mr May's career at the Inland Revenue Department has taken a similar turn to mine since these events. He has applied for a number of positions and has been declined. On one occasion he was recommended to a position by the Appointment Panel, only to have that recommendation overruled by head office."

According to May's boss, Norman Latimer, May was warned by Commissioner David Henry and told he'd been "naïve", but that he would get a chance to redeem himself.

Tony Bouzaid told the Winebox Inquiry that May had been "appropriately reprimanded (letter on file for 12 months) for his serious lack of judgment in attending the April 1992 Dr Molloy vineyard meeting without permission, and for his subsequent denials.

"He applied for several senior jobs in the Taxpayer Audit restructuring process – these jobs required a high degree of judgment and he was not successful. He was appointed as Team Leader at the same salary and grade."

But such considered comments from Bouzaid should be read in conjunction with the testimony from Norman Latimer, the IRD's number two in the Northern Region.

"Mr May applied for a job within the corporates unit within the department. The interviewing panel recommended Mr May for appointment. Mr Bouzaid had him taken off the list of candidates.

"After Mr May had been given his warning letter, Mr Bouzaid rang me up and said 'I understand that Mr May's warning letter is on file for 12 months. The letter should remain on his file indefinitely, he should not be with the department and Mr May should never get another job with us', or words to that effect.

"Mr May was later appointed to a position as a team leader in the department at Manukau, at a level below his abilities in my opinion. Mr Bouzaid rang me up and asked if I had had anything to do with the appointment, to which I replied 'no'.

"Mr Bouzaid has apparently rung the District Commissioner at Manukau a number of times and was most unhappy about the appointment."

Tim Bertram, a former IRD investigator in 1988 who'd later joined the Serious Fraud Office, praised the skills of the two Latimers and May in a brief of evidence prepared for the inquiry.

"Officers such as Mr and Mrs Latimer and Mr May had far more training and expertise in dealing with fraud than anyone else at head office.

"I can also say that under Mr Latimer, the Auckland branch of the Inland Revenue Department made arrangements to furnish its officers with the skills required to recognise and prosecute fraud. Head office did not do this.

"We used to get in people like Crown prosecutors and Police prosecutors to teach us evidence, investigation techniques and burden of proof requirements."

Bouzaid responded by calling Bertram "rather an unusual person and, frankly, I was pleased to see him leave. He was a risk to our organisation."

Given that May had attended the vineyard meeting in his own private time, in a private capacity, and had said nothing to breach IRD secrecy, his lawyer Paul Cavanagh QC demanded to know the answer to a basic question:

"Can you point to anything in your legislation," he told Bouzaid, "that governs work within the Inland Revenue Department, that gives to the Commissioner the right to direct how an employee shall conduct his private social life – if he is not breaching security in doing so?"

Bouzaid admitted that he had no legislative powers that he could put his finger on, but that a careful review of the various Acts might reveal something. Still, it seems that cross-examination in 1996 was the first time Bouzaid had considered that issue.

As for the Serious Fraud Office, it had by now completed what Dickie and others believed was a whitewash investigation of the *Merry Christmas Mr Lawrence* movie.

In a news release dated May 28, 1993, Sturt detailed his conclusions.

"The Serious Fraud Office has completed its investigation into the film partnership, Mr Lawrence Productions Ltd and Company.

"In a release dated 21 August 1992, I refuted a specific complaint that the Commissioner of Inland Revenue had been involved in a cover-up of a criminal conspiracy with partners of the lawfirm Russell McVeagh McKenzie Bartleet & Co.

"The full investigation has further confirmed that there is absolutely no basis for such an allegation. It is totally unfounded.

"The investigation into the formation, operations and business transactions of Mr Lawrence Productions Ltd and Company has shown that it was a special partnership comparable with many others set up in New Zealand and overseas at that time.

"Its purpose was to provide tax savings for the partners within the existing legislation. The partnership produced and marketed the film *Merry Christmas Mr Lawrence* in accordance with the accepted mechanisms for such undertakings.

"There is no evidence that the partnership was structured for any criminal purpose or that criminal frauds were perpetrated by the promoters or legal advisers.

"In particular, there is absolutely no foundation for the suggestions that Robin Lance Congreve, Geoffrey Thomas Ricketts and Paul Charles Carran committed criminal offences or were parties to a conspiracy to defraud. (They were at that time partners in the lawfirm Russell McVeagh McKenzie Bartleet & Co and were identified in parliamentary debate.)

"Such allegations against them are completely untrue. The file has now been closed."

Naturally, this news release caused a flutter of indignation in the henhouse, especially as Dickie and Molloy were steadily gathering evidence to pot Carran.

Significantly, a senior official within the Serious Fraud Office has since confirmed privately that the SFO statement was less than frank. "When Peters made a complaint regarding [IRD Commissioner] David Henry and corruption (alleged) [in the settlement of the Russell McVeagh film deals], no investigation was carried out. Yet, in a letter to Peters, Sturt found no corruption."

"Yet shortly after," continued our SFO mole, "D. Pain, as Deputy Director, assigned an investigator to check out the matter, calling for an inquiry in full. This was *after* the letter was sent to Peters." [author's emphasis]

The SFO staffer alleged Sturt suffered "impaired judgment as the Director in respect of any matters brought to the SFO's attention where he perceived a Peters influence."

The official described Sturt as having almost a pathological hatred for Peters, that dated back a long way before the winebox saga had blown up. That hatred allegedly clouded the SFO director's judgment.

"This is especially so in relation to the horse syndicate complaints by Dickie and Molloy.

"The Dickie /Molloy complaints is where it really started for the SFO. Sometime in 1990 or early 1991 Dickie and Molloy brought matters to Sturt /SFO attention, matters which suggested that members of Russell McVeagh & Co were involved in syndicate fraud.

"The SFO responded responsibly and began to pursue the complaints then, overnight almost, Sturt's demeanour towards the Dickie /Molloy complaints altered."

With Winston Peters on the bandwagon the whole case took on a new dimension, and there is certainly other evidence that Sturt appeared to be taking the bloodstock fraud allegations personally, as Ermine investor Pat Hadlee recalled.

"I sat next to Charles Sturt at a meeting much later in the piece, and I said to him 'I'm Pat Hadlee, how do you do? I'm involved in the bloodstock.'

"I thought this was my one and only chance to ask 'Why aren't you guys riding in like the cavalry and doing something?' "

But Sturt's response to Hadlee was caustic.

"You go back to your mate Dickie, and tell him from me that there's a big difference between civil/commercial fraud and criminal proceedings, and the sooner he understands and learns the difference, the better off all of you will be."

"This was Sturt," Hadlee told me, still astounded, "who'd never met me before, and we're sitting next to each other at a public function that Bolger was turning up at. I thought 'oh, I've just had my hand slapped', so I shut up."

Dickie, of course, was not investigating criminal fraud.

But as the Winebox Inquiry would discover, contemporaneous notes from this period clearly document the unravelling of Charles Sturt. When the SFO's John Hicks took the stand at the inquiry, it was his diaries that took centre stage.

Hicks' diaries contained fascinating references, such as claims that Sturt liked "providing bullets" for staff to fire "but not prepared to do it himself."

Hicks alleged that his boss made a habit of "putting down people in front of others", and "tends to favouritism" within the office.

Hicks told the inquiry that the SFO had done some kind of investigation into Merry Christmas and *The Little Prince*, but he wasn't sure who was involved.

As for the Peters factor, the tip that had come to me proved accurate.

"Was there a reaction in the SFO that Mr Peters was putting the heat on the SFO [by September 1992]?" asked Counsel assisting the Commission, Colin Carruthers QC.

Hicks admitted that was indeed one of the SFO's reactions. Pushed further, he conceded "I certainly got the impression Mr Sturt didn't like Mr Peters." The *Merry Christmas* complaint "was probably regarded as a bit of an irritant" because it involved Peters.

"We had the BNZ captive insurance allegations, we had Merry Christmas Mr Lawrence, we had the Commissioner of Inland Revenue, we had the Paul White affair. I suppose, if anything, it looked as though Mr Peters was trying to pick on us a little bit," said Hicks. "I would say, certainly, the Director was irritated in that period by Mr Peters.

"We have regular meetings, each Monday morning, for the whole of the staff. And it wouldn't be unusual for Mr Sturt to appraise the meeting of matters relating to Mr Peters.

"Mr Peters was a hot topic in that period," added Hicks, warming to it now, and the general thrust "was his personal dislike."

"Do we take it," asked Carruthers, "that there were disparaging comments about Mr Peters?"

"In that period, probably yes. Mr Sturt regularly makes comments about individuals in the office. I mean the common words that can be used are rat, mongrel, liar, cheat, but I am not saying that they were specifically used with Mr Peters. I have heard those over a number of years.

"My overall impression is that he didn't like Mr Peters."

John Hicks also admitted that he'd been ordered to take allegedly misleading and deceptive courses of action over the winebox affair by Charles Sturt.

In another diary note, dated June 2, 1994, Hicks wrote of an approach by SFO Senior Prosecutor Susan Pilgrim, who "asked me why no section 229A prosecution [in regard to the Magnum winebox deal*]."

Further on, Hicks said he told Pilgrim it was "not prudent to discuss at present. Susan said she was concerned if an inquiry occurred."

The Serious Fraud Office, of course, had gone on the record months earlier to say that there was no fraud in the Magnum deal, but at the time of its public utterances had done no determinative investigation on the issue.

But if Hicks' testimony was embarrassing to Sturt, that of former SFO Senior Prosecutor Susan Pilgrim was soul-destroying.

Pilgrim said her first concerns about the winebox came after seeing the 1994 *Frontline* documentary on the issue.

"At first sight it seemed to me that that transaction had all the hallmarks of an offence against section 229A of the Crimes Act, namely, using a document.

"I believed that my immediate reaction had to be completely wrong and

---

* See *The Paradise Conspiracy*.

terribly simplistic, because I knew that there had been a decision by the director that there was no fraud.

"I was curious to know what it was that I was missing. I assumed that there were a huge raft of facts which hadn't been described on the television programme but which would be known to the office, and I was curious to find out what they were.

"I clearly asked [Hicks] why, in the event, a charge under section 229 had not been brought. And my recollection is that Mr Hicks was very unsure of how to answer my questions. He almost, sort of, shrugged his shoulders.

"He didn't give me any answers which had any factual content about what had taken place in his examination of the documents."

"Well," asked Colin Carruthers QC, "were you satisfied in any way with what he told you?"

"Not at all. It simply confirmed my suspicions that a proper investigation hadn't taken place."

Pilgrim, the SFO's top staff prosecutor, went on to describe Charles Sturt's management style as "divisive" and that "he tended to have favourites".

"Was the issue of legal advice on the winebox exercise ever raised?" asked Carruthers.

"Yes. I recall that at one Monday meeting, the director said that he had heard rumours that staff were concerned that there had been no lawyer assigned to the winebox investigation.

"I recall he was very angry at this suggestion and reminded the staff that he was the lawyer on the winebox investigation."

"What was the reaction to that?"

"One of ridicule," said Pilgrim. "I don't believe that we thought that the director was competent to look through the winebox. . .he didn't give the impression of having an intimate working knowledge of financial transactions."

If Charles Sturt's reputation was already in tatters, worse was to come when Pilgrim described a conversation she'd had with the SFO's then-deputy director, former judge Trevor Maxwell.

"Mr Maxwell was expressing disquiet at something, I think, the director had done. And I said to Mr Maxwell: 'Do you really mean to be serious about trying to do something about this?'

"He said: 'If I tell you that every day I wonder whether I should ring Paul East or [State Services Commissioner] Don Hunn, do you realise I am serious?' "

As the heat turned up under the SFO even its senior legal counsel, Dr Willie Young QC, couldn't escape the flames, this time courtesy of Winston Peters.

Young had been hammering the politician on the witness stand at the Winebox Inquiry, demanding proof of the corruption the MP had talked about.

"I can't get past those agreements," snapped Peters, referring to the non-prosecution deal over the movies which fell outside the inquiry's terms of reference.

"These agreements encompass over 16 film operations. Many, many investors were obtaining very, very privileged treatment from the department. I have alerted the Serious Fraud Office to it and no action results."

Warming to the subject, the MP then went directly for Young.

"You asked me did I get my information from [a man in the pub named Harry] – I did get information the other day from a person like Harry. In fact, it came from a legal personality in Christchurch.

"It relates to a court case [in] which the judge felt compelled to make comment as to why the Serious Fraud Office had not prosecuted a certain party for conviction he felt would have been of certainty.

"I was alarmed to learn that the person acting for that certain party was the same person currently acting for the Serious Fraud Office, namely yourself."

"So," sneered a clearly annoyed Young back, "the cover-up and the conspiracy gets ever wider does it?"

"The judge thought it was rather unusual," continued Peters, "that here was a man who, which on the evidence he had seen should have been charged, he had not been charged by the Serious Fraud Office.

"The coincidence I discovered was that you acted for both the Serious Fraud Office and this man at the same time. . .a party that the judge referred to as one that should have been charged was not charged and that you were acting for both of them."

The exchange, as commissioner Sir Ronald Davison himself pointed out, was "interesting" but "not relevant" to the winebox corruption allegations.

And then there was arguably the most controversial decision that Sturt ever made, a decision taken in 1993. Evidence of the decision was given at the inquiry in 1997 by the SFO's Chief Investigator Geoff Downey, a man who'd been with the SFO virtually since its inception in 1990.

Prior to that he'd worked in the private sector, and also spent 16 years in the police force, rising to the rank of Detective Inspector.

Downey had been one of two SFO staff who attended the April 1992 vineyard meeting. The other was Neil Morris. He revealed that in June of 1992 he and Morris had been asked by Sturt to interview former BNZ employee Larry Johnson.

"The arrangement that was made was that Mr Johnson would go away and collate a summary and copy documents which he considered relevant to the matters he addressed, and he was going to call us back and bring them into the office."

Johnson, however, had felt the SFO was merely going through the motions in his interview, and never got back to them. But the SFO inquiry didn't end there.

Also in June, former BNZ senior manager Brian Perry wrote to the SFO in the wake of the ABC's *Four Corners* documentary on Fay Richwhite and the BNZ that marked the start of Winston Peters' BNZ campaign.

Perry enclosed details of what had happened to him in March/April 1989, when he stumbled across "a series of transactions for the Fay Richwhite /Capital Markets group.

"At that time I was involved in compiling and checking the bank's reported large exposures to major customers. I noted that the transactions for Fay Richwhite/Capital Markets did not appear to be included on the reporting lists for large exposures.

"If included, the exposure of BNZ to that group would have been in excess of $1 billion. I was told at the time by the head office executives that these transactions had been structured specifically so they did not need to be reported.

"My concerns about this matter related principally to what appeared to be a carefully constructed concealment of the true exposure of BNZ to that customer. This concealment appeared to be at the highest levels in the bank, and I was concerned to note that [BNZ CEO Lindsay] Pyne appeared to be aware of it, if not actually concurring with the concealment.

"I also believe it may be worthwhile exploring these transactions in respect of section 62 of the NZ Companies Act. This is the section that prohibits a company from providing funds or assistance for the purpose of purchasing its own shares.

"I am unable to offer any opinion on whether section 62 was breached, but merely make the observation that this should be investigated."

So it is quite clear that the Serious Fraud Office has been placed on notice to investigate by a former senior BNZ officer.

Imagine, if you will, that you have been alerted to billion-dollar dealings that are allegedly placing the very survival of the taxpayer-owned state bank in jeopardy.

Imagine next that you are suddenly given a huge carton of documents, most of them involving either said bank or the party allegedly behind the massive borrowing.

Would you, as a seasoned and sophisticated investigator, go through the windfall documents meticulously to see if there was any evidence to back up the earlier allegations?

One would think so, but not if you were Charles Sturt.

Hard physical evidence of the deals Perry had alerted the SFO to turned up in the winebox when Dickie and Lunn dumped it on the SFO's doorstep in October 1992. Page, after page, after page of hard evidence.

Appallingly, Charles Sturt admitted to the Winebox Inquiry that he'd failed to link the substantial evidence in the winebox with Perry's complaint, and so it went uninvestigated.

Massive borrowing, allegedly concealed from those with a right to know, involving the BNZ and its shareholder Capital Markets/Fay Richwhite, went *uninvestigated* because of – in my opinion – Sturt's utter incompetence!

Or was there a more sinister reason? The Winebox Inquiry would hear evidence that maybe there was.

Others, notably in the news media, did make the link between Perry's claims and the winebox deals.

Perhaps significantly, the Perry allegations were never shown to Geoff

Downey or even drawn to his attention during the time that he was investigating the BNZ.

As the inquiry heard, in October 1992 Downey said he was "contacted at home one evening by a person who was to be a witness in a trial that I was coordinating. He indicated that his brother-in-law was a former senior manager at the BNZ and that he had left the bank feeling uncomfortable about activities there. He also stated that Winston Peters was trying to locate his brother-in-law."

When Downey told Sturt of the tip-off, the director was keen to chase up on it and especially keen to beat Peters to the punch. The informant had indicated "that he strongly believed that his brother-in-law had left the BNZ because he was concerned at what he saw as fraudulent actions of members there."

The brother-in-law was a man codenamed at the inquiry as "Mr B", and on January 14, 1993, Downey tracked him down in the West African state of Gambia.

"I made arrangements for the office to fly him to London where I travelled on that and another, unrelated, matter."

Mr B told Downey he had 25 years' experience in world banking, including work for Natwest, Bank of America and the First National Bank of Chicago. He had served those institutions in London, Dublin, Nairobi, Saudi Arabia, Dubai, United Arab Emirates, Singapore and Nigeria.

He had been hired on a five year contract by the BNZ in August 1986 in the position later filled by Brian Perry, but had resigned less than a year into his contract.

Mr B told Downey he became suspicious of the bank's activities early in the picture. "Some of the transactions we were doing did not seem to add up to me and I was concerned about overall levels of group exposures.

"Banking is a sixth sense situation. When you smell something you don't like, one starts to become wary. It was a totally alien banking culture to me.

"I was concerned, for instance, that structures when drawn on story boards had to be taken down. These weren't to be left lying around offices. I know shredders were installed and there was a general air in the bank."

Growing increasingly concerned that the BNZ, a state owned bank, may have been "aiding and abetting" some form of tax trickery, Mr B found some of his colleagues also concerned that "these persons [were] really going too far, not just in the moral sense but perhaps in a legalistic sense."

He fingered Ron Diack at head office in Wellington as one of the prime movers in arranging these deals, and he told Geoff Downey the SFO should dig a lot deeper in search of the truth about what really went on in the BNZ.

Although Mr B could provide no specific instances of fraud, only suggestions of where to dig, he gave Downey two names of senior executives who may cooperate with the SFO – neither of the names was Johnson or Perry.

Returning to New Zealand, Downey briefed Charles Sturt in April 1993 and was shocked to discover a change of heart by Sturt.

"He indicated to me that he did not want the matter to go any further, whatsoever. He told me that our friends in Wellington would not appreciate the office inquiring into the Bank of New Zealand and, in particular, he did not want to give Winston Peters any further ammunition or cause in regards to his call for an inquiry into the bank."

Asked by Commission of Inquiry lawyer Colin Carruthers QC what he thought was meant by "our friends in Wellington", Downey answered "I clearly took that, and had no doubt, that he was referring to members of the National Party who were then in Government.

"It was a definite decision not to take it any further."

Downey says he specifically asked Sturt if he could interview the two other BNZ executives that Mr B had recommended talking to, and claims he was told "No." Downey says he was then ordered to hand over to Sturt all his files, documents and interview tapes on the now-quashed BNZ investigation.

"It is my understanding that the director placed it in the safe in his office."

For the record, Charles Sturt vehemently denied Downey's version of events, calling it "preposterous". He would not call Downey a liar, but claimed his Chief Investigator must have misheard or misunderstood.

Sturt's position was that no hard evidence of fraud had been forthcoming, and it was time to cut the losses and get on with other investigations.

Downey's evidence was the garnish to Sturt's main course, carved and served by Carruthers.

Highlighting an SFO media release on the winebox, Carruthers told Sturt "You will see it refers to 'accountants and investigators examining the documents over a period of several months'?"

"Correct," said the director.

"And do you see that it then goes on to deal with the conclusion that you, yourself, reached after examination?"

"Yes."

"Would you name the investigators that you were referring to, please?"

"Well, I could probably answer that in this way," began Sturt, starting to look flustered less than a hundred seconds into his cross-examination. "The accountants were Mr Hicks -"

"No," cut in Carruthers. "Let's deal with it in the way in which I asked you. Who were the investigators to whom you were referring?"

"I was wearing an investigator's hat for that particular purpose."

"There is only one of you Mr Sturt. Who were the investigators to whom you were referring?" Carruthers had the SFO director by the jugular, and he knew it. Sturt knew it too. Only a few weeks earlier he'd been boasting that it wasn't enough just to survive cross-examination by Carruthers, you had to "beat him". Senior partners at Russell McVeagh had gleefully bailed up Carruthers at a social function to tell him that Sturt was going to "destroy" him. Alas, their hero was on the verge of being destroyed himself.

There was a moment's hesitation as Sturt prepared to answer Carruthers' question.

"In the plural sense, that would not be correct," he admitted.

"And do we take it that you regarded yourself as an investigator for this purpose, and not a lawyer?"

"I regarded myself as wearing various hats, as I still do."

Sturt then conceded that the accountants were only Hicks and Gib Beattie – the latter only peripherally involved at the time.

"So," continued Carruthers, "do we get to the position that one accountant looks at the papers for, at the outside, 31 hours over a period, at the outside, of three weeks?"

"That one accountant, yes."

"And do you say that that state of affairs is accurately recorded and reflected to the New Zealand public by a statement that the winebox contained hundreds of documents which were examined by accountants and investigators in this office over a period of several months?"

After initially trying to claim the statement was correct, apart from the plural terms in it, Sturt then adopted a fallback position that it's easy to go back to old press release and "find errors in them. It is not misleading if that is what you are trying to infer."

But the inexorable advance of the Carruthers juggernaut continued. Another part of Sturt's news release "is not correct, is it?"

"Strictly speaking, it isn't," admitted Sturt.

Carruthers then read another paragraph "The investigation satisfied me that there was no evidence of criminal -"

"Sorry?" Sturt interrupted, "the examination?"

"The *investigation*," repeated Carruthers as he quoted the release, "satisfied me that there was no evidence of criminal fraudulent offending. Do you see that?"

"I see the word used, yes."

"There was never an investigation by the SFO involving accountants and investigators over a period of several months, was there?"

"There was an examination carried out specifically over the period in question," said Sturt, trying to fudge the issue again.

"Answer my question please."

"I am sorry Mr Carruthers, I am trying to give a proper answer."

"Mr Sturt," interrupted Sir Ronald Davison, "the question is capable of a simple answer, yes or no. You are obliged to answer it in that way."

The SFO director slumped in his chair. "There was never an investigation carried out, no."

The destruction of Sturt gained pace. Along the way there were allegations that he had misled various people, not the least of whom were parliamentarians.

"Mr Sturt, why are you telling Parliament that, given the office's statutory power to obtain copies of documents, the documents were photocopied the next day, when you are telling this Commission that you didn't have a statutory power?"

"It's a loosely structured paragraph," confessed the director. "There is not any intention there of giving any incorrect information or misleading any person."

"Well, you are telling the highest Court in the land something different from what you are telling this Commission, aren't you?"

Some of Sturt's supporters have, in the wake of his performance at the inquiry, tried to write it off to illness. I don't buy that. I was there. The demolition of the Serious Fraud Office boss began on a factual basis: had he made misleading statements or not? The evidence clearly shows that he had.

Now, whether the realisation that he was in for a hiding added to the stress that eventually cost him his job is another matter. Clearly, by day three of his cross-examination Sturt's mental capacity was shot, and he required medical intervention. Perhaps Sturt should have taken the advice he gave to his own staff: "If the oven's too hot, stay out of the chicken."

And now for the final coup-de-grace. After taking a pummelling at the Winebox Inquiry for allegedly shutting down the BNZ inquiry in 1993 for political reasons, Charles Sturt shut down the BNZ investigation again.

While Sturt had been away on sick leave, his senior staff had reactivated investigations into the BNZ, against the wishes of his loyal staff Gib Beattie and Steve Drain. Not only had it been reactivated, but it had proceeded to a full "Part II" investigation, which means that the SFO has strong suspicions that fraud is involved.

The day that Sturt returned to the office in March 1997, he shut it down for a second time.

In April, 1997, Sturt resigned as director of the Serious Fraud Office on health grounds. SFO sources say he was reluctant to leave.

The biggest issue in my view to come out of any of these events – the winebox, film, bloodstock, BNZ, Paul White affair – is not whether crimes were committed. It is whether those allegations were ever properly investigated by the Government agencies that the New Zealand public relies on to carry out their duties without fear or favour.

Because if the sorry state of affairs that passes for investigations at the SFO or the IRD, based on what we've heard from the Winebox Inquiry, has been repeated in other instances – who knows how many other people or incidents were never properly investigated, and for what reasons?

Under cross-examination from Colin Carruthers QC, Sturt admitted that failing to do one's duty for political reasons could be corruption.

In one of the Winebox Inquiry's more esoteric, but perhaps significant, moments, an essay from the besieged Burmese opposition leader, Nobel prizewinner Aung San Suu Kyi, was tabled into the record.

"It is not power that corrupts but fear," she wrote in 1991. "Fear of losing power corrupts those who wield it and fear of the scourge of power corrupts those who are subject to it.

"Most Burmese are familiar with the four *a-gati*, the four kinds of corruption. *Chanda-gati*, corruption induced by desire, is deviation from the right path in pursuit of bribes or for the sake of those one loves.

"*Dosa-gati* is taking the wrong path to spite those against whom one bears ill-will, and *moha-gati* is aberration due to ignorance.

"But perhaps the worst of the four is bhaya-gati, for not only does bhaya, fear, stifle and slowly destroy all sense of right and wrong, it so often lies at the root of the other three kinds of corruption.

"Just as *chanda-gati*, when not the result of sheer avarice, can be caused by fear of want or fear of losing the goodwill of those one loves, so fear of being surpassed, humiliated or injured in some way can provide the impetus for ill will.

"And it would be difficult to dispel ignorance unless there is freedom to pursue the truth unfettered by fear. With so close a relationship between fear and corruption it is little wonder that in any society where fear is rife corruption in all forms becomes deeply entrenched."

When we talk about corruption in New Zealand, too often we think only of palms crossed with silver – *chanda-gati*. As Aung San Suu Kyi compellingly points out, we need to expand our perception.

• The SFO had, by this time in 1993:

• Failed to investigate the winebox transactions.

• Apparently failed to investigate Winston Peters' allegation of IRD corruption over the film settlement deal, despite publicly claiming that it had investigated.

• Also claimed to have investigated the Paul White case, but hadn't,

• Issued a clean bill of health on *Merry Christmas Mr Lawrence*, and

• Quashed further inquiry on the BNZ affair.

The SFO's senior counsel now says the settlement deal was unenforceable, yet no further investigation has taken place, to my knowledge.

Little wonder, then, that the head of steam building underneath would soon find vent, firstly through winebox revelations about massive alleged tax fraud, and then through increasing behind the scenes fury in the bloodstock and film investigations.

CHAPTER 30

Collateral Damage

> "The Director-General of M.I.5, after exhaustive investigations into
> the claims about an attempted destabilisation of the Wilson
> Government in 1974-75 by members of the security forces and
> after lengthy interviews with serving officers and a thorough review
> of contemporary documents, has come to the following
> conclusions: 1. Everybody is innocent. 2. . . . .er 3. That's it."
>
> – *Private Eye* MAGAZINE

By the start of 1994, the genie was out of the bottle. What had begun at a
meeting of disgruntled bloodstock investors just over five years earlier had
mushroomed to become a major investigation involving numerous lawyers,
journalists and assorted individuals in what they perceived – rightly or wrongly
– as an anti-corruption drive.

By the very nature of such probes, it was inevitable that the massive resource
being expended on locating information would inevitably wash up other debris
from New Zealand's uncharted depths.

Chris Dickie, for example, needed to get a statement from a prominent
Auckland accountant working for a major international accounting firm, about
some of the intricacies involved in offshore company structures.

The accountant had recently been sent up to Hong Kong by his employer to
set up some offshore structures for clients in South Africa, Australia and, to a
lesser extent, New Zealand.

He gave Dickie a written statement, but informed the lawyer that it could
never be released.

"Why?" asked the perplexed lawyer.

"Because to do so would be signing my death warrant."

Over coffee, Dickie and I compared notes yet again. Always in search of the
big picture, and hoping that by discussing the evidence together we would gain
some new perspective on where it was all heading.

It had been over a beer, late one night in the offices of McVeagh Fleming,
that I had first briefed the lawyer on the workings of the infamous "JIF" tax
credit deals from within the winebox.

As the inquiry has now heard in evidence, US$1.2 *billion* was pumped through European Pacific Bank in the Cook Islands, Citibank in New York, the Bank of New Zealand and some major Japanese banks to create interest-earning deposits in the Cook Islands.

That interest income paid by the Japanese depositors was taxed in the Cooks, and a Cook Islands tax certificate issued. While the Japanese banks received a tax refund from their Government on presentation of the tax certificates, European Pacific, Fay Richwhite and the Cook Islands Government were plundering the Cooks Treasury and taking back out the tax money to split between themselves.* Dickie was entranced by the apparent intricacy of the arrangements, yet the sheer simplicity of the principle that drove them.

By mid-1994 all hell had broken loose. Top barrister, Julian Miles QC, had achieved an incredibly important victory on behalf of TVNZ, allowing the *Frontline* documentary to screen.

In the bloodstock litigation, both sides were now almost ready for their day in court – a full scale trial on the issues of how much the investors owed and whether in fact they owed nothing because of the alleged fraud involved.

Miles, who was also the barrister handling the litigation side of the bloodstock, was increasingly confident of victory there, too.

Certainly, Russell McVeagh was showing signs of weakening under Dickie and Molloy's unrelenting pressure.

Suddenly, a settlement deal was in the offing.

"Russell McVeagh to make amends for tax dodge deal gone awry," read the sub-heading on a front page lead in the *Independent*.

"Russell McVeagh McKenzie Bartleet & Co – this country's largest lawfirm – has, with others, offered to pay disgruntled bloodstock punters $14.5 million compensation in an out-of-court settlement.

"The punters," wrote Jenni McManus, "investors in the so-called Buckingham and Wicklow partnerships in the mid-1980s, filed High Court action in mid-1991, accusing the lawfirm of fraud, misrepresentation and taking a secret commission.

"The case was expected to go to trial early next year. The bloodstock partnerships were set up as tax dodges but collapsed with the sharemarket in 1987. Dunned for partnership debts, the investors mounted a group lawsuit, accusing Russell McVeagh of acting as entrepreneurs and promoters of the partnerships, rather than merely as solicitors – a claim the lawfirm vehemently denies.

"They also accused the syndicate managers of ripping off the Inland Revenue Department and breaching the Securities Act."

As a result of the legal action back in 1990 and 91, Westpac Bank had already received a payout from investors of about $15 million, representing the four/sevenths of the debt that made up the private investors' share of the burden.

---

* Outlined in detail in *The Paradise Conspiracy*.

"The worst part," remembers bloodstock investor Pat Hadlee, "was when I had to write a cheque for $824 every month, which I gave to Graeme and he gave to Westpac. We did that until we were both so broke I just said to Graeme 'well, I'm not going to pay any more. I can't afford to pay any more.'

"I never really believed it would get that bad. I'm a born optimist and I really thought it would sort itself out. It's been a very weird seven years because we haven't been able to control it. If something goes wrong in my life I sort it out, and this pissed me off because I could never do it. It was always there and you couldn't take control."

The total loss to the special partners from the collapse was estimated to be in the region of $30 million. The deal essentially meant that investors would only have to pay Westpac about a quarter of what the bank claimed they owed. Naturally, the investors would in turn claim reimbursement of that sum from the promoters and advisers.

The offer needed a 75 percent acceptance by investors, which didn't happen. They were hanging out for a much bigger financial return for their troubles than that.

"We are representing 304 clients and further persons have indicated a wish to join," Dickie told the *National Business Review* six weeks later when the offer deadline had expired.

"The vast majority of our clients have been in touch with us and have told us that any settlement must be based on principle and not expediency.

"In cases of this type the measure of damages is to restore the plaintiffs to the financial position they would have been in but for the behaviour complained of."

On the same front page was an article headed **"Controversial Show Rescheduled"**.

"Hidden transactions were given the codename "JIF" by executives of the European Pacific tax haven group. Five years later, those transactions are set to see the light of day in a Television New Zealand *Frontline* programme which its lawyers allege will expose suggested 'fraud on the IRD both in New Zealand, the Cook Islands and possibly Japan.'

"That's if TVNZ wins a battle currently being played out in the Auckland High Court against the Cook Islands tax haven company."

But as publicity surrounding the winebox documentary stormed through the news headlines throughout 1994, another sinister incident rated only a one-paragraph mention in the *New Zealand Herald*.

"Robbery at lawfirm" was the headline and, on this occasion, it wasn't referring to the fees being charged.

"A woman who disturbed burglars at an Auckland law firm last night was pushed to the ground and robbed.

"Police said the woman went into the offices of McVeagh Fleming in central Auckland about 5.30pm and found two men inside. They shoved her over and ran off with some money on to Wyndham St."

That was the newspaper version of what happened.

Now here's the real story, extracted from Dickie over a beer the day after the event:

McVeagh Fleming's offices had been broken into once before, and the office next to Chris Dickie's on the 15th floor had been jemmied open. But during this second break-in, the intruders were disturbed.

Dickie had locked away some key evidence in a hidden safe at the lawfirm. Normally such vital documents would have been in safekeeping elsewhere but he needed to refer to them frequently and wanted them close to hand. So he kept the originals there, and sent bulkier copies of the evidence to storage.

The documents included the original six cheques that had been written out to "pay" for the Wicklow syndicate's $2.966 million subscription in the Buckingham partnership. These cheques had never been passed to Buckingham and had sat in Dorothy Coates' drawer. They were, of course, central exhibits to the issue of the missing $3 million capital in Buckingham.

Also in the safe was an Anzon Ltd chequebook. The cheques had all gone but the chequebutts remained, providing a crucial time sequence of which cheques had been written out in the time leading up to and past the July 31, 1986 close-off for Buckingham subscriptions. This included, of course, the six cheques written to pay for Wicklow's subscription but never presented.

On this particular Friday evening, Dickie had returned to his office for a meeting at about 4.45pm.

"I saw a tall, very athletic-looking male waiting in the corridor. I remember thinking that it was an unusual place for a person to be, and his demeanour was unusual."

Dickie continued past the man and went into the meeting. At 5.00pm, two men, including Mr Athletic, fronted up to McVeagh Fleming's main reception desk. They told the receptionist they needed to see a lawyer, and were asking questions about trusts.

When the receptionist went to see if any of the lawyers were still in the building, the men jumped behind the counter. Dickie picks up the story again.

"They had removed two items of furniture which are kept in front of the safe so it's not visible. They had opened the safe. They had taken the material in it and were going for the door.

"How they could have got into that safe within the fraction of time remains a real enigma, but they had got into it.

"Billie [the receptionist], who's five foot nothing and very slim, went for one of the buggers! Went for him and bloody tackled him, and out of his hand dropped two white envelopes with my bloody evidence inside!"

The intruders escaped, and were not caught by the police, but at least Dickie's crucial exhibits of evidence had been retrieved.

Could it have been the random act of stair-dancers – people who lurk in stair wells and raid offices? Or was it something more sinister? There's no evidence either way.

"I've asked myself a thousand times about that," recalled Dickie, "but I'll never know."

Tony Molloy, meanwhile, began to highlight the film issues publicly for the first time, in a four page epic published in the *National Business Review* on March 31. He outlined a situation where promoters might push a movie deal for a film that had cost a million dollars to make, plus a quarter-million dollar fee to the promoter for putting the deal together. But, said Molloy, investors would be told that the film would "cost" five million plus the fee, and the full $5.25 could be claimed as a tax deductible expense.

"The only cash [investors] would have to put up would be $1million plus the $250,000 costs. The other $4 million was to be put up by a 'finance' company.

"Pay $1.25 million. Deduct $5.25 million against your income from other sources, and so pay no tax on that other income. Magic," wrote Molloy sarcastically.

"These promoters walk on water! And they are such self-proclaimed ethical paragons that it must all be above board. As Sir Joh Bjelke-Peters en used to say: 'Don't you worry about that!'

Molloy was scathing. Pointing out that most films never recoup their costs, he posed the question: why would any self-respecting finance company throw four million dollars down the gurgler knowing it would not be repaid?

"The answer of course is that the only real money with which the financier was to become involved in this deal was its cut of the $250,000 being shared with the promoter.

"The other $4 million was phoney money, the product of legerdemain. It was no more real money than the 'financier' was a real financier. The latter was a company just incorporated, or 'taken off the shelf' especially for the purpose of making the scheme look plausible."

Molloy then outlined the sleight of hand that had marked Komanti, although his example in the paper was purely hypothetical.

"This phoney $4 million was produced, on behalf of the phoney financier, by the promoter taking the clients' $1.25 million; opening a bank account in the name of the new company; paying the clients' $1.25 million into that account; withdrawing it again; deducting and paying itself and the financier their $250,000 just reward for the conception and execution of the scheme; re-depositing the remaining $1 million; withdrawing it again; re-depositing it yet again; withdrawing it yet again; re-depositing it yet again; and then withdrawing it once more and, at last, paying the vendor of the film the true cost of $1 million.

"Now, if you look at the bank statement generated by all this, and fold it vertically in such a way that the withdrawals column can't be seen, you would be able to say that it looks like there have been deposits into this account of $1.25 million + $1 million + $1 million + $1 million + $1 million = $5.25 million."

So, if the best that the best tax brains at Russell McVeagh could come up with was tax dodging by origami, you'd have to wonder how people like Paul Carran justified his incredible fees.

Molloy also took a swipe at the non-recourse lending arrangements of movie deals in the eighties.

"When they tired of promoting schemes which, by mere folding of bank statements, could conjure up funds in tranches of $4 million, promoters and financiers would arrange for variant schemes in which the phoney money component would come from non-recourse 'lending' to the hapless client.

"At one end of the scale, 'non-recourse' is the sort of lending that consortiums of banks might engage in for the finance of, say, a bauxite mine.

"After having done assays, and after having received geological reports as to the likely extent of the deposits; and following intensive studies of price trends in the aluminium industry, the banks might be completely satisfied that the revenue stream from the mining operation will be more than ample to meet the repayments of the, say, $500 million the consortium intends lending to the mining company.

"Being so satisfied, the consortium may lend on the basis of looking only to that forecast revenue stream, and not to the mining company itself, for the servicing of the debt."

In other words, as far as the miner was concerned it was a non-recourse loan, in as much as the initial profits from the mine would pay the debt. The banks, of course, fully expect repayment.

At the other end of the scale, said Molloy, were non-recourse loans of the type in the film and bloodstock industries which, as Russell McVeagh's Geoff Clews testified, would probably never be repaid. Fictitious loans, argued Molloy, because "who lends real money other than in the firm expectation that it will be repaid?"

"Here is where the full beauty of the trickle-down theory begins to shine in all its facets. J K Galbraith has described this as the theory that if the horse is fed enough oats, some will pass through to the road for the sparrows."

In this case, he says, the horse was the promoter eating the real money, while the sparrows were various company registration clerks who set up a myriad of offshore and shelf companies for each deal, clipping the ticket in fees all the way.

Molloy's epistle in the *National Business Review* sent corporate tax planners reaching for the migraine pills. It probably gave the Inland Revenue Department's head office heartburn. It also gave Molloy a profile that saw him appear, as a leading tax commentator, on the TV debate that followed the TVNZ winebox documentary.

Russell McVeagh's woes continued to grow. Fresh from defeat in its earlier offer to settle out of court, the country's largest lawfirm opened its *Independent* on May 20 to read that Equiticorp's statutory manager, Fred Watson from KPMG Peat Marwick, "is today expected to file a multi-million dollar lawsuit" against the Boys from the Black Stump, "over a bloodstock partnership dating back to the mid-1980s".

"The action relates to a full recourse, foreign currency loan believed to be in the region of $4 million to $5 million, Equiticorp made to the Ermine bloodstock partnership when it was floated in 1985."

Russell McVeagh's hired QC, Tony Lusk – brother of senior partner John – was obviously getting used to being asked by the media to comment on such matters.

"Russell McVeagh said any such claim would be denied for the same reasons as the present claims are being denied," said Lusk. "It's all very confusing to me. . .really, we're just speculating ourselves at the moment. It's a frustrating mystery."

In July of 1994 Russell McVeagh and its fellow defendants pitched another settlement offer at Dickie's clients, increasing the deal to nearly $17 million and dropping the need for a 75 percent acceptance by clients. But while some investors accepted, most continued to push for their day in court. They had developed a taste for blood, and they could sense their opponents were weakening.

Finally, for the first time in six years, a trial date was set. In September 1994, the High Court scheduled a twelve week trial on the massive case, to begin in February 1996, representing what had dwindled to 125 investors.*

Dickie, meanwhile, was continuing to firm up the evidence he needed to win his case. Mindful of the break-ins, and of the legal war that had broken out between TVNZ and European Pacific over possession of the winebox and the right to screen a TV documentary based on the winebox documents, Dickie decided to spend the summer of 1994/95 making sure that all his hard work could never be lost in a legal fight or, for that matter, a gunfight.

Sick of carrying the pistol around, and aware that if someone seriously wanted to do him over the gun would probably be useless, Dickie had handed the gun back months earlier, but the latest incidents did nothing to calm his nerves.

It got worse when he received a communique from Colin Nicholson QC, now a judge. Nicholson didn't beat around the bush.

"I have been told about some of the material that you have got," he said. "Chris, in my view you could be killed because of that. You are a prime candidate for a car bomb, and you should take some elementary steps. If something happens to you no one is going to know where to go or what to do. You need to do an affidavit, to set out some of the critical material."

Nicholson told Dickie that his only real protection was to have copies of the key evidence made and distributed to trusted individuals who could make use of it if anything happened to him. He told Dickie to seek advice from another QC, Colin Pidgeon, who revealed he too had had a close encounter of the sinister kind.

Pidgeon, by November 1994, had been appointed as Winston Peters' counsel for the initial stages of the Winebox Inquiry. During that month he had travelled to Wellington on another case.

---

* By a process of attrition through settlement, the number of die-hards hanging on for a day in court was dropping away.

Staying at the James Cook Hotel, the devout churchgoer and upright family man was surprised to be awakened by a knock on the hotel room door sometime between 11.00pm and midnight.

Dragging himself from the bed in his pyjamas, Pidgeon leaves the door chained but opens it slightly to see who has disturbed his sleep. His eyes went wide when he found "a very attractive brunette, dressed in a business suit but carrying an overnight bag" standing on the other side of the door.

"Aren't you going to let me in?" she smiled invitingly.

"No," replied the QC with fervour, at which point the woman tried to force her way in, despite the chain.

After a brief struggle, Pidgeon was able to close the hotel door on the female intruder, but as he listened he could hear her talking to a male companion, who'd apparently remained out of sight. When there had been silence for a few minutes, a shaken Pidgeon retreated back to bed.

But his feathers were to be ruffled again, when the phone rang at 1.30am.

"It was a woman's voice again, this time asking to speak to the woman who'd come to the room. I was hopping mad by now, and told her the woman wasn't here.

" 'What have you done with her?' came the response. I began to panic, wondering whether my mystery visitor was going to turn up dead somewhere and I'd be the prime suspect, so I told this woman that I hadn't let her friend in and had no idea where she'd gone.

"I later discovered from a person connected with European Pacific," said Pidgeon, "that it was a clumsy attempt to set me up with a call-girl."

So when Dickie told Pidgeon the kind of information he'd discovered, and the dangers apparently associated with it, Pidgeon was more than ready to accept that nasty things might happen to the unwary.

He agreed with Nicholson's earlier advice. So Dickie, who'd ditched the gun, took up the pen.

He grabbed every single file he could lay his hands on, and told his partners he was going back overseas. The lawyers at McVeagh Fleming assumed that Dickie was heading back to the Channel Islands but, as it transpired, Dickie's attempt to go incognito would prove, just like the All Black umbrella incident in Jersey, to be an abject failure.

He retreated to a bach on picturesque Kawau Island in Auckland's Hauraki Gulf. Hot summer evenings were spent gazing out over the water sparkling in the sunset as Dickie furiously dictated another affidavit, setting out everything that he'd discovered in what was now more than five years of investigation.

"I had my boat down on the mooring, and I kept looking at my boat and I kept looking at the lovely weather and I never went fishing. I dictated for four days. I worked peculiar hours and ate peculiar meals, and just went for it."

Perhaps he had lulled himself into a false sense of security. Perhaps it was the balmy weather and the lazy, hazy summer days. Whatever the reason, Chris Dickie was unprepared for the attack that came from the sea, and it almost killed him.

CHAPTER 31

Poisoned!

"The job of a professionally conducted internal enquiry is to
unearth a great mass of no evidence. If you say there was no
intention, you can be proved wrong. But if you say the enquiry
found no evidence of an intention, you can't be proved wrong."

– Sir Humphrey Appleby, *Yes Minister*

Chris Dickie stretched as he switched off the tape recorder. Four days straight without a break. Enough to make a boy yearn for some fresh air and seawater.

"On the afternoon that I finished – I remember it was a Wednesday at 4.00pm – I went for a walk along the jetty. One of the new residents on the island was walking along with me and bemoaning the fact that there – across on the other jetty – were beautiful oysters, but what a shame there weren't any mussels."

"Shivers, mate, I know where there are mussels!" exclaimed the lawyer, pointing at the floating pontoons a few metres out from the jetty they were standing on. "There are mussels everywhere down there, and if you stick your hand down under it you'll see they're huge."

So the two men stripped to their underwear and plunged in to the warm sea, harvesting mussels by the dozen from underneath the pontoon. It wasn't until they climbed back up on the wharf that they realised something was wrong.

"What in the hell's happened to you," queried Dickie's companion.

"I looked down at my chest," recalled Dickie, "and it was literally ballooning out as if someone was pumping air into it."

He presumed he was having an allergic reaction to something, but desperately wanted to cook up the mussels and oysters and enjoy a drink with his friends. "The thought of having a bourbon, and that I'd finished the affidavit, was great; so I went up, opened the bourbon bottle and took a few swigs, put the mussels on the barbie and didn't think much more about it until a few hours later when I started feeling decidedly giddy – and it wasn't an alcohol giddiness – and incredibly hot.

"I woke up in the morning and was viciously ill. I got into the shower and the first thing I saw was my feet. To my horror, blood and yellow muck was pouring down onto my feet, and when I saw my chest it was just an absolute mess."

Medical help was sought on the island and obtained, but Dickie wanted to tough it out and flesh out his affidavit some more. It wasn't to be. He felt like a walking corpse.

"The following week I started to feel extremely peculiar. I was falling asleep whenever I ate any food – just fell asleep, bang! – and I was starting to have difficulty walking."

Dickie's friends on Kawau convinced him to seek medical advice from Auckland Hospital.

"I was put through in the late afternoon to the people who deal with stings, and this person said 'I'm terribly sorry, Mr Dickie, but we only deal with stings you get from creatures on the land'."

"You bloody halfwit!," an exhausted and pained Dickie winced down the phone. "We are surrounded by water. We've got more water around us than any other country in the bloody world! We are surrounded by two bloody oceans – what the hell do you mean when you say you can't handle marine poisoning emergencies?"

More phone calls ensued, until a phone call from a quietly-spoken North Health medical officer.

"I would be grateful if you were prepared to listen to something that I want to read, and I would like you to tell me whether these are the symptoms that you feel."

"That's exactly what's happening to me," Dickie replied after the medic had finished.

"Then I don't want to alarm you, Mr Dickie, but you need help and you need it quickly."

Dickie had been stung by a kind of sea anemone. The creatures had fired thousands of tiny, living barbs when Dickie came close to the mussel pontoon. The organisms had burrowed into his skin, leaving visible trails and depositing a venomous neuro-toxin into his nervous system as they moved.

Anecdotally, he discovered that his own case was not isolated, and that several divers had nearly drowned after experiencing similar symptoms elsewhere around New Zealand. It became a matter of public health concern, and led to warnings about this venomous new type of sea anemone. Scientists speculated that it may have arrived in the warm northern waters from the hulls of ocean-going vessels. Doctors told Dickie that the dose of poison he received could have killed him.

With the attendant publicity – on *Holmes* and in the newspapers – the lawyer's hopes of an anonymous visit to Kawau vanished.

The *Independent* told how Dickie was back at his desk "after being stung by a mysterious sea creature".

Then came the jokes. A newspaper cartoon in the *Herald* showing two scientists inspecting a test tube, with a caption that read: "It must be an intelligent life form – it attacks lawyers."

The jibes from colleagues: "I know they have agents everywhere, but under the wharves at Kawau?" or "they'll do anything to stop you."

There was also some hate mail: a card addressed to Dickie, stamped but not franked with a postmark, and marked "private and confidential".

Somebody had inserted the word "don't" into the "Please Get Well" heading on the card. Inside, in a woman's handwriting: "Hope you aren't feeling better. Couldn't have happened to a more deserving person. Hope your recovery is slow! Thinking of you, and laughing!"

The price sticker of $4.25 was still attached to the card, and the sender had written "well spent" underneath it.

Chris Dickie was unable to work for ten weeks.

So 1995 started slowly and painfully, although not insignificantly: Dickie was to get a phone call from Hong Kong barrister David Gunson, the man who'd been involved in the massive MGM film studio deal with a client of European Pacific's.

Gunson wanted Dickie's help in the litigation over the Century Insurance collapse.

Dickie, in turn, found Gunson's Hong Kong contacts invaluable, and they would lead to the breakthrough that would – after seven years – solve the case. But as Dickie closed in on his prey, others were closing in on Dickie.

He had developed the irritating habit of going for a jog in the mornings in a bid to regain his fitness but, on one particular morning, he went an hour earlier than normal, at 5.20am.

"I've got a long driveway, and as I ran up the driveway I could see a vehicle, waiting. On the other side of the road, parked on the grass verge at an awkward, tilted angle was a white Toyota van with aerials sticking out of it, left, right and centre."

It was hard to tell whose eyes went widest – Dickie's or the van driver's. The lawyer recalled conversations he'd had with journalists about white vans and surveillance operations.

"I had exquisite pleasure in giving the driver, who looked at me with an air of dismay, the full fingers, with both hands! And then I continued jogging down the road."

Innocent van driver abused by passing jogger? A fantasy created by Dickie? Not according to the evidence.

Dickie had been forewarned that a surveillance operation might be in place against him, and the warning had come from a neighbour living in the house directly across the road from Dickie's.

"He's a doctor, and she's a teacher. Shortly before this van incident they'd invited Sue and I over for drinks."

"Chris," said the doctor, "I've been meaning to tell you – it's only from the press reports that I've become aware of the sort of work that you're doing – but I've been meaning to tell you for a long time that a while ago a group of people came to see me and asked whether they could use the facilities of our house for the purposes of setting up bugging equipment.

"They were, and these were their words, wanting to 'eavesdrop on a suspected drug operation that's taking place across the road.'"

"Of course, Chris," continued the doctor, "I'm very anti-drugs and I agreed to it, but I wonder now whether in fact they were bugging you!"

The lawyer spent that evening pacing the floor, swearing to himself every so often. "Bloody scumbags. Bloody scumbags!" So when he saw the white van bristling with aerials a few days later, he knew the two finger salute would be correctly interpreted by the recipient.

"I had become suspicious of, and certainly had no faith in, any enforcement agency. None whatsoever. It was clear that *hard evidence* was the only thing that was going to break it open."

"Hard evidence" is one of Dickie's favourite truisms. On cornering a journalist, or a lawyer who'd failed to scuttle away quickly enough, Dickie would regale them with the need to get *hard evidence*.

Even Mitchell McLeish – one of the men Dickie had been hunting – came to joke about it in a letter to a colleague in 1996, after he and the lawyer had begun cooperating on some parts of the investigation.

"Dickie has been in touch late this evening and is a bit huffed that you have not been in contact with him, as he only wants to help. I would like you to see him as soon as possible with his <u>hard</u> evidence!!"

Dickie, of course, knew that he was assembling the hard evidence. By the time of the surveillance van incident the man who'd been reduced to hiding in a dark garage with a gun had gone, replaced by a kind of avenging angel.

"People could listen to me as much as they bloody liked. I didn't care anymore. I wasn't going to be distracted from the finish line by silly diversions."

Sue Dickie, on the other hand, was terrified. She cried herself to sleep that night, wondering if someone was watching, or listening, from the street.

"Sue was immensely troubled by it, and one of the big worries that we had was that our bedroom window, because of the slope of the hill, was directly level with the roadway.

"We always wondered about the possibility of a firearm attack at night," Chris explained with a smile, "but I had a lot of comfort because Sue was closer to the window!"

CHAPTER 32

Lawyers, Gunson, Money

"The victor is not asked afterwards whether he has told the truth."
– ADOLF HITLER

It had been a bastard of a day for Dickie. Not in the sense of any difficulties with the case: he believed now that in the trial that was now just two months away he would win. No, it had just been the sheer volume of work that had worn the lawyer out, and the knowledge that another Christmas had snuck up on him unawares. It was December 8, 1995.

On his desk more evidence was emerging of strange transactions involving horses. There was, for example, Zorasong's purchase of the mare *Mrs Fitzherbert*, which had allegedly been on sold to Buckingham investors at a mark-up of nearly $200,000. More significantly, the evidence would come to show that Carran, Kirkham and McLeish had allegedly used money supplied by Ermine as a deposit, obtained extra funding from Westpac to complete the purchase, and then held onto the horse for three months before onselling the beast to Buckingham. During this time the mare did well in a series of races and the three men split the winnings personally.

In another deal, Zorasong had purchased a half share in two mares, *Royal Opera* and *Meadow Blue*, for US$390,000. Zorasong then sold *Meadow Blue* to Buckingham for US$390,000, but kept *Royal Opera* and its foal for itself. Effectively, Zorasong picked up a mare for free, arguably using Buckingham investors' money.

The evidence was becoming damning, on the face of it.

Leaning back in the chair and basking for a moment in the summer sun belting through the window behind him, Dickie paused to reflect on the way the tide appeared to have turned against the people who were once part of the "establishment" in New Zealand.

Not only was the Winebox Inquiry up and running, it was in top gear and firing on all cylinders. Even Dickie, who'd known about most of the allegations long ago through discussions with me, had nevertheless been stunned to hear the details emerge in an open hearing.

And then there had been the evidence regarding his own struggle, when rebel IRD officers Michael Scott, Denese Latimer and Norman Latimer had taken the stand to testify against head office. "Unbelievable," he muttered aloud, shaking his head ever so slightly and turning to pick up the ringing phone on his desk. He glanced at the clock. 5.34pm. Time to go home soon.

"Hello, Dickie speaking."

"Chris," said the voice, "I have obtained information and documents which I cannot give you."

"Oh fuck!" thought Dickie, "not another one of these conversations again."

"Is this your idea of a dirty phone call?" he hissed at the caller, half in jest and half in utter frustration. "Ringing up poor, stressed out lawyers just before they go home to tell them you can't talk to them?"

"No," sighed the caller, "but I can lead you in the direction you need to go.

"There is documentation in existence that indicates possible control of the offshore structures. I want to remind you about Hong Kong and your experiences there. I believe that you should start to think again about that source, and whether with the additional contacts you've got now in Hong Kong, you should try and get this material for your case."

Dickie's heart leapt and sank simultaneously. The Holy Grail. In Hong Kong. The place where he would be a dead man walking if he went back to do any serious digging. Now his tipster was indicating that the Grail existed in physical form, and Dickie had to find a way of locating it. The frustration of the previous seven years came flooding back, and he sobbed on his desk.

"The general tenor of his comments was exceptionally distressing," Dickie recalled. "Indeed, I went home and I can remember being really emotionally upset for about two hours, even physically thumping the walls. There is, in this case, an immense frustration – it's not just anger, it's frustration – at the immense difficulty of getting information."

For so long now, Dickie and Molloy had tried so hard to penetrate the secrecy of the world's tax havens to identify who owned and controlled the various tax haven companies used in the film and bloodstock deals.

This Herculean task had caused massive damage to Dickie's marriage and his health, but he and Molloy had nevertheless managed to compile plenty of circumstantial evidence which strongly indicated the offshore companies were really controlled by New Zealanders in New Zealand.

And now an opportunity had arisen to obtain "hard evidence", a mystery document from Hong Kong that might be the long sought-after Grail.

The call came at a tricky time for Dickie, who'd become embroiled in negotiations with Russell McVeagh to settle the dispute.

Those negotiations were being brokered by a man called David Bogan.

"Bogan told me he'd been approached by Russell McVeagh partner Laurie Mayne, who had inquired whether Chris Dickie was 'prepared to be commercial'."

Use of the phrase 'commercial' brought back some of Dickie's cynicism, as he wondered whether it was merely a euphemism for "You'll see things our way, my boy!", but he told Bogan he would agree to meet.

Bogan is a financial consultant who worked – at the time – in "The Black Stump" office tower. A former banker, he found he had a flair for commercial mediation, and is often called upon in Australia to mediate between banks and farmers.

He'd previously acted as mediator in some of the settlement negotiations between Russell McVeagh and individual investors, and both sides seemed to have confidence in him, which is important in mediation.

The first meeting between Dickie, Bogan and Laurie Mayne took place two days before the 21st birthday of Dickie's son. For the McVeagh Fleming lawyer it was a strange feeling. Mayne had been intimately involved in the defence for the Russell McVeagh team and, as such, was one of the targets of Dickie's fury about the missing documents. However, when they met for the first time, Dickie took an instant liking to the man.*

So the negotiations began. But then came the Holy Grail call and Dickie's dilemma. He solved it by placing a call to his Hong Kong contact, David Gunson.

Gunson had been involved with the setting up of the Cook Islands tax haven legislation, and Dickie found a delicious irony in that, especially as Gunson was "delighted" to help him nail the hard evidence he wanted.

"I want to get close to Deloittes," explained Dickie. "I was frightened off dealing with them on my last trip but I have reason to believe they're now in a position where they won't want to get dragged into the proceedings."

Over the intervening years since Dickie had been warned off, a lot more evidence had come to light. Evidence that put Deloittes firmly in the frame. Evidence that he figured the Hong Kong accounting firm wouldn't want being aired in a courtroom.

Together, they discussed the options and decided to use what was known as "letters of request", a procedure that was simpler and more appropriate to the turbulent Hong Kong tax haven jurisdiction than the Norwich Pharmacal order obtained in the Channel Islands.

But Dickie and Gunson had a trump card that went far beyond any legal manoeuvre: one of Gunson's closest friends was a senior partner at Deloittes Hong Kong, Peter Tosi.

"I'm confident," said Gunson, "that Peter will be utterly shocked by the fact that his company has been used as a vehicle to commit fraud."

Dickie began sending across some of the relevant background document-ation, so that Gunson could prepare himself for the approach to Tosi. It was the beginning of another "hook in the fish's mouth" operation.

Sure enough, Tosi was horrified at what Dickie had supplied implicating Deloittes partners Dermot Agnew and K K Yu in the schemes. These men were, of course, only agents for the real owners of the offshore companies but, because their names were on the documents, they were technically the ones in the hotseat.

---

* Dickie remains impressed at Mayne's abilities. He told one client that the Russell McVeagh partner had done a thoroughly professional job in the negotiations, especially given the heat that surrounded the issue on all sides.

After talking to Tosi, Gunson passed on to Dickie that there was a possibility he might get a chance to talk to a Mr K K Yu.

"What would you like me to ask him?" queried Gunson.

Dickie's blood froze. "K K Yu, as well as Dermot Agnew, had clearly played pivotal roles in the evidence which we had obtained to date," he told the author soon afterward.

"For example, Dermot Agnew's name appeared in many of the hidden companies as being one of the directors and/or shareholder, as had K K Yu. Agnew had signed the proof of debt for the Bonshow loan for a million dollars.

"There were a whole variety of reasons why I suddenly came to realise that Dermot Agnew and K K Yu, and the ability of Gunson to talk to them, that we were right up against people who in no way would I have gone to see alone. I would have been a babe in the woods."

Christmas Eve, as Dickie was preparing for festivities with his family, came another phone call from Gunson. He told Dickie that Yu was returning to Hong Kong from a business trip and would be back in his office on December 27. Gunson was planning to pay him a visit.

On the assigned day, Dickie received another call.

"It's David here, mate. Peter Tosi has just confirmed to me the existence of an internal memorandum between Dermot Agnew and K K Yu. Apparently they gave this memorandum to the New Zealand IRD some years ago. There are some other documents that are relevant as well."

Dickie was stunned. More so when Gunson explained that he was picking up a copy of the memo from Tosi, and that Deloittes would authenticate the document as having come from their records.

The fish was sniffing the bait, and Dickie fought an incredible urge to give Gunson a barrage of questions to ask. He didn't want to come so close and then scare the accountants away. So when Gunson rang back to say he was thinking about going over to Deloittes and asking for the whole file, Dickie hit the roof.

"For Christ's sake, don't do that! Whatever you do, David, get the hook in the fish's mouth – whatever you do! Don't try and land the bloody fish on the boat. Just get the document, get the memorandum. Just get that."

He calmed down a little, taking a breath. "Let's see it, let's digest it, then we can decide how we use it and what it says."

Gunson agreed, but Dickie did the electronic equivalent of getting down on his knees: he sent a begging letter by fax pleading with Gunson not to do anything silly.

"It's a pathetic fax," Dickie now admits.

And then the waiting began. As the hours ticked by and Dickie waited for the memorandum to appear on the fax, a sense of panic began to set in. Justifiably.

David Gunson rang. "They can't find their file."

The New Zealand lawyer went white. "I thought, uh oh, here we go again. Here comes the amnesia, here comes the 'we're here for some purposes but not for others', here come all the difficulties."

But it got worse.

"Dermot Agnew told me he was happy to provide a copy," said Gunson, "but that they've taken legal advice from a solicitor they used when they first ran into difficulties with Zorasong. Deloittes' lawyer has sent a copy of this memo to Russell McVeagh, asking whether it's going to be alright to provide it to a Hong Kong solicitor who is inquiring on behalf of certain New Zealand parties."

"Well that's it then," cursed Dickie, unable to hide his anger and disappointment. "Bye-bye, goodnight nurse. It's gone, David. It's over."

The New Zealander really didn't believe there was a snowball's chance in hell of retrieving the documents now.

"I was absolutely demoralised," he recalled, "because I had no doubt that we were very close to a document, or a series of documents, that must be mind-blowing.

"The expression that I came to hate was an expression 'go-down'. I'd never heard this expression before but, as I talked to people around me who were familiar with Hong Kong, apparently it's quite a familiar expression there.

"It's a reference to a warehouse where all the materials are kept. In my experience there are sudden disappearing acts, there are fires – like in the Cook Islands – when you want to get near the material, and the Hong Kong people used to say 'we'll go down and find it', only to return with an excuse like 'it's been eaten by rats.'

"But I had one ray of hope – that conversation with Peter Mourant as we walked along the turreted walls of Orgueil Castle in Jersey. He told me that the one thing which is always done, if you are taking instructions and operating an offshore entity on behalf of principals, is that you cover your own butt.

"You keep the records, because you never know the day that someone may come knocking on the door and say 'You've stolen our money', and you are able to show 'We were only the agent'."

David Gunson, too, was detecting a change of attitude. "We're going to have to be very low-key from here on," he told Dickie.

"We can't give up, we've got to keep trying," pleaded the New Zealander.

On New Year's Eve Gunson called again, telling Dickie that Agnew had agreed to authenticate certain documents for him.

"I was over the Moon," said Dickie, "but until I had them in my hot little hand I was torn between thinking that we might be very close to something or we might lose it completely."

The agony of waiting continued through the summer holidays until January 13, 1996. The trial was now only a month away, and settlement negotiations were continuing. But all Dickie could think about was the activity taking place somewhere far, far away.

Sick of waiting for a nervous Agnew to authenticate, Dickie decided to play the fish himself. He drafted a one line letter for Agnew to sign, which simply said 'I produce to you a copy of this document' and contained no other detail backgrounding the document or the circumstances behind its creation. He faxed it across to Gunson. A short time later the Hong Kong lawyer called again.

"He'll do it, Chris. Agnew's agreed to sign it and hand over the memorandum with it."

Dickie remained stuck on hot bricks for a further 48 hours. Then, on the night of the 15th, Gunson advised that Agnew had complied with the request.

"The letter has been done, and it's going to be posted," he said cheerfully.

"Bugger the post, Gunson," sputtered Dickie. "Run down the bloody street and get it!"

"Chris," admonished the Hong Kong lawyer, "we've got to remain cool."

"I know, David, I know, but bloody hell!" he whined.

On January 16th, at 3.00pm, Gunson was back in touch.

"I have spoken to his secretary. The letter is ready. I am to go down after lunch and pick it up."

"Shit! You bastard!" screeched Dickie, who'd only been waiting more than seven years for this document. "You're going to go and have lunch? For heaven's sake!"

"Yeah," grinned Gunson. "I'm off to have lunch. I'll call you with the result at 9.15pm your time."

Dickie's son, meanwhile, had just been advised through the mail that he'd scored an A bursary in his high school exams. "I decided that the only way I could kill the agony was to take my wife and son out to dinner."

The lawyer kept glancing at his watch, hoping his family wouldn't notice. Another family celebration marred by the intrusion of this case.

He arrived home at 9.02pm. At 9.07 the phone rang. For a moment Dickie had a flashback, back to another ringing phone in 1988. It had begun then – with any luck it would end here. In two paces he was there and lifting the receiver.

"David here, Christopher. I've got it!"

"Shit!" said Dickie eloquently.

"Get to your fax!"

If a battalion of paratroopers had stormed through the door with stun grenades and tear gas at that moment, Chris Dickie would not have been surprised. This was the document that would indicate who was behind all of this – the burning question that remained unanswered after more than seven years.

There was no bigger secret than this.

Dickie dialled a phone number.

"Howling At The Moon Productions, hello?"

"Yes, Ian, it's Chris. I am phoning to let you know that the document has arrived from Hong Kong. It is crucial to the offshore company structure, and I am leaving now to go to the office and collect it. I shall call you to confirm that I have it."

And he hung up, leaving a bemused journalist wondering what was in this particular document that appeared to have made Dickie so jumpy.

Sue Dickie, however, was crying in fear. She had seen her husband's rage after the Holy Grail call on December 8, 1995. She had lived through a nightmare Christmas with Chris as he tried to negotiate the release of this document. Hell, she had lived through the nightmare, fullstop.

They arrived at the McVeagh Fleming office around 9.25pm. There, on the fax machine, was the Holy Grail. Half expecting it to vanish in a puff of smoke, *Mission Impossible*-style, Dickie whipped out a camera and photographed it sitting there, as if seeing it on film would make it real. He was so nervous, however, that the shot was out of focus.

With all the hype, Sue Dickie was half-expecting someone to leap out from the shadows in the large office with a gun and swipe it

Wishart's phone rang again. "Ian, it's Chris. I've got it, and I've made arrangements to distribute copies. Meet me in the basement in town in 10 minutes."

The Dickies were in the office for less than four minutes. By the time I skidded to a halt on a wet Wyndham St outside the lawfirm's office tower, Sue had already gone. The orange streetlights melted into the rain cascading down onto the rough concrete driveway that led to the basement carpark. The clang of the huge metal gates unlocking and swinging open sounded incredibly loud.

There, waiting in the gloom beside a parked car in the shadows, was Dickie. "I've got the little fuckers, boy! I've got them."

He passed me a copy of the Hong Kong document. "This is my insurance policy. Keep it safe." When he finally got home, the lawyer sat down to peruse the evidence he'd waited for for so long.

Over the next few pages of this book you will see a reprint of that memo, as tabled at the Winebox Inquiry, but don't turn to it yet.

This was a significant document, and not just to Dickie. To put it in perspective, it might help if you knew how furiously lawyers for the IRD and SFO fought to stop it being tabled at the Commission.

Brian Henry, the lawyer for Winston Peters, had originally tried to get the memo entered into the evidence, but failed miserably. In fact, so vociferous had been the protests from the two departments that all copies of the memo had been seized and withdrawn by the Commission.

So when Paul Cavanagh QC introduced it to the hearing in November 1996, the response from the IRD's Tony Bouzaid was swift.

"I understood that this document was ruled out of evidence, from a question put by Mr Henry," he complained to Sir Ronald Davison.

"It is in, now, Mr Bouzaid," stated Cavanagh bluntly. "Were you aware that Mr Nash obtained that document in Hong Kong early in 1990?"

"I was aware he obtained documents from Hong Kong," replied a clearly startled Bouzaid.

IRD lawyer Graeme Lang tried to rescue his colleague, questioning whether the document had in fact been unlawfully leaked from within the IRD's files, and "if they have been disclosed other than in a proper way?"

"I assure the Commission," said Cavanagh, "that Mr Dickie, who is seated with me, personally obtained a copy of this document from the same source that the department obtained theirs. So this is not a document that has emanated from the department."

So that's a little of the flavour surrounding the emergence of this memorandum into the public domain. But before you read it, ponder this:

Since December 1988 Chris Dickie had been searching for a piece of evidence that would demonstrate who might have control of the schemes that had cost his investors money. Who was behind the secret tax haven entities that appeared to be clipping the ticket?

Everything the lawyer had gone through had been for this. Now would be a good time to make a cup of coffee. When you come back, read what follows.

Deloitte
·skins+Sells   225-564

Inter-Office Memorandum

From: K. K. Yu   Date: May 31, 1989
Subject:

To: Dermot Agnew

To facilitate your meeting with Paul Carran early June, 1989 I have pleasure to enclose herewith a list of companies/trusts which are benefically owned by Paul Carran or to which Paul Carran is the authorized person.

I also list underneath the points to be taken up with Paul Carran:

Z███████ LTD.

1. Fees - the company is indebted to us for app. HK$300,000.00 and STGS 575.00 to our London office. Kindly take this up with Paul Carran and ensure when these will be settled.

2. Audited financial statements - the final draft audited financial statements for the year ended March 31, 1987 has been sent to Paul Carran for approval. These are urgently required for UK filing purposes and we are still waiting for his approval to have this finalised.

3. Financial statements for the years ended March 31 1988 and 89 - enclosed please find a memorandum dated April 7 1989 to Paul Carran. This contains the necessary information required by us to finalise the financial statements for the years ended 31 March 1988 and 89. Kindly go throught this with Paul Carran and obtain an immediate answer.

4. Restructuring of the company - during the past few month: various correspondences have been entered into in respec: of the proposed restructuring of the company. To facilitate your meeting with Paul Carran, enclosed pleas: find a copy of these correspondences together with a.list of assets and libilities of the company.

5. Loans - in the above correspondences we have had instructions from Paul Carran to waive a loan for

US$500,000 to B██████ Ltd. In this respect, I enclosed herewith a letter of indemnity and should be obliged if you can arrange to be signed by Paul Carran.

6. Legal action taken by C█████ F█████ C██. Pty. Ltd. - a writ has been taken by C█████ F█████ C██. Pty. Ltd. against the company and Paul Carran is supposed to have dealt with this while he was in Jessey. Kindly take this up with Paul Carran to ensure what would be the subsequent development of this action.

We have also received instruction Paul Carran to close various Trusts and Companies on which he has control. These instruction are now being carried out and the following documents/information would be required:

K██████ TRUST

Forms of receipt and discharge for the years ended Dec 31 1987 and 88 have been sent to Paul Carran under cover of our memorandum dated Feb 17, 1987.

These have not been returned and enclosed please find a fresh copy for signature and return by Paul.

KOMANTI INVESTMENT LIMITED

1. Enclosed please find a copy of memorandum dated February 22, 1989. As the documents required have not yet been returned by Paul Carran, enclosed please find copies for his signature.

2. A letter of instruction and indemnity to liquidate the company is enclosed. Please also have this signed by Paul Carran.

3. Enclosed please find 6 letters for the purpose of assigning the film rights. Thought these would have to be signed by us as secretary to the company, I would like these to be approved by Paul Carran before having the same sent out.

4. Loan from C███ H█████ Ltd.- Paul Carran has given instruction to transfer the loan to R█████ Ltd. for US$ 38,100,000.00 to D███ H██ Ltd., nothing has been said concerning the same amount of loan received from Chary Holding Ltd. Kindly confirmed with Paul Carran whether if this loan should also be transfer to D███ H██ Ltd. as well.

5. Nothing has also been mentioned in respect of the loan to Z█████ Ltd. for UD$ 27,000.00. Please also obtain Paul Carran disposal on this amount. The company is still having a cash balance of around 55,000 US. In absence of instruction to the contrary, we would have to distribute this to the K█████ T████ on liquidation. Can you please obtain Paul Carran's view on this.

B█████ LTD.

1. Letter to E████ H█████ Ltd & Co. - please arrange approval from Paul Carran in respect of the letter to sent to E█████ H█████ Ltd & Co.

2. Letter of instruction and indemnity - enclosed please find such a letter for the purpose of liquidating the company. Kindly have this signed by Paul Carran and return to me for my further action.

R█████ LTD.

Enclosed please find a memorandum to Paul Carran recently. Kindly turn to point 2 of the memorandum and ask if Paul Carran would arrange a transfer in New Zealand.

D███████ LTD

Enclosed please find a letter of engagement and nominee
services agreement sent to Paul Carran previously, enclosed
please find a fresh copy for Paul Carran's signature and
return.

S███ R██ I█████████

Though S████ R██ I██████████ Ltd had been liquidated, we are
still unable to obtain their formal receipt and discharge from
R████ Trust. Since Paul Carran is the one who initiated this
issue, I shall be obliged if you can pass a copy of this
memorandum to Paul Carran and ask him to have this signed and
return.

We have also a fee note for HK$9,500.00 outstanding in
respect of this company and I shall be obliged if you can ask
Paul Carran to assist to have this collected.

K. K. Yu

Enclosures

From the first glance, Dickie could see that Paul Carran had some questions to answer.

"I have pleasure," K K Yu had written on May 31, 1989, to Dermot Agnew, "to enclose herewith a list of companies/trusts which are beneficially owned by Paul Carran or to which Paul Carran is the authorised person."

"Yeeeeeeessssss," screeched Dickie in a kind of primeval roar. Houston, we have lift-off.

In the office the next morning, Dickie dropped the memo on Peter Edwards with a big grin. His colleague was shocked.

"They've had it," he said, shaking his head. "It's over."

Dickie had taken steps to ensure that a number of copies were made and distributed swiftly. The original was to stay in Hong Kong under Gunson's control.

As part of the pre-arranged series of events, Gunson was to fax through another copy of the memorandum at certain times, and the next delivery was at 2.30pm. That became Peter Edwards' set.

"I have accepted for some time," Dickie said that day, "particularly since I saw the surveillance vehicle on the other side of my drive, that I must assume all the time that somebody was either going to get me or get the documents off me instantly I received them."

Journalist Frances O'Sullivan had, of course, been mugged in a lift in a city office tower by a man trying to snatch winebox documents from her. Her hotel room was later burgled and ransacked.

"If I'd been approached by anyone," said Dickie, "I'd have said 'tough luck, here's a copy. It's only a copy and you ain't gonna get the original'."

Tony Bouzaid would face heavy cross-examination at the Winebox Inquiry over the K K Yu memorandum, which had been in the possession of IRD investigator John Nash since 1990 – a year before the settlement.

"This memorandum," thundered the QC who, with Dickie as his junior, was representing Alan May and Michael Scott at the inquiry, "made it clear before you signed off the 16 film syndicates at the request of Mr Clews of Russell McVeagh McKenzie Bartleet & Co that a partner of his firm, Paul Carran, was involved in deceptive conduct – concealing the fact that these offshore entities were, in fact, controlled by him."

According to Bouzaid, the document needed to be put alongside other evidence which, he said, contradicted the memo in regard to entities like the control of Zorasong. He didn't elaborate on what evidence that might be initially, so he was invited by Cavanagh to produce it to the inquiry.

"What I have is extensive investigative work conducted by one of our investigators, probably containing many Eastlight folders, and I have relied on that," said Bouzaid.

"You are aware," asked Cavanagh, that the memorandum that I have referred to was made by the Hong Kong accounting firm that was carrying out Mr Carran's instructions?"

"I will accept that," replied Bouzaid after being asked to answer the question a second time. "Certainly."

"Are you alleging that the document is fraudulent, that it is not true in what it says?" quizzed the QC.

"I have no reason to doubt what it says is accurate – as a document on its own."

"The evidence clearly indicates that Mr Carran was controlling these offshore entities," continued Cavanagh. "Do you have evidence to the contrary?"

"We have," he answered. "I personally don't have it."

Pushed further, Bouzaid admitted he hadn't seen any particular document that contradicted the Deloittes memo.

"The Court would say, surely," exclaimed the lawyer, "that this is a document made as an internal memorandum by Mr Carran's Hong Kong agent. It must be correct unless it is a forgery."

"I accept that," conceded Bouzaid. "A Court would also look at other evidence that has been given by people under affidavit, or brought to New Zealand. My understanding is the weight of this document would need to be evaluated because it is a document emanating from offshore and may well require somebody coming to give evidence to attest to that document."

"You are aware that Mr Dickie got a whole lot of other documents, as well, that confirm Mr Carran's involvement in the management of these offshore companies. Documents that demonstrate such things as dramatic increases in the price of horses?"

"Yes," said Bouzaid. "We have also got other documents that conflict. That's what we have made judgments on."

"But we have got to trust you, don't we?" said Cavanagh sarcastically,

"Because we have never seen these documents that give you such confidence in the weakness of your case, have we?"

Bouzaid stuck to the party line, saying the IRD had extensively investigated, and adding that the department gave greater weight to claims made in affidavits than documentary evidence. Which, in my opinion, ignores the reality that humans can and do lie, even on oath, whereas document trails tend to be more revealing.

But Chris Dickie would never get the chance to use the memorandum in anger.

On a Friday afternoon in February 1996, just days before the bloodstock trial was due to begin, the last of the bloodstock investors finally settled. Not that it was a happy ending. The terms of the deal are confidential, but suggestions were made at the Winebox Inquiry that Russell McVeagh and the other defendants paid out 100 percent of the amount that the investors claimed they'd lost in the bloodstock partnerships.

Some of the multi-million dollar legal costs of the litigation were paid, but not all, and that became a bone of contention with a small group of the largest investors who, naturally, faced the largest legal bills.

Russell McVeagh McKenzie Bartleet and all other defendants have not admitted liability, and continue to deny that they have caused or contributed to any of the wrongs alleged by any of the three partnerships.

Dickie and Molloy had done such a good job of convincing the investors of the strength of their case that many had been looking forward to their day in court and were disappointed when it didn't happen.

"We went to Dickie's office at one point halfway through," remembered Graeme Hadlee, "and I said to him 'Chris, I believe, in my heart of hearts, that in the end you will make a settlement with these other guys.'

"He said 'Nothing in the world is going to make this settle. We're going to take them to the cleaners, Graeme.'

"Two years later we've all settled. Nobody's happy, but we've settled."

That weekend Dickie worked off his tension in the garden, communicating only in monosyllabic grunts with his family. He poured himself a bourbon on a mountain of ice, and slept as long as he could.

CHAPTER 33

The End Of The Beginning

"Between the possibility of being hanged in all innocence, and the
certainty of a public and merited disgrace, no gentleman of spirit
could long hesitate."

– ROBERT LOUIS STEVENSON, 1850–1894, *THE WRONG BOX*

With the civil litigation now disposed of, the skirmishing that had been sim-
mering between those directly involved turned into open warfare. Bloodstock
consultant Mitchell McLeish initiated legal action against Russell McVeagh over
what he believed was the firm's role in the problems faced by Zorasong and
Securelaunch.

For their part, Russell McVeagh were reaching for McLeish's testicles and
attempting to squeeze. "Russell McVeagh has bought my [personal guarantee]
from Westpac, which I expect means trouble," McLeish told his lawyer.

On March 22, 1996, Russell McVeagh lawyers Laurie Mayne and Chris
Brown – both now partners in the giant firm – met Chris Kirkham for a bit of
robust discussion about McLeish's planned action against the firm.

They allegedly told him that the lawfirm had insurance to cover fraud, and
that documents in the case had been passed to the insurers for perusal. They
said that they wouldn't be speaking to either Mitchell McLeish or their former
colleague, disgraced tax partner Paul Carran.

A lot of the discussion centred on Russell McVeagh's view of McLeish's role.
They allegedly told Kirkham they believed that McLeish had perjured himself
in a 1990 affidavit by stating he had nothing to do with Zorasong, and that
McLeish's interest "contravened his fiduciary duty to the Ermine, Buckingham
and Wicklow partnerships."

Mayne and Brown told Kirkham that the initial seed money for Zorasong
"came from film money belonging to Carran and yourself, and that's going to be
bad for you."

"That film money belonged to Chary Holdings, not me," protested Kirkham.
"It was just a loan from Chary!"

Kirkham claims he was told he would never get out of bankruptcy if he
helped McLeish. He also claims he was told that he might find it difficult getting
work if he chose to help his old friend.

As for Zorasong and Securelaunch, they told Kirkham that McLeish was welcome to the two companies and all the hassles that went with them. McLeish's fight with Russell McVeagh would be "drawn out and expensive" and, they claimed, "it was not Carran's or Russell McVeagh's fault that the stallion shares were not transferred – that fault lies with Bendelow and his people."

McLeish would certainly find the fight difficult, especially as, over the years, he claims to have followed advice from Carran and Kirkham to destroy documents. If nothing else, that is an object lesson to white collar wheeler dealers: if you think you're being clever by destroying records so that the authorities can't get hold of them, you'd better hope that your partners in the deal aren't going to do you like a dinner once the evidence is destroyed. After all, what's the point of having good documentation, if you can't use it in your defence?

By May 1996, the bankrupt Kirkham was back on the trail of the lost assets in Zorasong and Securelaunch. It wasn't going to be easy. The first step was a letter to the lawyer he'd been using in Eire, Pat O'Driscoll.

"You will recall that Coolmore refused to transfer the stallion interests to other companies which attempted to purchase them in 1990," wrote Kirkham on May 10, 1996.

"We presume that these interests are still in Zorasong Ltd. We understand Zorasong has been struck off for not filing returns.

"Mr McLeish and I are investigating the possibility of Zorasong taking action against Coolmore so that Zorasong can continue to own and use the stallion assets, including the unpaid dividends and service fees collected by Coolmore over the years, which by now is a substantial sum. These assets are also debt free."

The reply from the Irish lawyer was swift, but disappointing. O'Driscoll advised that the first hurdle would be getting Zorasong "reconstituted" – commercial-speak for getting a company that's been struck off put back on the company office registers.

Reconstitution is a bit like digging a dead body up and trying to breathe life into it – you run the risk of catching what ever disease killed it in the first place. In this case, warned the lawyer, a successful resurrection could see Kirkham and McLeish become instantly liable for Zorasong's unpaid debts, and forced to watch helplessly as creditors raided the treasure chest they'd just retrieved.

Undeterred, Kirkham fired back another letter on May 13.

"We now have a good opportunity to reconstitute Zorasong after several years of trying. The Auckland lawfirm of Russell McVeagh [Carran] effectively ran Zorasong – the Hong Kong entities did as they were told. The litigation in New Zealand is now settled so Russell McVeagh will now deal with Zorasong.

"The key aspect is – does Zorasong still own its stallion interests? We think it must do, as Zorasong did not [succeed in] sell [ing] these assets to Securelaunch."

You could sense Kirkham's frustration: here he was trying to emerge from bankruptcy, and he could see this pile of loot he felt certain he was entitled to.

"All we want to do is to continue to breed the stallion shares and collect the stallion fees which Coolmore has been collecting for years on behalf of Zorasong. These fees plus the current value of the shares would be approximately IR£1 million.

"Surely these monies are due to Zorasong as owner of the shares and its collection cannot be frustrated by the Statute of Limitations. Zorasong had few liabilities in 1990, so we cannot see how creditors could freeze the assets – they would be paid from the assets instead."

A series of faxes followed over the next two weeks, each becoming shorter and terser. Eventually Kirkham accused O'Driscoll and one of his juniors, Justin Fennell, of giving glib answers.

"I am sorry that you feel my letters are glib," wrote Fennell on May 30, 1996. "As you are aware, Zorasong transferred all its interest in the shares to Kanasawa in December 1989, and accordingly they no longer have any interests in the shares after that date.

"In any event," he concluded, "all claims up to 30 May 1990 are now statute barred."

So near, but so far. Kirkham was crushed, but if he'd known what was about to happen, he would have been absolutely terrified.

In June 1996, investigators from the Commerce Ministry, accompanied by police, launched an early morning raid on the home of Chris Kirkham. They seized 40 boxes of documents.

The raid ostensibly took place following information that Kirkham had been operating a business on his own account while bankrupt. Kirkham told the *Independent* he had no idea what was behind the raid by the Official Assignee's Office.

"But I said to them, 'Go for your lives'. I mean, there's nothing you can do about it," he said.

Many of the documents seized, however, related to the bloodstock and film deals.

At the Winebox Inquiry, the Inland Revenue Department's John Nash caused a sensation a few weeks after the raid by suggesting that maybe there was something to investigate after all.

"The department cannot prosecute non-revenue offences," he testified. "In my opinion, the offering documents for the bloodstock partnerships in particular raised serious issues as to the non-disclosure of material contracts involving either the promoter or its solicitor.

"However, securities fraud is the domain of the Securities Commission and the Serious Fraud Office, not the Inland Revenue Department."

In regard to the film deals, Nash told the inquiry that the decision to settle 15 of the 16 films without prosecution was proper, because the evidence might have been insufficient to stand up in court. The 16th film, he said, was settled with none of its expense claims being accepted, because it was a "black case".

"The perpetrator of the possible evasion had absconded offshore and so it was not possible to prosecute in this instance."

In addition, the Law Society has launched its own investigation into Russell McVeagh and its role in the film and bloodstock litigation.

Partners and former partners of the mega-lawfirm have been forced to dig deep into their pockets to help pay the massive costs of settling the bloodstock deals.

Not that settling may have been too severe a hardship for the rich men and women at Russell McVeagh.

"At one of the meetings a long time ago," remembered investor Pat Hadlee, "one of the questions was that if we were going to go for this enormous amount of money – we're talking $32 million here, I remember the figure – Russell McVeagh will go broke and they'll never be able to afford it.

"Chris and Tony had done their homework and they said 'Hang on a minute. 'There are sixty partners and they're all earning somewhere around $700,000 a year, minimum. If they each took a mortgage for $530,000, they'd have this paid off in six years.'

"The guys would have a mortgage for six years. I remember thinking 'Fuck, is that all?' My bloody mortgage is 15 years as it is!"

As Colin Pidgeon QC said when he read the Deloittes memorandum fingering Paul Carran as the beneficial owner or authorised person of the secret tax haven companies: "They brought a fine firm to its knees through greed, in my view! You have a duty to take this [memorandum] to the police and the Law Society," Pidgeon told Dickie.

But there were other things happening at this time that added to an almost surreal mood behind the scenes.

In March, 1996, observers close to both the winebox and the film and bloodstock affairs were stunned to learn of the mysterious death of former Cook Islands auditor, Richard McDonald.

"Cook Islands whistleblower Richard McDonald took his own life last Friday," wrote Frances O'Sullivan in the NBR, "deeply depressed after spending four months in exile in the small Queensland town of Blackbutt.

"Mr McDonald had been threatened with arrest by Sir Geoffrey Henry's government if he returned to Rarotonga in the wake of his decision to defy the Cook Islands government and give evidence to the Winebox Inquiry last October.

"The former Cook Islands director of audit had been sacked in 1987 after he travelled to New Zealand and Australia warning trans-tasman authorities that a tax credits scam was being orchestrated by the islands' government."

O'Sullivan wrote that McDonald was depressed because his fridge had blown up and he couldn't afford to get it repaired.

McDonald had told the Winebox Inquiry that things had become so bad for him in Rarotonga that he slept with an axe beside his bed for protection, and O'Sullivan wrote too of "a series of threats, obscene phone calls and standover tactics against the McDonald family."

McDonald had been a whistleblower to the bitter end.

"Now that he is safe from reprisal from Sir Geoffrey's regime," wrote

O'Sullivan, "I can reveal that it was Richard McDonald who also blew the initial whistle on the $.15 billion letters of guarantee scandal that rocked the Cook Islands [in 1995].*

The official cause of death was listed as suicide, but there were some discordant aspects to the case. Few people knew it, but McDonald was working on a book.

On January 22, 1996, he had written to New Zealand publishing company Nelson, Price Milburn Ltd of Wellington, touting his manuscript.

"It deals with the rise of the NZ welfare state over the first half of this century and its progressive destruction.

"I also had a lot to do with the Cooks, 1977-1995, often in a high place and that gave me a lot of feedback. I will succeed in annoying a lot of people, but who wants a dull book! I am on the second rewrite now and will have to do at least one more.

"I was involved in so much of this over the years and heard so much, both in New Zealand and Australia, I consider it a pity if I let my memories go down to the grave with me."

But go to the grave they did.

When McDonald's body was found by the eight year old son he treasured, missing from the scene were his manuscript drafts.

I have no evidence that McDonald's death was anything other than suicide, but as an investigative journalist I ask two fundamental questions: would a father who loved his eight year old son dearly kill himself and leave his body to be discovered by the child? And why would the manuscript go missing?

Maybe the questions are easily answered. Perhaps his death was accidental. Perhaps he had sent the manuscript to someone.

There was one other unfortunate death with winebox links only a few weeks later, this time in Auckland.

An ANZ bank employee, Patrick McMeekin, had allegedly told friends and neighbours that he wanted to testify to the Winebox Inquiry but had been unable to do so.

He died in a house fire in upmarket Herne Bay on Good Friday, 1996.

The ANZ's personnel manager Julie McDougall told the *NBR* that McMeekin had been on leave from the bank for several months when he died.

"He had been considering several options in relation to his employment with the bank. Patrick had at one stage been involved in helping the bank respond to inquiries from the winebox commission. He was one of several people at the bank involved from time to time," she said.

She added that the bank was unaware of any expressed desire by McMeekin to testify. It should also be noted for the record that the ANZ bank's involvement in winebox deals was peripheral, and restricted only to the fact that ANZ had bought Postbank, which had been heavily involved prior to the purchase.

---

* See *The Paradise Conspiracy*.

Police said they were not seeking anyone else in connection with McMeekin's death.

More detail on the film and bloodstock deals emerged at the Winebox Inquiry at the end of 1996, as the issue flared up again thanks to Tony Bouzaid pouring petrol on the barbecue.

"It has now been discovered that Mrs Latimer and Mr May breached secrecy by giving documents to Mr Dickie on at least three occasions.

"Some 33 documents have been identified as having been given to Mr Dickie to assist with the civil litigation proceedings. A number of these which were tabled by Mr Peters on 4 August 1992 can be identified as copies of those given to Mr Dickie." Extremely serious allegations to be making. But was there evidence to back up the claims? Or had head office got its facts wrong?

Unfortunately, Bouzaid was shooting blanks in an OK Corral showdown with the man representing the rebel IRD staff's interests and Dickie's, Paul Cavanagh QC, who explained why he needed to defend them and why the issues were relevant to the Winebox Inquiry.

"Northern staff took quite a different view of these [film] settlement proposals from that advanced by [IRD lawyer Angela] Satterthwaite, this witness and Mr Nash. And they were punished for it.

"I want to be able to demonstrate that that process in dealing with the people concerned was malicious, vindictive and unjustified."

In one example, Bouzaid had highlighted a section in Dickie's testimony where he referred to May showing him a document from the Lindsay Park Stud in Australia, complete with a receipt for bloodstock purchases.

Under cross-examination, Bouzaid admitted it would not be a breach of secrecy if May had shown it to the bloodstock investors' tax agent. To show it to Dickie was another matter.

"Would you be surprised, then, to know that he has written authority to act as their tax agent in negotiations with your department?" asked Cavanagh, who might also have added that Dickie was an investor, and therefore one of the affected taxpayers as well.

Bouzaid was surprised, and drew a distinction between special partners – who actually incurred any tax liabilities – and the general partner, which Bouzaid claimed was the only party entitled to see the documents. But he admitted he didn't know for sure what the position was, "I'm not an expert in special partnerships," he said.

"No," snapped Cavanagh, "but you have dared to criticise Mr May for breaching secrecy in relation to that matter when you don't know whether he did or not!"

As for the other documents allegedly supplied by the IRD to Dickie, Cavanagh pointed out that most of those were merely documents that Dickie had originally supplied, being returned to him.

On one occasion, where Bouzaid had alleged that May had handed over documents, he now admitted he had no evidence, especially as – on the date involved – May had actually been in hospital.

Bouzaid acknowledged that the real reason May's career was jeopardised was his attendance at the vineyard meeting, and the possibility that "his body language and his nodding of the head could have given impressions of approval as to what was being said at that meeting."

Bouzaid added that May's boss in Auckland, the then Regional Controller Patricia Housden, was "extremely disappointed" that May had attended.

It all prompted Cavanagh to question whether the IRD head office was aware of the Bill of Rights.

"This man has been pilloried for attending the meeting. And there is clear authority for the proposition that he cannot be challenged for his free association. There is law in Canada for a civil servant, that unless the department was satisfied that he breached secrecy or had done anything else at that meeting, he was perfectly entitled to attend it. And in fact it is the department who committed an offence in seeking to challenge him on it."

The IRD head office, which had complained so bitterly about Winston Peters allegations and challenging the politician to come up with evidence, appeared to be guilty itself of shooting first, as another Bouzaid attack on May showed.

The senior official recounted a tax case the department had lost where "the judge was most sarcastic to IRD and this was a case which I am told Mr May did this case, and the judge awarded very high costs [against] the department for acting irresponsibly."

Paul Cavanagh opened fire on the hapless Bouzaid, yet again.

"I am instructed that Mr May's evidence in the case was accepted by all parties and he wasn't even cross-examined on it. Are you aware of that?"

"Well," said Bouzaid hesitantly, "I can only read the judgment, and that's what [John] Nash referred to in reading the judgment."

"Well, Mr May is not mentioned in the judgment, is he?"

Bouzaid then admitted that May was mentioned nowhere in the judgment and, further, the case had been conducted by the IRD's legal team, not May.

To Bouzaid's credit, he then apologised for the criticism of May.

Again, if this is an example of the level and quality of investigative work by the IRD's head office staff – they cannot even make accurate allegations against their own employees – then it must, in my view, be a major cause for concern in regard to the IRD's ability to get it right in any of their investigations.

Also significant in my view: the IRD had the K K Yu memorandum a year before it decided to settle. Why didn't it use the memo and why did head office tell northern staff it had no evidence to support allegations of New Zealand control?

The ultimate question of what happened to the profits Zorasong made from marking up the prices in the bloodstock deals has never been satisfactorily answered.

While some of the mark-ups in Ermine were undoubtedly paper devices to soak up the paper loan of US$500,000 from Bonshow, there were no paper loans in the Buckingham or Wicklow syndicates that followed, and yet there is still evidence of price mark-ups – certainly in Buckingham's case.

Nor does this explain how more than US$300,000 ended up in the coffers of the Cook Islands company Investment Management Services Ltd, first identified by Dorothy Coates all those years ago. IMS was nominally administered by European Pacific staff, but there is evidence linking both Paul Carran and Chris Kirkham to it.

"She rang Hong Kong," remembered Molloy, "and she got absolutely carpeted by Carran when he found out, but she told us that there was money going up to the Cook Islands Trust Company, and I've just seen evidence this week that it was being sent to one AJ McCullagh* on the instructions of one Paul Charles Carran.

"The memo said that it was a procuration fee for having arranged for Zorasong to sell horses to Ermine and Buckingham, so they were not only milking the people on the prices through Zorasong, but they were charging a bloody procuration fee through another company in the Cook Islands, and taking it again."

There is also the issue of how Zorasong, a company with only a few dollars in capital, reached a point where it ostensibly owned US$1.8 million worth of horses in its own right. Company records show the assets they attempted to transfer to Securelaunch in 1990 included shares in the stallions *Lomond* and *Caerleon*, each stake valued at US$350,000, and a quarter-million dollar share of *Law Society*. These were, arguably, the three most valuable stallions in the world at the time.

Their broodmares included a 30 percent share of *Catopetl*, worth US$360,000, and full ownership of *Aces Full*, worth US$90,000. A scattering of foals, yearlings and two year olds made up the balance.

Liabilities were listed as only US$300,000. So where did the money come from?

"Well, Carran was in charge of raising funds," said McLeish, "but there were times when we borrowed money collectively, and we borrowed it from banks. Allied Irish Bank was a major supplier of funds, and we borrowed from British & Commonwealth Merchant Bank. I mean, there were a lot of places where money was borrowed – Hong Kong. But that was Carran's baby.

"Where the initial money came from, I've no idea really, but there was significant money there when we bought *Catopetl*. She was a serious animal and we could have virtually paid for her on the day, ourselves, if she'd made only £750,000 – but she made £800,000."

"I still have a few mares there, including probably the world's most valuable mare. We have just sold her foal for US$1 million," McLeish had noted in one document.

Paul Carran, for his part, wishes to stay silent about his own role.

"Well, I'm not seeking to get sympathy from anybody. I mean, life turns out

---

* See *The Paradise Conspiracy*.

like that. Some people get cancer, some people don't. I got bowled, there's nothing I can do about that. Talking about it is not going to solve it.

"All it does is, your electorate – the people that you write for – are not people that know me. They don't deal with me, they don't know who I am, so it's not going to change my life whether they feel sympathy or not.

"I got snookered, and that's all there is to it."

Over a period of months I made five phone calls to Paul Carran and sent one fax seeking his answers to the very serious allegations either made publicly or raised by virtue of the documentary evidence.

"Am I a crook? Did I commit fraud? The answer is no," he told me.

"Did I have a personal interest? [in the privately held Zorasong bloodstock] "No. Never did, never have. It is untrue. I've never had a partnership or a business involvement with Mitchell McLeish. I did put some capital into Scorten Investments with them, but chose to walk away from that.

"I regret investing in those partnerships I was involved in and I regret acting for them. It was a phenomenal ride, if I can use that analogy, and a lot of people fell off as we went over the hurdles. People lost heavily and I really, really regret that."

Carran refused to answer specific questions on the grounds of client confidentiality, but suggested I contact Laurie Mayne at Russell McVeagh and seek a clearance for Carran to talk. So I gave Mayne a call.

"Well," said Mayne, "I don't see why we or anybody would want one person who wasn't involved in it to be judge and jury of anything. So I don't know how helpful we can be, quite frankly."

"Well," I countered, "I've got 300 pages of a book -"

"Good on you. Publish it and we'll see," challenged Mayne.

"Well, I'd like to try and be as fair as possible."

"Well, I don't know how interested I am spending any time on it, quite frankly Ian. It's the last thing I want to start going back through. I'm onto other things, as are most other people, Paul and everybody.

"You'll have to make what you can of what you've got, I guess."

"Look, this is just one of those things in trying to get the other side of the story."

"Yeah, well, I don't know what other side of the story you're talking about," he said.

So, at the end of this venture, all I'm left with is Russell McVeagh and Paul Carran's general denials, reprinted where appropriate in this book, and the testimony of Geoff Clews and Robin Congreve at the Winebox Inquiry and in the Jersey proceedings. It is not that I didn't attempt to gain further cooperation, but for whatever reason it was not forthcoming.

Readers should not attempt to infer some kind of hidden meaning from their decision to stay silent. In a legal sense, Russell McVeagh and Carran do not have to say anything to me or anyone else. But from a journalistic point of view, it is a shame that this chapter in New Zealand history is being written without their input.

The central questions in this massive story are essentially simple ones:

- Why were investors not advised of price alterations?
- Were the various tax haven entities controlled from New Zealand?
- Who controlled those entities?
- Who was/were the beneficial owner(s)?
- Did the promoters have a financial interest in the secret company at the centre of the price mark-ups, which wasn't disclosed to the investors?

Those are the questions that essentially began this saga. We are all still waiting for the definitive answers.

The documents seized from Kirkham's home by Commercial Affairs investigators took a tortuous path. Passed to the police for investigation, the Serious Fraud Office stepped in and uplifted the material. On the last day of the Winebox Inquiry, we found out what the SFO had done with them, but only as a result of a sustained attack on Winston Peters and his lawyer, Brian Henry.

Henry had told the inquiry that some of Peters' allegations related to European Pacific's involvement with the film and bloodstock transactions.

In response, Fay Richwhite's lawyer Rhys Harrison QC told the inquiry "European Pacific did not participate in any film and bloodstock partnerships".

European Pacific's lawyer, Richard Craddock QC, echoed the point, and the SFO's Willie Young QC went even further.

"Confronted with the challenge to justify what was said as to the conspiracy not to prosecute EPI," said Young, "Mr Henry suggested that it related to the partnerships, but European Pacific had nothing to do with the film and bloodstock partnerships. The conspiracy alleged must have related to the winebox.

"But Mr Henry, rather than either put up or shut up, tried to slither away from the issue with the untrue evasion that the disgraceful allegations were related to something outside the Terms of Reference."

Brian Henry came out punching.

"The position sir," he told Sir Ronald Davison, "is I am instructed that some eight Eastlight folders of documents were delivered to you at lunchtime by the Commercial Affairs office, which shows that European Pacific and the Cook Islands Trust Corporation was involved in both bloodstock and film transactions.

"I was certainly aware of the company involved, [Investment] Management Services, which is a Cook Islands company and indeed it is a company referred to in *The Paradise Conspiracy*.

"I can indicate, sir, that the film involved, we believe, is one that is referred to in the settlement agreement that was produced to you during the course of the hearing."

Henry then quoted from a letter dated June 19, 1997, from the SFO to Commercial Affairs:

"You will be aware that our office is in receipt of a complaint in respect of the abovenamed entity, and that we have been assessing this matter with a view to ascertaining whether to launch an investigation.

"I write to formally advise you that after careful analysis, this office has determined that our file will be closed and we will not be undertaking a full investigation into this matter, nor into any other related or similar partnerships.

"The reasons for our decision are complex but include consideration of the age of the matter, with the inevitable loss of memory and documentation, the fact that other regulatory and investigative bodies have already traversed this ground; the impact of the Bill of Rights Act; the fact that a settlement was achieved between Inland Revenue Department and investors; the length of time involved; the difficulty and impracticality of unravelling intricate schemes implemented in numerous jurisdictions; a realistic assessment of the likelihood of attendance of overseas witnesses who will be required to produce admissible evidence and the prejudicial effect of the delay to date as well as future anticipated delay.

"As mentioned, this letter is a matter of courtesy, simply informing you of our decision, and is not intended to be a referral to you of a matter you should take further."

It was all, it would appear to me, just too difficult for the Serious Fraud Office to handle.

For the IRD, the final word comes in its closing submissions to the Winebox Inquiry in July 1997. The department quoted John Nash's testimony that "I have never doubted the legality of the December 1991 settlement agreement. . .The agreement was cleared for signing, with amendments, by Mr Peter Jenkin QC and Miss Satterthwaite.

"All concerns raised by Mrs Latimer were fully considered. I acted as Mr Bouzaid's principal adviser on film settlements and conveyed to him my opinion on the evidence held by the department in respect of the ventures being settled."

Nash also told the inquiry that he "advised Mrs Latimer and Mr May that summary documentation and unreliable witnesses would not stand against the evidence offered by taxpayers, and that evidence of some weight was required to disallow the expenditure claims either as to genuineness or excessiveness."

Like the SFO, Fay Richwhite and European Pacific before it, the IRD claimed "no bloodstock investigation touched upon events" in the Cook Islands, and "only one film transaction was ever structured so that funds passed through the Cook Islands (the film was made in the Cook Islands)".

"Ultimately," said the IRD legal team in their final submissions, "Mr Bouzaid had to decide between Mrs Latimer's advice and Mr Nash's advice, and he preferred the latter. It is sufficient to say that Mr Bouzaid was entitled to make a choice, and he preferred to accept the advice of Mr Nash. . .the advice was also demonstrably correct.

"On the evidence before the commission, there is no basis for any criticism or adverse comment regarding the manner in which the film cases were settled.

"The decision to settle the 'grey' cases was reached upon the basis that the extensive investigations which had been made over many years had failed to produce sufficient evidence to enable the objections to be determined by the court.

"No 'black' case was settled at less than 100%."

Specifically on the bloodstock, the IRD lawyers submitted that "Other difficulties also arose, such as the fact that the residence of the vendors of the stock was often arguably offshore, and there were conflicts in the evidence available to establish the identity of the persons controlling the offshore vendor companies.

"Often those companies also had no New Zealand-based assets which might be available to pay any tax which might be assessed."

As for Dickie, he continues to suffer from the seven year search for justice and two year wind-down. Some of his colleagues tell him what a great job he did, but he doesn't accept it. He feels genuine shame at being a lawyer, so much so that he has taken his practising certificate down from his office wall and will no longer display it.

"Let me tell you a story," he says, "of an incident a couple of years ago.

"I have a very strong sense of justice, which really is pretty naïve actually, being a lawyer. And if that sounds cynical it is the reason why I am now acutely embarrassed at being a lawyer.

"Anyway, Tony Molloy and I were at the investiture of a newly appointed High Court judge. Sitting in the front benches of the courtroom, as is the customary practice in such ceremonies, are the silks – the Queens Counsel.

"Behind them sit the barristers and solicitors who have had a common connection or an interest with the person who's leaving their ranks and being admitted as a judge. Behind them, and marked off by a counter, are the seats for the public.

"Sitting there in the public seats is Tony Molloy, with head bowed. This was not a mark of disrespect for the judge – in no way – it reflected Tony's embarrassment at the way the law had failed to protect the investors from being ground down. He could not bear to sit, as a leading silk, with the other Queens Counsel or lawyers.

"I get upset about it now, after this dreadful, dreadful seven years that we have had, that here is this person of the highest reputation, of the highest ethics, a person who has fought like hell with me – who was so moved, and so reduced by what we were coming up against, that he could not bring himself to say 'I can sit there and feel comfortable'.

"It's pretty bloody grim. I find that a very telling sign of the destruction that the case did to both of us."

Dickie says nothing more for a few moments, and in the sunlight as he looks away a tear glistens.